Angels - The Real Truth About All Types Of Angels

From Seraphim To Supernaphim And The Higher Personalities Of The Infinite Spirit

Angels - The Real Truth about all types of Angels

From Seraphim to Supernaphim and the Higher Personalities of the Infinite Spirit

by Dr. Roger W. Paul

Library of Congress Cataloging, in, Publication Data

Paul, Dr. Roger W.

Library of Congress Number:

ISBN: 979-8-9947653-2-6

Publisher Name is Dr. Roger W. Paul
Publisher Number For Title Management is: 2274327

Table of Contents

Publisher Information

ISBN: 979-8-9947653-2-6

Forward

When I first began studying The Urantia Book in 1973, I had no idea that a chance encounter with a stranger would fundamentally reshape my understanding of reality itself. I was seventeen years old, serving in the U.S. Navy, and attending Florida Keys College when someone approached me at a meeting, pressed a copy of this massive blue book into my hands, and said simply, "I think you're ready for this." Then he walked away, and the next time I saw him again, I had about a thousand question for him.

For the next nine months, I did little else but read. Page after page revealed a cosmos so vast, so intricate, so beautifully organized that my intended path toward seminary and traditional ministry became impossible. How could I return to conventional theology after glimpsing the architecture of eternity? The universe described in these pages wasn't the simple three-tiered heaven-earth-hell model I'd grown up with. It was something far more magnificent, a living, breathing hierarchy of beings and realms extending from our troubled little planet all the way to Paradise itself, and perhaps beyond.

Over the following decades, through multiple readings and thousands of hours of study, one particular revelation continued to capture my imagination: the angels. Not the greeting card variety with fluffy wings and halos, but real beings, organized into precise orders, each with specific duties and capabilities, working tirelessly throughout the grand universe to facilitate the spiritual progression of mortals like us. The Urantia Book dedicates several papers to these ministering spirits, and in my years of teaching, I've discovered that understanding the angelic hierarchy is absolutely essential for grasping how the universe actually functions.

This book represents the culmination of five decades spent wrestling with these concepts. I've taught them in study groups, explained them in countless YouTube videos, and watched students' eyes light up when they finally understand that we're not alone, that invisible companions walk beside us, record our choices, defend our interests in celestial courts, and will journey with us all the way to Paradise if we so choose.

The Challenge of Complexity

I won't mislead you, this material is dense. The Urantia Book presents seven major orders of seraphim, most with seven subdivisions, operating across multiple levels of universal reality. There are supernaphim serving on Paradise, seconaphim working in the superuniverses, and seraphim ministering in our local universe of Nebadon. There are cherubim, sanobim, and the mysterious midway creatures who exist between the material and spiritual realms. Each order has its own origin story, its own capabilities, its own sphere of service.

When I first attempted to diagram these relationships for a study group in the early 2000s, I filled an entire whiteboard and still didn't capture everything. One student looked at the tangle of lines connecting Paradise to Havona to the superuniverses to the local systems and finally down to our planet, and she said, "Roger, this looks like spaghetti thrown at a wall." She wasn't wrong. The organization of celestial beings is genuinely overwhelming at first encounter.

But here's what I've learned: you don't need to memorize every detail to benefit from this knowledge. What matters is understanding the fundamental principle, that the universe operates through intelligent, purposeful ministry carried out by real personalities who care about our welfare. The specifics support that core truth.

Why Angels Matter

Some people question whether studying angels is really necessary for spiritual growth. Shouldn't we focus on our relationship with God the Father, or on following the teachings of Jesus? Why spend time learning about celestial bureaucracy?

I understand that hesitation. I've felt it myself. But consider this: if you wanted to understand how the United States government functions, you'd need to know about the three branches, the system of checks and balances, the role of federal versus state authority. You don't need to memorize every department and agency, but grasping the basic structure helps you understand how decisions get made and how laws affect your life.

The same principle applies to universal government. Angels aren't just decorative additions to cosmic reality, they're the working components of divine administration. They coordinate spiritual influences in our minds. They transport us between worlds. They present evidence about our character before celestial tribunals. They teach us on the mansion worlds. They reflect divine wisdom to universe administrators. Understanding what they do helps us understand how our own ascension journey will unfold.

And perhaps most importantly, knowing about our guardian angels changes how we live right now. When you realize that two seraphim have been assigned specifically to you, that they observe your choices, celebrate your victories, and work tirelessly behind the scenes to create opportunities for your growth, it adds weight to every decision. You're not just making choices in private. You have witnesses who care deeply about your eternal welfare.

How This Book Is Organized

I've structured this book as a progressive journey through the angelic orders, starting with the beings we'll encounter first and moving toward those we'll meet much later in our ascension careers. We begin with the Seraphim, the angels most directly involved in our mortal lives, and examine their origin, nature, and the various orders of service they perform. We'll discover what guardian angels actually do (which may surprise you), how they differ from group guardians, and what it means to have celestial companions who will accompany us throughout eternity.

From there, we'll explore the Cherubim and Sanobim, those assistant angels who work alongside the seraphim, and the fascinating Midway Creatures who exist in that twilight realm between matter and spirit. These beings have played crucial roles in Earth's history and understanding them helps explain much about our planet's troubled past.

As we progress, we'll examine the higher orders: the Supernaphim who serve on Paradise and in Havona, the Seconaphim who minister throughout the superuniverses, and the specialized orders like the Solitary Messengers who travel at incomprehensible speeds carrying urgent communications across cosmic distances. We'll discover how reflectivity works, why the Ancients of Days can instantly know what's happening on millions of worlds, and how beings who have never met face-to-face can communicate as if standing in the same room.

Each chapter builds on previous concepts, gradually expanding our cosmic perspective. I've included detailed explanations where the text of The Urantia Book is particularly dense or technical, and I've drawn on decades of teaching experience to anticipate the questions that naturally arise. Throughout, I've tried to maintain the scholarly respect this material deserves while keeping the tone accessible and, I hope, occasionally even conversational.

A Word About Sources and Approach

The primary source for everything in this book is, of course, The Urantia Book itself, specifically Papers 23, 28, 37, 38, 39, and 113, which deal most directly with angelic beings. I've quoted extensively from these papers, always identifying the specific sections so you can verify the information and explore further on your own.

But this isn't merely a summary of those papers. I've attempted something more ambitious: a synthesis that connects concepts scattered across multiple sections, that addresses the practical implications for ascending mortals like us, and that doesn't shy away from the difficult questions these revelations raise. How could Lucifer, with full knowledge of Michael's authority, still choose rebellion? Why are we quarantined from certain universal circuits? What happens to guardian angels when their mortal charges fail to survive? These are the kinds of questions I've grappled with in decades of study, and I share my thinking, tentative as it sometimes is, throughout these chapters.

I should also mention my teaching methodology. For years, I've hosted study sessions via Zoom, working through The Urantia Book paper by paper with students across the country. Many of the insights in this book emerged from those discussions, from the questions people asked and the collective "aha!" moments when a particularly difficult concept suddenly clicked into place. I've incorporated some of those exchanges, because they often illuminate the material in ways my solo reflection wouldn't have achieved.

What You Won't Find Here

This book focuses specifically on angels and their ministry. It doesn't attempt to cover the entirety of Urantia Book cosmology. You won't find comprehensive discussions of the Paradise Trinity, the Seven Master Spirits, the local universe administrative structure, or the detailed descriptions of mansion world life, except where those topics directly relate to understanding angelic service. I have covered these concepts at length in my other three books.

I've also deliberately avoided the more speculative or controversial aspects of Urantia Book interpretation. You won't find me arguing about whether certain contemporary events fulfill prophecies from the text or engaging in the sometimes-contentious debates about how the book should be promoted or organized into study communities. My goal is simply to help readers understand what the revelation actually says about angels, presenting the information as clearly and accurately as I can.

A Personal Confession

I've read The Urantia Book more times than I can count, certainly well over a hundred complete readings, plus countless focused studies of specific papers. And you know what? I still discover new insights. I still encounter passages that suddenly make sense in ways they didn't before. I still feel that sense of awe when I contemplate the sheer scope of what's been revealed to us.

This humbles me. Despite five decades of study, despite teaching this material to hundreds of students, I remain a beginner in many ways. The universe is so much vaster than we can comprehend, the divine plan so much more intricate than our finite minds can grasp. I write this book not as an expert who has mastered the subject, but as a fellow student who has perhaps walked a bit farther down the path and wants to share what he's seen along the way.

If you find errors in my understanding, if you see connections I've missed or interpretations that seem questionable, I encourage you to dig deeper into the source material yourself. Don't take my word for it, verify everything against The Urantia Book itself. That's what good students do.

An Invitation

What follows is, I believe, one of the most comprehensive studies of angels from a Urantia Book perspective ever compiled. It represents not just my own work, but the accumulated insights of countless study group participants, the patient questions of students who pushed me to explain concepts more clearly, and ultimately, the magnificent revelation itself.

My hope is that by the time you finish this book, you'll see reality differently. You'll walk through your days aware that invisible companions observe your choices and work to create opportunities for your spiritual growth. You'll approach death without fear, knowing that guardian angels will carry your soul to the mansion worlds where your eternal adventure truly begins. You'll understand that the seemingly chaotic universe actually operates with perfect organization and purpose, administered by beings who never fail in their duties.

And perhaps most importantly, you'll realize that your life matters, not just to you, not just to your family and friends, but to the cosmic administration itself. You are known, you are valued, and you are accompanied every step of the way by celestial personalities who have devoted their existence to helping you achieve your divine potential.

That's not a comforting fantasy. According to The Urantia Book, it's revealed truth. And understanding the angels who serve us is the first step toward grasping just how loved and supported we really are.

Welcome to the study of the ministering spirits of the grand universe. I think you're ready for this.

Dr. Roger W. Paul
Dacula, Georgia
January 2026

Chapter 1: The Guardians of Destiny - An Introduction to Seraphic Ministry

When I first began studying Paper 113 of *The Urantia Book*, I had no idea how profoundly it would reshape my understanding of the unseen forces working in our lives. We often move through our days feeling alone, isolated in our struggles, unaware that celestial beings walk beside us, recording, guiding, and ministering to our spiritual growth. This chapter marks the beginning of our exploration into one of the most intimate and awe-inspiring relationships in all of creation: the bond between mortal humans and their guardian angels.

Throughout this fellowship series, my wife Reverend Diane Paul and I have welcomed students from across the country, from Alaska to the lower forty-eight states, joining us both in person and through online connections. Together, we've journeyed through the complex hierarchy of ministering spirits, using Don Estes' remarkable chart, "The Destiny of Universe Reality," as our guide. These visual aids, which I've made available on our website at fifthepochalrevelationfellowship.com, have helped us piece together the magnificent tapestry of celestial service that extends from the highest reaches of Paradise down to our humble planetary existence.

Tonight, or rather, in this study, we arrive at something special. After weeks of examining various orders of ministering spirits, we finally reach the seraphic angels, the beings most directly involved in our daily lives. We will address all the other orders of Angelic beings in the chapters to come. These are the traditional angels of heaven, the ones who have broken through into human consciousness throughout history, appearing in the sacred texts of cultures worldwide. While other celestial personalities have largely remained hidden from human awareness, the Seraphim have occasionally made themselves known when circumstances demanded direct intervention.

The Historical Recognition of Angels

It's worth noting that the Seraphim represent just about the only group of ministering spirits that humanity has consistently recognized throughout recorded history. Why is this? The answer appears quite simple when you consider it: they work most closely with us. They are, outside of the midway creatures and the physical controllers, the celestial beings nearest to our daily existence. When we read in the Old and New Testaments about people receiving divine messages, about angels appearing with warnings or guidance, we're likely reading accounts of seraphic ministry. These weren't abstract theological concepts; these were real encounters with real beings who served as intermediaries between the heavenly hierarchy and struggling mortals.

I find it particularly fascinating that this recognition of angels isn't limited to Judeo-Christian tradition. Cultures across the globe, separated by vast distances and operating independently of one another, have recorded experiences with angelic beings. This universal acknowledgment suggests something profound: the Seraphim have been faithfully ministering to humanity since the earliest days of our spiritual awakening, occasionally revealing themselves when the situation called for direct contact.

Now, I should mention that such direct appearances are rare. The revelation tells us that angels don't routinely materialize before us, and for good reason. Imagine the shock, the overwhelming fear that would grip most people if a celestial being suddenly appeared in their living room! Our evolutionary heritage has wired us for caution, for fear of the unknown. The Seraphim understand this, which is why they typically work through subtler means, through impressions, through synchronicities, through what we might call intuition or that small, quiet voice of conscience.

The Feminine Character of Ministering Spirits

Something else bears mentioning here, something we often overlook in our cultural conditioning: all seraphic ministers possess what *The Urantia Book* describes as a feminine character. This is significant. When we picture guardian angels, we shouldn't imagine stern, bearded patriarchs wielding flaming swords. The beings who watch over us, who record our spiritual progress, who gently guide us toward better choices, these beings embody feminine qualities.

To the women reading this study, I say: give credit where credit is due. The most intimate spiritual influence in our lives, apart from the Father fragment dwelling within us, comes from beings of feminine character. There's something profoundly beautiful about this arrangement, something that speaks to the balance and complementarity woven into the very fabric of universe reality.

The Question of Survival

In that opening paragraph of Paper 113, there's a phrase that stopped me cold the first time I read it: the Seraphim are "sent forth to do service for those who shall survive." Those four words, "who shall survive", carry enormous weight. They tell us something uncomfortable, something that contradicts certain popular theological assumptions: not everyone makes it. Not everyone survives the transition from mortal existence to the mansion worlds and beyond.

This is a difficult truth to confront. We live in an age that tends toward universalism, toward the comforting notion that everyone, regardless of choices or character, will somehow find their way to eternal life. But *The Urantia Book* presents a different picture. It affirms human free will in the most ultimate sense, we can choose survival, or we can choose non-survival. Even here on this planet, before we close our eyes in death, we can make a decision that becomes final.

Later in this paper, we'll encounter the sobering description of what the revelators call "the judgment of the unrighteous." Picture this: when roll call comes on the mansion worlds, the Seraphim appears with the mind patterns and memories of a particular individual. The name is called. The Seraphim responds. But the Thought Adjuster, that fragment of God himself, remains silent. That silence is the judgment. It means the soul has chosen, definitively and finally, to reject survival.

I mention this not to frighten anyone, but to underscore the genuine nature of our free will. The cosmic government doesn't override our choices. If a being decides, through persistent rejection of all that is good and true and beautiful, that they want no part of eternal existence, that decision is ultimately honored. The Seraphim are assigned to those who choose life, who choose to continue, who decide that the universe adventure is worth pursuing.

Jesus and the Angels

Jesus himself, speaking as Michael of Nebadon in human form, gave us insight into this angelic ministry. He said, "Take heed that you despise not one of these little ones, for I say to you, their angels do always behold the presence of my Father in heaven." We learned from the revelation that around age five or six, each child receives a Thought Adjuster, a fragment of the Universal Father who comes to dwell within the developing mind. Jesus is telling us that the angels see this Father fragment. They recognize it, honor it, minister to it.

But here's where it gets even more profound: who are "these little ones"? Yes, certainly children. But in a larger sense, aren't we all children of God? Every human being who has received a Thought Adjuster carries within them a fragment of Deity. When you harm another person, when you hate them or diminish them or destroy them, you're not just injuring a fellow mortal, you're acting against the Father himself, because he dwells within that person.

This is what Jesus meant by the Fatherhood of God and the brotherhood of man. It's not just a nice platitude. It's literal truth. We are brothers and sisters because we share the same Father, and that Father has placed a part of himself within each of us. The implications are staggering. Every act of violence, every word of hatred, every deed of selfishness is an offense not just against our fellow human but against the indwelling presence of God.

The guardian angels know this. They see the Father fragment glowing within each of their charges, and they labor tirelessly to help us recognize the same divine presence in others.

The Change That Christ Brought

Before Christ Michael completed his bestowal mission on our world, the angelic administration operated differently. The Seraphim served as group guardians, ministering to entire races or large populations rather than to individuals. But something changed after Christ's life, death, and resurrection. As sovereign ruler of our local universe of Nebadon, Michael made a decision: the ministry of guardian angels would become more personal, more intimate, more directly tailored to individual spiritual progress.

This was one of many adjustments Christ implemented in the wake of the Lucifer rebellion. Our world, Urantia, has suffered from isolation, from being cut off from normal universe circuits and communications. The default conditions here are far from ideal. But Michael, in his mercy and wisdom, made provisions to help compensate for our disadvantages. The individualization of guardian angels represents one such provision, a gift that brings celestial ministry closer to each struggling mortal.

Three Classes of Mortal Minds

As we delve deeper into Paper 113, we encounter a classification system that some may find uncomfortable. The revelation describes three broad categories of human minds: subnormal, normal, and supernormal. Let me address the first category with both honesty and compassion.

Subnormal minds exist on our world. These are individuals who, through no fault of their own, lack the mental capacity for intelligent worship of Deity. They cannot grasp abstract concepts. They cannot project into the future or imagine higher realities. Their understanding is limited to what is immediately present and tangible. The revelation describes them as having "corporeal natures," focused primarily on physical survival and immediate needs.

Now, here's what's important: an entire company of Seraphim, one battalion of Cherubim, is assigned specifically to minister to these individuals. Think about that. God hasn't abandoned them. These beings, who may seem to us to be disadvantaged or limited, are precious in the eyes of the universe administration. The angels watch over them, ensuring that justice and mercy extend to them in their life struggles.

And yes, some of them will survive to the mansion worlds. Even though they lack what we'd consider a "normal" mind, if they possess even a rudimentary concept of survival and a spark of faith in something greater than themselves, they will be given the opportunity to continue. When they awaken on the mansion worlds, they'll be treated as children, given patient instruction, allowed to develop at their own pace, eventually reaching the point where they can make an informed decision about their eternal destiny.

This brings us to a painful historical reality: these subnormal individuals should not exist in such numbers. What went wrong? The answer is the incomplete mission of Adam and Eve. Had our Material Son and Daughter succeeded fully in their biological uplift mission, had their superior genetic heritage been properly distributed throughout the human races, the number of subnormal minds would be dramatically reduced. But the Adamic default occurred. The mission failed. And so we're left dealing with problems that should have been corrected tens of thousands of years ago.

This doesn't mean we should harbor hatred or contempt for those with limited mental capacity. Rather, we should feel compassion and offer support where we can, knowing that the angels themselves are working to ensure these individuals receive fair treatment and genuine opportunity.

The Normal Mind and Psychic Circle Attainment

Most of us fall into what the revelation calls the "normal" category, average minds with average potential for spiritual growth. For us, the assignment of guardian angels follows a fascinating progression tied to something called the seven psychic circles of human achievement.

I need to pause here and explain what these circles represent, because they're central to understanding how angelic ministry evolves throughout our lives. The psychic circles aren't geographical locations or mystical zones; they're levels of spiritual and intellectual attainment. Circle seven represents the beginning stage, barely starting to grasp spiritual realities. As we grow in self-understanding, in self-mastery, in cosmic awareness, we progress through circles six, five, four, and so on, until we reach circle three.

Circle three is significant. It's the threshold at which something remarkable happens we're assigned personal guardian angels. Not group guardians who watch over hundreds or thousands of mortals, but two Seraphim dedicated exclusively to us, to our spiritual progress, to our eternal welfare.

Let me break down how this progression works. On circle seven, one guardian Seraphim oversees approximately one thousand human beings, assisted by 144 pairs of Cherubim who keep the records. That's a lot of mortals per angel, which tells you something about the level of individual attention available at this stage, minimal at best.

Move up to circle six, and the ratio improves: 500 mortals per two guardian Seraphim. Circle five narrows it further to about 100 individuals per pair of guardians. By circle four, we're down to ten mortals per two Seraphim. The closer we get to God, the more personalized the ministry becomes.

Then comes circle three, that crucial threshold. Suddenly, it's just you. Two Seraphim, one Cherubim, one Sanobim, all assigned to a single mortal. From that moment until you stand on the shores of Paradise itself, these celestial personalities will accompany you, guide you, serve you, and yes, come to love you with a depth of affection that we can barely comprehend.

Alternative Paths to Personal Guardians

But here's something fascinating: you don't have to reach circle three through the slow process of evolutionary growth to receive personal guardians. *The Urantia Book* describes three ways to qualify:

First, you can make the third circle through normal spiritual development, mastering yourself, understanding cosmic reality, learning to consistently choose the Father's will.

Second, you can be enrolled in what's called the Reserve Corps of Destiny. These are special individuals who possess the potential to perform significant service for God or for humanity without seeking personal glory or recognition. They're willing to be used as instruments without knowing it, without receiving credit, without ego gratification. If the Seraphim identify you as a candidate and you're accepted into this corps, you immediately receive personal guardians regardless of what psychic circle you're on.

Third, and this is the most direct path, you can make what the revelation calls a "supreme decision." You can make a wholehearted, unreserved commitment to do the will of God. You can pledge yourself to become Godlike, to follow the path of perfection attainment regardless of the cost. The moment you make that genuine, soul-deep decision, personal guardians are assigned. It doesn't matter if you're still struggling on circle seven. Your sincere consecration to divine will triggers immediate response from the seraphic ministry.

I suspect most of us in this study fellowship have already made that supreme decision. If you're reading these words, if you've committed time and energy to understanding *The Urantia Book*, if you've turned your face toward Paradise and said, "Yes, I will follow," then you likely have two Seraphim who have been walking beside you for some time now. You may not see them or hear them, but they're there. Recording your choices. Celebrating your victories. Working behind the scenes to open doors and create opportunities for your spiritual growth.

The Supernormal Mind

The third category, supernormal minds, represents individuals of exceptional spiritual capacity. These are men and women of "great decision, undoubted potential, and spiritual achievement." They maintain more or less conscious contact with their indwelling Thought Adjusters. Their lives demonstrate consistent dedication to truth, beauty, and goodness. They naturally gravitate toward service and worship.

Obviously, such individuals receive personal guardians. The universe doesn't waste exceptional potential. If you're someone who has genuinely advanced in spiritual understanding, who has developed the ability to discern divine guidance and follow it, the angels will provide maximum support for your continued growth.

Group Guardians Versus Personal Guardians

We need to understand the fundamental difference between group guardians and personal guardians, because the revelation makes a clear distinction. Group Seraphim serve temporary assignments. They may watch over you during your mortal life, but if you die before reaching circle three, they don't follow you individually to the mansion worlds. Instead, they hold your "soul trust", the record of your identity, the patterns of your mind, the essence of who you are, until the next dispensational resurrection.

This is what Jesus referred to when he spoke of "awakening my sleeping children." Most mortals who believe in God and choose survival but never quite make it to circle three become what the revelators call "sleeping survivors." They don't resurrect on the third day after death. They sleep, unconscious, unaware of the passage of time, until the next major resurrection, which might be decades or even centuries away.

Personal guardians, by contrast, form a permanent bond. Once assigned to you at circle three (or through enrollment in the Reserve Corps, or through a supreme decision), those Seraphim become your companions for eternity. They accompany you to the mansion worlds, celebrate your achievements on the morontia spheres, cheer your progress through the local universe educational system, and ultimately rejoice when you achieve Paradise and stand in the presence of the Universal Father.

For the Seraphim themselves, assignment as a personal guardian represents the highest aspiration. Every angel hopes for this posting, because it means they get to traverse the universe, experiencing worlds and systems and constellations they would never otherwise see. It means they get to participate in the supreme adventure of time, the ascent of an evolutionary mortal from animal origins to Paradise citizenship.

When the revelators announced the assignment of a guardian to a member of the Reserve Corps in Chicago (possibly someone like Sadler, though we can only speculate), one hundred qualified Seraphim applied for the position. Out of those hundred, twelve finalists were selected. And from those twelve, the celestial administrators chose the two who best matched the personality and temperament of the mortal in question.

Your guardian angels, if you have them, weren't randomly assigned. They were carefully selected from among many candidates specifically because their personalities harmonize with yours. They understand you. They think somewhat like you do. They appreciate your quirks and work effectively with your particular blend of strengths and weaknesses.

The Work of Recording Angels

Throughout this angelic ministry, records are being kept. The Cherubim and Sanobim serve primarily as recording angels, documenting everything of spiritual significance that occurs in your life. Every choice that has lasting value, every act of kindness or courage, every moment of authentic worship, every struggle against selfish impulses, all of it is recorded.

I want to be clear about what this means, because some people find the idea uncomfortable. The angels aren't recording your bathroom breaks or your grocery shopping trips or the color of socks you wore on Tuesday. They're not cosmic surveillance cameras capturing every mundane detail. What they record are the spiritually significant experiences, the moments that reveal character, that demonstrate growth, that show moral decision-making in action.

Why keep these records? Because you'll need them on the mansion worlds. Your personality survives death, but your mortal memories don't automatically transfer intact to your new morontia form. The records help reconstruct your identity, help you remember who you were and what you learned, help you pick up where you left off without having to start from scratch.

Think of it like this: your Thought Adjuster holds the spiritual transcript, the record of all God-knowing and God-seeking experiences. Your Seraphim and Cherubim hold the personal transcript, the record of your character development and life decisions. Together, these records provide everything needed to resurrect you as a recognizable, continuous personality.

The Dual Nature of Seraphic Assignment

Here's something I find particularly interesting: while the Seraphim serve as a pair, they function with remarkable flexibility. Both angels are fully capable of discharging all guardian responsibilities independently. This means one can take rest periods, recharging with the life energy of the universe circuits, while the other remains on duty. You're never left unattended.

The Seraphim rotate between active ministry and what we might call circuit maintenance. They need to periodically connect with the broader communications networks of the local universe, to refresh themselves with energy from universal sources, to receive updated instructions or information. During these rest periods, the Cherubim step up, temporarily assuming the role of recording angel alongside the Seraphim who remains on duty.

This arrangement shows both efficiency and redundancy. Nothing is lost. No opportunity for ministry is missed. One angel or the other is always watching, always available, always working on your behalf.

Day and Night Ministry

We should also understand that much of the Thought Adjuster's work occurs while you sleep. During those hours when your conscious mind is at rest, when the barriers of material consciousness are lowered, the Adjuster can accomplish spiritual transformations that would be difficult or impossible during waking hours. Dreams sometimes reflect this deeper work, though more often the results simply integrate into your character without your conscious awareness.

The Seraphim, by contrast, do most of their work while you're awake and active. They influence your environment, arrange circumstances, bring people into your life, suggest ideas through what seems like intuition, protect you from certain dangers, and generally orchestrate opportunities for spiritual growth. They work in the background of your daily experience, gently nudging, subtly guiding, occasionally intervening more directly when necessary.

Neither the Adjuster nor the Seraphim ever override your free will. They can suggest, but they cannot compel. They can arrange opportunities, but they cannot force you to take advantage of them. Every genuine spiritual decision must be yours, freely chosen, authentically willed, personally endorsed.

The Challenge of the Animal Legacy

Now I need to address something that often proves difficult for students: what the revelation calls the "animal legacy" or sometimes "the mark of the beast." This refers to the evolutionary baggage we carry from our animal origins, the primitive fears, the selfish impulses, the territorial instincts, the aggressive tendencies that served our pre-human ancestors but hinder our spiritual progress.

One of the primary tasks in early mansion world experience involves systematically removing this animal legacy. It's not accomplished in a day or even a year. The seven mansion worlds themselves represent, in part, seven stages of liberation from these primitive patterns.

I won't lie to you: this is hard work. Many students of *The Urantia Book* stumble over passages that describe the difficulty of spiritual transformation. We want to believe that once we accept God and commit to his will, everything becomes easy. But that's not how growth works, not on this world, not on the mansion worlds, not anywhere in the universe.

The supreme decision to seek God and do his will is just the beginning. After that comes the long, patient process of actually transforming your character, of replacing animal reactions with spiritual responses, of learning to love when instinct says to hate, to forgive when instinct says to retaliate, to serve when instinct says to hoard.

One of the most persistent animal patterns is fear. Throughout human history, we've been afraid, afraid of predators, afraid of enemies, afraid of starvation, afraid of darkness, afraid of spirits, afraid of death. Even now, in our supposedly enlightened era, fear drives so much of human behavior. We're afraid of government, afraid of change, afraid of other races and religions, afraid of economic collapse, afraid of loss and suffering and loneliness.

The Seraphim struggle to understand this fear. They've never experienced it. They exist in a reality where love and trust and confidence are the default states of being. When they look at humans constantly worrying, constantly dreading things that usually never happen, constantly living in anxious anticipation of disaster, they find it baffling.

But they're patient. They work with us despite not fully comprehending our fear-driven reactions. They gently, persistently encourage us toward courage and faith. And slowly, sometimes very slowly, we begin to change.

The Path Forward

As we close this introductory chapter, I want to return to something fundamental: none of us walks alone. Whether you've reached circle three or are still on circle seven, whether you have personal guardians or are still part of a group ministry, celestial beings are working on your behalf. The Thought Adjuster dwells within you. The Spirit of Truth of Christ Michael overshadows you. The Holy Spirit of the Divine Minister pervades your world. And the Seraphim, those magnificent angels of feminine character, coordinate all these influences, bringing them to bear on your daily experience in ways calculated to foster your spiritual awakening.

You don't have to see them or hear them or feel them for them to be real. They're there, as surely as the ground beneath your feet, as certain as the sun above your head. And if you've made that supreme decision, if you've genuinely pledged yourself to the Father's will, then you have two specific angels who know your name, who understand your struggles, who celebrate your victories, and who will stand beside you when you awaken on the mansion worlds.

In our next chapter, we'll explore more deeply how these guardian angels actually function, the techniques they employ, the limitations they work within, the results they achieve. We'll examine the fascinating question of survival and non-survival, looking honestly at what happens to those who choose to reject eternal life. We'll also delve into the experience of resurrection, both for those who achieve circle three during mortal life and for the sleeping survivors who await dispensational awakening.

But for now, let this truth settle into your consciousness: you are loved, you are guided, you are protected by beings of celestial origin who have voluntarily bound their destiny to yours. Whatever challenges you face, you don't face them alone. Whatever darkness surrounds you, the angels are there, working to bring light. Whatever uncertainty clouds your future, they are arranging circumstances to help you find your way.

This is the magnificent reality of seraphic ministry, the guardians of destiny who labor tirelessly, invisibly, lovingly on behalf of every mortal who chooses survival. And that, my friends, is where our study truly begins.

Chapter 2: Seraphic Guardians of Destiny - Our Companions on the Journey Home

When I first began studying Paper 113 of *The Urantia Book*, I'll admit I approached the concept of guardian angels with a mixture of curiosity and skepticism. Like many of you, I'd grown up with popular images of angels, winged beings hovering in clouds, or perhaps that gentle voice whispering in one ear while a devil whispers in the other. What I discovered in this revelation transformed everything I thought I knew about celestial ministry and our journey back to God.

Tonight, as my wife Diane and I continue our exploration of the Seraphic Guardians of Destiny, we're picking up where we left off in Section 3 of Paper 113. For those joining us for the first time, you can find our study slides at the Fifth Epochal Revelation Fellowship website, there's a link on the left-hand side near the top. We've created one for each paper we study, and I encourage you to follow along as we work through these profound concepts together.

The Integration of Spirit Influences

Let me start with something that really caught my attention when I first read this section. The text tells us that "one of the most important things a destiny guardian does for her mortal subject is to effect a personal coordination of the numerous impersonal spirit influences which indwell, surround, and impinge upon the mind and soul of the evolving material creature."

Now, think about what this means. We're not just dealing with one spiritual influence in our lives. We have multiple streams of divine ministry working simultaneously: the Thought Adjuster dwelling within us, the Spirit of Truth surrounding us, and the Holy Spirit, that circuit of the local universe Mother Spirit, also influencing our development. Each of these operates at different levels and in different ways.

The Thought Adjuster represents the prepersonal presence of the Universal Father. It's prepersonal because it hasn't yet achieved personality fusion with us. The Spirit of Truth and the Holy Spirit, on the other hand, are impersonal spirit influences. And here's where it gets interesting: these impersonal and prepersonal entities find it exceedingly difficult to make direct contact with our highly material and discretely personal minds.

This is where our guardian seraphim become absolutely essential. They act as coordinators, taking all these various spiritual influences and helping to unify them in ways we can actually appreciate and respond to. The Thought Adjuster influences us from within, working in the depths of our superconscious mind. The Spirit of Truth and the Holy Spirit influence us from without. The seraphim help integrate what's coming from the Thought Adjuster with these external spiritual circuits, creating a more coherent spiritual experience in our daily lives.

But here's something crucial: this integration works much more effectively when we develop what the book calls a "moral nature." If we're living barbarically, making immoral choices, engaging in selfish behaviors, these spirits struggle to communicate with us. Our guardian angels find their work infinitely more difficult when we resist moral growth. Conversely, as we expand our moral consciousness and make increasingly ethical decisions, we become more receptive to spiritual guidance from all these sources.

The Seraphic Ministry Through Universal Circuits

The seraphim don't work in isolation. They correlate "the manifold agencies and influences of the Infinite Spirit, ranging from the domains of the physical controllers and the adjutant mind-spirits up to the Holy Spirit of the Divine Minister and to the omnipresent spirit presence of the Paradise Third Source and Center."

Let's unpack this because it reveals the incredible scope of seraphic ministry. The Infinite Spirit, the Third Person of the Paradise Trinity, controls everything material throughout the universe, doesn't she? This control extends from Paradise itself down through all the superuniverses, local universes, and individual inhabited worlds. The seraphim operate within this vast domain, coordinating influences that include the Master Physical Controllers (who manage physical energy), the adjutant mind-spirits (which we'll discuss more in a moment), and the Holy Spirit circuit of our local universe Mother Spirit.

Before we reach the third psychic circle of spiritual attainment, we're primarily influenced through these adjutant mind-spirits. There are seven of them: intuition, understanding, courage, knowledge, counsel, worship, and wisdom. These are the mental circuits that connect our animal-origin minds to spiritual reality. The seraphim work particularly with the higher adjutants, worship and wisdom, as these are reinforced by the leadings of the Thought Adjuster.

What struck me most powerfully is realizing that the Infinite Spirit's ministry is fundamentally about mercy. Everything the Third Source and Center does for evolutionary creatures like us flows from divine mercy. The seraphim, as ministering spirits of the Infinite Spirit, embody this mercy ministry. They don't just deliver messages or protect us from danger; they're implementing God's merciful plan for our survival and eternal progression.

The seraphim take all these influences from the Infinite Spirit, the local universe Mother Spirit, the Holy Spirit, and the adjutant mind-spirits, and help us integrate them with the presence of the Father (the Thought Adjuster) and the presence of the Son (the Spirit of Truth). Think about that coordination for a moment. Your guardian angel is harmonizing the ministry of all three persons of the Trinity in your personal experience. No wonder the text says these "divine endowments are unified and coordinated on the lower levels of human spiritual experience by the ministry of the guardian seraphim."

Custodians of Identity and Soul

Now we come to what I consider one of the most beautiful and profound aspects of seraphic ministry. The text asks a question: why does the seraphic guardian eventually become "the personal custodian of the mind patterns, the memory formulas, and the soul realities of the mortal survivor during that interval between physical death and morontia resurrection"?

The answer reveals the exquisite precision of the universe plan. Mind is controlled by the Infinite Spirit. Who acts on behalf of the Infinite Spirit directly with us? The seraphic guardian. Therefore, only these beings of the Infinite Spirit family can preserve our mind patterns and memories during that transition between death and resurrection. It's a matter of spiritual jurisdiction, if you will.

When you die, three essential components of your identity must be preserved. First, your mind patterns, the entire neural network of your thoughts, reasoning abilities, and mental capacities. Second, your memory formulas, everything you've experienced, learned, and become through your mortal life. Third, your soul, that growing morontia reality jointly created by your material mind and divine Thought Adjuster throughout your lifetime of moral decisions.

The seraphim takes custody of all three. Meanwhile, the Thought Adjuster safeguards your personality, that unique gift from the Universal Father that makes you distinctly you. The Adjuster then meets the seraphim on the first mansion world, where you're given a new morontia body and reassembled. You wake up as yourself, same personality, same memories, same identity, but in a new form suited for the next stage of your journey.

I find it fascinating that even a supernaphim, a higher order of angel, (paradise level) shares this transit function with us later in our career. Just as the seraphim takes care of us during our first transition to the mansion worlds, when we eventually reach the circuits of Havona (the central universe), a supernaphim guarantees our transition from the Havona worlds to Paradise itself. They're both ministering spirits, one operating at the lower evolutionary level, the other at the higher perfected level. But here's what really matters: the seraphim who begins this journey with you actually accompanies you all the way to Paradise. She doesn't hand you off and disappear. Your guardian angel is in this for the long haul, the eternal haul, actually.

The Mystery of Seraphic Function

The revelators admit something remarkable: they don't fully understand how the seraphim accomplish all these complex functions. The text states plainly, "We do not really know, but we conjecture that this phenomenal ministry is in some undisclosed manner facilitated by the unrecognized and unrevealed working of the Supreme Being."

The Supreme Being represents God's evolving experiential presence in the time-space universes. Every experience we have, every moral decision we make, every spiritual step we take contributes to the actualization of the Supreme. The seraphim operate within this evolving reality, and their ministry appears to be somehow enhanced by the Supreme's presence and purpose.

What we can say with certainty is that "throughout the entire realm of progressive survival in and through the Supreme Being, seraphim are an essential part of continuing mortal progression." You cannot make this journey without them. They're not optional extras or occasional helpers; they're integral to the very mechanism of survival itself.

How Guardian Angels Guide Without Controlling

This brings us to a critical distinction that many people misunderstand. Seraphim are not mind invaders. They "spring from the same source that also gives origin to mortal mind, the Creative Spirit", but they function very differently than mind itself. The text describes them as "mind stimulators," but notice how they operate:

"from the outside inward, working through the social, ethical, and moral environment of human beings."

Think about the implications. Your guardian angel cannot reach into your mind and rearrange your thoughts. She cannot manipulate your will or force you to make certain decisions. What she can do is shape your environment, the circumstances, opportunities, and challenges you encounter, to promote "circle-making decisions." These are the moral and spiritual choices that advance you through the psychic circles of spiritual attainment.

The seraphim accomplish this through cooperation with other universe agencies. They work with the Master Physical Controllers to influence material circumstances. They coordinate with the midway creatures (those unique beings who can function in both material and spiritual realms) to manipulate terrestrial conditions. They can actually shape the physical environment you experience, but always in service of your spiritual growth and always respecting your free will.

Let me give you an example that might help clarify this. Suppose you're facing a significant career decision. Your guardian angel cannot make you choose the path that offers more spiritual growth opportunities. But she can arrange circumstances so that both options become clear to you. She might orchestrate a chance meeting with someone who shares their experience with one path. She might ensure you encounter information that illuminates the spiritual implications of each choice. She might even allow certain doors to close so that others open more clearly. But the decision? That remains absolutely yours.

This is why the text emphasizes that "mortal man subject to Adjuster leading is also amenable to seraphic guidance." We're subject to both influences, but neither controls us. The Adjuster represents "the essence of man's eternal nature," while "the seraphim is the teacher of man's evolving nature." In this life, we're usually unaware of our seraphic instructors. In the next life, the morontia existence on the mansion worlds, we'll be "conscious and aware of seraphic instructors," but here, their work happens mostly beneath our conscious awareness.

Teachers on the Path of Growth

When I first read that "seraphim function as teachers of men by guiding the footsteps of the human personality into paths of new and progressive experiences," I thought this meant they'd make my spiritual journey easier. I was wrong. The text continues: "To accept the guidance of a seraphim rarely means attaining a life of ease. In following this leading, you are sure to encounter, and if you have the courage, to traverse the rugged hills of moral choosing and spiritual progress."

This hit me hard. We often ask our angels for help, expecting them to smooth our path, remove obstacles, make things comfortable. But that's not their job. Their mission is to place us in situations where we must make moral choices, where we must struggle with ethical dilemmas, where spiritual growth becomes possible through challenge rather than comfort.

Think about how the Thought Adjuster works in conjunction with this. The seraphim creates the circumstances that require a decision. The Thought Adjuster, working from within, whispers, "This is the way." But we must choose. We must act. We must traverse those rugged hills ourselves. No one can do it for us, not even beings as advanced and devoted as our guardian angels.

The text makes a profound observation about worship and prayer. "The impulse of worship largely originates in the spirit promptings of the higher mind adjutants, reinforced by the leadings of the Adjuster." So, worship, that spontaneous up reach toward God, comes partly from the sixth and seventh adjutant mind-spirits (worship and wisdom), enhanced by the Adjuster's influence. "But the urge to pray so often experienced by God-conscious mortals very often arises as a result of seraphic influence."

Your guardian angel is constantly working to create cosmic insight in your mind, to help you recognize the Adjuster's presence more clearly, to encourage your cooperation with the divine presence within you. When you feel moved to pray, when circumstances drive you to your knees, when you suddenly sense the need for divine communion, that may very well be your seraphim orchestrating conditions to deepen your spiritual receptivity.

The Correlation of Ministry

I want to emphasize something the revelators stress repeatedly: the incredible cooperation between the Thought Adjuster and the guardian seraphim. "While there is apparently no communication between the indwelling Adjusters and the encompassing seraphim, they always seem to work in perfect harmony and exquisite accord."

We know the Adjuster is most active when we're asleep, during those hours when our conscious mind rests and superconscious spiritual work can proceed unimpeded. This suggests the guardian seraphim are probably most active during our waking hours, shaping our daily experiences and environmental encounters. Yet even though the Adjuster never truly sleeps, he steps back somewhat during our daytime lives, allowing the guardian angel to implement her ministry while he continues his deeper transformative work.

"Such superb cooperation could hardly be either accidental or incidental," the text notes. There's a divine choreography here, a coordination that transcends what we can fully understand. The Adjuster works from the inside, the seraphim from the outside, yet their ministries blend seamlessly in our experience.

And here's where the Supreme Being enters the picture again: "The ministering personality of the guardian seraphim, the God presence of the indwelling Adjuster, the encircuited action of the Holy Spirit, and the Son-consciousness of the Spirit of Truth are all divinely correlated into a meaningful unity of spiritual ministry in and to a mortal personality... these celestial influences are all integrated in the enveloping and evolving presence of the Supreme Being."

Do you see what this means? Every spiritual influence in your life, from the Father, the Son, the Spirit, the local universe Mother Spirit, and your guardian angel, becomes unified in the experiential reality of the Supreme. And because the Supreme is the God of experience, when you experience this coordinated spiritual ministry, the Supreme experiences it too. Your growth is his growth. Your struggles contribute to his actualization. Nothing in this universe happens in isolation.

The Sacred Boundaries

Now I need to address something crucial, something that eliminates a common excuse we humans like to use. "Angels do not invade the sanctity of the human mind; they do not manipulate the will of mortals, nor do they directly contact with the indwelling Adjusters."

Let me be absolutely clear: no angel, no demon, no spiritual being of any order has the power to make you do anything. "Neither angels nor any other order of universe personality have power or authority to curtail or abridge the prerogatives of human choosing."

So, when someone says, "The devil made me do it," they're simply wrong. When we blame our poor decisions on outside forces, we're refusing to accept responsibility. The seraphim can't invade your mind. They can't manipulate your will. They can't even directly influence the Thought Adjuster. All their work happens from the outside, through environmental circumstances and opportunities. The final choice always, always, remains yours.

"In no circumstances do these angels interfere with the free action of the human will." Free will is supreme in the universe. It's the one thing God himself will not violate. Your guardian angel, devoted as she is to your survival and growth, operates under the same constraint. She can guide, suggest, arrange circumstances, create opportunities, but she cannot and will not choose for you.

The text adds something touching: "Angels are so near you and care so feelingly for you that they figuratively 'weep because of your willful intolerance and stubbornness.'" Of course, seraphim don't shed physical tears, they don't have physical bodies, but "they do have spiritual emotions, and they do experience feelings and sentiments of a spiritual nature which are in certain ways comparable to human emotions."

Your guardian angel grieves when you persistently choose paths that lead away from spiritual growth. She rejoices when you make decisions that advance your soul. She's not a distant, dispassionate observer. She's intimately invested in your eternal destiny, even though she cannot force you toward it.

Independent Yet Responsive

Here's another important point: "The seraphim act in your behalf quite independent of your direct appeals; they are executing the mandates of their superiors, and thus they function regardless of your passing whims or changing moods."

Your guardian angel isn't sitting around waiting for you to pray before she acts. She has orders from higher authorities, likely the residential governor of your world and ultimately the Sovereign Creator Son of your local universe. Her mission is to guard you, guide you, and facilitate your survival and growth. She pursues this mission whether you acknowledge her existence or not, whether you pray or don't pray, whether you're consciously spiritual or completely oblivious to spiritual realities.

"This does not imply that you may not make their tasks either easier or more difficult, but rather that angels are not directly concerned with your appeals or with your prayers." You can definitely make your guardian's work easier by choosing spiritual paths and moral actions. You can make it more difficult through persistent selfishness and spiritual resistance. But her fundamental mission continues regardless.

The text explains: "In the flesh life the intelligence of angels is not directly available to mortal men. They are not overlords or directors; they are simply guardians." They guard you, but they don't chart your course. "You must chart your own course, but these angels then act to make the best possible use of the course you have chosen."

Let me give you a practical example. Suppose you choose a career path that has limited spiritual growth potential. Your guardian angel cannot redirect you to a different career. But she will work within the career you've chosen to create maximum opportunities for moral decisions, ethical challenges, and spiritual insights. She'll make the best of your choice, finding ways to advance your soul even in circumstances that seem spiritually unpromising.

The seraphim "do not therefore ordinarily arbitrarily intervene in the routine affairs of human life but when they receive instructions from their superiors to perform some unusual exploit, you may rest assured that these guardians will find some means of carrying out these mandates. They do not, therefore, intrude into the picture of human drama except in emergencies and then usually on the direct orders of their superiors."

Preparing for Eternal Association

Something that moves me deeply is this statement: "They are the beings who are going to follow you for many an age, and they are thus receiving an introduction to their future work and personality association."

Your relationship with your guardian seraphim isn't temporary. It's not like a teacher who instructs you for a semester and moves on. This relationship extends potentially throughout your entire ascension career, from this world through the mansion worlds, through the constellation and universe headquarters, through the superuniverse training spheres, and ultimately to Paradise itself.

Your guardian angel is learning about you right now. Every decision you make, every struggle you face, every triumph and failure teaches her about your personality, your tendencies, your potential. She's preparing for an eternal partnership. Later, on the mansion worlds and beyond, you'll become consciously aware of this companion who has been with you since you made your first moral decision as a child.

The Transition Called Death

When I first seriously considered what happens at death, I had more questions than answers. The revelation provides clarity that's both comforting and profound. "The instant the pilot light in the human mind flickers out, the spirit luminosity which the seraphim associate with the presence of the Adjuster appears to the attending angel."

Notice that phrasing, "the pilot light in the human mind." Death isn't complicated or mysterious from the universe perspective. It's simply the extinguishing of the mind's functioning. At that moment, the seraphim immediately recognizes the Adjuster's presence as a spiritual luminosity. The two custodians of your identity, angel and Adjuster, then proceed with their respective duties.

The seraphim "reports in person to the commanding angels, successively, of the group, company, battalion, unit, legion, and host." There's a clear chain of command in the angelic corps. Eventually, this report reaches "the planetary chief of seraphim for registry on the dispatches to be forwarded to the Evening Stars, or lieutenant of Gabriel, in command of the seraphic army of this candidate for universe ascension."

Here's something that surprised me: "It is not until you actually attain the personality status by the embracement of the immortal survival of your associated perfected soul that you finally and truly become one of the ascending family of the finaliter destiny." We don't automatically become survival candidates just because we're human. We become candidates when we die, but only if we've made genuine spiritual progress.

The guardian then receives certification and proceeds to the first mansion world, "where she will await the coconsciousness of identity of her former ward in the flesh." What beautiful phrasing, "coconsciousness of identity." She's waiting not just for your resurrection but for that moment of reunion when you become consciously aware of each other again.

When Survival Fails

Now I need to address something painful but important. What happens when a human soul fails to survive? "In case the human soul fails of survival after having received the assignment of a personal angel, the attending seraphim must proceed to the headquarters of the local universe, there to witness to the complete records of her complement as previously reported."

This explains what I mentioned earlier about the adjudication process. The seraphim goes before the tribunals of the archangels, the universe attorneys, essentially, to be examined regarding her service. Was she faithful? Did she do everything possible to facilitate survival? The records show her efforts, and she's "absolved from blame in the matter of the survival failure of her subject."

Then she returns to the worlds, either Earth or another planet, to be assigned another mortal of ascending potentiality or to some other division of seraphic ministry. But here's what troubles me: somewhere a soul that could have survived chose not to. A personality that could have continued eternally decided, through persistent rejection of spiritual guidance, to cease to exist.

The contrast is stark. If you're a survival candidate who has reached the third psychic circle and earned a personal guardian, she goes directly to the mansion world to await your resurrection. If you haven't survived, she must return to universe headquarters to account for her service before receiving a new assignment.

The Personal Coordination of Spirit Ministry

Let me return to something foundational that ties all this together. The seraphim achieve "a personal coordination of the numerous impersonal spirit influences which indwell, surround, and impinge upon the mind and soul." This coordination is absolutely essential because we exist at the intersection of multiple spiritual realities.

The Thought Adjuster dwells within us, prepersonal but profoundly personal in potential. The Spirit of Truth surrounds us, the spirit presence of our Creator Son, Michael of Nebadon, whom we knew as Jesus of Nazareth. The Holy Spirit circuit of the Divine Minister, our universe Mother Spirit, bathes us constantly in nurturing spiritual energy. The adjutant mind-spirits connect our material minds to spiritual possibilities.

Without the seraphim coordinating these influences, we'd be overwhelmed, confused, unable to integrate these various spiritual impulses into coherent spiritual experience. The guardian angels don't just guard; they integrate, correlate, unify. They're the divine coordinators making it possible for evolutionary creatures with animal-origin minds to progress toward spiritual perfection.

"More especially can and does this seraphic guardian correlate the manifold agencies and influences of the Infinite Spirit, ranging from the domains of the physical controllers and the adjutant mind-spirits up to the Holy Spirit of the Divine Minister and to the Omnipresent Spirit presence of the Paradise Third Source and Center."

Think about that range, from physical controllers managing material energy to the actual Paradise presence of the Infinite Spirit. Your guardian angel operates across this entire spectrum, bringing divine influences to bear on your personal experience in ways you can actually respond to and benefit from.

The Mercy Ministry

I want to emphasize something that's woven throughout this entire discussion: mercy. "The angelic servers are gifted in combining the love of the Father and the mercy of the Son in their administration to mortal creatures."

The seraphim embody divine mercy. They represent the patient, persistent, never-giving-up love of God for his ascending children. When we fail, they don't abandon us. When we stumble, they help arrange circumstances for recovery. When we wander, they work to bring us back to spiritual paths.

This mercy isn't weakness or sentimentality. It's the tough, enduring, practical love that gives us opportunity after opportunity to choose survival, to choose growth, to choose God. The seraphim serve us not because we deserve it, we're barely above the animal level when they first begin their ministry, but because God has decreed that every person of moral capacity deserves every possible chance to survive and progress.

"Herein is revealed the reason why the seraphic guardian eventually becomes the personal custodian of the mind patterns, the memory formulas, and the soul realities of the mortal survivor during that interval between physical death and morontia resurrection." Only through mercy could such an arrangement exist. Only through divine love would the universe invest such effort, such resources, such personal attention in creatures as primitive and unpromising as we are.

Looking Ahead

As we prepare to move forward in our study, I want you to understand what we've established in this chapter. Guardian seraphim are not optional additions to spiritual life. They're not supernatural security blankets for those who believe in such things. They're essential, integral components of the universe mechanism designed to raise evolutionary creatures from animal status to spiritual perfection.

Your guardian angel has been with you since you made your first true moral decision, probably in childhood. She's observed every choice, every struggle, every triumph. She's arranged countless circumstances you attributed to chance or coincidence. She's wept at your stubbornness and rejoiced at your progress. And she's preparing for an eternal association that will extend far beyond anything you can currently imagine.

In our next session, we'll explore the seraphic planetary government, how these celestial beings organize and administer their ministry to an entire world. We'll see how the angelic corps structures itself, how it coordinates with other universe agencies, and how it serves the grand plan of progressive spiritual civilization.

But for now, I want you to sit with this truth: you are not alone. You have never been alone. From the moment you became capable of making a genuine moral choice, a devoted personal or group guardian has been working tirelessly for your survival and advancement. The Father indwells you through the Thought Adjuster. The Son surrounds you through the Spirit of Truth. The Spirit ministers to you through the Holy Spirit and your guardian seraphim.

Every spiritual influence in the universe is coordinated and focused on one astonishing goal: helping you, yes, you personally, choose to survive, to grow, to ascend, to eventually stand in the presence of the Universal Father on Paradise as a perfected spirit being of eternal destiny… Can you think of anything more incredible than that?

Chapter 3: Seraphic Planetary Government - The Celestial Administration of Earth

Introduction

As we continue our exploration of the celestial beings who serve humanity, we arrive at a fascinating intersection, where the ministry of individual guardian angels meets the grand machinery of planetary administration. In our previous studies, we examined how seraphim work intimately with individual souls, guiding and protecting us through our mortal journey. Now, I'd like to shift our focus outward to consider something equally remarkable: how these same angelic beings participate in governing an entire world.

When I first encountered Paper 114 of *The Urantia Book*, titled "Seraphic Planetary Government," I'll admit I found myself wrestling with questions I hadn't fully considered before. We tend to think of government as a human institution, our legislatures, our courts, our administrative bodies. We look around at governments, institutions, and human leaders, and naturally assume they're running things. But what this paper reveals is something far more profound: there exists an intricate, highly organized celestial government working behind the scenes, guiding planetary destiny through spiritual forces we cannot see. This invisible administration doesn't override human free will, but it does shape circumstances, influence individual choices, and steadily, sometimes painfully slowly, move our world toward its ultimate destiny in light and life. But what if I told you that behind the visible structures of human civilization, there exists an invisible celestial government working constantly to guide our planet toward its destined purpose? This may sound like the stuff of mystical speculation, but *The Urantia Book* presents it as simple fact: our world operates under a sophisticated superhuman administration that coordinates the efforts of countless celestial personalities.

This chapter explores that hidden government. We'll examine who these celestial administrators are, how they organize their work, and perhaps most importantly, why our planet's governmental structure differs significantly from that of nearly every other inhabited world in our local universe. The story that emerges is one of remarkable adaptation, a celestial administration that has been forced to compensate for the tragic consequences of planetary rebellion while still working patiently toward the eventual establishment of light and life on our troubled world.

The Foundation of Celestial Rule

The opening statement of Paper 114 establishes a principle that appears throughout religious and philosophical traditions: "The Most Highs rule in the kingdoms of men." But *The Urantia Book* isn't speaking metaphorically here. This governance operates primarily through what the text calls "the ministry of the seraphim", those same angelic beings we've been studying, now viewed in their broader administrative roles.

Let me clarify something important right away. When we speak of the Most Highs, we're referring to specific celestial personalities, the Constellation Fathers known as Vorondadek Sons. These beings oversee entire constellations of local systems, and they exercise real authority over the direction of planetary affairs. This might seem to contradict our understanding of human free will and self-determination, but I think the relationship is more nuanced than it first appears.

The celestial government doesn't operate by overriding human choice or dictating every decision made by earthly leaders. Instead, it works through influence and circumstance. Guardian seraphim, as we learned in earlier chapters, can manipulate physical circumstances and gently influence individual thinking, always respecting the sacred zone of human will. When we scale this up to planetary governance, we find a similar pattern. The celestial administrators guide the overall trajectory of world events, ensuring that despite all our struggles and setbacks, our planet continues moving, however haltingly, toward its ultimate destiny.

Think about this for a moment. At noon on the day these revelations were compiled, Urantia hosted 501,234,619 pairs of seraphim, that's over one billion individual angels. Given the world's population in the 1930s, this suggests roughly one angelic presence for every human beings on the planet. Today, with our population approaching eight billion, we can reasonably assume the angelic host has grown proportionally. These beings aren't passive observers. They're actively engaged in thousands of different capacities: some serve as guardian angels to individuals, others work with groups and institutions, still others handle what the text mysteriously refers to as "transport, messenger, and death duty."

The sheer scale of this celestial presence humbles me. It suggests that no human being walks through life truly alone. Even those who feel most isolated, most forgotten by society, exist within the awareness and care of celestial ministers who understand their struggles and work constantly to create opportunities for growth and spiritual progress.

Why Urantia Is Different - Earth's Unique Status in the Universe

If you're familiar with *The Urantia Book*, you know that our planet occupies a unique, though not necessarily enviable, position in the universe. The text is quite explicit: "The planetary government is unlike that of any other world in the Satania system, even in all Nebadon." Seven specific factors contribute to this uniqueness and understanding them helps us grasp both our challenges and our strange privileges.

First, we're a **decimal planet**, one of the worlds where the Life Carriers experiment with modifications to the standard evolutionary patterns. Every tenth world in our local system serves this experimental function, making our world a laboratory of sorts for testing new approaches to life manifestation. which means our biological and even social evolution follows a somewhat different trajectory than most inhabited spheres. This alone would make us unusual, but it's just the beginning.

Second, and far more consequentially, we've endured the **Lucifer Rebellion**. Some 200,000 years ago, our System Sovereign, a being named Lucifer, led a rebellion against the universal government, and our Planetary Prince, Caligastia, joined that rebellion. The details of this upheaval are complex, but the result was catastrophic: our world became cut off from normal celestial circuits, isolated in a kind of spiritual quarantine that persists even now. Imagine a city suddenly disconnected from all outside communication and aid, left to manage its own affairs with only the barest external support. That's been Urantia's condition for two hundred millennia. Even today, we remain cut off from certain spiritual resources that normal planets take for granted.

The third factor compounds the second: the **default of Adam and Eve**. Even after the rebellion, celestial authorities sent a Material Son and Daughter, the biblical Adam and Eve, to help rehabilitate our world. But they too failed in their mission, defaulting on their responsibilities in ways that have been mythologized in various cultural traditions. Their default compounded our difficulties, leaving us without the full benefit of the violet race infusion that was meant to enhance human potential. Where we might have expected rescue, we experienced further setback. These two major celestial mishaps on one world, It's almost difficult to comprehend.

Fourth, and perhaps most significantly, **Urantia became the bestowal world of Christ Michael**, our universe sovereign. Yet from this apparent catalog of disasters emerges something extraordinary. Our world became the bestowal sphere of Christ Michael, the Creator Son who is sovereign of our entire local universe of Nebadon. When Michael chose to complete his seventh and final bestowal as a mortal on Urantia, appearing as Jesus of Nazareth, our troubled planet suddenly became what some call "the jewel of the universe." Michael's life, death, and resurrection here forever marked this world as special, the stage upon which the universe's Creator demonstrated the Father's love in its most complete form. Following his resurrection, the Union of Days, a Trinity-origin representative in our local universe, formally proclaimed Michael the Planetary Prince of Urantia. This designation is permanent and unprecedented.

Fifth, **the twenty-four planetary directors** function in ways unique to our world. These are former human beings who once lived on Earth, died, ascended through the mansion worlds, and eventually became citizens of Jerusem, our system capital. They proved their trustworthiness so thoroughly that Gabriel and higher authorities appointed them to this special council. Every hundred years, one of the twenty-four serves as resident governor-general on Urantia, administering planetary affairs in Michael's name. What makes this arrangement even more remarkable is that these twenty-four Urantia counselors don't just govern our world, they oversee the administration of all thirty-seven rebellion-isolated planets in our system.

The remaining factors flow from this bestowal. We're governed by this unique council of twenty-four, the same elders mentioned in the Book of Revelation, composed of former Urantians who have proven themselves worthy of this trust. And we have Machiventa Melchizedek, known in scripture as the priest-king Melchizedek who appeared to Abraham, designated as our Vicegerent Planetary Prince, though he has not yet assumed full administrative authority.

Sixth, an **archangel circuit is stationed on our planet**. The archangels are a unique order of celestial beings, something like the military or security forces of the local universe. They don't answer to Gabriel as other angelic orders do but report directly to Michael through their own command structure. Not a single archangel joined the Lucifer rebellion; their loyalty proved absolute. These beings are responsible for maintaining accurate records of every ascending mortal from birth through universe ascension. They certify identities, guarantee the integrity of resurrection records, and essentially ensure the entire ascension plan functions without corruption. That the archangel circuit headquarters operates from Earth speaks volumes about our world's significance in the aftermath of Michael's bestowal.

Seventh, and Finally, **Machiventa Melchizedek has been designated vicegerent Planetary Prince**. This extraordinary being materialized on Earth nearly 4,000 years ago to preserve the concept of one God when that truth was in danger of being lost entirely. He taught Abraham and established the foundation upon which Jesus would later build. As a reward for his faithful emergency service, Machiventa received appointment as acting planetary prince, though interestingly, he has not yet assumed full authority in that role. Some speculate he's waiting for Michael's second coming, or perhaps for the conclusion of the Lucifer rebellion adjudication. Others think he may simply be allowing the twenty-four counselors to gain administrative experience before taking up permanent duties. We don't know for certain, but his presence in this capacity marks yet another way our world stands apart.

This constellation of circumstances makes our world administratively complex in ways that are, apparently, without parallel. We're simultaneously a troubled rebel sphere and a sacred planet of special significance. We're isolated from normal celestial communications while hosting unusual concentrations of celestial ministry. We're struggling with the consequences of ancient betrayals while being slowly prepared for unprecedented destinies.

The Council of Twenty-Four

At the heart of Urantia's celestial government stands the Council of Twenty-Four, a group that should fascinate anyone interested in the intersection of human and divine governance. These aren't abstract spiritual entities disconnected from human experience. They were once mortals like us, walking the same earth we walk, facing similar challenges, making choices that eventually qualified them for extraordinary responsibilities.

I find myself wondering about them often. Who were they? The text doesn't reveal their mortal identities when they are on duty as the Governor general, perhaps wisely, since we humans have an unfortunate tendency to venerate our heroes to the point of worship. But we know they were recognized leaders during their earthly lives, individuals who demonstrated exceptional qualities of character and judgment. After their deaths and subsequent resurrection on the mansion worlds, they continued their spiritual progression through the educational spheres of our local system. Somewhere along that journey, they were identified as candidates for special service.

The process of their selection reveals much about how the celestial government operates. They were nominated by the cabinet of Lanaforge, our current System Sovereign who replaced Lucifer after the rebellion was adjudicated. The Most

Highs of our constellation approved these nominations. The Assigned Sentinel of Jerusem, the capital sphere of our local system, concurred. Finally, Gabriel himself, the chief executive of our local universe, made the formal appointments under the authority of Christ Michael. This isn't a casual process. It represents careful evaluation by multiple levels of celestial authority, ensuring that only the most trustworthy individuals receive these responsibilities.

Among these twenty-four, tradition and hints in the text suggest we might recognize at least one: John the Baptist. Remember Jesus's words about John? He would be given charge of many things in the heavenly kingdom. If John indeed sits among the twenty-four, it demonstrates something important: these positions aren't rewards for perfect lives but recognition of extraordinary faithfulness. John's life was cut short violently, his mission seemingly incomplete. Yet his unwavering commitment to truth, his courage in the face of danger, and his willingness to subordinate his own recognition to Jesus's mission apparently qualified him for this eternal trust.

One of the twenty-four always resides on Urantia, serving a term of one hundred years as Resident Governor-General before rotating back to Jerusem. The current governor isn't identified by name, again, to prevent inappropriate veneration, but we know he or she functions as the coordinator of all superhuman administration on our planet. This person doesn't possess dictatorial authority. Instead, the Resident Governor-General serves more as a coordinator and advisor, respected by all orders of celestial beings functioning here.

What strikes me most about this arrangement is its wisdom. Rather than installing a celestial being from some higher order to govern our planet, a Melchizedek or a Lanonandek Son, for example, Michael chose to entrust this responsibility to proven humans. Former mortals govern mortals, bringing to their administration an understanding born of lived experience. They remember what it means to face temptation, to struggle with doubt, to make difficult moral choices with imperfect information. This empathy undoubtedly makes them more effective administrators than any celestial being who has never walked in human shoes.

The Archangel Circuit

Now we should address something that initially puzzled me: the significance of Urantia hosting an archangel circuit. To understand why this matters, we need to grasp what archangels are and what they do.

Archangels are an order of beings created by Christ Michael and the Divine Minister, the Creative Mother Spirit of our local universe. Unlike most other orders of angels who ultimately answer to Gabriel, archangels maintain a somewhat independent command structure. They're organized more like a military force, and in fact, that comparison isn't far off. During the Lucifer Rebellion, it was the archangels who remained absolutely loyal, serving as Michael's primary defenders against the rebel forces.

Their primary responsibility focuses on what the text calls "the ascension career of time", the entire journey from mortal life to Paradise. They're concerned with record-keeping, certification, and the judicial processes that govern our survival and progression. When a guardian seraphim must account for their care of a mortal soul, they stand before an archangel tribunal. When you awaken on the mansion worlds after death, it's archangels who certify that you are indeed who you claim to be, that your records are accurate and complete. Think of them as the guarantors of the entire survival plan, the beings who ensure the system operates with absolute integrity.

During the rebellion, not a single archangel defected. Not one. This perfect loyalty in the face of sophisticated arguments from Lucifer and his sympathizers speaks volumes about their character. They couldn't be swayed by promises of liberty, couldn't be confused by clever philosophical arguments, couldn't be intimidated by threats. This absolute trustworthiness makes them ideal for their judicial and certification roles.

Now, here's what makes Urantia special in this context: we host one of the division headquarters for the archangel circuit. This means archangels use our world as a hub for their operations throughout our entire local system of inhabited planets. They come and go from here, coordinating activities across hundreds of worlds. Why Urantia? The text suggests it's precisely because this world is where Michael completed his terminal bestowal, making it symbolically and practically appropriate as an administrative center for beings whose primary loyalty is to Michael himself.

I confess this gives me goosebumps when I really think about it. Our troubled, rebel planet, isolated and struggling, also serves as a headquarters for some of the most trusted beings in the entire local universe. It's as if our very difficulties and the triumph that occurred here qualify us for special administrative functions. The planet where Michael faced his greatest challenge and achieved his greatest victory becomes a center for ensuring that his plan for ascending mortals proceeds without compromise.

Machiventa Melchizedek: The Waiting Prince

No discussion of Urantia's government would be complete without considering Machiventa Melchizedek, and I find his story particularly moving. The Melchizedeks as an order are teachers, beings created to serve as educators throughout the local universe. They staff the schools on the mansion worlds and system capitals, guiding ascending mortals through increasingly complex levels of cosmic understanding. But Machiventa did something extraordinary.

Nearly 4,000 years ago, the concept of one God was dying on our world. The religious insights that had been carefully cultivated were fragmenting into polytheism and superstition. In response, Machiventa incarnated, appeared as a fully adult human being without going through birth or childhood, and established himself in Salem (later Jerusalem). For nearly a century, he taught Abraham and others about the one true God, laying foundations that would eventually influence Judaism, Christianity, and Islam.

This wasn't part of normal Melchizedek duties. It was an emergency mission, a response to our world's desperate spiritual condition. And having successfully completed it, Machiventa was eventually designated as Urantia's Vicegerent Planetary Prince, essentially the acting prince, holding the position for Christ Michael who serves as actual Planetary Prince.

Here's what I find fascinating: Machiventa hasn't yet assumed his full responsibilities. The designation has been made, the position is his by right, but he apparently waits for the proper moment to take up active administration. Some speculate he'll appear when Michael returns to Urantia for his second coming. Others think he might wait until the Lucifer Rebellion is formally concluded by the higher courts of the superuniverse. Still others, including the narrator of Paper 114, expect he might appear "any day or hour."

Why the delay? The text suggests it might allow the Council of Twenty-Four to continue gaining valuable administrative experience. Machiventa's restraint appears to be another act of service, allowing others to grow and learn rather than immediately claiming the authority that is rightfully his. This pattern of self-subordination for the good of others echoes throughout these celestial administrations. It stands in stark contrast to the grasping ambition of Lucifer and Caligastia, doesn't it?

When Machiventa does assume active control, it will mark a significant shift in our planetary administration. We'll have, for the first time since Caligastia's betrayal, a visible planetary prince, though whether he'll make himself visible to the general population remains unclear. The text hints at profound changes ahead: the conclusion of the rebellion's adjudication, Michael's return, the lifting of our spiritual quarantine. These events will likely occur in concert, ushering in a new dispensation for our long-struggling world.

The Angelic Population of Earth

When this material was transmitted in the mid-1930s, the revelators provided specific numbers that stop you in your tracks. At noon on the day of transmission, there were 501,234,619 pairs of seraphim assigned to Urantia, meaning just over one billion individual angels serving our planet. The registry showed slightly more than that total, indicating nearly 200 million angels were temporarily absent on transport duty, messenger assignments, or what they call "death duty", the solemn work of transporting departed souls to the resurrection halls.

Think about what this means. The human population in the 1930s was approaching two billion. The angelic population was roughly half that number. Today, with over eight billion people on Earth, the seraphic complement has undoubtedly grown proportionally. There are enough angels to assign guardian seraphim to every soul, plus vast orders of seraphim dedicated to other ministries: group guardianship, planetary supervision, administrative functions, and specialized services we're only beginning to understand.

Beyond the seraphim, there are similar numbers of cherubim, the assistant angels who work alongside their seraphic superiors. And then we have the midwayers, those unique beings descended from the corporeal staff of the original Planetary Prince. The midwayers exist in a realm between material and spiritual reality, able to manipulate matter and remain invisible to human eyes. They work constantly alongside the seraphim, executing tasks that require physical intervention in ways pure spirits cannot accomplish.

Many of the rebel midwayers who followed Caligastia into rebellion were removed from Earth at the time of Jesus' resurrection. The loyal midwayers, both primary and secondary orders, united into a single working corps and continue their faithful service to this day. We owe them an enormous debt. It was the midway commission that provided much of the detailed information about Jesus' life found in Part IV of *The Urantia Book*. Without their careful observation and record-keeping, we would have lost countless precious details about Michael's life in the flesh.

I want to be clear about something that troubles me when I hear people misunderstand the midwayers. Not all midwayers were evil. Not all became demons. Yes, some joined the rebellion and wreaked havoc, giving rise to many of the "devil and demon" legends in human folklore. But the loyal midwayers remained true, and they are holy, dedicated servants of the celestial government. They love humanity deeply and work tirelessly for our benefit. We shouldn't confuse the actions of rebels with the character of those who stayed faithful.

The Superhuman Government in Action

So how does this celestial administration actually function? What we're dealing with is what the revelators call "superhuman government", a term that captures both its invisible nature and its authority over planetary destiny. This government doesn't replace or directly control human governments. Rather, it works through influence, through the manipulation of circumstances, and especially through the ministry of guardian seraphim who attend individual human beings.

Guardian seraphim can't control groups of people or force specific decisions. They work with individuals, gently nudging, arranging circumstances, creating opportunities for moral and spiritual growth. When government leaders face crucial decisions, their guardian seraphim work behind the scenes to illuminate better choices, to bring certain information to attention, to create moments of reflection. The results aren't always what the angels hope for, human free will remains sovereign, but over centuries and millennia, this patient ministry moves civilization forward.

The resident governor-general serves as the coordinating director of all superhuman activities on the planet. He doesn't possess absolute authority in the way a human dictator might, but he hands down scores of decisions daily that all celestial personalities accept as final. His role is more that of a wise father-advisor than a technical ruler, which makes sense when you consider these governors are former humans who lived mortal lives just as we do. They understand human nature from the inside. They remember struggle, doubt, faith, and perseverance. This experiential wisdom makes them ideal administrators, not distant, theoretical authorities, but beings who have walked the path they now oversee.

The governor-general also represents multiple levels of universe administration simultaneously. He speaks for Jerusem, our system capital, since he serves on behalf of the twenty-four counselors who are Jerusem citizens. He represents Gabriel, the chief executive of our local universe. He maintains contact with Salvington, the headquarters world where Michael himself resides. And working alongside the governor-general is a Vorondadek observer, one of the constellation fathers who directly represents the Most Highs of Norlatiadek.

This Vorondadek observer has maintained a station on Earth ever since the Caligastia betrayal. That's when the Most Highs assumed direct oversight of our planet, ensuring that no further catastrophic defaults could occur without immediate intervention. The presence of this observer guarantees that constellation authorities remain intimately informed about planetary developments.

Michael's Hands-Off Approach

One detail that fascinates me is Michael's restraint in exercising his authority as Planetary Prince. When the Union of Days proclaimed him to that office following his resurrection, Michael could have immediately reorganized everything. He possessed, and possesses, absolute authority to restructure planetary administration however he sees fit. Yet he has made virtually no changes to the existing system.

Why? I suspect it's because the plan already in place is sound. Michael established the twenty-four counselors, gave them clear authority, and trusts them to do their work. He doesn't micromanage. He doesn't interfere unnecessarily. This is consistent with his entire approach to universe administration, he delegates appropriately, empowers capable beings, and allows experience to teach its lessons.

It's also possible that major changes await future developments: the completion of the Lucifer rebellion adjudication, the full assumption of authority by Machiventa Melchizedek, or Michael's return to Earth in visible glory. Any of these events could trigger significant administrative reorganization. Until then, the current system functions efficiently under the steady guidance of beings who have proven their capability and loyalty.

The Reserve Corps of Destiny

I should mention briefly a group we'll study in more depth in the next section, the reserve corps of destiny. These are human beings living on Earth today who have been recruited and trained for special service during times of planetary crisis. They don't usually know they're part of this corps. They live normal lives, pursue ordinary careers, raise families, and serve their communities. But they possess certain qualities of character, certain steadfastness of purpose, that make them reliable in emergencies.

When events threaten to push civilization too far off course, when war, economic collapse, or social disintegration looms, members of the reserve corps may find themselves inexplicably positioned to make crucial differences. A decision here, an intervention there, a moment of moral courage at just the right instant, these seemingly small acts, coordinated across thousands of reservists worldwide, can shift the trajectory of history. The seraphim work intensively with these individuals, preparing them, positioning them, and activating them when the hour demands.

This is one more way the celestial government operates without overriding human free will. Reservists make their own choices. They're not puppets or robots. But they've been identified as trustworthy souls whose decisions, when influenced by their guardian seraphim during critical moments, tend toward wisdom, courage, and service rather than panic, selfishness, or despair.

The Blessing of Struggle

I want to touch on something that might seem contradictory at first. If there's this vast celestial government working for our benefit, why doesn't it simply fix everything? Why do we still experience war, poverty, injustice, suffering, and all the other evils that plague human civilization?

The answer lies in understanding the purpose of mortal existence. We're not here to live in paradise, that comes later, in the morontia realms and beyond. We're here to grow, to develop, to forge character through the experience of choosing good over evil in circumstances where evil is a real and present option. If everything were easy, if every problem were solved for us, we wouldn't grow. We'd become spiritually lazy, atrophied, incapable of the kind of robust faith that survives universe challenges.

The struggle is the blessing. I know that's a hard pill to swallow when you're in the midst of genuine suffering. But looking at it from the cosmic perspective, every moral decision we make, every time we choose love over hate, service over selfishness, truth over deception, these choices are building something eternal within us. They're developing the kind of soul that can survive death, that can continue ascending through universe after universe, eventually standing in the presence of the Universal Father himself.

The celestial government could intervene more forcefully. It could make life easier. But in doing so, it would rob us of the very experiences that make us who we're becoming. So instead, it guides, it influences, it supports, but it allows us to walk the path ourselves, to stumble, to get back up, to learn, to grow stronger.

Why Study This Material?

You might wonder why we spend time studying these complex organizational details. Who cares about Vorondadek observers and archangel circuits when we're trying to live good lives and serve our fellow humans? I'll tell you why it matters: because understanding the reality of celestial government transforms how we see our world and our place in it.

When you know that a vast, loving, incredibly competent administration is guiding planetary destiny, you can face the news each day with hope instead of despair. When you understand that your guardian seraphim is working behind the scenes to help you make wise choices, you pay more attention to those intuitive nudges toward better decisions. When you realize that your life, your choices, your service, your growth, contributes to the experiential reality of the Supreme Being, the evolving God of time and space, then even small acts of kindness take on cosmic significance.

We're not alone. We're not forgotten. Despite appearances, despite the chaos and confusion that sometimes seem to dominate human affairs, there is a plan. There is direction. There is divine purpose working itself out through human history, and we get to participate in it. Not as passive observers, but as active co-creators of the age of light and life that will eventually dawn on this world.

The Broader Administrative Structure

Before we conclude, I want to step back and consider the full scope of celestial administration on Urantia, because it's easy to lose sight of the forest while examining individual trees.

At the top, we have Christ Michael himself, our Creator Son and Universal Sovereign, who serves as Planetary Prince though he doesn't personally administer daily affairs. His will and his love for our world, however, permeate everything that happens here. He delegates authority downward through multiple channels.

The Most Highs, the Vorondadek Sons who govern our constellation of Norlatiadek, maintain ultimate administrative authority over Urantia as they do for all worlds in our constellation. They issue mandates and directives that shape broad policy. On our world, they're represented by a Vorondadek observer who maintains constant presence here, monitoring conditions and reporting back to constellation headquarters.

Our local system of Satania is governed by Lanaforge, who replaced Lucifer after the rebellion. Lanaforge maintains close oversight of all the rebellion-affected worlds, and he works through the Council of Twenty-Four for day-to-day administration of Urantia. The Resident Governor-General serves as his direct representative here.

But remember: this superhuman government doesn't operate in isolation from other celestial ministers. The midwayers, beings halfway between physical and spiritual, work closely with the seraphim to accomplish material tasks that angels cannot directly perform. The various orders of seraphim, from the supreme seraphim who work with universe-wide concerns down to the guardian angels who care for individual mortals, all coordinate their activities under the direction of the Resident Governor-General.

It's worth emphasizing that this isn't a government imposed upon unwilling subjects. It's a coordinating structure designed to help all these diverse orders of beings work together effectively. The seraphim don't resent taking guidance from the Governor-General; they welcome the coordination. The midwayers don't chafe under angelic supervision; they've worked together for millennia. This is celestial administration functioning as it should, diverse personalities unified by common purpose and mutual respect.

Living Under Celestial Government

So, what does all this mean for us, for those of us living our mortal lives under this invisible celestial administration? I think several implications deserve consideration.

First, we can take profound comfort in knowing that our world, despite all its troubles, operates under wise supervision. When we look at human affairs, the wars, the injustice, the suffering, it's easy to despair, to think we're alone and abandoned to our own devices. But we're not. Countless celestial beings work tirelessly behind the scenes, creating opportunities for progress, gently influencing events toward better outcomes, ensuring that despite every setback, we continue moving toward light and life.

This doesn't mean we can passively wait for celestial intervention to solve our problems. That's not how it works. The celestial government respects human agency absolutely. They create opportunities; we must choose to take them. They arrange circumstances; we must respond wisely. They inspire ideas; we must act on them. The partnership between human effort and celestial ministry produces progress. Neither alone is sufficient.

Second, we should recognize that spiritual growth often comes through struggle rather than ease. If the celestial government could simply impose perfection on our world, they would, wouldn't they? But that would defeat the very purpose of our existence. We're here to grow, to make moral choices, to develop characters that can endure into eternity. The difficulties we face, both personal and planetary, provide the resistance against which we build spiritual muscle. This doesn't justify cruelty or excuse injustice, but it does help us understand why celestial intervention isn't more obvious and dramatic.

Third, I think we should approach life with greater humility about what we think we know. We're living in a context vastly more complex than we can perceive with our physical senses or comprehend with our finite minds. When events don't make sense, when prayers seem unanswered, when good people suffer and evil people prosper, we might remember that we're observing a tiny fragment of an enormously complex whole. The celestial administrators see connections and consequences we cannot begin to imagine. This doesn't mean we shouldn't question or struggle with difficult experiences, but it might temper our certainty that we fully understand what's happening around us.

Finally, we might live with greater hope. The administration described in Paper 114 isn't temporary or provisional. These structures will remain in place until our world finally achieves light and life, a state of spiritual and social advancement that seems impossibly distant from our current condition. But it will come. The celestial government guarantees it. Not tomorrow, probably not in our lifetimes, but eventually. Every small act of kindness, every choice for truth over convenience, every moment of genuine spiritual growth contributes to that eventual triumph.

Looking Ahead

In this chapter, we've examined the invisible government that guides our world, a government composed of angels, former mortals, Melchizedeks, and other celestial beings all working together under the ultimate authority of Christ Michael. We've seen how Urantia's unique history has shaped an equally unique administrative structure, one that reflects both our challenges and our unexpected privileges.

But celestial government involves more than structure and hierarchy. In our next chapter, we'll examine the specific functions that various orders of angels perform, the actual work of planetary ministry. How do seraphim influence human institutions? What role do they play in preserving and advancing civilization? How do they coordinate with midwayers and other orders of beings to accomplish tasks that neither could manage alone?

But even more importantly, we'll begin to understand how we can cooperate with this celestial administration in our daily lives. How can we make ourselves more accessible to seraphic ministry? How can we align our decisions with the overarching plan these beings are working to implement? What does it mean to be a conscious participant in planetary progress rather than just a passive recipient of whatever circumstances come our way?

These aren't abstract theological questions. They're deeply practical concerns that can transform how we live each day, how we treat other people, and how we contribute to building a better world, not just for ourselves, but for generations yet unborn who will inherit what we leave behind.

Our planet has been through extraordinary trials. We've stumbled badly at times. But we're also the world that Michael chose for his final bestowal, the world where he revealed divine love in its most complete form. That makes us special, perhaps more challenged than most worlds, yes, but also more blessed, more watched over, more intimately connected to the heart of universe administration itself.

These questions will lead us deeper into the practical operations of celestial ministry on our world. We'll discover that angels aren't idle in some distant heaven but actively engaged in every aspect of human life and social progress. Their ministry touches everything from education to politics, from religion to industry, from individual salvation to planetary destiny.

The picture that emerges is one of extraordinary complexity and beauty, a vast, coordinated effort involving millions of personalities all devoted to helping us, despite our shortcomings, to achieve our divine potential. Understanding this ministry can transform how we see both the world around us and our place within it.

As we continue this study, I encourage you to hold that truth close: you are a citizen of a universe teeming with intelligent, loving beings who want nothing more than to see you succeed in your eternal adventure. The angels are real. The government is real. The plan is real. And you, right now, right where you are, have a part to play in its unfolding.

Chapter 4: The Seraphic Planetary Government and Earth's Spiritual Administration

When I first began studying Paper 114 of *The Urantia Book*, I have to admit I was somewhat overwhelmed by the complexity of what it revealed. Here was a detailed blueprint of an entire celestial government operating right here on Earth, invisible to most of us, yet intimately involved in guiding our world's spiritual evolution. The more I explored this material with my study group, the more I realized how much we've misunderstood about the spiritual forces that surround us. We're not alone. We've never been alone. And despite the challenges our planet has faced, rebellion, default, isolation, we remain deeply connected to a vast universe teeming with purpose and divine care.

In this chapter, I want to walk you through the incredible revelation of Earth's seraphic planetary government. We'll explore who these celestial administrators are, how they function, and why their work matters profoundly to each of us. More importantly, I'll share how this knowledge transformed my understanding of what it means to be a citizen of the cosmos, even while living out my days on this seemingly isolated world.

The Current State of Urantia's Government

Let me start with something that might surprise you: Earth, or as *The Urantia Book* calls it, Urantia doesn't have a "normal" planetary government. At least not in the way other inhabited worlds in our local universe do. The reason traces back to what the book describes as the Caligastia rebellion, which occurred roughly 200,000 years ago. Caligastia was our Planetary Prince, assigned to guide our world's development. For about 200,000 years, he served loyally. Then something went terribly wrong. He aligned himself with Lucifer's rebellion against the established order of our local universe, and in doing so, he abandoned his post and betrayed the trust placed in him.

When a Planetary Prince defaults, it creates an administrative crisis. The normal channels of spiritual guidance become disrupted. Think of it like this: imagine a ship losing its captain mid-voyage during a storm. Someone has to step in, and quickly. That's essentially what happened to our world. The constellation government, specifically, the Most Highs of Edentia, immediately dispatched a Vorondadek Son to assume emergency oversight of our planet. This celestial being is known as the Most High Observer, and he represents a higher level of universe authority than even our Planetary Prince would have held.

Here's what struck me when I first learned this: we're currently being overseen by the twenty-third Most High Observer since the rebellion. That means twenty-two others have served before him. If we do the math, and I did, with my study group's help, that works out to roughly one observer every 10,000 to 11,000 years. These aren't short-term assignments. These celestial administrators commit to lengthy service on our behalf, maintaining stability while our world slowly recovers from its spiritual setbacks.

The Most High Observer functions primarily as an observer, as the title suggests, but he's empowered to do much more when necessary. During times of grave planetary crisis, and the book records thirty-three such occasions in our history, this observer can seize direct control of planetary affairs. When that happens, he essentially becomes the regent of Earth, exercising unquestioned authority over all celestial ministers and administrators stationed here. The only exception is the divisional organization of the archangels, which operates somewhat independently.

Now, you might wonder what constitutes a "grave planetary crisis." The book doesn't give us a detailed list, but we can make some educated guesses. A nuclear war threatening to destroy civilization would certainly qualify. Or imagine a scenario where the light of spiritual truth was about to be extinguished entirely, where atheism or materialism had so completely overtaken human thought that the very concept of God was dying out. That kind of spiritual emergency would likely trigger intervention. The arrival of Machiventa Melchizedek during Abraham's time appears to have been one such intervention, a response to the fading knowledge of the one God.

The Resident Governor General: Christ's Representative on Earth

While the Most High Observer represents the constellation government, there's another key figure in Earth's spiritual administration: the Resident Governor General. This role fascinates me because it's held by a former human being, someone who once walked this Earth just as we do now.

The Resident Governor General is one of the twenty-four counselors stationed on Jerusem, the headquarters world of our local system. These twenty-four are exceptional individuals who lived extraordinary lives on Urantia and, after their resurrection and ascension, were selected to serve in this unique capacity. They maintain close contact with our world, and one of them, the Resident Governor General, actually resides here, though not in physical form.

This governor general serves as the direct representative of Christ Michael, Jesus of Nazareth, who is also Michael, the Creator Son of our local universe. Let that sink in for a moment. The risen Christ, now sovereign over the entire universe of Nebadon, maintains a personal representative on Earth at all times. We are not forgotten. We are not abandoned. The sovereign of 3.8 million inhabited worlds keeps his attention focused on this single, struggling planet because this is where he lived his final bestowal life, where he died and rose again, and where he poured out the Spirit of Truth nearly two thousand years ago.

The governor general works closely with the Most High Observer, but they represent different levels of authority. The observer represents Edentia and the constellation government, which ultimately answers to the superuniverse of Orvonton. The governor general represents Salvington (the universe headquarters) and Jerusem (the system headquarters). In most matters, the governor general functions as a provisional and advisory chief executive, but he possesses veto power vested in the Most High Observer. It's a system of checks and balances, much like we see in human governments, designed to ensure wisdom and prevent the concentration of too much power in any single office.

The Archangels: Guardians of the Ascension Plan

There's a third major player in Earth's celestial government that deserves our attention: the archangels. I'll be honest, before studying *The Urantia Book*, my understanding of archangels came almost entirely from traditional religious art and vague biblical references. I pictured mighty warriors with flaming swords, dramatic and powerful but ultimately mysterious. The reality, as revealed in Paper 114, is both more specific and more profound.

The archangels maintain a divisional headquarters right here on Urantia. This headquarters was established relatively recently, about two thousand years ago, on the day of Pentecost, following Jesus's resurrection. The timing is significant. The book explains that the archangels are primarily concerned with the ascension plan for human beings. Their mission is to ensure that mortal creatures like you and me have every opportunity to survive death, continue our existence on the mansion worlds, and eventually progress all the way to Paradise and the presence of the Universal Father.

What gives the archangels their unique authority is that they operate somewhat independently of the regular planetary government. Even when the Most High Observer seizes control during a crisis, the archangels' organization remains separate. In matters of purely spiritual concern and certain personal affairs, the supreme authority is actually vested in the commanding archangel attached to the divisional headquarters. That's remarkable when you think about it. The archangels answer to a higher authority than even the Most High Observer in specific domains, particularly those involving individual human destiny and spiritual progression.

This arrangement makes sense once you understand the archangels' role. They're not primarily concerned with managing planetary affairs, social evolution, or political systems. Their focus is laser-sharp: ensuring that every human being who desires eternal life and chooses to follow the Father's will receives every possible assistance in that journey. They work closely with our guardian seraphim, with our Thought Adjusters (the indwelling presence of God), and with the vast network of celestial personalities dedicated to the ascension plan.

The Twelve Corps of Master Seraphim

Now we come to what I consider one of the most beautiful and intricate aspects of Earth's spiritual government: the twelve corps of master seraphim who serve under the supervision of the Resident Governor General. These aren't guardian angels in the traditional sense, those who watch over individual human beings. Instead, these are specialized seraphic groups, each dedicated to a specific aspect of planetary progress and stability.

Let me introduce you to these twelve groups and explain what each one does. I think you'll be amazed at how comprehensive this celestial administration is and how much care has gone into ensuring that every dimension of human life receives spiritual support and guidance.

1. The Epochal Angels

These are the angels of the current age, the dispensational group. They're responsible for overseeing and directing the affairs of each generation, making sure that events and developments fit into the larger mosaic of the age in which they occur. Every generation has its own character, its own challenges, its own opportunities. The epochal angels work to ensure that each generation fulfills its potential and contributes to the ongoing evolution of civilization.

The book tells us that the current corps serving on Urantia is the third group assigned during our present dispensation. When I think about the epochal angels of our time, I imagine they're working overtime. We live in the age of the internet, instant global communication, unprecedented access to information, and also unprecedented opportunities for distraction, misinformation, and spiritual confusion. These angels are guiding us through a transformation that would have been unimaginable just a century ago.

2. The Progress Angels

If the epochal angels focus on the present, the progress angels look toward the future. These seraphim are entrusted with initiating evolutionary progress across successive social ages. They foster the development of civilization's inherent progressive trends, and they labor constantly to make things what they ought to be. I find their mission statement particularly compelling: they work to make things what they *ought* to be.

Think about the great social movements that have advanced human dignity over the centuries, the abolition of slavery, the recognition of human rights, the expansion of education, advances in justice and equality. The progress angels don't force these changes upon us, but they create conditions favorable to their development. They manipulate circumstances, if you will, so that when courageous human beings choose to act for justice and progress, the environment supports their efforts.

The current group serving on Earth is the second corps assigned to our planet. They work in dynamic tension with other seraphic groups, sometimes pushing for change, sometimes being held in check by forces that seek to preserve valuable traditions and prevent reckless disruption.

3. The Religious Guardians

These are the angels of the churches, though I should immediately clarify what that means. The religious guardians are not concerned with denominational divisions, sectarian disputes, or debates over doctrine. They're not championing one church over another or one faith tradition against another. Instead, they work to maintain the ideals that have survived across epochs, the imperishable values of spiritual truth, and to help translate those values from one generation to another in forms that people can understand and embrace.

Their task is delicate. They're the checkmates of the progress angels, maintaining a creative tension between preservation and innovation. On one hand, they don't want valuable spiritual insights and moral teachings to be lost in the rush toward novelty. On the other hand, they're not trying to fossilize religion or trap it in outdated forms. They seek to preserve the essence, the living truth, while allowing the container to evolve.

The book emphasizes that these angels are "not the source of ultra-sectarianism and meaningless controversial divisions of professed religionists." That line has stayed with me. When religious people fight over trivial differences, when denominations treat each other with hostility, when believers claim exclusive access to truth, that's not the work of the religious guardians. That's human ego and spiritual immaturity. The angels of the churches work for something much higher: the recognition that all genuine faith, all authentic spiritual experience, all sincere seeking after God is part of one great human family, the brotherhood of man under the Fatherhood of God.

4. The Angels of National Life

Sometimes called the "angels of the trumpets" in biblical literature, these seraphim are the directors of political performance on Earth. They work with international relations, with the rise and fall of nations, with the slow evolution of human governance from tribalism toward more enlightened forms of global cooperation.

Here's what's important to understand: these angels are not managing human political systems in the way a puppeteer controls a puppet. They can't override human free will or force leaders to make wise decisions. But they can influence conditions, create opportunities, and work behind the scenes to prevent catastrophic outcomes. The book says quite directly: "The Most Highs rule in the kingdoms of men." This doesn't mean divine tyranny. It means there's a wisdom and purpose at work in human history that transcends the limited vision of any single nation or leader.

The current corps serving on Urantia is the fourth group assigned to oversee international relations. I sometimes wonder what they must think as they watch human beings struggle with nationalism, tribalism, and the false belief that one nation's prosperity must come at another's expense. The angels of national life are surely working toward the day when we recognize ourselves as one planetary family, when international law reflects spiritual principles, and when the welfare of all people, not just the citizens of powerful nations, becomes the standard by which we measure political success.

5. The Angels of the Races

These seraphim work for the conservation of the evolutionary races, regardless of their political entanglements or religious groupings. On Earth, there are remnants of nine human races that have intermingled and combined into the peoples of modern times. The angels of the races remain closely associated with the race commissioners, special celestial administrators who monitor the genetic and cultural development of these racial groups.

The corps now serving on Urantia is the original group assigned shortly after the day of Pentecost. Their long tenure suggests the importance and complexity of their work. They're not trying to prevent the blending of races; that's a natural and beneficial process. Rather, they're working to ensure that the positive contributions of each racial heritage are preserved and that all peoples are treated with dignity and justice.

This is deeply personal to me because racial injustice remains one of humanity's most persistent failures. When I read about the angels of the races, I'm reminded that every ethnic group, every cultural heritage, every human family has value in the eyes of God. The prejudice and discrimination we see in our world are affronts not just to human dignity but to the divine plan for our planet's evolution.

6. The Angels of the Future

These seraphim fascinate me. They're the projection angels, the ones who forecast future ages and plan for the realization of better things in new and advancing dispensations. They're called the architects of successive eras. Just think about that for a moment. There are celestial beings whose entire mission is to envision what humanity can become and to work toward making that vision reality.

The angels of the future don't see the future as fixed or predetermined. They're working with probabilities, with human potential, with the slow unfolding of the divine plan. They see trends we can't see, possibilities we can't imagine, and they're constantly adjusting their plans based on the choices we make. When human beings make wise choices, when we choose cooperation over conflict, when we choose spiritual growth over material obsession, when we choose love over fear, we're aligning ourselves with the vision these angels hold for our world's future.

7. The Angels of Enlightenment

If there's one seraphic group whose work I see most clearly in our contemporary world, it's the angels of enlightenment. These are the angels dedicated to fostering planetary education, mental and moral training for individuals, families, groups, schools, communities, nations, and entire races. Their mission encompasses everything from a child learning to read to a civilization grappling with ethical questions raised by new technologies.

The book notes that we're now receiving help from the third corps of enlightenment angels assigned to Urantia. Their work must be challenging in an age when information is abundant, but wisdom is scarce, when entertainment is everywhere but genuine education is undervalued, when people have access to all the world's knowledge through their smartphones yet remain profoundly ignorant of spiritual realities.

I see the angels of enlightenment at work whenever someone has that moment of insight, that sudden clarity when confusion gives way to understanding. I see them in the teacher who inspires a student to think deeply, in the book that changes someone's worldview, in the conversation that opens someone's mind to new possibilities. They work with our Thought Adjusters, with our guardian seraphim, with the Spirit of Truth, to illuminate our minds and guide us toward higher understanding.

8. The Angels of Health

These seraphic ministers assist mortal agencies dedicated to promoting health and preventing disease. The current corps is the sixth group to serve during this dispensation. Their work becomes especially poignant when we remember what happened to our world. On a normal planet, an Adam and Eve, a Material Son and Daughter, arrive to biologically uplift the human races. They contribute their superior genetic heritage, slowly raising the physical standards of the entire population and making humanity more resistant to disease, more vigorous, and longer-lived.

Our Adam and Eve defaulted on their mission. Instead of the patient, gradual work they were supposed to do, they made a fateful mistake that cut short their mission and limited the biological benefit we would have received. As a result, we're more susceptible to disease, more physically limited, and shorter-lived than we would have been if their mission had succeeded.

The angels of health work to compensate for this loss. They assist doctors, nurses, researchers, public health officials, anyone genuinely dedicated to alleviating suffering and improving human wellbeing. They can't violate natural law or perform miracles, but they can inspire insights, guide research, and create conditions favorable to healing and health.

9. The Home Seraphim

These angels may be the most underappreciated of all the seraphic groups, yet their mission is fundamental. They're dedicated to the preservation and advancement of the home, which the book calls "the basic institution of human civilization." The current corps is the fifth group to serve in this capacity.

I emphasize this point in my teaching because our culture sometimes forgets how foundational the family is. The home is where children first learn love, where they develop their capacity for relationships, where they form their earliest concepts of fairness, responsibility, and moral behavior. A stable, loving home is the best predictor of a child's future success, not wealth, not privilege, but simply the presence of parents or caregivers who provide consistent love and guidance.

The home seraphim work to support marriages, to help parents raise children with wisdom, to preserve the bonds that hold families together even through difficult times. They're not trying to impose a single-family model or to judge people whose families don't fit conventional patterns. Rather, they're supporting the principle that human beings thrive when they live in relationships of mutual commitment and care.

10. The Angels of Industry

This seraphic group focuses on fostering industrial development and improving economic conditions. They've been reassigned seven times since the bestowal of Michael, since Jesus lived and died on Earth. That's more turnover than most other groups have experienced, which suggests the rapid pace of industrial and economic change in our world.

These angels must be incredibly busy in our era of globalization, automation, and technological disruption. They're working to ensure that economic development serves human welfare rather than enslaving it, that industry creates opportunity rather than exploitation, that wealth generates shared prosperity rather than grinding inequality.

On a normal world, one where Adam and Eve fulfilled their mission, industrial development would have been guided by semi-material beings who understood both spiritual principles and material needs. They would have helped us avoid many of the mistakes we've made environmental destruction, unsafe working conditions, economic systems that generate enormous wealth for a few while leaving billions in poverty. The angels of industry are doing their best to steer us toward better outcomes, but they work within the constraints of human free will and human error.

11. The Angels of Diversion

When I first encountered this seraphic group, I smiled. There are angels whose mission is to foster the values of play, humor, and rest. They seek to uplift our recreational diversions and promote the more profitable use of human leisure. The current corps is the third to serve on Urantia.

This reveals something profound about the spiritual life. God is not a stern taskmaster demanding constant seriousness. Play, creativity, joy, laughter, these are gifts, and they're important to our wellbeing. A life that's all work and no rest, all duty and no delight, is an impoverished life. The angels of diversion remind us that renewal is as important as productivity, that leisure is not wasted time but necessary time, that play is how we reconnect with the spontaneous joy that children naturally possess but adults too often lose.

I think these angels must have worked overtime to help humanity develop music, art, sports, dance, literature, and all the other forms of creative expression that make life beautiful. Every time we laugh with friends, every time we lose ourselves in a good book, every time we play a game or go for a walk in nature simply for the pleasure of it, we're responding to the ministry of the angels of diversion.

12. The Angels of Superhuman Ministry

The final group serves not humans directly but other celestial beings. These are the angels who minister to angels, a fascinating concept. The seraphim themselves need support, guidance, and care. They're not omnipotent or omniscient. They're finite beings with their own needs and challenges. The angels of superhuman ministry ensure that all the other celestial personalities serving on our world have what they need to do their work effectively.

This corps has served since the beginning of the current dispensation. Their presence reminds us that ministry is universal, that service flows in all directions, that even the highest beings in creation serve those above them and beside them, that the entire universe operates on principles of mutual care and cooperation.

How the Government Functions: Checks, Balances, and Cooperation

Now that we understand who the key players are, let's look at how they actually work together. The spiritual government of Earth doesn't operate like a dictatorship or even like a conventional monarchy. Instead, it functions through a system of councils, consultations, and carefully distributed authority.

Every administrative day on Urantia, and we're talking about Earth days here, twenty-four-hour periods, begins with a consultative conference. This gathering includes the Resident Governor General, the planetary chief of archangels, the Most High Observer, the supervising supernaphim, the chief of resident Life Carriers, and various invited guests from among the high Sons of the universe or student visitors who might be present on our world.

Picture this: the highest celestial authorities governing our planet meet daily to coordinate their efforts, share information, and make decisions. No single administrator rules by fiat. Decisions emerge from discussion and consensus. When disagreements arise among the master seraphim, the Resident Governor General typically mediates. If his ruling proves controversial, it can be appealed to conciliating commissions or even to the System Sovereign of Satania.

The conciliating commissions deserve special mention. These are celestial tribunals that handle disputes and make judgments throughout the universe. When a conciliating commission makes a decision, it's rarely overturned. These commissions operate at the intersection of wisdom, experience, and spiritual insight, and their rulings command enormous respect.

What strikes me about this governmental structure is its humility. Even the Most High Observer, who possesses vast authority, operates within a framework of accountability. Even the Resident Governor General, Christ's personal representative, doesn't make unilateral decisions on matters of importance. The system is designed to prevent abuse of power, to ensure that multiple perspectives inform decisions, and to guarantee that justice and mercy temper the administration of law.

The Reserve Corps of Destiny: Heaven's Secret Agents

There's one more dimension of Earth's spiritual government that I need to address, and it's perhaps the most mysterious and personally relevant of all: the Reserve Corps of Destiny. This is the point where celestial government intersects most directly with human life, where ordinary people become extraordinary instruments of divine purpose.

The Reserve Corps of Destiny consists of living men and women who have been admitted to special service in the superhuman administration of world affairs. These are not famous people, for the most part. They're not celebrities or political leaders or religious authorities. Most of them don't even know they've been chosen for this unique role. They live ordinary lives, work ordinary jobs, face ordinary challenges. But something about them, their character, their spiritual receptivity, their dedication to truth and service, makes them valuable to the celestial administrators of our world.

The book identifies three characteristics of Reserve Corps members. First, they have a special capacity for being secretly rehearsed for numerous possible emergency missions in the conduct of various world activities. Second, they demonstrate wholehearted dedication to some special social, economic, political, spiritual, or other cause, coupled with a willingness to serve without human recognition or reward. Third, they possess a Thought Adjuster of extraordinary versatility, probably with pre-Urantia experience in coping with planetary difficulties.

Let me unpack these characteristics because they're crucial to understanding what the Reserve Corps actually is and what it isn't.

Secret Rehearsal and Unconscious Training

Reserve Corps members are trained unconsciously, usually during sleep. Their Thought Adjusters, the indwelling fragments of God that all normal-minded humans receive, work in cooperation with guardian seraphim and secondary midwayers to provide this training. The training occurs in what the book calls "the deep mind," below the threshold of conscious awareness.

This is not channeling. I can't emphasize this strongly enough because there's tremendous confusion on this point. Channeling involves a person consciously receiving messages from a spiritual source and then communicating those messages to others. The channeler is aware of what's happening. They remember the experience. They can describe it.

The Reserve Corps experience is entirely different. These individuals have no conscious memory of their training. They don't know they're being prepared for special service. They don't receive voices or visions or special revelations. When they wake up in the morning, they simply feel rested, nothing more. Yet during the night, their Thought Adjusters have been working with them, preparing them for potential future service.

This unconscious training is crucial because it prevents ego involvement. If someone knew they were part of the Reserve Corps of Destiny, they'd be tempted to pride. They might tell others about their special status. They might expect recognition or authority. They might begin to trust their own opinions more than they should simply because they know they've been chosen for something significant.

By keeping the training unconscious, the celestial administrators ensure that Reserve Corps members remain humble, that they continue to test their ideas against reason and experience, that they don't confuse their personal opinions with divine guidance. These individuals serve precisely because they don't know they're serving. Their egos remain out of the way.

Wholehearted Dedication and Selfless Service

The second characteristic, wholehearted dedication to a cause combined with willingness to serve without recognition, is equally important. Reserve Corps members aren't people seeking fame or status. They're not motivated by applause or reward. They're the ones who show up day after day to do good work simply because it needs doing.

Think about the social reformers who fought for decades to change unjust laws, often without seeing the fruits of their labor in their lifetimes. Think about the teachers who pour their lives into students, knowing they'll never be wealthy or famous. Think about the parents who sacrifice their own ambitions to raise children with integrity and love. Think about the scientists who pursue truth for its own sake, the artists who create beauty because they must, the religious believers who serve God without fanfare or recognition.

These are the kinds of people who might be, though they'll never know for certain, members of the Reserve Corps of Destiny. They're committed to something larger than themselves. They're willing to invest their lives in causes that might not pay off until long after they're gone. And they do all this not for glory but because they believe it's right.

Exceptional Thought Adjusters

The third characteristic involves the Thought Adjuster itself. Not all Adjusters are equally experienced. Some are indwelling a mortal for the first time. Others have guided multiple personalities through the ascension journey and bring vast experience to their work. Reserve Corps members apparently receive Adjusters with unusual versatility and probably pre-Urantia experience, meaning these Adjusters have successfully guided other mortals on other worlds through similar challenges.

This makes sense when you think about it. If celestial administrators need to prepare someone for a crucial mission, perhaps to prevent a catastrophe, or to introduce a new idea at precisely the right moment, or to make a critical decision that will affect millions, they'll want an experienced Adjuster who knows how to work effectively with the human mind and who can handle complex, high-stakes situations.

The book mentions that these Adjusters sometimes function as "self-acting Adjusters," a term that requires explanation. Normally, Adjusters work with us, respecting our free will and guiding us gently. A self-acting Adjuster can, in special circumstances and with proper authorization, temporarily take full control of a person's mind and body. The human personality essentially steps aside, or rather, is put into a state like deep, dreamless sleep, while the Adjuster uses the body and mind for specific tasks.

This is precisely how *The Urantia Book* itself was transmitted. A human subject, whose identity was never revealed and who apparently had no conscious memory of the transmissions, served as the channel through which celestial beings communicated the papers that became the book. The subject's Thought Adjuster, working with secondary midwayers, facilitated this communication while the human personality slept peacefully, unaware of what was happening.

How Many Reserve Corps Members?

The book provides specific numbers. On Urantia, there are twelve Reserve Corps groups, one for each of the twelve divisions of master seraphim we discussed earlier. The combined corps consists of 962 people. The smallest group numbers 41, and the largest 172.

Think about that. Fewer than a thousand people, scattered across the entire planet, constitute the Reserve Corps of Destiny. You might live next door to one and never know it. You might be one yourself and not realize it. These individuals are living normal lives, but they've been prepared for extraordinary moments, moments when a single person's decision or action might tip the scales of history.

With the exception of "less than a score of contact personalities," the book says all these Reserve Corps members are unconscious of their preparation. That phrase "contact personalities" is intriguing. It suggests that perhaps twenty or fewer people worldwide have some conscious awareness of their role. These might be individuals who work directly with celestial administrators in ways that require conscious cooperation, though even here, the book gives us no details.

The Reserve Corps in Action

When do Reserve Corps members actually serve? The book explains that they function during times of emergency or crisis, situations where normal celestial manipulation of planetary conditions isn't sufficient. These might be social emergencies, spiritual exigencies, moments when evolutionary culture is on the verge of breakdown, or times when the light of living truth is in danger of being extinguished.

Sometimes, a Reserve Corps member might be prompted to take a specific action: to speak at a crucial meeting, to write an influential article, to make a decision that changes the course of events. They won't necessarily know why they feel compelled to act. They might just have a strong intuition, an unshakable conviction that something needs to be done. They'll act on that conviction, and only later, if ever, will they realize how significant their action was.

Other times, the Reserve Corps functions more subtly. The book mentions that these individuals serve as "conservators of essential planetary information." When a reservist is about to die, their Thought Adjuster transfers certain vital data from their mind to a younger successor's mind through a liaison of the two Adjusters. This ensures that important knowledge, understanding, or insights aren't lost with the passing of a generation. It's a form of spiritual and intellectual inheritance, invisible to human observation but crucial to planetary progress.

Channeling Versus Reserve Corps Service: A Critical Distinction

I want to return to the issue of channeling because it's so important. In recent decades, numerous individuals have claimed to channel spiritual beings, ascended masters, angels, extraterrestrials, you name it. Some of these people may be sincere. Others are clearly fraudulent. But regardless of their sincerity, channeling as it's commonly practiced is not the same as Reserve Corps service.

Channeling typically involves:

- Conscious awareness of receiving messages
- Memory of the channeling experience
- The ability to describe who or what is being channeled
- Public disclosure of the channeling activity
- Often, a desire for recognition or status as a channeler

Reserve Corps service involves:

- Complete unconsciousness during training or transmission
- No memory of the experience afterward
- No knowledge of being part of the Reserve Corps
- No public disclosure (because there's nothing to disclose)
- No desire for recognition (because the person doesn't know they're serving)

The difference is profound. Channeling centers the human ego. Reserve Corps service eliminates the ego from the equation entirely. Channeling invites pride and can easily become a form of spiritual one-upmanship: "I channel Archangel Michael!" "Well, I channel Jesus himself!" "That's nothing, I channel the Universal Father!"

Reserve Corps members can't engage in that kind of spiritual competition because they don't know they're members. If someone announces, "I'm part of the Reserve Corps of Destiny," you can be fairly certain they're not. Real Reserve Corps members have no such knowledge, and even if they suspected it, they would never proclaim it because the second characteristic of Reserve Corps service is willingness to serve without recognition.

This is why the transmission of *The Urantia Book* is so different from channeled material. The human subject who facilitated the transmission never knew what was happening. Never wrote a book about their experiences. Never gave lectures claiming special authority. Never founded a movement or sought followers. The subject's identity was protected, and to this day, most students of *The Urantia Book* don't know who that person was, which is exactly as it should be.

We Are Not Forgotten: The Promise of Divine Care

As we've explored the complex spiritual government of Urantia, one theme emerges repeatedly: despite our planet's troubled history, despite the rebellion and default that have left us partially isolated from universe circuits, we are not forgotten. We are not abandoned. We are not cosmic orphans.

The book makes this explicit in some of the most beautiful language found anywhere in its pages. Let me quote it at length because these words deserve to be savored:

"Your isolated world is not forgotten in the councils of the universe. Urantia is not a cosmic orphan stigmatized by sin and shut away from divine watchcare by rebellion. From Uversa to Salvington and on down to Jerusem, even in Havona and on Paradise, they all know we are here. You mortals now dwelling on Urantia are just as lovingly cherished and just as faithfully watched over as if the sphere had never been betrayed by a faithless Planetary Prince, even more so. It is eternally true, 'the Father himself loves you.'"

Even more so. Those three words stop me every time I read them. We're not just as loved as worlds that never experienced rebellion, we're loved *more*. Our struggles, our limitations, our courageous persistence in seeking God despite the spiritual darkness that has sometimes enveloped our world, all this evokes special care and attention from the celestial hosts.

Think about what's been invested in this one small planet. A Material Son and Daughter came here, and though they defaulted, they still contributed their biological heritage. Machiventa Melchizedek came during a spiritual emergency, living among humans to keep alive the knowledge of the one God. And then Jesus himself, Christ Michael, the Creator and sovereign of a universe containing millions of inhabited worlds, chose Urantia as the place for his final bestowal. He lived among us, taught us, died here, and rose again here.

The archangels established their divisional headquarters on our world, a mark of special status. The Most High Observer maintains constant vigilance. The Resident Governor General coordinates daily with the other celestial administrators. Twelve corps of master seraphim labor to advance every dimension of human life. Guardian angels attend each of us individually. The Spirit of Truth, poured out by Jesus, connects us to the circuit of the Creator Son. The Holy Spirit, the presence of the Divine Minister, the creative mother spirit of our universe, surrounds us with loving care. And dwelling within our minds, the Thought Adjusters, actual fragments of the Universal Father, guide us toward eternal destiny.

No, we're not forgotten. We're remembered with love, watched with care, and guided with patient wisdom by an entire hierarchy of celestial beings who have devoted their lives to our welfare.

Looking Ahead

In this chapter, we've explored the visible structure of Earth's spiritual government, the administrators, the seraphim, the Reserve Corps. But there's more to the story. In the next chapters, we'll turn our attention to all the angels most directly involved in our individual lives: the guardian seraphim, the Cherubim and Sanobim who watch over us from birth to death and beyond. We'll discover how these remarkable beings work, what they can and cannot do, how we can cooperate with their ministry, and what happens when we finally meet them face to face in the world to come.

The revelation of Earth's spiritual government should change how we see our world and our place in it. We're not alone. We're not adrift. We're part of a vast, loving universe where countless beings labor for our benefit. Every time we choose truth over falsehood, every time we choose love over fear, every time we reach toward God in prayer or worship, we align ourselves with this great work. We become, in our small way, collaborators with angels and archangels, with the Most Highs and the Creator Son himself, in the transformation of this world.

That's a privilege beyond measure. And it's an invitation to live with hope, with purpose, and with the quiet confidence that comes from knowing we're held in the arms of infinite love.

Chapter 5: The Ministering Spirits of the Local Universe

Introduction: Understanding Our Celestial Companions

When I first began studying Paper 38 of *The Urantia Book*, I have to admit I was unprepared for how profoundly it would shift my understanding of the unseen universe surrounding us. We tend to think of angels in the vague, somewhat sentimental terms handed down through religious tradition, winged figures on Christmas cards, perhaps, or distant guardians mentioned in passing during prayers. But what *The Urantia Book* reveals is something far more intricate, far more real, and infinitely more personal than anything I had previously imagined.

This chapter explores the nature, origin, and function of the ministering spirits who serve throughout our local universe of Nebadon. These beings, seraphim, cherubim, and sanobim, are not mythological constructs or symbolic representations of divine care. They are actual personalities with distinct characteristics, specific duties, and a profound investment in our spiritual development. Understanding who they are and how they function within the divine plan can transform not only our comprehension of cosmic administration but also our sense of connection to the larger spiritual family to which we belong.

As we examine Paper 38 together, I want you to approach this material with both intellectual curiosity and personal openness. These are the beings who walk beside us, quite literally, throughout our mortal journey and beyond. Getting to know them, their origins, their nature, their limitations, and their remarkable capabilities, is getting to know some of our closest companions in the universe.

The Three Orders of the Infinite Spirit

Before we can properly understand the seraphim and their role in our local universe, we need to establish the broader context of angelic orders throughout creation. *The Urantia Book* tells us there are three distinct orders of personalities created by the Infinite Spirit, and this classification helps us see where our local universe angels fit within the grand scheme of things.

The text references an ancient understanding that appears in Christian scripture, where the Apostle wrote of Jesus "who has gone to heaven and is on the right hand of God, angels and authorities and powers being made subject to him." Now, the Apostle's concept of heaven was quite different from what we now understand through *The Urantia Book*. He wouldn't have known about the mansion worlds, the constellation headquarters, or the vast architectural spheres that constitute the morontia career. His notion of heaven was simpler, more immediate, Jesus sitting literally at God's right hand. Yet despite this limitation in cosmological understanding, he was remarkably accurate in identifying three distinct categories of celestial beings.

Let me break down what these three orders actually represent:

Angels refer to the ministering spirits of time, the seraphim and their associates who serve primarily in the evolutionary realms. These are the beings most directly concerned with mortal creatures like ourselves. They work within the time-space universes, accompanying us through our planetary existence and continuing their ministry as we progress through the mansion worlds and beyond.

Authorities designate the messenger hosts of space, beings like the supernaphim and seconaphim who serve at higher levels of universe administration. These personalities function as messengers, administrators, and coordinators across the vast distances of space, maintaining the communication networks and administrative efficiency of the superuniverses and the central universe.

Powers represent the higher personalities of the Infinite Spirit, the Seven Master Spirits, the Supreme Executives, and other exalted beings who operate at the highest levels of universe coordination and direction. These are personalities of such elevated status and function that we can barely comprehend their sphere of activity.

What strikes me about this ancient classification is how much the Apostle got right, even if his understanding was necessarily incomplete. He grasped something fundamental about the hierarchical yet coordinated nature of spiritual administration. The universe isn't chaotic or random; it's organized with remarkable precision, and that organization reflects the character of the Gods who created it.

The Angelic Core of Nebadon

Just as the supernaphim serve as the primary angelic order in the central universe of Havona and Paradise, and just as the seconaphim and tertiaphim function as the angels of the seven superuniverses, so the seraphim, along with their associated cherubim and sanobim, constitute the angelic core of our local universe.

I want to emphasize this point because it helps us understand the scope and scale of divine organization. Each level of creation has its appropriate order of ministering spirits. The pattern repeats across different domains, yet each order is specifically suited to the realm in which it serves. The seraphim are perfectly adapted for service in Nebadon, just as we mortals are perfectly suited to begin our careers on evolutionary worlds like Urantia.

If you're interested in exploring this further, I highly recommend using the topical index feature available in many digital versions of *The Urantia Book*. When you click on "supernaphim," for instance, you'll find a detailed breakdown of all the different types, primary supernaphim who serve on Paradise and in Havona, secondary supernaphim who minister in the superuniverses, and tertiary supernaphim who work with ascending mortals. Each category has distinct functions and seeing them laid out systematically really helps clarify the magnificent order of things.

Similarly, if you look up "angels" in the index, you'll see the complete hierarchy:

1. Supernaphim (central universe)
2. Seconaphim (superuniverse)
3. Tertiaphim (superuniverse)
4. Omniaphim (superuniverse)
5. Seraphim (local universe)
6. Cherubim (local universe)
7. Sanobim (local universe)

The list even includes the midwayers, who occupy a unique position as permanent citizens of the evolutionary worlds. This organizational chart, if you will, reveals the thoughtful structure underlying all spiritual ministry.

One detail from Paper 38 particularly fascinated me: when the Infinite Spirit first began creating our local universe alongside Creator Son Michael, there weren't yet any native angels available. The solution? A neighboring local universe, one that was apparently further along in development, loaned Nebadon a group of about one hundred omniaphim to serve as an initial angelic core. Additionally, seraphim were loaned from the local universe of Avalon.

That name, Avalon, might sound familiar. These are the same surgeons of Avalon who created the specialized bodies for the Caligastia one hundred and for Adam and Eve when they arrived on our world. It appears that Avalon is a more mature local universe, one that has progressed significantly beyond where Nebadon currently stands. The fact that entire groups of ministering spirits can be temporarily reassigned from one local universe to another speaks volumes about the cooperative nature of universe administration.

This loan arrangement was necessary because when a Creator Son first embarks on the adventure of creating his local universe, he doesn't automatically have all the support personnel he needs. The same appears to be true for archangels, Michael was loaned some archangels from another local universe to help establish the foundations of Nebadon. It's a remarkable picture of mutual assistance, of more advanced universes helping younger ones get started. We see this same principle operating at every level of creation, those who have gone before reach back to help those who follow.

The Origin of the Seraphim

Understanding when and how the seraphim came into existence requires us to grasp some foundational concepts about local universe creation. When Michael first began creating Nebadon, he worked in partnership with the Creative Mother Spirit, what we sometimes call the Universe Mother Spirit or the Divine Minister of Nebadon.

Their initial creative work was collaborative. Together, they brought forth all the orders of local universe Sons, the Melchizedeks, the Vorondadeks, the Lanonandeks, the Life Carriers, and numerous other orders of divine Sons. This was a joint creative endeavor, combining the creative prerogatives of both the Creator Son and the Universe Mother Spirit.

But then something shifted. Once these foundational orders were established, Michael and the Mother Spirit embarked on separate creative projects. Michael began the creation of the Material Sons and Daughters, the Adams and Eves who serve as biological uplifters on evolutionary worlds. These were the first of the sex creatures, beings with reproductive capacity designed to improve the physical and mental qualities of evolving mortal races. The Material Sons and Daughters came entirely from Michael; they are single-origin beings, created by the Creator Son alone.

While Michael was creating the Material Sons and Daughters, the Universe Mother Spirit undertook her "initial solitary effort at spirit reproduction." This was the beginning of the seraphic hosts. Every seraphim, every cherubim, every sanobim in Nebadon comes from her creative action alone. They too are single-origin beings, their origin is the Mother Spirit.

The text tells us that seraphim are "projected in unit formation, 41,472 at a time." I find that specific number intriguing. It's not a round figure like 40,000 or 50,000, but a precise count that must have some significance in the mathematics of spiritual creation. And this creative process hasn't stopped. The Mother Spirit continues to create seraphim periodically as Nebadon grows and develops. We're told that Nebadon is only about one-third complete, we're working toward a total of ten million inhabited worlds, and we're nowhere near that number yet. Every time a new world comes into the system, every time a new population requires spiritual ministry, more seraphim are needed. And so the Mother Spirit continues her creative work.

One clarification the revelators make is important: the creation of seraphim dates from what they call the "attainment of relative personality" by the Universe Mother Spirit, not from her later attainment of full personality. This distinction might seem technical, but it matters. The Mother Spirit existed in a state of relative personality from very early in Nebadon's history, she had personality and creative capacity, but it wasn't fully developed. Her personality reached its complete expression only after Michael completed his seventh and final bestowal on our world about two thousand years ago. When he returned and was declared Sovereign of Nebadon, something fundamental changed for the Mother Spirit. She became fully personalized, stepping into the totality of her identity and function.

But seraphim were being created long before that moment. Millions of years before Michael walked on Urantia as Jesus, the Mother Spirit was already bringing forth the angelic hosts that would serve throughout our universe. That's what they mean by "relative personality", she had sufficient personalization from the beginning to engage in creative ministry, even though her personality would later blossom into something even more complete.

Single-Origin and Dual-Origin Beings

This might seem like a tangent, but I think understanding the concept of single-origin versus dual-origin beings illuminates something profound about the divine plan, not just for angels, but for us as well.

As I mentioned, the Material Sons and Daughters are single-origin beings because they come from Michael alone. The seraphim, cherubim, and sanobim are single-origin beings because they come from the Mother Spirit alone. But what about us? What about ascending mortals?

Here's where it gets interesting. When human life first appears on an evolutionary world, that life comes from the action of the Life Carriers, but the spark that animates it, the gift of life itself, comes from the Universe Mother Spirit. She is the one who breathes life into material forms. In that sense, the very first humans on any world are single-origin beings. Their life springs from one source: the Mother Spirit.

But then the Material Son and Daughter arrive, Adam and Eve on our world, and they too are single-origin beings, created by Michael. The divine plan calls for these Material Sons and Daughters to biologically uplift the evolutionary races through the gradual infusion of their superior heredity. When Adam and Eve's descendants intermarry with the native populations, something remarkable happens single-origin beings from two different sources combine to produce dual-origin offspring.

On our world, of course, this plan was compromised by what we call the Adamic default. Eve, through well-intentioned but misguided reasoning, short-circuited the carefully designed program of racial uplift. The consequences were significant. Instead of the violet race systematically mingling with all the other races according to a divine timetable, the process became haphazard and incomplete. We received only a fraction of the Adamic inheritance that was intended for us.

Even so, the principle remains. As Adamic blood gradually spreads through the human population over thousands of generations, we move from being single-origin toward becoming dual-origin beings. It's an agonizingly slow process now, much slower than it should have been, but it continues. Eventually, perhaps millions of years in the future, every human being born on Urantia will carry enough of the Adamic inheritance to be considered a dual-origin being.

Why does this matter? Because dual-origin beings possess certain advantages. They have a richer genetic heritage, greater spiritual capacity, enhanced intellectual potential. The mingling of origins creates something stronger, more resilient, more capable than either origin alone. This pattern appears throughout the universe, the combination of different origins, different perspectives, different streams of inheritance produces greater possibility.

And here's what moves me most about this: even though the default disrupted the plan, it didn't destroy it. God's purposes are patient. They work through setbacks, adapt to complications, and continue moving forward across vast stretches of time.

The divine plan for our world is still unfolding, just on a different timeline than originally intended.

The Nature of Angels

So what are seraphim actually like? What is their nature, their mode of existence?

The first thing to understand is that angels do not have material bodies. They are definite and discrete beings, real personalities with individual identities, but they exist on a spiritual level of reality that normally remains invisible to mortal eyes. We can't see them because our physical senses are limited to a narrow band of reality. They perceive us perfectly well, however. They see us "in the flesh," as the text puts it, without needing any transformers or translators. They understand how we think, how we feel, how we experience the world.

What's remarkable is how much angels share with us emotionally and intellectually. They understand mortal life from the inside, you might say. They comprehend our moral struggles and spiritual difficulties. They appreciate our efforts in music, art, and genuine humor. The text specifically mentions "real humor," which suggests they can distinguish between humor that uplifts and humor that degrades. They love human beings, and the revelators assure us that "only good can result from your efforts to understand and love them."

There is one significant limitation, though. Angels don't experience what the text calls "sensuous emotions." They have no sexuality, no reproductive capacity, and therefore no sex drive or sexual feelings. This isn't a lack or deficiency; it's simply part of their nature. Since they don't reproduce, they have no need for the complex emotional and physiological systems associated with sexuality. They can observe our experiences in this realm, but they don't personally understand them from within.

This is why when it is said, the Angels fell from Heaven during the Lucifer rebellion, and mixed with the daughters of men, this is totally incorrect. Angels are spiritual beings and have no sexual organs or tendencies. The beings that mixed with the daughters of men were the rebellious sixty of the Caligastia 100, they had physical bodies created for them from our DNA for their mission, so they had the capability to reproduce like humans, and this is where the Nephilim or giants came from.

I find this both humbling and oddly comforting. These magnificent beings who know so much, who have such advanced capacities in so many areas, have a blind spot when it comes to one fundamental aspect of human experience. It reminds me that every order of being has its own unique perspective, its own strengths and limitations. No single type of creature embodies all possible experiences. We each contribute something distinctive to the cosmic tapestry.

The text mentions that angels can, with permission, make themselves visible to mortals. I suspect this explains some of the genuine spiritual experiences people report, moments when they sensed or even saw an angelic presence. Not every such report is authentic, of course, but I'm inclined to think that angels do occasionally reveal themselves when circumstances warrant it and when permission is granted by higher authorities.

What about ghost sightings and paranormal phenomena? The revelators make clear that there are no "ghosts" in the traditional sense, no human personalities lingering on Earth after death. When we die, our souls are either taken by seraphic transport to the mansion worlds or, in cases where immediate survival isn't assured, put into a state of sleep to await the next dispensational resurrection. Either way, there's no human consciousness left behind to haunt old houses or familiar locations.

That said, I've wondered whether some paranormal phenomena might be explained by what we could call "metaphysical loops", recordings, if you will, in the fabric of space-time itself. Perhaps certain events of sufficient intensity create impressions that can replay under specific conditions. These wouldn't be actual entities, just echoes of things that happened. It's also possible that angels, going about their duties, are occasionally perceived by sensitive individuals and misinterpreted as ghosts or spirits. We simply don't know enough to rule out various possibilities.

The main point is this: seraphim are not ghosts, and they don't contribute to superstitious beliefs about the dead lingering on Earth. They are living, active personalities with important work to do, and that work is always oriented toward service and progress, never toward frightening people or encouraging false beliefs.

Comparing Angels and Mortals

One of the most encouraging statements in Paper 38 concerns the relationship between angels and ascending mortals. The text says that in nature and personality endowment, seraphim are "just a trifle ahead" of mortal races in the scale of creature existence. Just a trifle ahead. Not vastly superior, not infinitely beyond us, but only slightly more advanced.

Think about what this means. When we arrive on the mansion worlds and receive our morontia forms, those transitional bodies that are part material, part spiritual, we become "very much like them." The gap between us and the angels isn't as large as we might have imagined. On the mansion worlds, we'll begin to appreciate seraphim in new ways. On the constellation spheres, we'll enjoy their companionship. On Salvington, the capital of our local universe, we'll share their places of rest and worship.

The text promises that throughout "the whole morontia and subsequent spirit ascent, your fraternity with the seraphim will be ideal; your companionship will be superb." I love that word, superb. Not just good, not merely adequate, but superb. The seraphim will become some of our dearest friends, companions we'll treasure throughout eternity.

This speaks to something I've come to appreciate more and more: the universe is designed for relationships. It's not a hierarchy where those above look down on those below with disdain or indifference. It's a family, vast and diverse, where different orders of beings recognize each other as brothers and sisters engaged in a common enterprise. The angels don't see themselves as our superiors, even though they possess certain advantages. They see themselves as our companions and helpers, fellow servants of the same God.

And here's another crucial point: angels don't judge us. They observe us, certainly. They keep detailed records of our spiritual progress. But they don't sit in judgment. When your guardian seraphim presents your life record before the Ancients of Days after your death, she simply reports the facts. She doesn't editorialize. She doesn't say, "This person was terrible, I don't see how you could possibly let them continue." She just says, "Here's the life as it was lived. Here's where they were spiritually. Here's what they achieved and what they struggled with." Other beings, divine judges of incomprehensible wisdom, make the determination about survival. The angels only report.

The text draws a pointed lesson from this: "Angels do not sit in judgment on mankind; neither should individual mortals prejudge their fellow creatures." If beings as advanced as the seraphim refrain from judging us, who are we to judge each other? It's a principle that, if we actually lived by it, would revolutionize human relationships.

I'll be honest, I find this one of the hardest teachings to embody. It's so easy to make snap judgments about people, to categorize them, to decide we know what they're really like based on limited information. The angels, who know us far better than we know ourselves, who can count the hairs on our heads, as Jesus once said, even they withhold judgment. Surely we can try to do the same.

Guardian Angels and Personal Ministry

When do we acquire personal guardian angels? This is a question many people ask, and the answer has to do with something called the psychic circles.

The psychic circles are levels of spiritual achievement that we pass through during our mortal careers. There are seven of them, and we start in the seventh circle as young children when we first begin making moral decisions. As we grow spiritually, as we learn to love more deeply, think more clearly, serve more effectively, and commune more consistently with our indwelling Thought Adjuster, we progress through the circles.

When we reach the third psychic circle, something significant happens: we're assigned personal guardian seraphim. Actually, we're assigned two seraphim, because these beings always work in pairs. Along with the seraphim come two other Angels, a cherubim and sanobim, a total of four angels, or two pairs, dedicated specifically to our spiritual welfare.

Before reaching the third circle, we're still under angelic care, but it's group care. One pair of seraphim might be responsible for dozens or even hundreds of people who are all at similar levels of spiritual development. It's not that they neglect us, but their attention is necessarily divided. Once we reach that third circle, though, we become their full-time assignment. They're with us constantly, guiding, protecting, inspiring, and preparing us for the next stage of our journey.

I should mention that the cherubim and sanobim are helper orders. They're not as advanced as the seraphim, but they're essential parts of the angelic team. The cherubim assist the seraphim in various duties, while the sanobim handle more routine tasks. It's a beautifully coordinated effort, with each order contributing according to its particular capacity.

What exactly do these guardian angels do? They work behind the scenes in countless ways, most of which we never consciously perceive. They coordinate spiritual influences, arrange circumstances to maximize our growth opportunities, protect us from dangers we don't even know exist, and preserve our souls when we die. They're present during our most difficult trials and our highest achievements, always working to help us move forward.

And here's something that amazes me: the text says seraphim possess "inherent and automatic" powers of knowing things about us that would require tremendous effort for mortals to track. The example given is that they know exactly how many hairs are on our heads, and they keep that count updated as we lose hair and grow new hair. To us, that would be an impossibly tedious task. To them, it's effortless. It's just part of their nature.

The point isn't really about hair counting, of course. It's about demonstrating how thoroughly they know us. They're not distant overseers who check in occasionally. They're intimately familiar with every aspect of our being, our thoughts, our struggles, our progress, our setbacks, our potential. They know us better than we know ourselves.

Yet they never use that knowledge to control us or override our will. They respect our freedom absolutely. They can guide and suggest, but they can't compel. The sovereignty of our will remains inviolate, even in the face of superior knowledge and wisdom.

Life Beyond the Flesh

Since we've been discussing angels and their role in our lives, I should address something that often comes up: what happens to relationships when we reach the mansion worlds?

The text is quite clear: "You will neither marry nor be given in marriage but will be as the angels of heaven." This means there's no sexual reproduction on the mansion worlds, no marriages initiated there. Our morontia bodies don't have reproductive capacity. That entire dimension of life, so central to our existence here, simply doesn't apply there.

Now, this raises obvious questions. What about married couples who've built their lives together, who've loved each other deeply? Are they just separated, their bond dissolved?

Not at all. If you're married on Earth and both you and your spouse survive to the mansion worlds, you can certainly choose to remain together as companions. The bond you've formed can continue indefinitely if you both wish it. You're not bound by legal marriage anymore, that's an institution designed for reproductive societies, but you can maintain your partnership based on genuine affection and shared purpose.

The relationships we form here, with spouses, with children, with parents, with siblings, all continue to have meaning beyond death. Your mother is still your mother; your brother is still your brother. These connections remain real and valuable. What changes is that we're no longer limited to these relationships or defined primarily by them. The family of the universe opens up before us, infinitely larger and richer than we can now imagine.

For those who never married on Earth, or who never found a partner, there's no "making up for lost time" on the mansion worlds by finding a spouse there. That opportunity is unique to our mortal existence. But this isn't a loss, because the forms of companionship and love available on the mansion worlds transcend anything we've known here. We won't feel deprived; we'll feel expanded.

There's another requirement I should mention, one that often surprises people: every ascending being must gain the experience of raising at least three children to the age of decision. This applies to everyone, regardless of whether they had children on Earth.

For those of us who never had children, this experience will come either through assignment to the nursery worlds, where children who died before reaching the age of decision are raised, or through apprenticeship with Material Sons and Daughters, observing and assisting them in child-rearing. The age of decision on the nursery worlds is typically somewhere between sixteen and twenty years old, the age at which the young person must make a permanent choice about their eternal future.

Why is this experience required? Because parenting develops capacities essential to universe citizenship, patience, unconditional love, long-term commitment, the ability to guide without controlling, the wisdom to let go when appropriate. These aren't optional skills; they're fundamental to the kind of beings we're becoming. Everyone needs to develop them.

Those who've already raised children on Earth will have a head start, though they may still be assigned to mentor additional children on the nursery worlds. Those of us without that experience will need to acquire it. Either way, we'll all eventually possess the wisdom that comes from shepherding young souls through their formative years.

I find this requirement both daunting and deeply meaningful. It suggests that universe citizenship isn't about intellectual achievement alone. It's about heart development, about becoming the kind of beings who can nurture and guide others with wisdom and love. That takes practice, and God ensures we all get that practice, one way or another.

The Unrevealed Angels

Before we close this chapter, I want to mention something intriguing: Paper 38 refers to six other orders of angelic beings that function in our local universe but are not revealed to us in detail. We know they exist, we know they're called ministering spirits, but we're given almost no information about them.

Why? Because these six orders "are in no manner connected with the evolutionary plan of Paradise ascension." They handle administrative and logistical functions that don't directly involve mortal ascenders. Their work is essential to the operation of the universe, but it's not relevant to our personal spiritual journey.

This is an important principle that appears throughout *The Urantia Book*: we're told what we need to know for our current stage of development. Information that doesn't serve our immediate growth or understanding is withheld, not from secrecy or elitism, but simply because we're not ready for it and don't need it yet.

Even on our own world, there are twelve orders of seraphim assigned to various planetary functions that have nothing to do with human salvation or the ascension plan. They manage other aspects of planetary administration, things we wouldn't understand and don't need to concern ourselves with at our current level.

This selective revelation actually comforts me. It means God isn't trying to overwhelm us with data. The revelators are thoughtful teachers who portion out truth according to our capacity to receive and use it. As we grow, more will be revealed. For now, we're given enough, more than enough, to orient our lives toward the highest goals and to walk confidently into an eternity of discovery.

Conclusion: Companions for Eternity

As I reflect on everything we've explored in this chapter, I'm struck by a profound sense of gratitude. We're not alone in this universe. We're not fumbling through life with only our limited understanding to guide us. From the moment we made our first moral decision as children, invisible companions have been with us, watching, helping, hoping for our success.

These seraphim are not distant, austere beings looking down on us from lofty heights. They're friends, really, friends who know us completely and love us anyway. They're invested in our progress because they've chosen to be. They celebrate our victories and sustain us through our defeats. When we finally wake up on the mansion worlds and begin to perceive them clearly, I believe we'll feel like we're being reunited with companions we've known forever, because we have.

The Universe Mother Spirit continues her creative work, bringing forth new angels as Nebadon grows toward its destiny of ten million inhabited worlds. Millions of years from now, when our local universe stands complete and settled in light and life, the angels created today will still be serving, still ministering, still helping younger souls find their way home to Paradise.

And we'll be there too, further along our own journey, perhaps serving as mentors to others who are just beginning. The patterns repeat at every level, those who've gone ahead reach back to help those who follow. It's a family, this universe of ours. A vast, diverse, ancient, and ever-growing family. And the angels are our elder siblings, watching out for us with patience and affection.

In the next chapter, we'll explore the specific orders and functions of seraphim in greater detail. We'll look at the seraphic worlds, the organization of angelic ministry, and the various specialized roles that angels fulfill throughout the local universe. We'll discover just how intricate and thoughtful the divine plan of ministry really is, and how perfectly adapted these beings are to their sacred work.

For now, though, I want to leave you with this thought: you're known, you're loved, and you're accompanied every moment of your life. The angels are real. They're here. And they're on your side.

Chapter 6: The Seraphic Realms - Understanding the Ministering Spirits of Our Local Universe

When I first encountered the descriptions of angelic beings in The Urantia Book, I'll admit I was skeptical. My background in science had conditioned me to approach supernatural claims with caution. Yet as I studied Paper 38 more deeply, something shifted. The organizational precision, the functional clarity, the sheer coherence of what I was reading, it began to feel less like mythology and more like cosmology. Tonight, as we continue our journey through this remarkable revelation, I want to share with you what I've come to understand about these beings who walk beside us, invisible yet profoundly present in our spiritual lives.

The Geography of Heaven: Seraphic Worlds and Their Purpose

Let me paint a picture for you. Imagine the architectural spheres surrounding Salvington, the headquarters of our local universe of Nebadon. The ninth group of seven primary spheres in the Salvington circuit belongs entirely to the seraphim. Each of these seven worlds has six tributary satellites orbiting around it, creating a constellation of forty-nine spheres dedicated to angelic training and habitation.

Now here's what fascinated me when I first studied this arrangement: the seraphim of Nebadon, our local universe angels, occupy only the first cluster. That's one primary world and its six satellites. The remaining six clusters, with all their satellites, house six orders of angelic associates that have never been revealed to us on Urantia. Think about that for a moment. We're being told that there are entire classifications of celestial beings whose very existence remains unknown to us. It's a humbling reminder that the universe is far more populated, far more complex, than our limited perspective can grasp.

These seraphim have access to all forty-nine spheres, of course. They can visit and learn from their angelic cousins. But their true home, the place where each seraphim has an actual residence, exists on that first primary sphere and its surrounding satellites. The Urantia Book tells us that each seraphic estate is characterized by both beauty and vastness, and that every seraphim has a real home. When the text uses the word "home," it means something specific: the domicile of two seraphim, because these beings live and work in pairs.

This pairing isn't arbitrary. It reflects something fundamental about their nature.

The Mystery of Positive and Negative: How Seraphim Function

One of the questions I get asked most frequently is this: "Are angels male or female?" The answer might surprise you. Seraphim are neither male nor female in the way we understand those terms. They are, instead, positive and negative, complementary forces that complete a functional circuit. But all Angels are of the female inclination.

Let me explain what I mean by this, because it's crucial to understanding how guardian angels actually work. When seraphim are encircuited, connected to the spiritual presence of the local Universe Mother Spirit, it requires two angels to accomplish most tasks. One carries a positive charge, if you will, and the other carries a negative charge. Together, they complete a spiritual circuit, much like the way electrical current requires both positive and negative poles to flow.

Think of it this way: you can't have a functioning atom without both protons and electrons. The structure requires both elements to maintain stability and perform its function. Seraphim operate on a similar principle. When they're encircuited and actively ministering, both partners must be present for the circuit to function properly.

However, and this is where it gets interesting, when they're not encircuited, they can work alone. The text tells us that "when stationary," they don't require their complement of being. What does this mean in practical terms? Well, consider the work of your guardian seraphim. Their job isn't what most people think it is. They're not hovering around you like Clarence in *It's a Wonderful Life*, keeping you from stepping in front of buses. That's not their function at all.

The actual work of a guardian seraphim involves placing opportunities, sometimes difficult ones, in your path so you can learn spiritual lessons. They don't manipulate physical matter directly. Instead, they influence your thoughts, gently nudging you toward choices that will benefit your soul's growth. For this kind of work, only one of the pair needs to be actively engaged at any given moment. The other can rest. But here's the key: they're both always present. One works while the other rests, and then they switch. You're never without both of them nearby.

Now, when we're assigned guardian seraphim, and not everyone has personal guardians right away, we'll get to that later, we're actually assigned two pairs. That's two seraphim plus a cherubim and a sanobim. These latter two serve as the "guardians of record." They're the ones maintaining a complete chronicle of your life, recording every decision, every spiritual choice, every moment of growth or stagnation. When one seraphic pair is resting, the cherubim and sanobim take over the recording function. This means there's never a gap in your spiritual record. Every moment of your life is witnessed and documented.

Some people find this unsettling, the idea that invisible beings are constantly observing and recording. But I've come to see it differently. These beings aren't judging you. They're not tallying up your sins. They're witnessing your growth, celebrating your victories, and yes, noting your struggles. They're invested in your success because your spiritual progress is their mission. You might even say it's their joy.

The Guardian Angel Myth: What They Actually Do

I need to address something that troubles me about popular culture's portrayal of guardian angels. My mother, bless her, used to pray for guardian angels every time we took a long trip. She imagined them as divine bodyguards, cosmic seatbelts that would keep us safe from physical harm. I hate to disappoint anyone who shares that belief, but that's not what guardian angels do.

Let me be blunt: if you walk into your house and there's a gas leak and you light a match, it's going to explode. Your guardian angel will not stop you. If a drunk driver runs a red light and hits your car, your guardian seraphim will not intervene. I learned this firsthand a few weeks ago when my wife Diane and I were in a serious accident. A truck slammed into us. The airbag deployed, and for a terrifying moment, I couldn't breathe. I genuinely thought I was dying. My guardian angels didn't prevent that accident.

So, what were they doing? They were guarding what actually matters: my soul, my spiritual destiny, my continued existence beyond this physical life. You see, guardian angels are more accurately called "guardians of destiny." Their job is to ensure that your soul makes it to the mansion worlds. Whether your physical body survives to eighty-five or dies at thirty-five is, from an eternal perspective, almost irrelevant. Either way, you continue. Either way, your spiritual journey proceeds.

This might sound cold but think about it logically. If we truly are eternal beings, if death is merely a transition from one phase of existence to another, then the timing of that transition matters less than the quality of the spiritual preparation we've achieved before it happens. Guardian angels focus on that preparation. They put challenges in your path that will strengthen your soul, deepen your faith, and expand your capacity for love and service.

Now, there are exceptions to the non-intervention rule. In cases involving individuals who are part of the Reserve Corps of Destiny, about a thousand humans at any given time who are being trained during sleep to handle planetary emergencies, the midwayers or even seraphim might intervene physically to preserve that person's life. But this is rare, and it's always authorized by higher authorities, typically an archangel.

Let me give you an example from the life of Jesus himself. When Jesus was a young boy, he was playing on the roof of his house when a sandstorm blew in. Sand got in his eyes, he lost his footing, and he fell down the stairs. Two midwayers were assigned specifically to protect Jesus. Yet they did nothing. They let him fall. Why? Because they understood that this minor accident wouldn't kill him or permanently harm him. It wouldn't interrupt his mission. And accidents of time, random physical mishaps that don't threaten spiritual destiny, are generally allowed to proceed. Joseph, being a good carpenter and father, responded by installing railings on the stairs. That's how wisdom works in the physical realm.

The midwayers later had to justify their non-intervention to their superiors. They were cleared because their reasoning was sound. This tells us something important: even celestial beings operate under rules, under principles of non-interference except when absolutely necessary.

The Training of a Seraphim: From Observer to Commissioned Minister

How does a seraphim become qualified for the work of guiding human souls? The process is lengthy and, I think, rather beautiful in its thoroughness.

When seraphim are first created by the local Universe Mother Spirit, and they're created in groups of 41,472, a number we'll return to later, they spend their first millennium as non-commissioned observers on Salvington. That's a thousand local universe years, mind you, which is considerably longer than our years. During this entire first age of their existence, they simply watch. They observe the functioning of universe administration. They see how decisions are made, how problems are solved, how spiritual ministry actually works in practice.

After this millennium of observation, they spend their second millennium on the seraphic worlds of the Salvington circuit, those training spheres we discussed earlier. Here they receive formal education. The first 100,000 Nebadon seraphim were actually trained by angels from Avalon, the local universe nearest to ours. Once that initial corps was fully trained, they took over the education of all subsequent seraphic orders. The Melchizedeks also play a significant role in angelic education, teaching all local universe angels, seraphim, cherubim, and sanobim alike.

But here's where it gets really interesting for us. After completing their formal training, seraphim are sent out as observers to the lowest of the evolutionary worlds. Now, what constitutes a "low" evolutionary world? I'd say we probably qualify, wouldn't you? We're a decimal planet, a world of experimentation. We've been isolated for 200,000 years due to the Lucifer rebellion. We're still dealing with war, poverty, corruption, and all manner of spiritual immaturity. We're not exactly the showcase planet of the local universe.

So, when young, uncommissioned seraphim come here to observe, they're assigned to work alongside experienced guardian seraphim who are already active. This means that you and I might actually have four seraphim attending us at any given time, two experienced guardians and two trainees, plus the cherubim and sanobim keeping records. We're walking training grounds for the angelic orders. I find that both humbling and oddly comforting. Our struggles, our growth, our daily spiritual choices, they're not just important to us. They're lessons for beings who are learning how to minister to ascending mortals.

After this period of field observation, the trainee seraphim return to the constellation headquarters for advanced studies. Then they're sent to one of the local systems for further practical experience. Only after all of this, millennia of observation, study, and apprenticeship, are they finally commissioned as full-fledged ministering spirits.

The thoroughness of this training tells me something important: the work of guiding ascending mortals is considered complex, delicate, and critically important. Angels aren't just thrown into service. They're prepared carefully, educated thoroughly, and given extensive hands-on experience before they're entrusted with the spiritual destiny of will creatures like us.

The Architecture of Heaven: Seraphic Organization and the Armies of God

Now I want to turn to something that initially struck me as almost military in its precision: the organizational structure of the seraphic hosts. When I first read these numbers, I thought, "Why in the world does heaven need a military organization?" But as I studied deeper, I began to understand.

After their second millennium on the seraphic headquarters, seraphim are organized into groups of twelve pairs, that's twenty-four individual angels. Twelve such groups constitute a company of 144 pairs, or 288 individuals. Twelve companies form a battalion: 1,728 pairs, or 3,456 angels. Twelve battalions create a unit: 20,736 pairs, or 41,472 individuals.

Wait, that last number should ring a bell. It's the exact number in which seraphim are created. This isn't coincidence. It's elegant design. Each creation batch forms one complete organizational unit.

The structure continues upward. Twelve units make a legion, 248,832 pairs, or nearly half a million individual angels. Twelve legions constitute a host: almost three million pairs, or nearly six million angels. And twelve hosts form an army: over thirty-five million pairs, or more than seventy-one million individual seraphim.

These armies are under the supreme command of Gabriel, the Bright and Morning Star, chief executive of the Sovereign of Nebadon. He's called "the Lord God of hosts" for good reason.

When Jesus was arrested in the Garden of Gethsemane, he told his disciples, "I can even now ask my Father, and he will presently give me more than twelve legions of angels." People read that and think it's poetic exaggeration. It's not. Jesus was being quite literal. Twelve legions would be nearly six million angels. That's real power. He could have called them down at any moment. He chose not to, and we'll explore why that matters in a moment.

But first, why does heaven need this kind of organizational capacity? Think about what happens during a systemic rebellion. When Lucifer rebelled, he didn't just spread ideas, he began using rebellious beings to cause actual physical disruption in the local universe. If such a situation escalates, Gabriel has the authority to deploy entire legions or even armies of angels to physically restrain the rebellious forces.

Seraphim, you see, aren't merely spiritual entities. They can exert physical force when necessary. An archangel sent to retrieve someone doesn't ask permission, they have the power to physically transport that being wherever they need to go. If the situation demanded it, an entire legion could be deployed to a planet to physically restrain every rebellious individual simultaneously. There are enough angels in a single army to assign one angel to every human being on Earth and still have tens of millions left over.

This isn't about intimidation. It's about capacity. The universe is designed with safeguards, with backup systems, with the ability to contain and correct problems before they spiral into catastrophe. The angelic hosts are one such safeguard.

But, and this is crucial, these powers are almost never used. Why? Because the Creator Son and his administrators respect the free will of creatures. They allow evolutionary worlds to work through their problems, to learn from their mistakes, to grow through struggle. Intervention happens only when absolutely necessary to prevent complete collapse or when a planetary mission of supreme importance is threatened.

The Question of Divine Intervention

This brings us to one of the most challenging questions I get asked: Why didn't God intervene during World War II? Why doesn't God stop Putin? Why didn't my guardian angel prevent my accident? Why do children suffer?

These are painful questions, and I won't pretend to have complete answers. But I can share what I've come to understand from studying these papers.

First, this planet is on a normal evolutionary trajectory, even though it might not feel that way to us. Every inhabited world goes through similar stages: tribal conflict, national wars, ideological struggles, and eventually, hopefully, planetary unification and the age of light and life. We're still in the messy middle stages. The wars we experience, as horrible as they are, represent the growing pains of a species learning to govern themselves, learning to value peace over conquest, learning that wisdom is better than violence.

Divine intervention in every crisis would short-circuit that learning process. We would become dependent children, never developing the spiritual strength and wisdom necessary to take our place as mature citizens of a vast universe. So, the policy, generally speaking, is non-interference. Let the planet evolve. Let the creatures learn.

There was a fascinating historical example someone brought up during one of our study sessions. During Operation Barbarossa, Hitler's invasion of the Soviet Union, winter arrived a full month earlier than normal. The Germans were caught completely unprepared, and the early winter contributed significantly to their defeat. Could that have been divine intervention? Could the midwayers have manipulated weather patterns? It's possible. We'll probably never know for certain.

But it illustrates the point: if intervention happens, it's typically subtle, working through natural mechanisms rather than obvious miracles.

Now, there are exceptions. The Reserve Corps of Destiny I mentioned earlier represents one such exception. These are approximately a thousand individuals at any given time who are trained during sleep to handle planetary emergencies. If a situation arises where a physical human must perform a specific task to prevent catastrophe, one of these trained individuals might be used, sometimes without conscious awareness that they're doing anything unusual.

Let me give you a hypothetical example. Suppose someone at a military base decided to launch an unauthorized nuclear weapon. A member of the Reserve Corps working on that base, someone with proper clearance and access, might suddenly feel compelled to enter a restricted area and prevent the launch. Their Thought Adjuster would assume control, perform the necessary action, and then return control to the human, who might have no memory of what they just did.

Is this manipulative? Perhaps. But consider the alternative: the unnecessary death of millions of people. The universe isn't run by simplistic rules. There's wisdom at work, weighing competing values and making decisions for the greater good.

And here's something else to consider: if our planet faced imminent complete destruction, say, if our moon were somehow knocked out of orbit and headed toward Earth, the spiritual administration has emergency protocols to evacuate every human being. We would simply wake up on another planet, our lives continuing as if nothing had happened. The physical destruction of Earth wouldn't end our spiritual journey. It couldn't, because we're spiritual beings having a physical experience, not physical beings hoping to become spiritual.

This realization changed how I think about death. When I was in that accident, unable to breathe, certain I was dying, I wasn't afraid. I knew, deeply knew, that my existence would continue. Yes, it would matter to Diane, to the students I teach. But *I* would go on. My work would continue, just in a different form, in a different place. That's not fatalism. It's perspective.

Why Jesus Didn't Call Down the Legions

So why didn't Jesus call down those twelve legions of angels? He had the power. He had the authority. Gabriel would have instantly deployed them. Jesus could have ended his arrest, his trial, his crucifixion with a single word.

He didn't, because doing so would have defeated the entire purpose of his bestowal. He came to live a human life, to experience what we experience, to show us that a human being, empowered by faith and indwelt by God, can triumph spiritually even in the face of physical defeat and death. If he'd called down the angels, he would have been acting as the Creator Son, not as Jesus the man. The whole mission would have been compromised.

More than that, he understood something we often forget physical survival isn't the point. Spiritual growth is the point. The Kingdom of God isn't built by force or power or angelic intervention. It's built one transformed soul at a time, through faith, through service, through love freely chosen in the face of hardship.

This is why the angelic armies, as vast and powerful as they are, remain largely invisible and inactive in our daily lives. The goal isn't to create a perfect world through force. The goal is to help us become perfect beings through growth. And growth requires struggle. It requires challenge. It requires the freedom to fail, to learn, and to try again.

A Personal Reflection on Life, Death, and Destiny

Let me return to my own experience for a moment, because I think it illustrates something important. When that truck hit us and I couldn't breathe, I told Diane, "I am dying here. I am not going to make it through this." I really believed that was the end.

In the days that followed, after I'd recovered enough to think clearly, Diane kept saying, "You're still here because your work isn't finished. You haven't completed your destiny on this planet." Maybe she's right. Maybe there are students I haven't taught yet, lessons I haven't learned, contributions I haven't made. Or maybe the timing was simply arbitrary, a quirk of circumstance, nothing more profound than the excellent response time of our local EMS.

The truth is, I don't know. And here's what I've realized: it doesn't matter which explanation is correct. What matters is what I do with the time I have, however long or short that might be. The most important work in my life right now is teaching The Urantia Book, helping others understand these profound truths that have transformed my own thinking. Whether I continue this work for two more years or twenty, I'm going to do it with full commitment, because this is my contribution to the spiritual progress of this planet.

And when my time here does end, whether it's next week or decades from now, I'll wake up on the mansion worlds and continue the same journey, just in a different setting. Death is a doorway, not a wall. My guardian seraphim understand this. They're not trying to extend my physical life indefinitely. They're trying to maximize my spiritual growth while I'm here, and then they'll escort me to the next phase when this one concludes.

That's their job. That's what they've been trained for across millennia. And they're very, very good at it.

The Immensity of It All

Sometimes I sit with these numbers, millions of angels, thousands of worlds, entire orders of beings we don't even know exist, and I'm overwhelmed. The universe is so much larger, so much more complex, so much more populated than we generally imagine. And yet, in the midst of all this cosmic machinery, there are beings specifically assigned to you and me. Individuals who know us intimately, who are invested in our success, who will journey with us from this troubled planet all the way to Paradise itself.

I find that simultaneously humbling and empowering. Humbling because I'm forced to confront how small I am in the grand scheme of things. Empowering because I realize I'm not alone, have never been alone, and never will be alone. We're surrounded by invisible helpers, spiritual ministers, cosmic administrators who care deeply about our progress.

The seraphim aren't distant, impersonal forces. They're personalities. They form friendships. They have homes on beautiful worlds. They gather for reunions every millennium, catching up with their companions, celebrating their achievements, reflecting on their service. And someday, when we reach the mansion worlds, we'll finally meet them face to face. We'll see the faces of those who walked beside us through our darkest moments and our greatest triumphs. I can't wait for that day.

As we close this chapter on the seraphic worlds and organization, I hope you've gained not just information but perspective. These aren't dry theological concepts. They're descriptions of real beings, real places, real structures of ministry that surround and support us every day. In our next chapter, we'll look more closely at the cherubim and sanobim, those faithful record-keepers who ensure that nothing of spiritual value in your life is ever lost or forgotten. We'll also explore the various orders of seraphic service and how they function in the broader work of the local universe.

But for now, sit with these ideas. Think about the angels who are with you at this very moment. They know you better than you know yourself. They see potential in you that you might not yet recognize. And they're committed, absolutely, eternally committed, to helping you achieve your destiny as a perfected son or daughter of God.

What a gift. What an incredible, undeserved, magnificent gift.

Chapter 7: Cherubim, Sanobim, and the Midway Creatures - Guardians Between Worlds

When I first began studying the celestial hierarchy described in *The Urantia Book*, I must admit I was overwhelmed by the sheer number of spiritual beings involved in our lives. We've already explored the Seraphim, those magnificent guardians who accompany us throughout our mortal journey and beyond. But tonight, as we continue our examination of Paper 38, we turn our attention to beings who work alongside the Seraphim in ways that are perhaps even more intimate and mysterious: the Cherubim, the Sanobim, and the remarkable Midway Creatures.

These aren't distant, abstract entities. They're here, working behind the scenes of our daily existence, bridging the gap between the material world we can touch and the spiritual realms we can barely imagine. Understanding them helps us grasp something profound about how the universe actually operates, not through random chance or cold mechanism, but through an intricate web of ministering spirits, each playing their appointed role in the grand design.

Cherubim and Sanobim - The Essential Pairs The Nature and Origin of These Beings

In all essential qualities, Cherubim and Sanobim bear a striking resemblance to Seraphim. They share the same origin, emerging from the creative will of the Universe Mother Spirit, yet their destinies don't always mirror those of their Seraphic cousins. What strikes me most about these beings is how wonderfully intelligent they are, how marvelously efficient, and, this touches something deep, how touchingly affectionate and almost human in their nature.

They represent the lowest order of angels, which paradoxically brings them closest to us. Because they occupy this position nearest the boundary between spiritual and material existence, they understand us in ways that higher orders might not. Think about that for a moment: beings specifically designed to work at the edge of human experience, capable of understanding our struggles because they themselves exist at a threshold.

The Complementary Partnership

Just as we discovered with the Seraphim, Cherubim and Sanobim always work in pairs. They're inherently associated, functionally united in a way that seems essential to their very nature. One serves as the energy-positive personality, the

Cherubim, who acts as the senior or controlling personality, what the text calls the "right deflector." The other, the Sanobim, functions as the energy-negative complement, the "left deflector."

Neither can function effectively alone. When separated from their partner, their capabilities become severely limited. This isn't a weakness, it's a design feature. The universe, it appears, operates on principles of complementarity and balance. These angelic pairs model something we would do well to remember that isolation diminishes us, while partnership amplifies our potential.

When serving independently of their Seraphic directors, Cherubim and Sanobim become even more dependent on mutual contact. They must always function together, their energies harmonizing to accomplish their assigned tasks. The parallel to the Seraphim is unmistakable, one positive, one negative, one considered the complement of being, working in perfect synchrony.

Creation and Classification

The Universe Mother Spirit brings these beings into existence, and she creates them in two distinct types. First, there are the regular Cherubim and Sanobim who serve throughout the local universe. Second, she creates the Morontia Cherubim and Sanobim, beings who exist at a semi-material level, straddling the boundary between pure spirit and physical matter.

Here's something fascinating: every fourth Sanobim is what we call quasi-material or Morontia. Why? Because when we ascenders arrive on the Mansion Worlds without a partner, and many of us will, these Morontia Cherubim are assigned to keep us company. They need to exist on a level closer to our newly morontia selves, more physical than the regular Cherubim, able to relate to beings who are just beginning their transition from material to spiritual existence.

Efficient Assistants to Seraphic Ministers

Cherubim and Sanobim serve as invaluable assistants to Seraphic ministers, and all seven orders of Seraphim are provided with these subordinate helpers. This bears repeating because it's significant: *all seven orders*, including the five orders not fully revealed to us in *The Urantia Book*, have Cherubim working alongside them.

These beings serve for ages in their capacities, but they never accompany Seraphim on assignments beyond the confines of the local universe. They remain here, in Nebadon, carrying out their duties without venturing into the larger cosmos. Their service is local, intimate, and thoroughly connected to the specific needs of our universe.

Now, here's where it gets personal. When you reach the third psychic circle in your spiritual development, that crucial threshold, both Cherubim and Sanobim are assigned to you alongside your Seraphic guardians. They become part of your spiritual entourage, working behind the scenes, recording your choices, assisting in ways you may never consciously recognize.

Some researchers have wondered whether these beings might account for certain paranormal phenomena, the shadowy figures people report seeing, the sense of a presence in the room. Could they be? Perhaps. They're described as being close enough to our dimension that we might, under certain circumstances, perceive their influence. I'm not claiming every ghost story involves Cherubim, but the possibility is worth considering.

Their Role and Limitations

These beings handle the routine spiritual work on individual worlds throughout the systems. In emergencies, they can even serve in place of a Seraphic pair. But, and this is crucial, they *never* function as attending angels to human beings, even temporarily. That privilege belongs exclusively to the Seraphim.

Think of it this way: while Cherubim and Sanobim are assigned to individual humans once we reach the third circle, they're never totally in charge. They take up the extra work that the Seraphim can't get to, recording, organizing, assisting, but the primary guardian relationship belongs to the Seraphim alone. You'll never find a human being without one of the Seraphim accompanying them. Once Cherubim and Sanobim are assigned to you, they remain with you until death. Normally, they don't continue with you to the Mansion Worlds, their service is planet-bound.

There are Cherubim and Sanobim on the Mansion Worlds, certainly, but they're not serving as individual Guardians of Destiny. That role remains the exclusive privilege of the Seraphim.

Training and Continuous Improvement

When assigned to a planet, Cherubim enter local courses of training that include studying planetary customs and languages. These ministering spirits of time are all bilingual, speaking both the language of their local universe of origin and that of their native superuniverse. They acquire these linguistic abilities through the schools of the realms.

What strikes me here is the emphasis on continuous self-improvement. Cherubim and Sanobim, like Seraphim and most other orders of spirit beings, are continuously engaged in efforts at self-betterment. Only the subordinate beings of power control and energy direction, those who manage the mechanical operations of the universe, are incapable of progression. Everyone else, every creature possessing actual or potential personality volition, seeks new achievements.

The text mentions something intriguing about superuniverse languages. If Cherubim learn their "native superuniverse" language, this suggests each of the seven superuniverses may have its own distinct linguistic patterns. We live in one superuniverse among seven, and each appears to have developed its own form of communication. The diversity of creation extends even to language itself.

The Morontia Level and Borderline Work

By nature, Cherubim and Sanobim exist very near the morontia level of existence. This positioning makes them extraordinarily efficient at what the text calls "borderline work", operating at the boundaries between physical, morontial, and spiritual domains.

These children of the Local Universe Mother Spirit are characterized by what we might call "fourth creatures." Just as the Havona Servitals and the Conciliating Commissions have this characteristic, every fourth Cherubim and every fourth Sanobim are quasi-material, very definitely resembling the morontia level of existence. This quality makes them feel closer to us, more relatable. They can easily function in morontia existence, which becomes important as we transition from material to morontia life.

These angelic fourth creatures provide great assistance to Seraphim in the more literal phases of universe and planetary activities. The Morontia Cherubim perform many indispensable borderline tasks on the morontia training worlds, and they're assigned to serve the Morontia Companions in large numbers. In fact, they relate to morontia creatures much as Midway Creatures relate to evolutionary mortals on inhabited worlds.

On inhabited worlds, these Morontia Cherubim frequently work in liaison with the Midway Creatures, which we'll discuss shortly. Though Cherubim and Midway

Creatures are distinctly separate orders with different origins, they display remarkable similarity in nature and function.

The Evolution of Cherubim and Sanobim

Not all Cherubim and Sanobim are created equal, and their evolutionary potential varies significantly. The Universe Mother Spirit can transform these beings from one type to another through what's called "the Embrace." This Divine Embrace represents a crucial moment of advancement, a transformation that opens new pathways of service and growth.

There are three great classes with regard to evolutionary potential:

1. Ascension Candidates

These beings represent the highest potential among Cherubim and Sanobim. By nature, they're candidates for Seraphic status. While they may not equal Seraphim in inherent endowment, through application and experience they can attain full Seraphic standing.

These are the brilliant ones, the achievers, the beings who demonstrate the capacity for growth that will eventually qualify them for promotion. They're working toward something greater than their current station, and the possibility of becoming Seraphim drives their service.

2. Mid-Phase Cherubim

Here's where we encounter inherent limitations. Not all Cherubim and Sanobim possess equal ascension potential. Most of these mid-phase beings will remain Cherubim and Sanobim throughout their service careers. However, and this offers hope, the more gifted individuals among them may achieve limited Seraphic service.

If they're exceptionally good at their work, if they demonstrate unusual gifts, they might advance to join the Ascension Candidates. It's possible, though not guaranteed. Their future depends partly on merit, partly on capacity, and partly on factors we don't fully understand.

3. Morontia Cherubim

These fourth creatures of the angelic orders always retain their quasi-material characteristics. They will continue as Cherubim and Sanobim, along with the majority of their mid-phase brethren, until something extraordinary happens, the completed factualization of the Supreme Being.

When the Supreme Being comes into full fruition, an event still in our future, something will change for these beings. We don't know what, exactly. The text doesn't specify their destiny beyond that cosmic milestone. But their future is somehow tied to the completion of the experiential God, the Supreme, who gathers all evolutionary experience into unified reality.

The Path to Paradise

For Ascension Candidate Cherubim and Sanobim, the path forward becomes clearer when we understand what happens to those who serve alongside ascending Seraphim. The more experienced of these Cherubim are attached to the Seraphic Guardians of Destiny, placing them in direct line for advancement to the status of Mansion World Teachers.

Here's how it works: When their Seraphic seniors, the Guardians of Destiny, are deserted by their mortal wards who attain morontia life, and when other types of evolutionary Seraphim are granted clearance for Seraphington and Paradise, they must leave their former subordinates behind. Cherubim and Sanobim cannot pass beyond the confines of Nebadon with them.

But these deserted Cherubim and Sanobim aren't abandoned. The Universe Mother Spirit embraces them, and through this embrace they achieve a level equivalent to Mansion World Teachers in their attainment of Seraphic status.

This is profoundly important. The embrace transforms them, opening the possibility of advancement to Paradise. Once they become Seraphim, they can potentially attach themselves to Seraphic Guardians of Destiny or serve as single Seraphim assigned to groups of finaliters. The doors of eternity swing open before them.

The Second Embrace and Full Seraphic Status

Once these transformed beings have served long and faithfully as Mansion World Teachers on the morontia spheres, from the lowest to the highest, something remarkable occurs. When their corps on Salvington becomes over-recruited, the

Bright and Morning Star (Gabriel himself) summons these faithful servants to appear in his presence.

The oath of personality transformation is administered. Then, in groups of seven thousand, these advanced and senior Cherubim and Sanobim are re-embraced by the Universe Mother Spirit. From this second Embrace, they emerge as full-fledged Seraphim.

The full and complete career of a Seraphim, with all of its Paradise possibilities, now opens before these twice-embraced beings. They may be assigned as Guardians of Destiny to mortal beings, and if their mortal ward attains survival, they become eligible for advancement to Seraphington and the seven circles of Seraphic attainment, even to Paradise and the Corps of the Finality.

Can you imagine what this means to them? For ages, they've served in subordinate roles. Now they stand on the threshold of the Paradise adventure, equal in status to those they once assisted. Their goal becomes clear: serve as Guardians of Destiny, guide their mortal ward to survival, and thereby earn their own passage to eternal service.

The Stakes of Guardian Service

But here's something that makes the stakes intensely personal: if their mortal wards do not survive, if the human they're assigned to guard ultimately rejects eternal life, these Seraphim must start over with another person. All that investment, all that careful guidance, ends without the reward of advancement.

When someone decides not to continue into eternal life, it disappoints these celestial helpers in ways we can barely comprehend. They haven't just lost a companion; they've failed in their sacred duty. The repercussions extend throughout the celestial hierarchy.

This is why our choices matter so profoundly. We're not deciding in isolation. Our eternal destiny affects beings who have invested themselves in our spiritual success. When we refuse to continue, we don't just cease to exist, we impact the Paradise journey of beings who have served us faithfully.

The Midway Creatures: Bridges Between Worlds

Now we come to one of the most fascinating revelations in all of *The Urantia Book*, the Midway Creatures. These beings occupy a unique position in the cosmic hierarchy and understanding them helps explain much about our planet's unusual history.

Classification and Nature

The Midway Creatures have a threefold classification that reveals their complex nature:

First, they're properly classified with the ascending Sons of God. Their destiny, ultimately, involves the Paradise ascent alongside mortal ascenders.

Second, they're factually grouped with the orders of permanent citizenship. Unlike angels who serve and move on, Midwayers are assigned to specific planets for vast ages, becoming intimately connected to the worlds they serve.

Third, and this is why they appear in this paper, they're functionally reckoned with the ministering spirits of time. Their intimate and effective association with the angelic hosts in serving mortal humans on individual worlds makes them spiritual ministers in the truest sense.

When our planet lost forty thousand Primary Midwayers during the Lucifer Rebellion, the tragedy extended far beyond numbers. We lost forty thousand ministering beings who were supposed to help humans throughout the ages. That's a staggering deficit, a spiritual resource we've been operating without for hundreds of thousands of years.

Origins and Characteristics

These unique creatures appear on the majority of inhabited worlds. They're always found on decimal planets, those experimental worlds where the Life Carriers try new approaches to developing life. Urantia, our world, is one such decimal planet, which partly explains our unusual history.

Midwayers come in two distinct types: Primary and Secondary. Their methods of origin differ dramatically, as do their characteristics and capabilities.

Primary Midwayers

The Primary Midwayers constitute the more spiritual group. They're a somewhat standardized order of beings, uniformly derived from the modified ascending mortal staff of the Planetary Princes. Every planet that enjoys their ministry has exactly fifty thousand Primary Midway Creatures, no more, no fewer.

On our world, these beings descended from the Caligastia One Hundred, that staff of modified humans who served under our Planetary Prince before the rebellion. The *Urantia Book* explains in earlier papers how this happened. The staff discovered, somewhat accidentally, how to produce these beings, and Caligastia encouraged all of them to continue creating these Midwayers. Eventually, fifty thousand came into existence.

What's crucial to understand: Primary Midwayers are energized intellectually and spiritually by the angelic technique. They maintain a uniform intellectual status, but here's something startling, the seven adjutant mind-spirits make no contact with them whatsoever. They exist entirely outside that circuit of mind ministry that you and I depend upon.

Only the sixth and seventh adjutant spirits, the spirit of worship and the spirit of wisdom, are able to minister to the Secondary group. But the Primaries? Nothing. They operated without that fundamental connection to the Local Universe Mother Spirit's mind ministry.

Is it any wonder so many of them rebelled? Without the stabilizing influence of the adjutant mind-spirits, without that connection to spiritual sanity that the mind circuits provide, they were vulnerable in ways we can barely comprehend.

Secondary Midwayers

The Secondary Midwayers are more material, more like us. They vary greatly in numbers on different worlds, though the average is around fifty thousand. They're derived from the planetary biological uplifters, the Adams and Eves, or from their immediate progeny.

There are no less than twenty-four diverse techniques involved in producing Secondary Midway Creatures on evolutionary worlds. The mode of origin on Urantia was, as the text diplomatically puts it, "unusual and extraordinary."

Because of Adam and Eve's default, their failure to fulfill their mission completely, we didn't receive our full quota of Secondary Midwayers. Not even close. If I recall correctly, every fourth child born to Adam and Eve's descendants produced an invisible being, visible to celestial personalities and the Prince's staff, but not to normal humans.

Can you imagine raising an invisible child? Your family could see them, the celestial supervisors could see them, but your neighbors couldn't. It would have been quite an experience, I suspect.

Essential Features, Not Accidents

Neither the Primary nor Secondary Midwayers are evolutionary accidents. Both represent essential features in the predetermined plans of the universe architects. The Life Carriers know, perhaps a million years in advance, that these beings will appear at specific junctures in a planet's evolutionary development.

Their appearance at opportune moments aligns with the original designs and developmental plans of the supervising Life Carriers. Everything was planned. These beings were meant to exist, meant to serve, meant to help humanity navigate the difficult transition from animal origins to spiritual potential.

The tragedy, then, is not that they exist but that so many of them were lost to rebellion. We might spend years theorizing about why the Midwayers rebelled in such large numbers during the Caligastia Rebellion. Were they resentful of their half-existence between worlds? Were they proud of their unique abilities? Did they grow frustrated with the slow pace of human progress?

Without physical bodies like ours, they could observe everything, influence much, but participate in physical existence only partially. That kind of existence might generate its own frustrations. And their capacity to create mischief, what they might have considered harmless fun, could have gotten out of hand, contributing to the breakdown of planetary administration.

Different Capacities and Limitations

Primary Midwayers are not candidates for Thought Adjusters. Neither are the Secondary Midwayers. Not a single one has ever received an indwelling fragment of the Universal Father. They progress through different mechanisms, follow different paths to spiritual growth.

Secondary Midwayers are physically energized by the Adamic technique, spiritually encircuited by the seraphic order, and intellectually endowed with the morontia transition type of mind. They're divided into four physical types, seven orders spiritually, and twelve levels of intellectual response to the joint ministry of the last two adjutant spirits and the morontia mind.

These diversities determine their differential of activity and planetary assignment. They're not carbon copies of one another. Just as humans vary in intellectual capacity and spiritual receptivity, so do Secondary Midwayers. They exist along a spectrum of capability, and their assignments match their abilities.

Complementary Abilities

Here's where it gets fascinating. Primary Midwayers resemble angels more than mortals. Secondary Midwayers are much more like human beings. Each renders invaluable assistance to the other in executing their manifold planetary assignments.

Primary Midwayers can achieve liaison cooperation with morontia and spirit-energy controllers and mind circuits. They work in the higher dimensions of reality, interfacing with spiritual forces and morontia mechanisms.

Secondary Midwayers can establish working connections only with physical controllers and material-circuit manipulators. They work in the lower, more material dimensions.

But, and this is the crucial point, when each order establishes perfect synchrony of contact with the other, they achieve practical utilization of the entire energy gamut. From gross physical power all the way up through transition phases of universe energies to the higher spirit-reality forces of the celestial realms, they can operate anywhere.

Working together, they control and manipulate multiple dimensions of reality. They're perfect beings to have on a planet because they can function across the entire spectrum from physical to nearly spiritual. This is why they could appear as the demons and devils of ancient lore, manifesting in forms that terrified our ancestors.

Even before the Spirit of Truth arrived on our world, some Midwayers could invade human minds. They could literally enter your consciousness against your will, though the text notes that even then, if you were spiritually minded, they couldn't do this. Spiritual integrity provided protection.

After the Spirit of Truth was poured out at Pentecost, this kind of invasion became impossible. The rebellious Midwayers were removed from our planet, taken in chains to the Father's prison worlds along with Satan and the other rebels. Since Pentecost, genuine demonic possession cannot occur. Any cases of "possession" we hear about today have other explanations, mental illness, psychological disorders, fraud, but not actual spiritual invasion by rebel Midwayers.

Bridging Material and Spiritual Worlds

The gap between material and spiritual worlds is perfectly bridged by a serial association that's quite beautiful when you think about it:

Mortal man → Secondary Midwayer → Primary Midwayer → Morontia Cherubim → Seraphim

In the personal experience of an individual mortal, these diverse levels are undoubtedly unified and made personally meaningful by the unobserved and mysterious operations of the Divine Thought Adjuster.

Everything comes together through that fragment of God dwelling within you. The Thought Adjuster coordinates the ministry of all these beings, weaving their influences into a coherent spiritual experience. You may never consciously recognize their individual contributions, but they're all there, working in concert to guide you toward eternal life.

Service on Normal and Abnormal Worlds

On normal worlds, planets that haven't suffered rebellion and default, the Primary Midwayers maintain their service as the intelligence corps and celestial entertainers on behalf of the Planetary Prince. The Secondary Midwayers continue their cooperation with the Adamic regime, furthering the cause of progressive planetary civilization.

But when the Planetary Prince defects and the Material Son fails, as happened on Urantia, the Midway Creatures become wards of the System Sovereign. They serve under the directing guidance of the acting custodian of the planet.

Only three other worlds in our local system of Satania have Midwayers functioning together under unified leadership as they do here. Our unusual circumstances, the double tragedy of rebellion and default, forced the Primary and Secondary Midwayers to cooperate in ways not necessary on normal worlds.

The United Midwayer Commission, working together despite their different origins, brought this revelation to the attention of universe authorities and Michael.

They suggested that *The Urantia Book* be given to our world. Without their unified advocacy, we might not have this revelation today.

Diverse Activities

The planetary work of both Primary and Secondary Midwayers varies considerably on different worlds throughout a universe. On normal, average planets, their activities differ dramatically from their duties on isolated spheres like Urantia.

On a normal world, you'd have a brilliant Planetary Prince leading evolutionary progress, coordinating development, guiding civilization toward light and life. The Midwayers would assist this well-functioning administration, their work streamlined and purposeful.

Here, without that ideal leadership for most of our history, the Midwayers have shouldered burdens they were never meant to carry alone. They've compensated for our missing planetary government, done their best to guide confused and struggling humanity, worked to maintain whatever progress they could despite enormous handicaps.

Historians and Archivists

The Primary Midwayers serve as planetary historians. From the time of the Planetary Prince's arrival to the age of settled light and life, they formulate the pageants and design the portrayals of planetary history for the exhibits on system headquarters worlds.

When we eventually reach the headquarters world, Jerusem, we'll be able to experience these pageants. They'll show us what happened in our planet's past, what's happening now, and what will happen in the future. The Midwayers have been recording everything, preserving our story, creating a comprehensive historical record that transcends mortal memory.

Ultimate Destiny

Midwayers remain for long periods on inhabited worlds. But if faithful to their trust, they will eventually, and most certainly, be recognized for their age-long service in maintaining the sovereignty of the Creator Son. They'll be duly rewarded for their patient ministry to material mortals on their world of time and space.

Sooner or later, all accredited Midway Creatures will be mustered into the ranks of the ascending Sons of God. They'll be duly initiated into the long adventure of the Paradise ascent in company with those very mortals of animal origin, their earth brethren, whom they so jealously guarded and so effectively served during the long planetary sojourn.

Think about that. The beings who watched over primitive humans hundreds of thousands of years ago, who witnessed all our struggles and failures and occasional triumphs, will eventually ascend to Paradise alongside us. We'll journey together, former guardians and former wards, all of us headed toward the same eternal destiny.

The Fate of Rebel Midwayers

Someone asked what happened to the Midwayers who rebelled. It's a sobering story. At Pentecost, all of them were taken away in chains to the Father's prison worlds, along with Satan and the other rebels. They were removed by force, taken to await adjudication by the Ancients of Days.

Unlike mortals, who sleep unconsciously if they're found unsalvageable, these rebel Midwayers will be conscious during their adjudication. They'll know they're being judged. If they don't repent, they'll also be conscious when that which makes them who they are is taken away. They'll cease to exist, fully aware of their own annihilation.

It's a terrible fate. The wages of sin is death, not the temporary death we experience, but permanent obliteration of personality. Yet even here, mercy operates. They have time to repent. The adjudication hasn't happened yet. The possibility of redemption remains, though we don't know how many, if any, will choose that path.

Reflections on Reality Insurance

As we close this chapter, I want to return to something that came up in discussion with the study group. We were talking about survival, about waking up on the Mansion Worlds, and someone asked about belief in Jesus.

The *Urantia Book* doesn't explicitly say you must believe in Jesus to reach heaven. But Jesus himself said, repeatedly, "No one comes to the Father but by me." He said, "I am the way, the truth, and the life."

Here's how I think about it: If I wake up on the Mansion World and discover Jesus isn't the Creator Son, that he's not the Sovereign of the universe, then I've lost my way. Because he was my way to get there. But that won't happen. Jesus is who he said he was, Michael of Nebadon, our Creator, our guide, our path to the Father.

Why take the chance of not waking up because of stubbornness or pride? Why risk missing eternity because you refused to recognize your own Creator? At minimum, even if you're skeptical, it's what I call "reality insurance." Acknowledge Jesus, research who he was, understand who God is, and you've secured your passage to the next level of existence.

God forgives sins. That's what divine mercy is about. I don't believe Jesus died to pay for everyone's sins, that's a theological construct that doesn't make sense in light of *The Urantia Book*. God forgives sins because God is merciful. Jesus came to show us a perfect life, to reveal himself as the Creator Son, to demonstrate the way to eternal life.

But you have to recognize your Creator. You have to acknowledge reality. That's not too much to ask.

Looking Ahead

We've covered remarkable ground in this chapter, exploring beings most people have never heard of, Cherubim who can become Seraphim, Sanobim who work in complementary pairs, Primary and Secondary Midwayers who bridge worlds and witness ages.

These aren't mythological creatures or theological abstractions. According to *The Urantia Book*, they're real beings, working right now, some of them assigned to you personally if you've reached the third psychic circle. They're recording your choices, assisting your guardians, doing their part in the vast plan to bring you safely to Paradise.

In our next chapter, we'll turn to the Seraphic Hosts, the full organization and function of the Seraphim across the local universe. We'll discover how these magnificent beings are organized, what their various orders accomplish, and how they coordinate to minister to mortals like us across millions of inhabited worlds.

The celestial hierarchy continues to unfold in beauty and complexity. Each level we study reveals new dimensions of care, new evidences of divine planning, new reasons to trust that we're not alone in this universe.

This paper 38 was presented by a Melchizedek acting by request of the Chief of the Seraphic Hosts of Nebadon.

Chapter 8: The Seraphic Hosts - Understanding the Angels Among Us

When I first began studying Paper 39 of *The Urantia Book*, I have to admit, I felt overwhelmed. This isn't one of those papers you can breeze through in an evening. It's dense, layered, and packed with information that doesn't always reveal itself on the first reading, or even the second. But here's what I've come to understand: if we want to grasp the true nature of angels and their role in our spiritual journey, we need to slow down and really think about what's being presented. So, before we dive into the details, let me offer you a word of caution and a bit of encouragement.

This paper is divided into numerous sections, each describing different orders of seraphim, angels who serve in various capacities throughout the local universe and beyond. There are seven major classifications, and under most of these, there are seven subcategories. Yes, you read that right. It's a lot to keep straight. But I promise you, if we take it step by step, it will all begin to make sense. My goal in this chapter is not just to relay information, but to help you see the bigger picture: how these celestial beings are intimately involved in our lives, our growth, and our eventual ascension to Paradise.

The Question Everyone Asks First

Right off the bat, I know what you're wondering. I get this question every time I teach this material: "Which one of these seraphim become our Guardian Angels?" It's a natural question. After all, most of us have grown up with the idea of guardian angels watching over us, and we want to know where they fit into this elaborate hierarchy.

Here's the answer, and it may surprise you: *any or all of them*. That's right. Any seraphim, from any of these classifications, can potentially become a Guardian of Destiny if they qualify. The path to becoming a guardian angel isn't limited to one particular order. Instead, it's about experience, training, and desire. Many seraphim start in one classification and, through education and service, move into others. Over time, they gain the skills and wisdom necessary to be entrusted with the sacred duty of guiding a mortal soul from birth to eternity.

Think of it this way: when seraphim are first created by our local universe Mother Spirit, they're born with the innate abilities needed for a specific role. But they're not stuck there. Through study, testing, and hands-on experience, they can qualify for other assignments. A Supreme Seraphim can become a Superior Seraphim. A Supervisor Seraphim can train to be an Administrator Seraphim. And yes, any of them can aspire to become a Guardian of Destiny, the role that offers the deepest, most personal connection to ascending mortals like you and me.

So, as we explore these various orders, keep in mind that we're not looking at a rigid hierarchy where one type of angel is "better" than another. We're looking at different functions, different areas of service, all equally valuable in the grand scheme of the universe.

How Angels Begin

Here's something fascinating that the revelators share with us: when seraphim are created, they emerge fully formed. There's no childhood for an angel. No learning to walk, no learning to talk, no diapers or tantrums or teenage angst. One moment they don't exist, and the next moment they awaken, complete, aware, and ready to serve.

I sometimes compare it to waking up from anesthesia. When I had surgery recently, they injected the sedative, and within seconds, I was gone. No memory of falling asleep, no sense of time passing. Then, just as suddenly, I was awake again, fully myself, with all my faculties intact. That's probably the closest we can come to understanding what it's like for a newly created seraphim. They wake up as adults, so to speak, with the skills and knowledge they need for their initial assignment already in place.

But, and this is important, they don't have a past. No memories, no childhood experiences to draw from, no history of mistakes and lessons learned. They're a blank slate in that sense. And while they're born with the abilities required for their specific role, anything outside that role has to be learned. If a seraphim is created as a Son-Spirit Minister, for example, they know how to relay messages and coordinate activities for the Creator Son and the Creative Mother Spirit. But if they want to serve in another capacity, say, as a Court Advisor or a Teaching Counselor, they have to go through training, just like we do.

This is where the comparison to human experience becomes really interesting. When we die and wake up on the mansion worlds, we find ourselves in a similar situation. We have all our memories from Earth, but we lack so much knowledge about the universe, about God, about the cosmic reality we're now part of. Most people arrive there with little or no understanding of the Father, the Son, the Spirit, or the vast structure of creation. They have to start at square one, taking classes on cosmology, theology, history, all the things we're learning right now through *The Urantia Book*.

And guess what our job will be when we get there? Teaching. That's right. Those of us who've studied this revelation, who've wrestled with these concepts and worked to understand them, we'll be helping those who arrive after us. We'll be sharing what we've learned, guiding them through the same confusion we once felt. It's humbling, really. We're not just studying for our own benefit, we're preparing to serve.

The Seven Orders of Seraphim

So let's lay out the structure. According to Paper 39, seraphim are classified into seven major groups:

1. **Supreme Seraphim** – Closely associated with the Seraphic Corps of Completion
2. **Superior Seraphim** – Stationed at Salvington, our local universe headquarters
3. **Supervisor Seraphim** – Stationed at the constellation headquarters
4. **Administrator Seraphim** – Stationed at the system headquarters
5. **Planetary Helpers** – Serving both at the system capital and on inhabited worlds
6. **Transition Ministers** – Ministering on all inhabited worlds and the mansion worlds
7. **Seraphim of the Future** – Reserved for future assignments, particularly as worlds advance toward light and life

Each of these groups (except the Seraphim of the Future, about which we're told very little) is further divided into seven subgroups. That gives us a total of 42 distinct categories of seraphic service in the local universe. It's a lot, I know. But the more you sit with it, the more you begin to see how beautifully organized and purposeful it all is.

What strikes me most is that this isn't a hierarchy of importance. It's a division of labor. Each order serves a vital function, and none is inherently superior to another. They're all necessary. They're all honored. And they all work together to facilitate the spiritual growth of ascending mortals and the smooth operation of the universe.

The Supreme Seraphim: Angels of the Highest Service

Let's start at the top, not because Supreme Seraphim are more important, but because they offer a clear picture of what angels can become. These are seraphim who have completed the entire ascension journey. They've gone all the way to Paradise, been embraced by both the Eternal Son and the Infinite Spirit and become part of the Seraphic Corps of Completion. Think of them as the finaliters of the angelic realm.

And here's the beautiful irony: after achieving this exalted status, many of them choose to return to service at the most basic level. They *want* to be assigned as Guardian Angels. Why? Because that's where the most meaningful experience lies. That's where they can have the deepest impact. It's not about prestige or status for them, it's about service, growth, and connection.

Within the Supreme Seraphim, there are several specialized roles, and I want to highlight a few that directly impact us:

Son-Spirit Ministers

These angels serve as the intelligence corps for the Creator Son (Christ Michael) and the Creative Mother Spirit. They relay messages, coordinate activities, and ensure that the will of our universe parents is carried out efficiently. If you imagine the local universe as a vast organization, these are the executive assistants, the communication officers, the ones who keep everything running smoothly.

Bestowal Attendants

This is one of the most fascinating groups. When a Paradise Son, whether an Avonal Son or our own Creator Son, comes to a world on a bestowal mission, they're accompanied by 144 of these specialized seraphim. The number 144 appears several times in religious texts, and now we understand why. These aren't just symbolic figures, they're real, highly trained angels who organize and direct the spiritual work associated with the mission.

Jesus himself alluded to this when he said he could call upon legions of angels if needed. He wasn't exaggerating. There were legions at his disposal, all coordinated by these 144 Bestowal Attendants. And these weren't inexperienced angels. Every single one of them had completed the journey to Paradise and back. They were seasoned, wise, and fully capable of handling the immense spiritual challenges of an incarnation mission.

Court Advisors

Now this is where things get deeply personal. Court Advisors are the angels who defend us. They're the ones who stand up for us when we make mistakes, when we stumble, when we fail to live up to our potential. And here's what I want you to understand: they don't defend us because we're innocent. They defend us because we're *redeemable*.

Justice demands that every mistake be acknowledged and addressed. But mercy, divine mercy, requires that we be judged not just by our actions, but by our intentions, our nature, our circumstances. Court Advisors ensure that mercy is applied fairly. They examine our motives, our background, our struggles, and they present the best possible case for our continued spiritual existence.

This happens throughout our ascension journey, not just at the end. Every time we make a significant error, every time we default on our responsibilities, every time we act in ways that contradict the divine will, there's an adjudication process. And our angels, our Court Advisors, are there, making sure we're given every opportunity to learn, grow, and continue forward.

Let me be clear about something: there's only one unforgivable sin, and that's outright rebellion against God. Everything else, murder, theft, betrayal, cruelty, these are mistakes. Terrible mistakes, yes. Mistakes with serious consequences. But they're not unforgivable. If a person genuinely desires to change, to grow, to align themselves with the Father's will, they can be redeemed. The Court Advisors make sure that opportunity isn't taken away unfairly.

Where Angels Are Trained

Here's something I find absolutely intriguing: somewhere on Earth, right now, there's a facility where angels are being trained. We can't see it. We can't touch it. We can't walk into it even if we stumbled right through the middle of it. But it's there.

The Urantia Book tells us that on every inhabited world, there are celestial schools attached to the headquarters of the Planetary Prince. These schools train seraphim in the languages, cultures, and customs of the mortal races they'll be serving. Even though our Planetary Prince's regime fell into rebellion, the training facility remains. And it's likely connected to the archangel headquarters that's also located somewhere on this planet, perhaps in the Redwood forests of California, though that's speculation.

Imagine that. You could be hiking through the woods, and without knowing it, pass directly through a classroom full of angels studying human psychology, learning how to guide us more effectively. It's a humbling thought. It reminds us that we're not alone, and we're not unnoticed. The universe is alive with purpose, and we're part of something far greater than we usually realize.

The Path to Becoming a Guardian

So how does a seraphim become a Guardian of Destiny? It's not automatic. It requires desire, training, and qualification. And interestingly, many angels who achieve this honor do so only after serving in other capacities for a long time.

The process appears to work like this: a seraphim is created with the skills for a specific role. Through education and experience, they learn additional roles, gaining a broader understanding of how the universe operates. Eventually, they may enroll in the celestial schools on an evolutionary world like ours, where they study the intricacies of mortal life. If they succeed in their training and demonstrate the necessary qualities, patience, compassion, wisdom, dedication, they're assigned to a mortal soul.

From that point forward, their destiny is tied to ours. Where we go, they go. When we sleep in death, they remain awake, carrying our identity and our potential forward. When we're resurrected on the mansion worlds, they're there with us, continuing to guide and teach. And if we make it all the way to Paradise, they ascend with us, sharing in the triumph.

It's a partnership unlike any other. We help each other grow. We challenge each other. And in the end, we become something neither of us could have been alone.

A Personal Note

I've been studying *The Urantia Book* for years now, more times than I can count. And every time I come back to Paper 39, I find something new. Some detail I missed before. Some connection I hadn't made. This material is layered, and it rewards patience.

If you're feeling overwhelmed right now, that's okay. I was too when I first encountered it. But stick with it. Ask questions. Reread sections that confuse you. And remember that the goal isn't to memorize all these classifications, it's to understand the bigger picture. Angels are real. They serve in countless ways. And they're deeply, personally invested in our spiritual success.

In our next session, we'll continue exploring the other orders of seraphim, the Superior Seraphim, the Supervisor Seraphim, and all the rest. We'll see how they work together, how they serve on different levels of universe administration, and how they ultimately support the same goal: helping us, mortal creatures of time and space, find our way home to God.

But for now, let this sink in you are not alone. You've never been alone. From the moment of your first moral decision, you've been accompanied by celestial beings who care about you, who defend you, who work tirelessly to ensure you have every opportunity to succeed. That's the real revelation of Paper 39. Not just the organizational details, but the profound love and commitment that permeates every level of angelic service.

And that, I believe, is worth taking the time to understand.

In the next chapter, we'll examine the specific functions of each seraphic order in greater detail, exploring how they interact with us at different stages of our journey and what their presence means for our daily lives.

Chapter 9: The Superior Seraphim and the Ministry of Angels

Introduction: Understanding the Angelic Hierarchy

When I first began studying Paper 39 of *The Urantia Book*, I'll admit I found myself somewhat overwhelmed by the sheer complexity of the angelic orders. Seven levels of seraphim, each with seven subdivisions, it's enough to make anyone's head spin. Yet as I've spent years working through this material with study groups, I've come to appreciate that this intricate organization reveals something profound about the divine administration of our local universe. These aren't just abstract concepts or theological speculation. We're talking about real beings who will greet us on the Mansion Worlds, guide our education, and transport us across space as we journey toward Paradise.

Tonight, I want to take you deeper into section one of Paper 39, specifically focusing on what the text calls the Superior Seraphim. We're picking up at paragraph 13, which introduces us to the Teaching Counselors, a group of angels that may already be assisting teachers right here on our planet. I realize this material can seem dense at first but stay with me. Understanding these angelic orders helps us grasp how the universe actually functions, and more importantly, it prepares us for what lies ahead when we awaken on the first Mansion World.

The Teaching Counselors: Invaluable Assistance on the Path

Let me read directly from Paper 39, section 1, paragraph 4: "The Teaching Counselors: These angels are the invaluable assistants to the spiritual teaching corps of the local universe. Teaching counselors are secretaries to all orders of teachers, from the Melchizedeks and the Trinity Teacher Sons down to the morontia mortals who are assigned as helpers to those of their kind who are just behind them in the scale of ascendant life."

What strikes me about this passage is its scope. These Teaching Counselors don't just work at the highest levels with the Melchizedeks and Trinity Teacher Sons at our local universe capital, Salvington. They extend all the way down to the seven Mansion Worlds, where they assist us, newly awakened morontia beings, as we learn to teach those coming behind us. Think about that for a moment. The revelation tells us we won't simply be thrown into teaching roles unprepared. We'll have seraphic helpers guiding us, showing us how to communicate what we've learned to others who are just beginning their ascension journey.

The text continues: "You will first see these associate teaching seraphim on some one of the seven Mansion Worlds surrounding Jerusem." Jerusem, of course, is the headquarters of our local system. So, our first encounter with these particular angels happens relatively early in our morontia career. They're there to help us adjust, to learn, and eventually to teach. I find this deeply reassuring. The universe doesn't expect us to figure everything out on our own.

During one of our study sessions, Rodney asked an interesting question: "Could they be helping us right now?" And honestly, the answer appears to be yes. The passage says these counselors assist "morontia mortals who are assigned as helpers to those of their kind who are just behind them in the scale of ascendant life." While we're still in the flesh, we don't fully perceive this assistance, but it's quite possible that as I teach this material, or as any sincere teacher tries to communicate the truths in this book, we may have unseen helpers making the task a bit easier.

Let me tell you, trying to make sense of a paper like this, with seven different levels and seven sub-levels under each, becomes genuinely confusing. I often feel the weight of responsibility when attempting to relate these complex hierarchies in a way that's understandable. Perhaps that's where these teaching counselors come in, even now.

The text goes on: "These seraphim become associates of the division chiefs of the numerous educational and training institutions of the local universes, and they are attached in large numbers to the faculties of the seven training worlds of the local systems and of the seventy educational spheres of the constellations. These ministrations extend on down to the individual worlds. Even the true and consecrated teachers of time are assisted and often attended by these counselors of the supreme seraphim."

Notice how the revelation emphasizes that these ministrations extend "on down to the individual worlds", meaning planets like ours, Urantia. Even here, "true and consecrated teachers of time" receive assistance. If you're someone who teaches *The Urantia Book* sincerely, trying to help others grasp its truths, you may well have invisible companions supporting your efforts.

There's one more detail I want to highlight. The fourth creature bestowal of our Creator Son, the being we know as Jesus, but whose universe name is Michael of Nebadon, was made in the likeness of a Teaching Counselor of the Supreme Seraphim. Michael chose to experience life as this particular order of angel during his fourth bestowal. That's a remarkably humble choice, wouldn't you say? It tells us something about the value and importance of teaching, and of the beings dedicated to that ministry.

The Five Directors of Assignment

Moving to the next subdivision, we encounter what the revelation calls the Directors of Assignment. The text tells us: "A body of 144 Supreme seraphim is elected from time to time by the angels serving on the evolutionary and on the architectural spheres of creature habitation. This is the highest angelic council on any sphere, and it coordinates the self-directed phases of seraphic service and assignments. These angels preside over all seraphic assemblies pertaining to the line of duty or the call to worship."

What we're looking at here is essentially the governing council of angels on any given world or sphere. One hundred forty-four Supreme seraphim, elected by their peers, form this council. They coordinate assignments and, significantly, they preside over assemblies related to worship. This will be our first real opportunity to experience authentic worship when we awaken on the Mansion Worlds. These seraphim will be leading or directing that worship.

I want to pause here because worship is, in many ways, the highest activity we can engage in. It's more important than learning, more important than service, though those are vital too. Worship is that direct, personal connection between the creature and the Creator. On our planet, hampered as we are by material limitations and spiritual confusion, genuine worship can be difficult. But on the Mansion Worlds, guided by these Directors of Assignment, we'll finally understand what it means to truly worship. I find myself looking forward to that experience with a mixture of anticipation and, I'll be honest, a bit of nervousness. How will it feel to worship with such clarity?

The Recorders: Keeping the Universe's Memory

The next group we encounter is the Recorders. Here's what the text says: "These are the official recorders for the Supreme seraphim. Many of these high angels were born with their gifts fully developed; others have qualified for their positions of trust and responsibility by diligent application to study and faithful performance of similar duties while attached to lower or less responsible orders."

This passage reveals something fascinating about how angels develop. There are two classes of Recorders. Some are created already possessing the full capacity to perform their duties, they essentially come "out of the box" ready to record. Others, however, have earned their way into this position through study and faithful service in lesser roles. In other words, there's a merit-based progression even among angels. Some advance by proving themselves capable and trustworthy.

While we're discussing recorders, it's worth remembering that everything of significance is recorded, both in our personal lives and in the larger universe. Every important event, every meaningful decision, every genuine spiritual experience gets preserved in one form or another. These Recorder angels are responsible for maintaining that vast repository of information. When I think about my own life, knowing that the truly important moments are being recorded, it gives me pause. Not in a fearful way, but with a sense that my choices matter. They're not lost to time; they become part of the permanent record of the universe.

The Unattached Ministers: A Versatile Reserve

The seventh and final group of Supreme seraphim mentioned in this section is the Unattached Ministers: "Large numbers of unattached seraphim of the supreme order are self-directed observers on the architectural spheres and on the inhabited planets. Such ministers voluntarily meet the differential of demand for the service of the Supreme seraphim, thus constituting the general reserve of this order."

The Unattached Ministers function as a reserve corps. They're versatile enough to fill in wherever needed, whether as Recorders, Teachers, or in any other seraphic capacity. If there's a sudden need for additional help in one area, these ministers can step in. I think of them as the universe's way of ensuring flexibility in administration. Not everything can be planned perfectly in advance, especially in an evolving universe like ours. Having a reserve of capable, adaptable beings makes practical sense.

Understanding the Superior Seraphim

Now we arrive at the Superior Seraphim proper. The name might suggest they're somehow better than other angels, but that's not quite right. The text clarifies: "Superior seraphim receive their name, not because they are in any sense qualitatively superior to other orders of angels, but because they are in charge of the higher activities of a local universe."

They're called "superior" because of their assignments, not their inherent worth. They handle high-level responsibilities. The passage continues: "Very many of the first two groups of this seraphic corps are attainment seraphim, angels who have served in all phases of training and have returned to a glorified assignment as directors of their kind in the spheres of their earlier activities."

Here's where it gets really interesting. Attainment seraphim are those who have served in all seven types of angelic ministry. Many of them have journeyed all the way to Paradise, been embraced by the Eternal Son, and then returned to serve in the local universe, much like finaliters do. The text notes: "Being a young universe, Nebadon does not have many of this order." Our local universe hasn't been around long enough to produce vast numbers of these accomplished beings. But they do exist, and they bring with them the wisdom of complete experience.

During our study group discussion, Gary asked whether seraphim are ascending beings. That's a nuanced question. Angels aren't ascending in the same way we are, they're not evolutionary creatures starting from animal origin. They're created beings, made by the Infinite Spirit through our local universe Mother Spirit. However, they do have an ascension plan of their own. They can progress through service in the various seraphic orders, or, and this is the preferred path for many, they can become guardian seraphim.

Why would an already accomplished angel choose to become a guardian? Because it guarantees them the experience of starting at the very bottom, accompanying an evolutionary mortal through all the ups and downs of material existence, and then journeying with that soul all the way to Paradise. It's the surest path to complete experiential knowledge. Many Superior Seraphim who have already been to Paradise actually choose to return and become guardians so they can gain this fundamental experience. That level of dedication and humility impresses me deeply.

Someone once pointed out that this makes us, humans, the lowest type of being in the grand scheme, and that's technically true. But as I like to say, at least we're not pond scum. We may start at the bottom, but we have the potential to ascend all the way to Paradise and beyond. That's no small thing.

The Seven Groups of Superior Seraphim

The Superior Seraphim function in seven distinct groups and understanding their organization helps us see how the universe administration flows from the highest levels down to individual planets. Let me walk you through each group, because they follow a logical hierarchy.

1. The Intelligence Corps

"The Intelligence Corps belong to the personal staff of Gabriel, the Bright and Morning Star. They range the local universes gathering the information of the realms for his guidance in the councils of Nebadon. They are the intelligence corps of the mighty hosts over which Gabriel presides as vicegerent of the Master Son. These seraphim are not directly affiliated with either the systems or the constellations, and their information pours in direct to Salvington upon a continuous, direct, and independent circuit."

Gabriel serves as the chief executive of our local universe, second only to Michael himself. The Intelligence Corps reports directly to him, gathering information from across all the inhabited worlds and architectural spheres. They operate on what's called the intelligence circuit, one of the seven circuits of the local universe.

This brings up an important point about circuits that often confuses people. There are local universe circuits, controlled by our Divine Minister (the local universe Mother Spirit), and there are superuniverse circuits that extend beyond our local universe. The intelligence circuit we're discussing is local, it originates at Salvington and extends throughout Nebadon's worlds. It's separate from the superuniverse intelligence circuit, which originates with the Infinite Spirit and flows through the Master Spirits.

During our study, I showed a diagram of the three local universe circuits: the bestowal spirit of the Son (the Spirit of Truth, which is Michael's circuit), the circuit of the Divine Minister (the Holy Spirit), and the intelligence ministry circuit (which includes the seven-adjutant mind-spirits). These circuits work together to unify and administer the local universe.

The Intelligence Corps feeds information directly to Gabriel through this circuit. Every significant event, every development worth noting, flows to Salvington continuously. It's a remarkable system when you think about it, real-time intelligence gathering across millions of worlds.

2. The Voice of Mercy

"Mercy is the keynote of seraphic service and angelic ministry. It is therefore fitting that there should be a corps of angels who, in a special manner, portray mercy. These seraphim are the real mercy ministers of the local universes, being the inspired leaders who foster the higher impulses and holier emotions of men and angels. The directors of these legions are now always completion seraphim who are also graduate guardians of mortal destiny; that is, each angelic pair has guided at least one soul of animal origin during the life in the flesh and has subsequently traversed the circles of Seraphington and has been mustered into the seraphic corps of completion."

The Voice of Mercy represents something beautiful. These angels have earned their position through direct experience, they've served as guardian seraphim, accompanying at least one mortal through life, death, and the journey to Paradise. They've seen us at our worst and our best. They've witnessed the struggles, the failures, the small victories, and the eventual triumph of faith. That experience qualifies them to be ministers of mercy because they truly understand what it means to be patient with imperfect, evolving beings.

The text says they're "completion seraphim", angels who have gone all the way to Paradise, traversed the circles of Seraphington (the seraphic training world), and been mustered into what amounts to the seraphic equivalent of the Corps of Mortal Finaliters. They've achieved the highest possible status for an angel, yet they've chosen to return and serve as mercy ministers. Why? Because having guided mortals through the messy, painful, glorious process of spiritual growth, they've learned what mercy really means.

I find this deeply moving. These aren't angels who simply understand mercy as an abstract principle. They've lived it. They've had to exercise enormous patience with whom they were assigned to guard, someone like you or me, stumbling through life, making mistakes, occasionally getting it right. That's what gives them the experiential foundation to truly minister mercy.

3. Spirit Coordinators

"The third group of Superior seraphim are based on Salvington but function in the local universe anywhere they can be of fruitful service. While their tasks are essentially spiritual and therefore beyond the real understanding of human minds, you will perhaps grasp something of their ministry to mortals if it is explained that these angels are entrusted with the task of preparing the ascendant sojourners on Salvington for their last transition in the local universe, from the highest morontia level to the status of newborn first-stage spirit beings."

The Spirit Coordinators have a specific and critical function: they help us make the transition from morontia existence to spirit existence. This happens at the very end of our local universe training, on Salvington itself. We've progressed through all the Mansion Worlds, through the constellation training spheres, and we've finally arrived at the local universe capital. We're at the highest level of morontia development possible. But to move forward to the superuniverse, we must become first-stage spirits.

That's not a simple transition. Our entire mode of existence changes. The text compares their work to what the Mind Planners do on the Mansion Worlds: "As the Mind Planners on the mansion worlds help the surviving creature to adjust to, and make effective use of, the potentials of morontia mind, so do these seraphim instruct the morontia graduates on Salvington regarding the newly attained capacities of the mind of the spirit."

When we leave Salvington, we're leaving behind the direct influence of our local universe Mother Spirit. We no longer have the seven-adjutant mind-spirits guiding our thinking. Instead, we step into what's called the cosmic mind, a higher level of mental functioning that comes through the Master Spirits and ultimately from the Infinite Spirit. The Spirit Coordinators help us make that enormous adjustment. They coordinate our thoughts, our understanding, our very consciousness as we transition from morontia to spirit.

4. Assistant Teachers

"The assistant teachers are the helpers and associates of their fellow servants, the teaching counselors. They are also individually connected with the extensive educational enterprises of the local universe, especially with the sevenfold scheme of training operative on the mansion worlds of the local systems. A marvelous corps of this order of seraphim functions on Urantia for the purpose of fostering and furthering the cause of truth and righteousness."

The Assistant Teachers work closely with the Teaching Counselors we discussed earlier, but their focus is more directly on the educational structure itself, particularly the "sevenfold scheme of training" that operates on the seven Mansion Worlds. Each Mansion World has specific concepts and lessons we must master before progressing to the next. Years ago, I studied these seven levels in detail with groups, though I suspect most people don't remember all the specifics now. The point is that there's a structured curriculum, and the Assistant Teachers help us navigate it.

What caught my attention is the statement that "a marvelous corps of this order of seraphim functions on Urantia." Right here, on our planet, these angels work to foster truth and righteousness. They're busy here, remarkably busy, given the confusion and spiritual darkness that often seems to prevail. When someone has a breakthrough in understanding, when truth suddenly becomes clear, when righteousness actually becomes attractive rather than burdensome, that may well be the work of these Assistant Teachers, operating behind the scenes.

Their work centers on truth and righteousness. Not rules and regulations, but genuine understanding of what's true and what's right. That's the foundation they're trying to help us build, both here and on the Mansion Worlds.

5. The Transporters

Now we come to what I consider one of the most fascinating groups: the Transporters. "All groups of ministering spirits have their transport corps, angelic orders dedicated to the ministry of transporting those personalities who are unable, of themselves, to journey from one sphere to another. The fifth group of the superior seraphim are headquartered on Salvington and serve as space traversers to and from the headquarters of the local universe."

When you wake up on Mansion World One, you don't automatically sprout wings and fly to Mansion World Two. It doesn't work that way. You remain dependent on angelic transport throughout your entire morontia existence. These Transporter seraphim carry you from sphere to sphere, from world to world, even from Salvington to the superuniverse capital of Uversa.

The text explains: "The energy range of seraphim is wholly adequate for local universe and even for superuniverse requirements, but they could never withstand the energy demands entailed by such a long journey as that from Uversa to Havona. Such an exhaustive journey requires the special powers of a primary seconaphim of transport endowments. Transporters take on energy for flight while in transit and recuperate personal power at the end of the journey."

Think of it like a rechargeable battery, as someone in our study group suggested. These angels consume energy while transporting passengers across space. They can handle trips within the local universe and even to the superuniverse capital, but the enormous distance from Uversa to Havona requires a more powerful class of angel, primary seconaphim, which belong to the superuniverse order. Local universe angels simply don't have the energy capacity for that journey.

This brings up an intriguing question we discussed: What about UFO sightings? Could some of these mysterious lights people see be transport seraphim? It's an interesting thought. After all, student visitors from other worlds do come to our planet, and they would need transportation. The book doesn't mention spaceships for such visits; it talks about transport service.

But then Gary raised a practical objection: "Why would they zigzag around?" That's a good point. If transport seraphim are simply carrying passengers from one place to another, why would they zip over a mountain, stop in mid-air, then take off in another direction? That kind of behavior doesn't fit with orderly, purposeful transport. It seems more likely that the erratic movements people report in UFO sightings represent something else, perhaps actual physical craft from other inhabited worlds in our region of space.

There's another consideration. Transport seraphim primarily carry morontia beings, not material creatures. They can't transport "combustion bodies, flesh and blood such as you now have," as the text explicitly states. So, if beings are visiting our planet in physical form, they would need actual vehicles. The transport seraphim would be relevant only for morontia visitors, who would have to be reassembled on arrival.

Someone asked about the Tree of Life, how did it get here? That's a legitimate mystery. We know it came from either Edentia (the constellation capital) or Jerusem (the system capital). But it was physical, a living plant. Transport seraphim can't carry physical objects without them disintegrating. So, either it came as a seed (as Jane suggested—that's a good thought), or it was transported in some kind of physical vehicle that took the long route, perhaps requiring five hundred thousand years to arrive.

If our planet was being prepared a million years in advance for Prince Caligastia's arrival, and they knew the Adamic mission would follow later, they might have planned the Tree of Life's journey long before it was actually needed. They could have sent it in a mechanical transport, something like a drone, programmed with its destination, equipped with life support systems to keep the plant alive during the centuries-long journey. Our own military has vehicles like that now. It's not hard to imagine the celestial administrators having something far more sophisticated.

Anyway, I'm speculating. The point is that transport seraphim are essential to our morontia career, and we'll become very familiar with them as we journey from world to world.

The text adds one more crucial detail: "Even on Salvington, ascending mortals do not possess personal transit forms. Ascenders must depend on seraphic transport in advancing from world to world until after the last rest of sleep on the inner circle of Havona and the eternal awakening on Paradise. Subsequently you will not be dependent on angels for transport from universe to universe."

So the good news is that once you make it to Paradise, once you complete that final, long sleep and wake up on the Isle of Paradise itself, you gain the ability to transport yourself. You become a finaliter, and finaliters have personal transport capability. That's when we finally get our "wings," so to speak, probably not actual wings.

6. The Recorders

We've already touched on the Recorders when discussing the Supreme seraphim, but they appear again here as part of the Superior order. Their function remains the same: maintaining the official records of the local universe. Everything that matters gets recorded, and these angels are responsible for preserving that information.

7. Unattached Ministers

Similarly, we encountered the Unattached Ministers earlier. They serve as a flexible reserve, able to fill any position when needed. Their versatility makes them invaluable to the smooth functioning of the universe administration.

The Process of Being Enseraphimed

I want to spend some time on the actual experience of seraphic transport, because the text provides fascinating details. "The process of being enseraphimed is not unlike the experience of death or sleep except that there is an automatic time element in the transit slumber. You are consciously unconscious during seraphic rest. But the Thought Adjuster is wholly and fully conscious, in fact, exceptionally efficient since you are unable to oppose, resist, or otherwise hinder creative and transforming work."

When you're "enseraphimed", wrapped in the protective cocoon of a transport seraphim for a journey, you enter a state the text calls "consciously unconscious." You're aware that you went to sleep, and you're aware when you wake up, but you have no consciousness of the time that passed in between. It's similar to being under anesthesia for surgery. You close your eyes, and in what seems like the next instant, you're waking up somewhere else. It could have been hours, days, or even years, but to you it feels instantaneous.

What's remarkable is that while you're unconscious, your Thought Adjuster is fully awake and "exceptionally efficient." Why? Because your conscious mind isn't in the way. The Adjuster can do creative and transforming work without your usual resistance or opposition. I find that both humbling and encouraging. Even during transport, when we're completely checked out, spiritual progress continues.

The text elaborates: "When you are enseraphimed, you go to sleep for a specified time, and you will awake at the designated moment. The length of a journey when in transit sleep is immaterial. You are not directly aware of the passing of time. It is as if you went to sleep on a transport vehicle in one city and, after resting in peaceful slumber all night, awakened in another and distant metropolis. You journeyed while you slumbered."

The analogy is perfect. You board a train in one city, fall asleep, and wake up in another city hundreds of miles away. You made the journey, but you weren't conscious of it. The same thing happens with seraphic transport, except the distances are vastly greater, potentially light-years.

"And so you take flight through space, enseraphimed, while you rest, sleep. The transit sleep is induced by the liaison between the Thought Adjusters and the seraphic transporters."

Your Thought Adjuster and the transport seraphim work together to put you into this transit sleep. It's a coordinated effort between your indwelling divine fragment and the angelic being carrying you. You're completely safe, surrounded by friends, both your guardian angels and the transporter, as you zip through space toward your destination.

What Happens When We Die?

This discussion of transport leads naturally to a question many people have: What happens at death? The text addresses this directly: "The angels cannot transport combustion bodies, flesh and blood such as you now have, but they can transport all others, from the lowest morontia to the higher spirit forms. They do not function in the event of natural death. When you finish your earthly career, your body remains on this planet. Your Thought Adjuster proceeds to the bosom of the Father, and these angels are not directly concerned in your subsequent personality reassembly on the identification mansion world. There your new body is a morontia form, one that can enseraphim. You 'sow a mortal body in the grave; you reap a morontia form on the mansion worlds.'"

Let me break this down step by step, because it's important to understand the process clearly:

When you die:

1. Your physical body remains on this planet. It goes back to the dust, as the saying goes. The flesh and blood body cannot be transported, it's too dense, too material.
2. Your Thought Adjuster takes your personality, everything that makes you uniquely *you*, and proceeds to the "bosom of the Father." This means your personality pattern, your identity essence, goes to Paradise for safekeeping.
3. Your guardian angel takes your soul and the complete transcript of your life, every memory, every experience of survival value, and heads to Salvington or possibly directly to the Mansion Worlds.
4. Through reflectivity (a technique we'll discuss another time), you're judged by the Ancients of Days on the superuniverse capital. If you're deemed salvageable, if you've made the minimum spiritual progress required, then your resurrection is authorized.
5. Three days later (or three "periods," which might be Mansion World days totaling about eighteen of our days, or it might be literal days, the text leaves this open to interpretation), you awaken on Mansion World One in a completely new body. This body is morontia, part material, part spiritual, and it can be enseraphimed for transport.

During those three periods before your resurrection, a broadcast goes out across Mansion World One announcing that you'll be arriving at a specific location at a specific time. This allows your family members and friends who arrived before you to gather and be there when you wake up.

Who greets you?

Your guardian angels are the first beings you see. They know you best, they've been with you your entire life, guiding, protecting, recording. They're there to make you feel comfortable and welcome. But there's also an archangel present. Why? Because the archangel has a duplicate of your life transcript. The archangel's role is to guarantee that the transcript your guardian brought matches the personality pattern your Thought Adjuster brought back. Everything must align perfectly.

Your guardian angel guarantees the accuracy of the transcript. The archangel verifies it. Your Thought Adjuster ensures that the person who wakes up is truly *you*, the same personality, the same identity. Your soul, that repository of spiritually valuable experiences, is reunited with your personality and installed in the new morontia body.

Gary asked during our study: "When we wake up, we'll have two guardian angels, right?" That's correct. You'll have both of them there, your guardian pair.

He also asked about the Spirit of Truth and the Holy Spirit: "Are they there too?" They don't participate in the resurrection process directly, but you're automatically re-encircuited into them when you awaken. Think of it as being reconnected to a broadcast. You never really left the circuit; you just weren't conscious of it for those three days. When you wake up, you're back online, so to speak, with all the spiritual circuits functioning normally.

As someone in our group pointed out, we're remarkably multifaceted beings. Our identity involves so many components: the physical body (left behind), the personality (preserved by the Adjuster), the soul (carried by the guardians), the memories (in the transcript), and our connection to various spiritual circuits. The resurrection process skillfully reassembles all of this into a coherent, conscious being on a new level of reality.

You might even have hair again on the Mansion Worlds. Maybe a beard. Then again, you might be rather ugly by Mansion World standards, who knows? The important thing is that you'll be *you*, recognizably yourself, ready to continue the great adventure.

One of our participants made an interesting observation: "Our brain is like an antenna tuned to the energies of the spiritual world." That's actually a useful way to think about it. While we're in the flesh, our physical brain provides the interface for consciousness. But consciousness itself, mind, personality, soul, isn't physical. When the brain dies, consciousness doesn't end. It's translated to a different medium, a morontia form, and continues uninterrupted.

Conclusion: Preparing for What Lies Ahead

As we wrap up this portion of Paper 39, I hope you're beginning to see how carefully organized and thoughtfully administered the universe truly is. The angelic orders aren't random. Each group has specific functions, specific areas of responsibility. From the Intelligence Corps gathering information for Gabriel, to the Voice of Mercy ministering to struggling mortals, to the Spirit Coordinators preparing us for first-stage spirit existence, to the Transporters carrying us across space, every order plays an essential role in the grand plan of ascension.

These aren't distant, abstract beings we'll never encounter. We're going to meet them. We'll work with them. We'll benefit from their guidance and service throughout our morontia career and beyond. Understanding who they are and what they do prepares us mentally and spiritually for that future. When we wake up on Mansion World One and see our guardian angels waiting with welcoming expressions, we won't be completely disoriented. We'll have some idea of what's happening and what comes next.

I'll admit, some of this material is challenging. Seven levels of seraphim, each with seven subdivisions, creates a lot of complexity. But stick with it. The reward is a clearer picture of reality, a universe that makes sense, that's run with intelligence and compassion, that's designed to help evolutionary creatures like us survive death and progress toward perfection.

In our next session, we'll continue with the remaining groups of Superior Seraphim and begin examining the Supervising Seraphim, who operate at the planetary and system levels. We'll explore how these angels work more directly with humans still in the flesh, and how they'll assist us during our early days on the Mansion Worlds.

Thank you for joining me in this study. As Jane beautifully prayed at the close of our session: "We give thanks for this hour spent learning. We thank you for the inspiration given, which is passed on to us. We do our best to learn, and we know you're generous and merciful, and that we have plenty of time to fully integrate everything we're trying to understand. Most of all, we give thanks for Jesus of Nazareth, Michael of Nebadon. We thank you, we love him, and we're grateful for being created in such a perfect creation. Amen."

Chapter 10: The Seraphic Hosts - Ministers of the Local Universe

Introduction

As we continue our journey through Paper 39 of *The Urantia Book*, I find myself increasingly amazed at the intricate organization of celestial beings who work tirelessly on our behalf. Tonight, I want to share with you what may be one of the most practical revelations in the entire book, the nature and function of the seraphic hosts who serve throughout our local universe of Nebadon.

When most people think of angels, they picture beings with wings and halos, perhaps strumming harps on clouds. The reality, as revealed in this remarkable text, is far more sophisticated and purposeful. These celestial ministers form a vast administrative network that extends from the universe capital of Salvington down to our very planet. They record our decisions, transport morontia beings across space, defend our free will in legislative assemblies, and even organize us into social groups designed to help us grow spiritually.

What strikes me most powerfully about this section is how intimately these angels are involved in our daily lives, not in some vague, mystical sense, but in concrete, administrative ways. They literally speak for us in courts we'll never see during our mortal lives. They work to bring us together with others who can help us accomplish tasks important to the universe. They defend our right to make our own choices, even when those choices might inconvenience higher beings.

In this chapter, we'll examine three orders of seraphim: the Superior Seraphim stationed at Salvington, the Supervisor Seraphim assigned to the constellations, and the Administrative Seraphim who serve in the local systems. Each order has seven distinct divisions, and each division performs functions critical to the smooth operation of universe government. Understanding these orders gives us insight into just how organized, how thoughtful, and how personal the universe administration really is.

The Superior Seraphim: Ministers of Salvington - The Recorders

Let me start with what might seem like the most mundane function, record keeping. The sixth order of Superior Seraphim are the Recorders, and they're particularly concerned with the reception, filing, and redispatch of records from Salvington and its associated worlds. Now, you might wonder why I'm excited about celestial filing clerks but consider this: everything is recorded at every level of the universe. Every decision you make, every choice that has moral significance, every interaction that affects your spiritual growth, all of it is documented.

These Recorders also serve as special recorders for resident groups from the superuniverse and higher personalities. They act as clerks of the courts of Salvington and as secretaries to the rulers thereof. When the traveling courts move throughout the local universe making decisions about various matters, these Recorders are there, ensuring that everything is properly documented and available for future reference. It's a system that guarantees justice, continuity, and accountability across vast stretches of time and space.

I've often thought about the implications of this. Nothing is lost. No good deed goes unnoticed. No sincere decision is forgotten. For those of us who sometimes feel invisible or insignificant, this should be tremendously encouraging.

The Broadcasters

The Broadcasters represent a specialized subdivision of the seraphic reporters, and their work fascinates me. They're concerned with the dispatch of records and the dissemination of essential information throughout the universe. The book tells us their work is of such a high order that 144,000 messages can simultaneously traverse the same lines of energy. Think about that for a moment, not 144,000 messages total, but 144,000 messages on a single energy circuit. There are probably thousands of these circuits operating at any given time.

These Broadcasters adapt what the book calls "the higher ideographic techniques of the superaphic chief recorders," which suggests a form of communication far more sophisticated than anything we possess on this planet. They maintain reciprocal contact with intelligence coordinators at higher levels, creating a network that keeps information flowing smoothly throughout the local universe and beyond.

What impresses me here is the sheer volume of communication required to coordinate a universe containing millions of inhabited worlds. The Broadcasters ensure that vital information reaches those who need it, when they need it. They're the nervous system of the local universe, if you will, transmitting signals that keep the whole body functioning in harmony.

The Intelligence Network

The seraphic Recorders of the superior order maintain what we might call a liaison, a close working relationship with the intelligence corps of their own order and with all subordinate recorders. Meanwhile, the Broadcasts enable them to maintain constant communication with the higher recorders of the superuniverse, and through this channel, with the recorders of Havona and even the custodians of knowledge on Paradise itself.

This creates an intelligence network that extends from our local universe all the way to the very center of all creation. If an issue arises in Salvington that requires clarification, these Recorders can reach out to the custodians of knowledge on Paradise and ask, essentially, "What's the standard procedure? How is this done in Paradise?" The answer comes back down through the network, ensuring that the rule of Paradise touches even our level of existence.

Many of these superior order Recorders are seraphim who ascended from similar duties in lower sections of the universe. They worked their way up, gaining experience and wisdom as they went. This suggests something important about the universe administration: it values experience. Those who serve in high positions often started at the bottom and learned every aspect of their work along the way.

The Reserves

Large reserves of all types of Superior Seraphim are held on Salvington, instantly available for dispatch to the farthest worlds of Nebadon. These reserves respond to requisitions from the directors of assignment or upon request from universe administrators. The reserves also furnish messenger aids when requisitioned by the chief of the Brilliant Evening Stars, who is entrusted with the custody and dispatch of all personal communications.

Here's something I find particularly interesting: while a local universe has adequate means of intercommunication through various circuits and technologies, there's always a residue of messages that require dispatch by personal messengers. Some communications are too sensitive, too personal, or too important to be broadcast over the circuits. For these messages, the Creator Son can give a sealed communication to one of these seraphim, and the Brilliant Evening Star will dispatch that seraphim personally to deliver the message to its intended recipient.

The basic reserves for the entire local universe are held on the seraphic worlds of Salvington, and these corps include all types and all groups of angels. It's a system that ensures flexibility and rapid response to any need that might arise across the vast expanse of Nebadon.

The Supervisor Seraphim: Ministers of the Constellations

As we move down one level in the universe organization, we encounter the Supervisor Seraphim. This order of universe angels is assigned to the exclusive service of the constellations. These capable ministers make their headquarters on the constellation capitals, but they function throughout all Nebadon in the interests of their assigned realms.

Supervising Assistants

The first order of Supervising Seraphim are assigned to the collective work of the constellation fathers, the Most Highs. These seraphim are the ever-efficient helpers of the Most Highs, and they're primarily concerned with the unification and stabilization of a whole constellation.

Now, let me give you some context. The Most Highs are Vorondadek Sons, and there are three of them in charge of each constellation. Under normal circumstances, these rulers rotate regularly, bringing fresh perspectives and preventing stagnation. However, something unusual happened in our constellation of Norlatiadek. The book tells us plainly: "The rotation of the Most Highs on Edentia was suspended at the time of the Lucifer Rebellion."

We now have the same rulers who were on duty when Lucifer rebelled, and the book infers that no change in these rulers will be made until Lucifer and his associates are finally disposed of by the Ancients of Days. Our constellation fathers remained loyal during that terrible crisis, and they've maintained their posts ever since, providing stability in the aftermath of rebellion. They probably still have the same Supervising Assistants who served them during that crisis, seraphim who proved their loyalty when it mattered most.

Law Forecasters

The second order of Supervisor Seraphim are the Law Forecasters, and their work touches on something I consider absolutely fundamental to universe government, the protection of free will.

The intellectual foundation of justice is law, and in the local universe, law originates in the legislative assemblies of the constellations. These deliberative bodies codify and formally promulgate the basic laws of Nebadon, laws designed to afford the greatest possible coordination of the whole constellation while maintaining a fixed policy of non-infringement upon the moral free will of personal creatures.

Here's where it gets really interesting for us as mortals. It's the duty of the Law Forecasters to place before the constellation lawmakers a forecast of how any proposed enactment would affect the lives of freewill creatures. They're well qualified to perform this service by virtue of long experience in the local systems and on the inhabited worlds like ours.

These seraphim seek no special favors for one group or another. Instead, they appear before the celestial lawmakers to speak for those who cannot be present to speak for themselves, and that includes us. Mortal men may actually contribute to the evolution of universe law, because these seraphim faithfully and fully portray not necessarily man's transient and conscious desires, but rather the true longings of the inner man, the evolving morontia soul of the material mortal on the worlds of space.

Let me make this personal. When you make a moral decision in your life, a decision that reflects your deepest values and your sincere desire to do what's right, that decision matters beyond your immediate circumstances. If the constellation is considering a law that might somehow affect the moral free will of creatures like you, these Law Forecasters will be there to represent your viewpoint. They'll explain to the constellation fathers why you think the way you do, what your true spiritual aspirations are, and how this proposed law might impact your growth.

You have a voice in universe government, even at this early stage of your existence. That's remarkable when you stop to think about it. It underscores something I've come to believe deeply: the universe respects and protects your right to choose. The Father wants you to freely choose to do His will, not to be compelled or coerced. These Law Forecasters exist, in part, to safeguard that fundamental principle.

Social Architects

The third order of Supervisor Seraphim are the Social Architects, and I need to spend some time here because their work directly impacts all of us, right now, in this life.

From individual planets up through the morontia training worlds, these seraphim labor to enhance all sincere social contacts and to further the social evolution of universe creatures. These are the angels who seek to divest the associations of intelligent beings of all artificiality while endeavoring to facilitate the interassociation of will creatures on a basis of real self-understanding and genuine mutual appreciation.

Now, listen to this next part carefully: "Social Architects do everything within their province and power to bring together suitable individuals that they may constitute efficient and agreeable working groups on earth, and sometimes such groups have found themselves reassociated on the mansion worlds for continued fruitful service."

Let me make this practical. You're part of a study group right now, listening to this teaching. Have you ever wondered how you found this group? How you happened to encounter *The Urantia Book* at just the right time in your life? How certain people seem to come into your life exactly when you need them?

The Social Architects are at work. They influence us individually to put us in groups where we can grow spiritually or accomplish some task important to the universe. Many of these groups, once formed, will continue their work when they reach the mansion worlds. What we start here, we may be privileged to finish there, with better brains and clearer understanding.

The book is honest about the limitations, though. It says, "But not always do these seraphim attain their ends; not always are they able to bring together those who would form the most ideal group to achieve a given purpose or to accomplish a certain task." Under these conditions, they must utilize the best of the material available.

Still, the implications are profound. These angels continue their ministry on the mansion worlds, where they're concerned with any undertaking having to do with progress on the morontia worlds that involves three or more persons. You see, two beings operate on the mating, complemental, or partnership basis. When you work with a partner constantly, like my wife Diane and I do, you get to know each other so well you can almost finish each other's sentences.

But when you add a third person, the dynamics change completely. That person's personality doesn't interact the same way as a partnership does. Their background is different, their perceptions are different, they're at a different spiritual level. When you have something like our study group tonight with six people, the dynamics become even more complex because each of us brings different experiences, different ways of understanding, different strengths and weaknesses to the group.

That's why the Social Architects get involved when there are three or more. The social interaction of a group is fundamentally different, and more challenging, than a simple partnership. These seraphim are organized in seventy divisions on Edentia, and these divisions minister on the seventy satellites that circle the constellation headquarters, what the book calls the "morontia progress worlds."

Ethical Sensitizers

The fourth order of Supervisor Seraphim are the Ethical Sensitizers, and their mission is to foster and promote the growth of creature appreciation of the morality of interpersonal relationships, "for such is the seed and secret of the continued and purposeful growth of society and government, human or superhuman."

These enhancers of ethical appreciation function anywhere and everywhere they may be of service. They serve as volunteer counselors to planetary rulers and as exchange teachers on the system training worlds. However, we won't come under their full guidance until we reach what the book calls "the Brotherhood schools on Edentia," where they will quicken our appreciation of fraternal truths through the actual experience of living with the Univitatia in the social laboratories of Edentia.

The Univitatia are permanent citizens of the constellation, beings native to that level, and we'll live with them to learn their social habits and interact with them. Our ethics coming from a mortal background will be different from theirs, and that's where these Ethical Sensitizers will help us. They'll buffer our reactions, help us modify our responses, and guide us in developing a more universal sense of ethical behavior.

There's a pattern here that's worth noting. Just as we have to learn to integrate with people from other cultures here on earth, people who have different values, different customs, different ways of seeing the world, we'll face similar challenges as we ascend through the universe. The Ethical Sensitizers help ease those transitions, helping us become truly cosmic citizens rather than provincial mortals who can only understand our own narrow perspective.

The Transporters

The fifth group of Supervisor Seraphim operate as personality transporters, carrying beings to and from the headquarters of the constellations. These transport seraphim, while in flight from one sphere to another, are fully conscious of their velocity, direction, and astronomic whereabouts. They're not traversing space as an inanimate projectile would. They may pass near one another during space flight without the least danger of collision.

These beings are fully able to vary their speed of progression and to alter their direction of flight, even to change destinations if their directors should instruct them at any space junction of the universe intelligence circuits.

These are the constellation-level transporters. They transport both morontia and spiritual beings, not material mortals like us. Our bodies couldn't survive the transit; they'd burn up in the atmosphere. But once we become morontia beings on the mansion worlds, we'll book transport on one of these seraphic carriers to travel from world to world throughout our constellation and beyond.

The book describes how these transit personalities are organized to simultaneously utilize all three of the universally distributed lines of energy, each having a clear space velocity of 186,280 miles per second, the speed of light. These transporters can superimpose velocity of energy upon velocity of power until they attain an average speed on their long journeys varying anywhere from 550,000 to almost 559,000 miles per second.

The velocity is affected by the mass and proximity of neighboring matter and by the strength and direction of the nearby main circuits of universe power. What's particularly interesting is that these Transporters ride the energy circuits, they hop on these power lines, if you will, and ride them all the way to their destinations. It's an elegant solution to the problem of space travel, using the existing infrastructure of universe energy to facilitate movement.

Constellation Recorders

The sixth order of Supervising Seraphim act as special recorders of constellation affairs. A large and efficient corps functions on Edentia, the headquarters of our constellation of Norlatiadek, to which our system and planet belong.

Notice the pattern here. At every level of universe administration, local universe, constellation, system, and planet, there are recorders. The work of accurate record-keeping appears to be absolutely fundamental to the functioning of universe government. Without these detailed records, justice would be impossible, coordination would break down, and the accumulated wisdom of billions of years of experience would be lost.

The Reserves

General reserves of the Supervisor Seraphim are held on the headquarters of the constellations. These angelic reservists are in no sense inactive. Many serve as messenger aids to the constellation rulers. Others are attached to the Salvington reserves of unassigned Vorondadek Sons. Still others may be attached to Vorondadek Sons on special assignment, such as the Vorondadek observer and sometimes Most High regent of Urantia.

We have a Vorondadek observer stationed on our planet at all times, and one of these reserves may be assigned to him permanently, assisting him in his observation and reporting duties. It's another example of how closely the universe administration monitors our world, especially given our troubled history with two defaults and a rebellion.

The Administrative Seraphim: Ministers of the Local Systems

Now we arrive at the fourth order of seraphim, the Administrative Seraphim, assigned to the administrative duties of the local systems. They're indigenous to the system capitals, but they're stationed in large numbers on the mansion worlds, the morontia spheres, and the inhabited worlds like ours.

Fourth-order seraphim are by nature endowed with unusual administrative ability. They're the capable assistants of the directors of the lower divisions of the universe government of a Creator Son, and they're mainly occupied with the affairs of the local systems and their component worlds.

Administrative Assistants

These able seraphim are the immediate assistants of a system sovereign, and before the Lucifer rebellion, that sovereign was Lucifer himself. They're invaluable in the execution of intricate details of executive work at the system headquarters. They also serve as personal agents of the system rulers, journeying back and forth in large numbers to the various transition worlds and to the inhabited planets, executing many commissions for the welfare of the system and in the physical and biological interests of its inhabited worlds.

Here's where the Lucifer rebellion becomes deeply relevant to understanding these angels. Lucifer was the system sovereign, and as he traveled from planet to planet, from sphere to sphere, propagating his concepts of rebellion along with his assistant Satan, many of these Administrative Seraphim got caught up in the rebellion themselves. They were loyal to their immediate superior, and when he rebelled, they followed him, at least initially.

The rebellion wasn't put down immediately. It continued for quite some time while celestial beings on various planets and spheres made their decisions about which side they would support. Only after all these decisions were made did the universe authorities send out a replacement for Lucifer, Lanaforge, a Lanonandek Son who brought his own staff with him.

Lucifer's assistants had been Lanonandek Sons as well, and many of them went into rebellion with him. When Lanaforge arrived to take over the sovereign administration of our system, he brought loyal Lanonandek Sons to serve as his assistants. Once that transition was complete, Lucifer was taken away in chains to one of the Father's prison worlds, and Lanaforge became our system sovereign. He has held that position ever since.

The Administrative Seraphim who remained loyal became attached to Lanaforge and his administration. A corps of one thousand of this versatile order now assists the acting ruler of our planet, working to help overcome the lingering effects of rebellion and default.

The same seraphic administrators are also attached to the governments of world rulers, the planetary princes. The majority of planets in a given universe are under the jurisdiction of a secondary Lanonandek Son serving as planetary prince. But on certain worlds, such as ours, there has been what the book diplomatically calls "a miscarriage of the divine plan."

When a planetary prince defaults, as our prince Caligastia did when he joined the Lucifer rebellion, these seraphim become attached to the Melchizedek receivers and their successors in planetary authority. Let me walk you through what happened on our world, because it illustrates how the Administrative Seraphim adapt to changing circumstances.

When Caligastia rebelled, twelve Melchizedek receivers immediately came to the planet and took over the government. The Administrative Seraphim who had been attached to Caligastia were reassigned, those who remained loyal, that is. Many had followed Caligastia into rebellion and had to be replaced. The loyal seraphim became attached to the twelve Melchizedek receivers.

This arrangement lasted until the arrival of Adam and Eve, our Material Son and Daughter. At that point, the Administrative Seraphim became attached to them. After a hundred years, Adam and Eve defaulted in their mission. What happened? The Melchizedek receivers came back, and the Administrative Seraphim were reattached to them.

This continued until about 1,900 years before Christ, when Machiventa Melchizedek incarnated on our world as an emergency Son. The Administrative Seraphim became attached to him during his mission. After he left, they went back to being attached to the twelve receivers.

Then came Jesus, Christ Michael, our Creator Son, incarnated as a mortal of the realm. During his incarnation, the Administrative Seraphim were attached to him as the recognized sovereign of our planet. There's actually a nuance here worth mentioning during the thirty years Jesus lived as an ordinary mortal before beginning his public ministry, Immanuel, another high Paradise Son, the Union of Days, served as substitute regent, and the Administrative Seraphim would have been attached to Immanuel during that period.

Upon the death and resurrection of Jesus, these angels became attached to the first of the twenty-four counselors who came down to manage the planet. The arrangement now is that one of these counselors serves as acting planetary governor, rotating every hundred years, and the Administrative Seraphim are attached to whomever holds that position at any given time.

This arrangement will continue until Machiventa Melchizedek makes his move to become the permanent vicegerent Planetary Prince, serving in place of Christ, who has now become our Planetary Sovereign but doesn't reside here permanently. When that happens, and no one knows exactly when it will, the Administrative Seraphim will be permanently attached to Machiventa's administration.

Why is it taking so long? Well, there's no hurry in the universe. A thousand years to these beings is like a weekend to us. The southern United States is known for its slow pace of life, but if you think the South is slow, wait until you experience universe time. Things move at the pace required for perfection, not at the pace of mortal impatience.

Justice Guides

The second order of Administrative Seraphim are the Justice Guides, and these angels present the summary of evidence concerning the eternal welfare of men and angels when such matters come up for adjudication in the tribunals of a system or a planet.

They prepare the statements for all preliminary hearings involving mortal survival, statements which are subsequently carried with the records of such cases to the higher tribunals of the universe and superuniverse. The defense of all cases of doubtful survival is prepared by these seraphim, who have a perfect understanding of all the details of every feature of every count in the indictments drawn by the administrators of universe justice.

These are the lawyers of the celestial realms. They come into play in two different situations. First, they represent angels or other celestial beings who have rebelled or are charged with some serious offense. If a celestial being is found guilty of rebellion, the Justice Guides are there to represent them in their defense. Unlike us mortals, who are unconscious during the adjudication of our survival, these celestial beings are fully conscious during their trials. They appear, probably through reflectivity, before the Ancients of Days on the superuniverse capital, and these Justice Guides present their defense.

The second situation involves us. When we die and our guardian seraphim goes through the process of justifying our life and advocating for our survival, we're not conscious of this proceeding. We're asleep, awaiting resurrection. Our guardian angel represents us, presenting the evidence of our life, our decisions, our growth, and our potential.

Usually, the guardian seraphim can handle this alone. But if there's some question, some complication in our case, the Justice Guides may assist in our defense. They'll work alongside our guardian seraphim to justify something in our life, to explain the context of our choices, to argue for our survival. We won't be aware that this is happening, but it may make the difference between survival and extinction.

The book makes a sobering point here. If an angel is found guilty and does not repent, they'll be erased from existence, just as we will be if we persistently and finally reject survival. Jesus brought up the Old Testament principle when he said, "The wages of sin is death." That remains true for angels and humans alike. Every being is given every opportunity for repentance, every chance to choose life over extinction, but the universe respects free will completely. If a being chooses extinction, whether consciously or through persistent rejection of all that is good and true, that choice is honored.

Reflections on Angelic Ministry

As I've studied these orders of seraphim, certain themes emerge that I think are worth reflecting on as we close this chapter.

First, there's the theme of protection. These angels are not primarily concerned with making our lives comfortable or successful by worldly standards. They're concerned with protecting our free will, defending our rights, and ensuring we have every opportunity for spiritual growth and survival. The Law Forecasters speak for us in legislative assemblies. The Justice Guides defend us in survival hearings. The Social Architects work to place us in groups where we can flourish. This is protection of the deepest, most meaningful kind.

Second, there's the theme of organization. The universe is not chaotic or haphazard. It's organized with stunning precision, with clear lines of authority, specific functions for each order of beings, and built-in redundancy through the reserve corps. This organization serves a purpose: it ensures that every world, every system, every constellation receives the ministry it needs to progress toward light and life.

Third, there's the theme of experience. Many of the higher-ranking seraphim ascended from lower orders, gaining experience as they progressed. The universe values hands-on experience. Those who rule or administer have often served in subordinate positions and understand the challenges from personal experience. This seems to be a universal principle: leadership comes through service, and wisdom comes through experience.

Fourth, there's the theme of adaptation. When Caligastia rebelled, the Administrative Seraphim adapted by attaching themselves to the Melchizedek receivers. When Adam and Eve defaulted, they adapted again. When Jesus completed his mission, they adapted once more. These angels are not rigid or inflexible. They respond to changing circumstances while maintaining their core mission of faithful service.

Finally, there's the theme of persistence. Our constellation fathers have remained in their positions since the Lucifer rebellion, perhaps for two hundred thousand years or more. The Administrative Seraphim continue their work despite two planetary defaults and a system rebellion. The Justice Guides continue to defend beings whose cases are "doubtful," never giving up on anyone who shows the slightest potential for survival. This kind of persistence, patient, faithful, unwavering, characterizes the entire celestial administration.

Conclusion

We've covered a great deal of ground in this chapter, examining the Superior Seraphim who serve at Salvington, the Supervisor Seraphim assigned to the constellations, and the Administrative Seraphim who minister in the local systems. Each order has seven divisions, each division has specific functions, and all work together in a coordinated system of universe administration.

What I hope you take away from this study is a sense of how intimately you're connected to this vast celestial organization. You're not alone, struggling through life with no help or recognition. You're surrounded by angels who record your decisions, defend your rights, organize your social relationships, and advocate for your survival. They work behind the scenes, invisible to mortal eyes but ever-present and ever-faithful.

In our next chapter, we'll continue with Paper 39, examining the remaining orders of seraphim who serve on the inhabited worlds themselves. These are the angels who work most directly with us during our mortal lives, the guardian seraphim and their associates. We'll explore how they're organized, how they function, and how they prepare us for the life to come on the mansion worlds.

The journey from mortality to Paradise is long, but you don't walk it alone. The seraphic hosts accompany you, guide you, protect you, and celebrate with you as you make each step forward in your eternal career. Understanding their ministry should give you confidence, comfort, and courage as you face the challenges of mortal existence, knowing that the universe is truly organized for your success, your growth, and your eternal survival.

In our next session, we'll explore the planetary seraphim, the angels who serve directly on inhabited worlds like ours, working with mortals in their daily struggles and preparing them for the great adventure of eternal life.

Chapter 11: Administrator Seraphim - Guardians of Justice and Cosmic Citizenship

Introduction: Understanding the Unseen Ministers of Justice

As we continue our exploration of Paper 39 in *The Urantia Book*, we come to a section that reveals something quite remarkable about the celestial order, how justice, mercy, and spiritual education are administered across the vast systems of inhabited worlds. In this chapter, we examine the Administrator Seraphim, a specialized order of angels who function primarily at the system and planetary levels, ensuring that every ascending mortal receives fair treatment, proper guidance, and the opportunity to grow into cosmic citizenship.

I've spent years studying these passages, and what strikes me most is how practical these celestial beings are. They're not distant, abstract concepts. These angels work directly with us, even now, in this life, preparing us for the next stages of our eternal journey. When we talk about Administrator Seraphim, we're talking about beings who understand both divine law and human frailty, who balance justice with mercy, and who see our potential even when we can't see it ourselves.

Let me share what I've learned about these remarkable ministers and why understanding their work matters for anyone serious about their spiritual growth.

The Justice Guides: Defenders in the Courts of Heaven

When we think about justice, most of us picture courtrooms, judges, and lawyers arguing cases. The universe has something similar, though infinitely more compassionate. The Justice Guides are seraphic angels specifically assigned to present evidence concerning the eternal welfare of mortals and angels when such matters come before the tribunals of a system or planet.

Here's what makes them different from any defense attorney you'll find on Earth: they have perfect understanding. These angels comprehend every detail of every feature of every count that might be brought against an ascending soul. They prepare statements for all preliminary hearings involving mortal survival, statements that eventually carry forward to the higher tribunals of the universe and superuniverse.

The Urantia Book makes clear that these Justice Guides aren't working to defeat justice or delay it. Their mission is to ensure that unerring justice is dealt out with generous mercy and fairness to all creatures. Think about that for a moment. Perfect justice combined with generous mercy. That's the standard they work to uphold.

I find it fascinating that many of these Justice Guides actually served in conciliating commissions before taking on their current roles. These commissions are like traveling courts, made up of three beings who move from system to system, planet to planet, universe to universe, resolving disputes and addressing cases of doubtful survival. The experience they gain in these commissions prepares them perfectly for their work as Justice Guides. They've seen it all, every type of case, every manner of misunderstanding, every kind of spiritual struggle.

The Justice Guides commonly appear before referee trios of the conciliating commissions on local worlds. These are the courts that handle minor misunderstandings and disputes. Later, many of these same angels appear as what the book calls "Voices of Mercy" in the higher spheres, including on Salvington, the headquarters of our local universe.

From the Urantia Book:

"In each superuniverse the Universal Conciliators find themselves strangely and innately segregated into groups of four, associations in which they continue to serve. In each group, three are spirit personalities, and one, like the fourth creatures of the servitals, is a semimaterial being. This quartet constitutes a conciliating commission and is made up as follows:

> (275.6) 25:2.6 1. *The Judge-Arbiter.* The one unanimously designated by the other three as the most competent and best qualified to act as judicial head of the group.
>
> (275.7) 25:2.7 2. *The Spirit-Advocate.* The one appointed by the judge-arbiter to present evidence and to safeguard the rights of all personalities involved in any matter assigned to the adjudication of the conciliating commission.
>
> (276.1) 25:2.8 3. *The Divine Executioner.* The conciliator qualified by inherent nature to make contact with the material beings of the realms and to execute the decisions of the commission. Divine executioners, being fourth creatures—quasi-material beings—are almost, but not quite, visible to the short-range vision of the mortal races.

(276.2) 25:2.9 4. *The Recorder.* The remaining member of the commission automatically becomes the recorder, the clerk of the tribunal. He makes certain that all records are properly prepared for the archives of the superuniverse and for the records of the local universe. If the commission is serving on an evolutionary world, a third report, with the assistance of the executioner, is prepared for the physical records of the system government of jurisdiction.

(276.3) 25:2.10 When in session a commission functions as a group of three since the advocate is detached during adjudication and participates in the formulation of the verdict only at the conclusion of the hearing. Hence these commissions are sometimes called referee trios."

The Lucifer Rebellion: A Test of Loyalty

One of the most telling aspects of the Justice Guides comes from their behavior during the Lucifer Rebellion. Very few of them were lost to that catastrophic uprising. In contrast, more than one quarter of the other administrator seraphim and lower orders of seraphic ministers were misled and deluded by what the book calls "the sophistries of unbridled personal liberty."

Why did the Justice Guides fare so much better? I believe it's because they work so closely with the mercy and justice systems of the universe. They see firsthand how divine mercy operates. They understand the consequences of rebellion, not as abstract theory, but as lived reality in the cases they defend. They know what happens when beings choose selfishness over service, personal liberty over cosmic responsibility.

The Lucifer Rebellion is difficult for us to fully grasp from our limited earthly perspective. We experience wars here on our planet, and they're terrible, no question about it. But wars on Earth, as devastating as they are, don't compare to the wars in heaven. When you die in an earthly war, you wake up on the mansion worlds and continue your eternal journey. When celestial beings rebel and are judged non-salvageable, there's no second chance. That's permanent extinction. It's about as serious as existence gets.

Lucifer's message was deceptively simple: unbridled personal liberty. You can do anything you want, anytime you want, to anybody you want. Anyone with genuine love and respect for other beings would immediately recognize the flaw in this philosophy. When you take away someone else's liberty through your selfish actions, you're actually diminishing your own freedom. You're harming not just that individual but every being in the universe, including yourself.

What baffles me most about the Lucifer Rebellion, and I'll be honest, I still struggle to understand it, is how anyone could reject Michael, our Creator Son. He's such a magnificent, compassionate being. Why would anyone not want to be part of his universe? The only explanation I can come up with is what I call the "me syndrome." It's when someone becomes so consumed with themselves that everyone else becomes irrelevant. Nothing matters except what they want, what serves their interests, what elevates their status.

This is selfishness in its purest, most destructive form. And it's the opposite of what Jesus taught when he walked this Earth.

The Foundation of Cosmic Morality: Love and Family

During one of my study sessions, someone asked an interesting question about self-love. They wanted to know if loving yourself is wrong. My answer was simple: it's not wrong to love yourself, but it is wrong to adore yourself. There's a significant difference.

When we talk about God the Father and the Creator Son, we're talking about adoration, a level of love that's millions upon millions of times larger than mere self-regard. We're talking about loving God the Father, all of creation, and every being he's brought into existence. That's why Jesus continually emphasized the Fatherhood of God and the Brotherhood of Man. You can't have one without the other. You cannot properly love or adore God the Father without loving every creature he has created.

Someone in that same study session brought up people who say, "I'll do whatever I want as long as it doesn't hurt anybody." Even that statement reveals a self-centered orientation. It's still all about what "*I*" want. True spiritual maturity means considering others first, recognizing that we're all part of one universal family.

And that brings us to something important: the highest institution on this planet is the family. Not governments, not corporations, not even religious organizations, the family. Why? Because the family unit is the closest thing we have to understanding our relationship with God and all other beings. When we understand family dynamics, how parents love children, how siblings support each other, how families grow and change together, we begin to grasp the cosmic concept of divine relationships.

I have a close relative who exemplifies that "me first" mentality. I suspect we all know someone like that. It's one of the hardest things to witness because you can see how their selfishness limits them, how it damages their relationships, how it prevents their spiritual growth. But recognizing that pattern in others helps us identify and root it out in ourselves.

Interpreters of Cosmic Citizenship: Learning Our Place in Creation

After completing the mansion world training, that first intense apprenticeship in the universe career, ascending mortals reach an important milestone. They're permitted to enjoy what *The Urantia Book* calls "the transient satisfaction of relative maturity" as citizens on the system capital.

Now, let me explain what that means. Each goal we achieve in our ascension is a genuine, factual achievement. But in the larger picture, these schools and milestones are simply steps on the long path to Paradise. We can't skip them, and we shouldn't want to. Each one matters. However relative our success may be at any given stage, no evolutionary creature is ever denied the full satisfaction, even if temporary, of reaching their goal.

Think of it this way: there's a pause in the Paradise ascension, a short breathing spell where the universe horizons stand still, our status stabilizes, and our personality gets to taste the sweetness of accomplishment. We need these pauses. Without them, the journey would be overwhelming.

Someone asked me once, "So when we're on our way to the mansion worlds, it's not constant grinding effort?" Exactly right. At each level, we have periods of rest and reflection where we can enjoy what we've achieved. The revelation doesn't specify exactly how long these pauses last, but I imagine they're substantial enough for us to truly appreciate where we are and prepare ourselves mentally and spiritually for what comes next.

The Interpreters of Cosmic Citizenship help us during these transition periods. They help us understand not only the goals we've reached but how we fit into the larger cosmic picture. They explain why we're where we are, how we got there, and what significance this particular stage holds in our eternal journey. That's a lot to process, which is why these pauses are so necessary.

The first major pause in a mortal's ascension career occurs on the capital of the local system. For those of us from Earth, that would be Jerusem, the headquarters of our system, Satania. During this pause, we attempt to express in creature life everything we've acquired during eight preceding life experiences, our life on Earth plus the seven mansion worlds.

I like to ask waitresses a question when we go out to eat. My wife knows this routine well. The waitress inevitably comes to the table and asks, "Do you have any questions?" And I always respond, "Yes. What's the meaning of life?" Not one has ever given me an answer. They usually just stare at me for a moment and then move on to the specials.

But someone in my study group did have an answer. They said the meaning of life is to take care of cats. I appreciate the humor but let me share what I've learned from *The Urantia Book*: the meaning of life is to do the will of God the Father. That's it. That's what it all comes down to. And that meaning extends through every life as we journey through the dimensional worlds, always doing God's will, always seeking to align ourselves with divine purpose.

The seraphic Interpreters of Cosmic Citizenship serve as guides to new citizens of the system capitals. They quicken our appreciation for the responsibilities that come with universe government. These angels work closely with the Material Sons in system administration, and they portray the responsibility and morality of cosmic citizenship not just to ascending mortals but also to material mortals still living on inhabited worlds.

We're learning cosmic morality, how to be good citizens of a universe built on love, service, and cooperation.

Quickeners of Morality: Understanding Liberty Through Loyalty

On the mansion worlds, we begin learning self-government for the benefit of all concerned. Our minds learn cooperation, learn how to plan alongside other, wiser beings. Then, at the system headquarters, the seraphic teachers, called Quickeners of Morality, take our education further. They quicken our appreciation of cosmic morality, particularly the intricate relationship between liberty and loyalty.

Isn't it interesting that these specific angels teach about the interactions of liberty and loyalty? Lucifer clearly missed this lesson. He championed unbridled liberty instead of understanding that true liberty only comes through loyalty. He skipped the class, so to speak, and look what happened.

So, what is loyalty? *The Urantia Book* gives us a beautiful definition: loyalty is the fruit of an intelligent appreciation of universe brotherhood. You can't just take from the universe and give nothing back. As we ascend the personality scale, we first learn to be loyal, then to love, then to be filial, that means having the devotion of a child to a parent, and only then can we be truly free. But that freedom doesn't fully arrive until we become finaliters, until we've attained perfection of loyalty.

Let me say that again because it's crucial: you cannot self-realize the finality of liberty until you've achieved perfection in loyalty. Only through loyalty do you learn to love others, to interact with them genuinely, to become part of their lives. Liberty isn't the same as freedom. Liberty is the ability to be loyal to your friends, your loved ones, God the Father, and all your brothers and sisters throughout the universe. It's a responsibility, not just a privilege.

That's what these Quickeners of Morality teach us, what loyalty truly means and how to apply it in our interactions with all beings, including God the Father. Someone asked me what "self-realizes finality of liberty" means. It's essentially self-understanding, a deep, permanent grasp of loyalty and liberty that never fades. Unlike our limited human minds where we forget things shortly after learning them, this understanding stays with us indefinitely. That's what "finality" signifies. Forever.

We won't be free in the fullest sense until we become finaliters. We won't have attained perfection of loyalty until we reach Paradise and take the finaliter oath. And here's something remarkable: we don't have any finaliters who ever rebel. Not one. Why? Because when you fuse with your Thought Adjuster, you're fusing with God himself. To rebel after that would be to rebel against yourself. And when you take the finaliter oath, you become totally, irrevocably dedicated to God. Nothing will ever come between you and the Father because you've become permanently part of him, and he's become permanently part of you.

The Fruitfulness of Patience

The Quickeners of Morality teach us something else that's equally important: the fruitfulness of patience. They explain that stagnation leads to certain death, but overly rapid growth is equally suicidal. There's a natural pace to spiritual development.

The Urantia Book offers a beautiful analogy. A drop of water falls from a higher level to a lower one, flowing onward and passing downward through a succession of short falls. Just like that, progress in the morontia and spirit worlds happens slowly, gradually, through distinct stages. We move one drop at a time, one small step at a time. It's a long journey to Paradise, but that's how it's designed to work.

Someone asked about the ego during one of my sessions. What they meant was self-importance, and I told them plainly: there's no room for self-importance on the Paradise journey. Self-importance becomes a thing of the past because it doesn't support growth. When you become self-important, you replace God's will and the wisdom of others with your own limited perspective. That's a dead end.

One of my students has been watching some Hindu teachings lately, and they often talk about the ego. Sometimes they say things like, "If I'm angry, it's not really me." There's some truth there, but sometimes it seems like they're denying the personality itself, which I think is a mistake. You have to identify something before you can improve it. You have to acknowledge your flaws before you can overcome them.

Think about alcoholism. It's a disease, and once it takes hold, you have to retrain your mind and change how you think about alcohol. You replace destructive patterns with constructive ones. The same principle applies to spiritual growth. You have to replace bad habits and negative tendencies with good ones, and that's how you grow.

To mortals still living on inhabited worlds, the Quickeners of Morality portray mortal life as an unbroken chain of many links. Our short time here on Earth, on this sphere of mortal infancy, is only a single link, the very first one in a long chain that will stretch across universes and through the eternal ages.

Here's the key: it's not so much what you learn in this first life. It's the experience of living it that matters most. Even the work of this world, paramount though it is, isn't nearly as important as the way you do this work. There's no material reward for righteous living, but there's profound satisfaction in the consciousness of achievement. And that transcends any conceivable material reward.

This reminds me of a quote from *The Urantia Book* that I often share: "Life is but a day's work—do it well." Every single day is your responsibility. Do your work as well as you possibly can. If you think about this cosmic chain we're building, each link matters. This life is the smallest link in the entire chain, the shortest of all the lives we'll experience. So, if you do well with this little link, you'll be prepared when you move on to the bigger ones.

Someone mentioned how the book talks about taking "a short breathing spell" and keeps emphasizing how short this life is. That's absolutely true. When you arrive on the first mansion world, the first thing that happens is they give you ten days to get your bearings. Now here's an interesting detail: they don't specify whether those are Earth days or mansion world days. Mansion world days are about eighteen times longer than ours. So, if it's mansion world days, that's quite a substantial period to adjust.

During those ten days, if you're not suited for the first mansion world, meaning you've already learned those lessons during your Earth life, they graduate you to the second mansion world. You get another ten days there. If you're beyond that level too, they move you to the third. This continues until you reach the mansion world where you're psychologically prepared to learn what you need to learn next.

Now, even if you graduate directly to, say, the third mansion world, you still have to go back and teach on the first and second worlds. So, you don't miss those experiences entirely, you just approach them from a different angle. Your residence is on the third mansion world, but you're still involved with the earlier worlds as an instructor.

The breathing spells between each stage give you time to understand your new body, your new surroundings, and how you fit into them. Nobody rushes you. You get to reunite with friends and family who've gone before you. Some of them might be on the first mansion world, others on the second, third, fourth, fifth, or sixth. Everyone progresses at their own pace, and these pauses allow us to celebrate our achievements together before moving forward.

Somebody mentioned that in an earlier paragraph, the book says no creature is ever denied the full satisfaction of goal attainment, and there's always a pause where you can truly appreciate what you've accomplished. You're not just shoved into the next room. You get to enjoy what you've done, and you get to revel in that success with your friends and relatives who are sharing the journey with you.

I also want to point out something from that passage about righteous living: "There is no material reward for righteous living." What you have in this world has nothing to do with whether you live a righteous life. If you're rich, you're simply fortunate in that regard. If you're poor, you're fortunate in a different way, because honestly, you'll learn better lessons being poor than being rich. If everything's handed to you, you won't struggle. If you struggle, you learn. So, in a spiritual sense, those who struggle may actually be one step ahead of those who've had it easy.

The Keys to the Kingdom: Sincerity, Decisions, and Humility

Let me share something I consider one of the most important passages in this entire section. I have it highlighted in my copy of the book, and I want you to really listen to this:

"The keys to the kingdom of heaven are sincerity, more sincerity, and more sincerity. All men have these keys. Men use them, advance in spirit status, by decisions, by more decisions, and by more decisions. The highest moral choice is the choice of the highest possible value, and always, in any sphere, in all of them, this is to choose to do the will of God. If man thus chooses, he is great though he be the humblest citizen of Jerusem or even the least of the mortals on Urantia."

I've taught two critical lessons in this chapter. The first is the purpose of life: to do the will of God the Father. The second is how to live that life: "Life is but a day's work—do it well."

If you're not actively doing the work every day, you can't make decisions. If you're not sincere about what you're doing, regardless of what it is, you're not progressing. And if you're not doing those two things, how can you possibly choose to do the will of God? It becomes impossible.

God has a purpose for each of us. No matter how you look at it, we all fit into a larger divine plan.

Dealing with Talent, Ego, and Humility

Someone asked a thoughtful question about people born with exceptional talents, skills, or even genius-level abilities. How do you deal with ego when following up on those talents requires some degree of self-confidence? It's a fair question.

Yes, pursuing excellence in your field requires confidence and dedication. But the higher you climb in skill and intelligence, the easier it becomes to develop what I call "big head syndrome." You get very good at what you do, and suddenly it's tempting to think it's all about you.

The key is setting self aside and recognizing why you've become skilled in the first place: because of your sincerity and because you're doing the will of God in your life. When you stop doing God's will and make it all about yourself, all about what you want, all about your success, that's when the big head takes over.

Here's the truth: all human beings, all creatures in the universe, have certain skills they can develop. Almost anybody can learn to do almost anything if they apply themselves properly and consistently. I'm a perfect example. I wasn't born with the ability to become a doctor. I wasn't born with the ability to teach *The Urantia Book*. None of this came easily. It took work.

If I had developed big head syndrome when I was younger, thinking it was all about me, that people should send me money and make me rich, that I should be on television, I would have missed the point entirely. Maybe I should stop talking now before I sound too preachy, but here's what matters: unless you humble yourself and recognize that your skills and talents are nothing without God, you've got it all wrong. None of it comes from us alone. We're able to do things because God has blessed us with certain abilities. If we apply those abilities, we can provide tremendous benefits to our brothers and sisters throughout the universe.

But you've got to be willing to do that.

If you have a skill and you're very good at your job, it's crucial not to be self-important. Leave yourself out of it. Your mental state should be: "I want to glorify God. I want to use this skill because he's given it to me, but I want to keep myself out of the equation."

Someone asked what you should think about mentally to avoid getting a big head. First, you can't get the idea that it's all about you. Just because you have a skill and perform it well doesn't make you especially unique. Many people have that same skill and do it just as well as you. There's always someone smarter than you, no matter how intelligent you become. Always. The key is to share that knowledge, to teach anyone and everyone around you.

If you're doing a job and you do it well, teach your coworkers how to do it as well as you do. That's real leadership. Not bossing people around or being selfish, but showing them, trusting them, and trusting God to glorify whatever you're teaching in his name, not yours.

I saw a program once about a manager on a boat who constantly bossed people around. She wouldn't even trust her crew to complete simple tasks like preparing juice for a client without hovering over them. That's not leadership, that's revealing your own inability to trust yourself, and you're projecting that mistrust onto others.

When you do that, people will never reach their full potential under your supervision.

Think about it like a mother bird with her chicks. If she held onto them and never pushed them out of the nest to make them fly, they'd always be dependent on her. You have to push your coworkers, your students, your children out of the nest so they can develop their own wings and fly on their own.

A lot of progressing spiritually comes down to helping others progress and teaching them to be better. That's what sincerity means, being honest with yourself about your goals and motivations. Are you sincere in everything you do, everything you share, everything you teach? Are you sincere in what you believe to the point where you can give it away freely?

If you can't give it away, it's not worth having.

Transport Seraphim: The Reality of Spiritual Travel

Each category of seraphim has its own transport specialists, and the Administrator Seraphim are no exception. These Transport Seraphim function within local systems, carrying passengers back and forth from the system headquarters and serving as interplanetary transporters.

In our system, Satania, seldom does a day pass when a transport seraphim doesn't deposit some student visitor or traveler of spirit or semi-spirit nature on the shores of our planet, Earth. These same space travelers will eventually carry you to and from the various worlds of the system headquarters group. When you finish your assignment on Jerusem, they'll carry you forward to Edentia, the headquarters of our constellation.

But here's something crucial, something that has enormous implications for how we understand spiritual reality: under no circumstances will they carry you backward to the world of human origin. A mortal never returns to his native planet during the dispensation of his temporal existence. And if he should return during a subsequent dispensation, perhaps thousands of years later, he would be escorted by a transport seraphim from the universe headquarters group, not the local system.

Let me be very clear about why this matters. This single restriction demolishes entire religions built on supposed visitations from deceased individuals.

The Problem with Visitations from the Dead

People have sworn up and down throughout history that they've seen God the Father. They've claimed Jesus appeared to them. They insist Elijah came back and spoke to them, or Melchizedek, or Abraham, or their deceased grandmother who stood at the foot of their bed in the middle of the night.

According to *The Urantia Book*, is that possible? No. It's not allowed. And the reason is profound: if it were allowed, it would destroy faith.

Jesus said we're saved by faith. If you eliminate the need for faith, if departed loved ones or ancient prophets can return and confirm everything for you, you remove one of the few opportunities you have in this life to exercise genuine spiritual faith. It steals your opportunity to believe without seeing, to trust without proof, to hope without guarantee.

Everyone wants to see their dead relatives. I understand that longing completely. But let me give you a historical example of why this restriction exists.

Harry Houdini, the famous magician, spent much of his life trying to contact his dead mother. He had a good friend, another magician named Thurston, and together with Dr. William Sadler, yes, the same Dr. Sadler involved with *The Urantia Book*, they went around investigating and disproving mediums who claimed to speak with the dead.

This was during the same period when *The Urantia Book* was being revealed. Even with all his expertise, even knowing every trick used by fraudulent mediums, Houdini never found a genuine, honest medium who could actually contact the dead. He tried for years. He desperately wanted to speak with his mother. He died without ever succeeding.

Dr. Sadler documented case after case of fraudulent mediums, false spiritualists, and delusional claims. In every instance, there was a natural explanation, trickery, self-deception, or mental illness.

So, when someone tells you they've started a religion based on a vision where Jesus appeared to them and told them all other religions are false, should you believe them? What about near-death experiences where people claim to have visited heaven or hell?

Here's what I think happens in many near-death cases: people sometimes see their Guardian Seraphim as they're dying, but they see them according to their preconceived ideas. If you believe seraphim have wings like birds, you'll see a seraphim with bird wings. If you understand that seraphim use friction shields during transport, you might perceive that instead. It's a representation filtered through your existing beliefs.

I've seen diagrams showing a transport seraphim with a sleeping mortal inside, friction shields open. That's one representation. There are others. The point is, what people see during near-death experiences is often their mind interpreting something real through the lens of their cultural and religious conditioning.

Medical research has shown that after death, it takes at least one hour for all brain function to cease completely. During those sixty minutes, while the Thought Adjuster is preparing to depart, a lot could be happening neurologically. People can imagine all sorts of things during that transition period.

I'm not dismissing near-death experiences entirely. Something real may be happening. But we have to be appropriately skeptical, especially when people build entire religious movements on the foundation of a single subjective experience.

The book tells us many people see their Guardian Seraphim before death. That's a real phenomenon. But the Guardian Seraphim isn't delivering messages from dead relatives or ancient prophets. They're doing their job, preparing to transport your soul to the mansion worlds.

The Case of Paul and the Damascus Road

This brings us to a difficult question: what about the Apostle Paul? He claimed to have seen Jesus on the road to Damascus. He went blind, had a dramatic conversion experience, and that encounter became the foundation of much of his theological teaching.

Did Paul actually see the resurrected Jesus after Jesus had already left the planet on his final departure? According to the book Jesus had just 19 appearances to mortals after his death, then he left the planet back to Salvington. No mention is made to elude to the fact of him making a exception to come back to speak with Paul or anyone else.

I'll be honest with you: I don't buy it. I'm sorry but based on what *The Urantia Book* teaches about these restrictions, I can't accept Paul's account at face value. You're free to believe something different, that's your choice. But if I have to choose between believing Paul's interpretation of events and what the revelation tells us about how the universe operates, I'm going with the revelation.

The Urantia Book itself says that Paul did more to advance Christianity than any other person except Peter. But it also acknowledges that Peter wasn't strong enough to stick completely to what Jesus taught him. So, what we have in the New Testament is largely the story of Jesus according to Paul. Not the life of Jesus, as told in *The Urantia Book*.

And Paul was wrong about several very important things:

Paul was wrong about women and how they should be treated in the community of believers. Paul was wrong about the sacrificial system. The very beginning of *The Urantia Book* makes this crystal clear: God requires no sacrifice for your sins. If you had to sacrifice something, an animal, another person, even Jesus himself, to gain God's mercy, then what would be the purpose of mercy? It would be meaningless. You can't have mercy if someone has to die to purchase that mercy.

But that's what Paul taught, and it's ingrained in traditional Christian theology. Why did Paul teach it? Because it was embedded in the Jewish religious system of his time. For centuries, people throughout the world, not just Jews, were sacrificing animals and even human beings for sin. Any logical person should question whether God really requires you to kill someone else because you did something wrong. Does that make any sense at all?

No. But that's what much of the New Testament teaches, and I can tell you this from years of study, both in college and on my own. Before *The Urantia Book* came into my life, I was convinced the sacrificial atonement doctrine was true. I was wrong. Let me say that again, I WAS WRONG, And I can admit that now.

Regarding Paul's Damascus road experience: historical evidence suggests there was an earthquake during his journey. He fell off his horse. Did he hit his head? Quite possibly. Could that explain the blindness and the vision? It's certainly more plausible than believing the resurrected Jesus violated the universe's own protocols to appear to someone who had been persecuting his followers.

Look, Paul may have had a profound spiritual experience. His conversion was real, his life changed completely. But whether it was literally Jesus appearing to him or something else entirely, I can't say with certainty. What I can say is that *The Urantia Book* is very clear about the restrictions on departed mortals returning to their native worlds during the dispensation of their temporal existence.

And there's a reason for that final detail in the passage we read: if a mortal ever does return to his planet during a subsequent dispensation, thousands of years later, he must be escorted by a transport seraphim from the universe headquarters group. There has to be an escort. Why? To keep that returning individual from revealing something to someone that would destroy their faith journey.

It all comes back to protecting faith. Faith is that precious commodity we exercise in this life, perhaps our most important spiritual muscle. Without it, we can't grow properly. Without it, we can't truly choose to trust God without absolute proof.

Conclusion: Preparing for the Journey Ahead

In this chapter, we've explored the vital work of Administrator Seraphim, those specialized angels who serve at the system and planetary levels, ensuring justice, teaching citizenship, quickening morality, and providing transport between worlds. We've seen how these celestial beings balance perfect justice with generous mercy, how they survived the Lucifer Rebellion through their deep understanding of universal law, and how they prepare us for each new stage of our eternal journey.

We've learned that the keys to spiritual progress are surprisingly simple: sincerity, decisions, and choosing to do God's will. We've discovered that patience, humility, and loyalty are not just virtues but necessities for advancement. And we've confronted some uncomfortable truths about visitations, near-death experiences, and how easily human beings can be misled by subjective experiences that contradict established cosmic protocols.

The restrictions on departed mortals returning to Earth aren't arbitrary rules meant to disappoint us. They're protections, safeguards for our spiritual development. They preserve our opportunity to exercise faith, that essential quality without which our entire journey would be compromised.

As we move forward in our study, we'll next examine the Planetary Helpers, another category of seraphim whose work directly touches our daily lives here on Earth. We'll explore how these angels minister to us right now, in our current mortal state, preparing us for that first great transition to the mansion worlds.

But for now, take time to reflect on what we've covered. Think about your own sincerity, your daily decisions, and whether you're truly seeking to do God's will in your life. Remember: life is but a day's work. Do it well. Every single day is your opportunity to build another small link in that eternal chain stretching all the way to Paradise.

The Administrator Seraphim are already working on your behalf, preparing the way for your arrival on the mansion worlds. The Justice Guides are ready to defend you when the time comes. The Interpreters of Cosmic Citizenship are waiting to help you understand your place in the universe. And the Transport Seraphim stand ready to carry you forward on the greatest adventure any mortal can experience.

Your journey is just beginning.

Chapter 12: The Seraphic Planetary Helpers and Transport Angels

Introduction: Understanding Our Celestial Companions

When I first began studying the seraphic orders described in The Urantia Book, I was struck by how detailed and practical the descriptions were. These weren't abstract theological concepts or mystical beings existing in some distant realm beyond comprehension. Instead, the revelators presented a working universe filled with purpose-driven celestial personalities who interact with humanity in specific, tangible ways. In this chapter, we're going to explore two particular classifications of seraphim: the Planetary Helpers and the Transport Angels. Both groups play crucial roles in the spiritual development of our world and the broader administrative structure of our local system.

Before we dive into the specifics, I want to set some context. We're continuing our study of Paper 139, which falls within a larger section detailing the ministering spirits of the local universe. By this point in the revelation, we've already encountered several orders of angels, each with distinct responsibilities and capabilities. What makes the Planetary Helpers particularly fascinating is their direct connection to our world's unique history, including the tragic default of Adam and Eve and the subsequent Lucifer Rebellion. These events, which might seem like ancient mythology to some, actually shaped the very nature of angelic ministry on our planet.

The Record Keepers: A Threefold System of Universal Archives

Let me start with something that might surprise you: everything that happens in our local system is recorded. Not just the major events, the rebellions, the arrivals of divine Sons, the epochal revelations, but apparently everything of significance. The seraphim responsible for maintaining these records are appropriately called the Recorders, and they operate out of the system capital, which in our case is Jerusem.

Now, here's where it gets interesting. The Temple of Records on Jerusem isn't constructed from a single type of material. Instead, it exists in three distinct states simultaneously. One-third of this structure is made from what the revelators describe as "luminous metals and crystals", material substances that we, as ascending mortals, will be able to perceive when we first arrive on the mansion worlds. This is probably similar to what the apostle John was trying to describe in the Book of Revelation when he spoke of streets of gold and crystalline structures. He simply didn't have the vocabulary to describe what he was seeing.

The second third of this temple consists of morontia material. If you're new to The Urantia Book, morontia refers to a state of existence between material and spiritual, a kind of bridge realm where ascending mortals gradually transition from physical to spiritual reality. As we progress through the mansion worlds, our perception expands, and we begin to recognize morontia structures and materials that were previously invisible to us. The Material Sons and Daughters, beings like Adam and Eve, can also access these morontia records because they exist on this intermediate level of reality.

The final third of the Temple of Records is purely spiritual. Only beings who have attained spiritual status, seraphim, higher angels, and other spirit personalities, can perceive and access this portion of the archives. What strikes me as remarkable about this arrangement is its elegant inclusivity. The same physical location accommodates beings at vastly different stages of development. When we first arrive on the mansion worlds as newly resurrected mortals, we'll see only the material portion of this temple. As we progress, our vision will expand to include the morontia sections. Eventually, if we advance far enough, glimpses of the spiritual architecture may become accessible to us as well.

I should mention that the revelators indicate there are times when the controlling mechanisms of the universe allow certain beings to experience an extended range of perception. During these special occasions, we might be able to see all three aspects of the Temple of Records simultaneously, which must be quite an extraordinary experience.

But what exactly is being recorded? The answer appears to be the history of everything significant that occurs within the local system. Take the Lucifer Rebellion, for instance. Every aspect of that catastrophic event has been meticulously documented. When visitors from other systems come to Satania, our local system, they can literally review what happened during the rebellion. I imagine they can watch something akin to videos or holographic recreations showing Lucifer's arguments, the choices made by various planetary princes, and the devastating consequences that followed.

Why would they want to do this? The answer reveals something profound about how the universe educates its citizens. Systems that have never experienced rebellion want to understand what went wrong here. They want to see how easily reasonable-sounding arguments can lead to spiritual disaster. They want their citizens to appreciate the wisdom of divine governance by witnessing what happens when that governance is rejected. In other words, our tragedy becomes a teaching tool for the rest of the universe. There's something both humbling and hopeful about that realization.

The Planetary Helpers: Angels of a Broken World

When we turn our attention to the Planetary Helpers, we're dealing with seraphim whose primary mission centers on assisting the Material Sons and Daughters. Under normal circumstances, on worlds where the Adamic mission proceeds according to plan, these angels would work alongside Adam and Eve to biologically uplift the evolutionary races, harmonize diverse cultures, and gradually advance civilization toward the stages of light and life.

Our world, however, doesn't operate under normal circumstances. The Adamic default changed everything. When Adam and Eve failed in their mission, the majority of the Planetary Helper seraphim were reassigned. The revelators tell us that much of their work devolved upon three other orders: the Administrator Seraphim, the Transition Ministers, and the Guardians of Destiny. That last group might sound familiar, they're our guardian angels, the seraphim who watch over individual human beings throughout our mortal lives.

Despite this massive disruption, some Planetary Helpers remained on our world and continue their specialized ministries even today. Let me walk you through each classification and what they do.

The Voices of the Garden

This designation carries a poignancy that's hard to miss. When Adam and Eve established their headquarters, the Garden of Eden, their personal seraphim became known as the Voices of the Garden. These angels served as advisors and helpers in the tremendous task of physically and intellectually uplifting the evolutionary races.

Here's a detail that often gets overlooked: one of these Voices of the Garden specifically warned Eve before she defaulted. The angel apparently told her quite clearly that she was about to violate the divine plan. Eve chose to proceed anyway. I suspect Adam received a similar warning when he made his fateful decision to join Eve in default rather than remain loyal to the original mission. These angels tried to prevent the disaster, but they couldn't override free will.

After the default, some of these seraphim remained and were reassigned to assist the twelve Melchizedek receivers who took over planetary administration. They're still here, working quietly in the background, doing what they can to salvage what remains of the Adamic mission.

The Spirits of Brotherhood

If there's one classification of angels that seems particularly challenged by conditions on our world, it's the Spirits of Brotherhood. Their mission is to foster racial harmony and social cooperation among the diverse peoples of an evolutionary world. Under ideal circumstances, this would be difficult enough. On a world scarred by rebellion and default, it's nearly impossible.

The revelators don't mince words about this. They note that "seldom do these races of different colors and varied natures take kindly to the plan of human brotherhood." That's putting it mildly. Primitive humanity only gradually comes to realize the wisdom of peaceful cooperation, and that realization typically requires ripened human experience and the faithful, persistent ministry of these seraphic spirits.

What I find remarkable, and the revelators express this as well, is that despite the Adamic default, these angels have managed to foster and bring about even as much brotherhood as we currently experience. Think about that for a moment. We complain, rightfully, about ongoing prejudice, tribalism, and ethnic conflict. We look at our world and see division everywhere. But the angels look at our world and see miraculous progress considering where we started and what obstacles we've faced.

That said, I can't help noticing that over the past few decades, something seems to have shifted. For much of the twentieth century, we appeared to be making steady progress toward greater tolerance, cooperation, and mutual understanding. But in recent years, perhaps the last ten or twenty years, things have started to fragment again. Old prejudices have resurfaced. New divisions have emerged. Political tribalism has intensified. The Spirits of Brotherhood must be working overtime right now, trying to hold things together.

The Souls of Peace

The early history of evolutionary worlds is, frankly, violent. War is the natural state of primitive humanity. Peace has to be learned, cultivated, and defended. That's where the Souls of Peace come in. Their ministry becomes especially important during the era when a planetary Adam and Eve are trying to establish a new paradigm of cooperative living.

On our world, these angels faced severe setbacks due to the Adamic default. But here's a beautiful detail: the chief of the Souls of Peace in Adam's day was named Vevona, and this angel remained on our world after the default. Vevona was attached to the staff of the resident Governor General, one of the twenty-four counselors who serve as planetary administrators.

You might wonder why I'm telling you this. Here's why: it was this same Vevona who, when Michael of Nebadon was born as Jesus of Nazareth, heralded to the world, "Glory to God in Havona and on Earth peace and good will among men."

Yes, that Vevona. The angel who announced Jesus's birth wasn't just any random celestial being. It was the chief of the Souls of Peace who had been faithfully serving our troubled world for thousands of years, working to establish the very peace that the birth of Christ would ultimately make possible. The traditional rendering says, "Glory to God in the highest," but the actual proclamation referenced Havona, the central universe, the eternal dwelling place of the Universal Father. It's a small detail, but it connects the birth of Jesus to the entire cosmic reality, not just to heaven as some vague location above the clouds.

The Spirits of Trust

Here's something to consider trust doesn't come naturally to primitive humanity. Think about the survival struggles of early human societies. Trusting strangers could get you killed. Trusting the tribe in the next valley could lead to ambush. Suspicion was a survival mechanism.

The Spirits of Trust work to overcome this inherent suspicion and help evolving humanity develop the capacity for trust. Their ministry centers on a profound truth: the gods are trustworthy. More specifically, the Universal Father is so trustworthy that he literally places a fragment of himself, the Thought Adjuster, within the mind of every normal human being. If God can trust us that much, perhaps we can learn to trust one another.

This entire group of seraphim was transferred to new assignments after the Adamic miscarriage, but they've continued their work on our world. The revelators note, and remember, this was written in 1934 or 1935, that they haven't been wholly unsuccessful, because a civilization was then evolving which embodied much of their ideals concerning confidence and trust.

That's worth pausing over. In the 1930s, despite the Great Depression and the approaching shadow of World War II, the angels saw progress. Our civilization was developing naturally, incorporating higher values of trust and cooperation. It wasn't until Hitler and the Second World War that things got seriously derailed again. There's even a rumor in Urantia Book study groups that the revelators specifically instructed the contact commission not to publish the book until after 1955, possibly because they didn't want Hitler or other totalitarian leaders to get their hands on it. The concepts in this revelation are powerful, potentially dangerous in the wrong hands, but they require a certain level of spiritual maturity to appreciate properly.

The Agents of Uncertainty

In the more advanced stages of planetary evolution, these seraphim help humanity appreciate something that might seem counterintuitive: uncertainty is actually valuable. They work to enhance our understanding that uncertainty is "the secret of contented continuity."

Think about it this way: if we knew exactly what was going to happen in our future, what would be the point of effort, creativity, or moral choice? The revelators put it bluntly: "when ignorance is essential to success, it would be a colossal blunder for the creature to know the future." These angels help philosophers and thinkers appreciate the sweetness of uncertainty, the romance and charm of an indefinite and unknown future.

This actually explains something important about The Urantia Book itself. People sometimes complain that the revelation doesn't tell us everything. It leaves questions unanswered. It provides frameworks but not exhaustive details. Why? Because if we knew everything, we wouldn't think for ourselves. We wouldn't experiment, dream, or create. We wouldn't develop the capacity for faith, the willingness to act on incomplete information while trusting in divine guidance.

The universe wants us to grow, and growth requires uncertainty. It requires challenges that we can't simply look up the answers to in some cosmic textbook. That's not cruelty or withholding on the part of our celestial teachers. It's wisdom.

The Transporters: Cosmic Travel Explained

Now we come to one of the most fascinating topics in the entire revelation: how do celestial beings actually move from one world to another? The answer involves the

Transport Seraphim, angels specifically designed to carry other beings across interplanetary and even interstellar distances.

Let me be clear about something right from the start: this method of transportation is not for mortals in their physical bodies. We don't get transported anywhere after we die. When we experience the sleep of death, our bodies decompose, and our personality, along with our soul, awaits resurrection. The transport seraphim carry celestial beings, those who already have morontia or spiritual forms.

Here's how it works. When a celestial being needs to travel from one world to another, let's say from the mansion worlds back to our planet, or from Jerusem to some other system capital, they come to the headquarters of the sphere they're departing from. After proper registration, they're "inducted into the transit sleep." That's the technical term. Essentially, they're put into a state of unconsciousness.

Meanwhile, the transport seraphim positions itself horizontally above what the revelators call "the universe energy pole of the planet." I understand this to be something like the center point of the planet's magnetic field, probably the north or south pole, or possibly a spiritual energy center that corresponds to the magnetic poles.

The seraphim has what appear to be two sets of wings extending from head to foot. But here's the thing: these aren't actually wings in the biological sense. They're energy insulators, friction shields. When the transport seraphim is ready to receive a passenger, these shields open at angles to the body of the angel. The sleeping personality is then carefully deposited by officiating seraphic assistants directly onto the top of the transport angel. Once the passenger is positioned, both the upper and lower pairs of shields are carefully closed and adjusted.

Do you see where our traditional concept of angels with wings comes from? Ancient peoples who witnessed Adam and Eve being transported to our world saw these friction shields and interpreted them as wings. The stories got passed down through generations, and eventually, every depiction of angels in human art included wings. It's a beautiful example of how limited mortal perception tries to make sense of celestial realities.

Now, here's what I want to emphasize: the being who is transported is completely unconscious during the entire journey. They don't see themselves leaving one world. They don't experience the transit through space. They don't see themselves arriving at their destination. They fall asleep on one world and wake up on another. The entire journey happens outside their conscious awareness.

Why is this important? Because when people have near-death experiences and claim they traveled through a tunnel of light or flew through space or visited other realms, they're not describing seraphic transport. That's not how it works. What they're experiencing is something else, probably reflective phenomena in their own mind, projections of their own expectations and beliefs about what death and the afterlife should be like.

The revelators actually address this directly. They explain that just prior to physical death, a reflective phenomenon sometimes occurs in the human mind. The dimming consciousness seems to visualize something of the form of the attending angel, and this immediately gets translated into terms of whatever concept of angels that individual holds. If you grew up believing angels have wings and halos, that's what you'll "see." If you believe in beings of light, you'll see beings of light. If your culture tells you that your ancestors come to escort you to the afterlife, you'll see your ancestors.

None of this is actual seraphic transport. It's the mind interpreting experiences through the filters of belief and expectation. I don't say this to diminish anyone's experience, these moments can be profoundly meaningful and spiritually significant. But we need to distinguish between subjective experience, and the actual mechanics of how the universe operates.

Contemporary Implications: Technology and Moral Development

Before I close this chapter, I want to address something that's been on my mind lately, and I suspect it's been on yours as well. We live in an era of staggering technological advancement. In the last seventy years, really, in the last thirty, we've experienced changes that would have been incomprehensible to previous generations. We went from rotary phones to smartphones, from libraries to the internet, from manual typewriters to artificial intelligence.

Here's my concern: our technological and scientific capabilities have vastly outpaced our moral and spiritual development. We've created tools, social media, surveillance systems, genetic engineering, artificial intelligence, that require wisdom and restraint to use properly. But we haven't developed the collective wisdom fast enough. We're like children playing with matches in a room full of gasoline.

The revelators understood this danger. They note that the replacement of the atonement idea with the concept of divine attunement represents a spiritual advancement. But look at what's happening in some parts of our world: there are places where animal sacrifice is still practiced, where ancient rituals persist despite thousands of years of spiritual progress. Just recently, I read about a city in Michigan where animal sacrifice has been legally permitted again. That's not progress. That's regression.

The same dynamic plays out in larger social patterns. We had been making real progress toward brotherhood, toward the ideals that the Spirits of Brotherhood have been fostering. For most of the twentieth century, despite terrible setbacks like the World Wars, the overall trajectory seemed positive. But in the last couple of decades, something has shifted. We're fragmenting again. Political tribalism has intensified. Misinformation spreads faster than truth. People can't seem to have civil conversations about important issues.

I don't think this is primarily a political problem, and I don't think one political party, or another is solely to blame. This is a spiritual problem. When societies advance technologically faster than they advance morally, chaos results. When we develop the capacity to instantly communicate with millions of people before we develop the wisdom to use that capacity responsibly, we get what we have now: a society that's technically sophisticated but spiritually immature.

What's the solution? The same solution that's always worked: the teachings of Jesus. The Fatherhood of God and the brotherhood of man. If we could genuinely embrace those two simple concepts, most of our problems would resolve themselves. Not instantly, not easily, but eventually and inevitably.

The angels are still here, still working. The Spirits of Brotherhood haven't given up on us. The Souls of Peace continue their ministry. The Spirits of Trust keep trying to help us develop confidence in divine guidance and in one another. But they can't force us. They can inspire, encourage, and create opportunities, but they can't override our free will. The choice to slow down, to prioritize what matters, to teach our children the things that are truly important, that choice remains ours.

Conclusion: Continuing the Journey

As we close this chapter, I hope you have a clearer picture of the seraphic orders that serve our world and how they fit into the larger administrative structure of our local universe. The Recorders maintain the threefold archives that preserve our history for all eternity. The Planetary Helpers, despite overwhelming setbacks from rebellion and default, continue their specialized ministries. The Transport Seraphim move celestial beings across vast distances using methods that ancient peoples could only interpret as miraculous flight.

These aren't abstract theological concepts. They're descriptions of how our universe actually functions. Real beings with real responsibilities are working right now to help our world recover from its tragic history and move forward toward its divine destiny.

In our next chapter, we'll continue our exploration of the seraphic orders, examining additional classifications and their specific functions in the ascending mortal career. We'll discover how these angels prepare us for mansion world life and how their ministry continues even as we progress through the morontia realms toward eventual spirit status.

For now, I'll simply encourage you to sit with these concepts. The next time you feel discouraged about the state of the world, remember that armies of angels are working behind the scenes, fostering brotherhood, peace, trust, and spiritual growth. We're not alone in this. We never have been.

Editor's Note:

Dr. Roger Paul continues his systematic study of The Urantia Book's revelation concerning the ministering spirits of the local universe. His approach combines scholarly analysis with practical spiritual application, making these profound concepts accessible to students at all levels of familiarity with the text.

Chapter 13: The Seraphic Ministry - Transport, Destiny, and the Eternal Partnership

Introduction: The Unseen Companions of Our Journey

When I first began studying Paper 39 of *The Urantia Book*, I'll admit I found myself overwhelmed by the intricate details of angelic organization and function. The text presents layer upon layer of celestial hierarchy, each order with its specific duties and destinations. Yet as I worked through this material with study groups over the years, something remarkable happened. What initially seemed like an exhaustive catalog of celestial bureaucracy transformed into something deeply personal and profoundly hopeful: a revelation of the invisible companions who walk beside us, now and forever.

This chapter continues our exploration of the seraphic hosts, focusing specifically on the extraordinary mechanisms by which angels traverse the cosmos and the even more extraordinary destiny they share with us. We're moving beyond organizational charts here. What we're really examining is a partnership, one that begins the moment we make our first genuine decision to follow the will of God and continues throughout eternity.

I want you to understand something right from the start: if you're reading this book, if you've made a sincere commitment to seek God's will in your life, you already have guardian angels assigned to you. Not one, but at least two seraphim, along with their cherubim and sanobim assistants. That means as I write these words and as you read them, we're not alone. There are celestial personalities present, invested in our growth, patient with our failures, and committed to our ultimate success. That reality changes everything.

The Mechanics of Seraphic Transport: Navigating the Universe Circuits

Before we can appreciate the destiny that angels share with mortals, we need to understand something that initially seems far removed from our earthly experience: how seraphim actually move through the cosmos. This isn't mere technical detail. The transport mechanisms reveal fundamental truths about the structure of reality itself and our place within it.

The Universe Circuits: Rivers of Divine Energy

When *The Urantia Book* speaks of "universe circuits," it's describing something that has no direct parallel in our everyday experience, though we might think of them loosely as cosmic highways or energy streams that connect all inhabited worlds to Paradise. These circuits aren't physical structures in any sense we'd recognize. They're better understood as channels of spiritual energy, living conduits that radiate from the presence of the Universal Father, the Eternal Son, and the Infinite Spirit.

Everything in the organized cosmos depends on these circuits. Angels don't eat or drink as we do; instead, they draw sustenance directly from the spirit energy that flows through these divine pathways. The circuits maintain connection, enable communication, and provide the framework for all cosmic travel. There are gravity circuits that govern matter itself, mind circuits that connect all intelligent beings to the Infinite Spirit, and personality circuits that link each unique individual directly to the Universal Father.

Our world, Urantia, presents a unique situation. Because of the Lucifer rebellion and the subsequent default of Adam and Eve, we've been partially isolated from certain circuits, spiritually quarantined, in a sense. We're not completely cut off; the Spirit of Truth and the ministry of the Thought Adjusters ensure we're never truly alone. But we don't have the same ease of communication with the system capital that other inhabited worlds enjoy. This isolation makes the ministry of angels to our world all the more remarkable. They serve as bridges, maintaining connections that would otherwise be severed entirely.

Enseraphiming: The Process of Celestial Travel

Now here's where things get genuinely fascinating. Transport seraphim, a specialized order of angels, can move through space at extraordinary velocities. We're not talking about anything approaching the speed of light here; seraphic transport far exceeds those limitations. But mortal beings, even morontia beings on the mansion worlds, cannot survive such transit on their own. The friction and energy involved would simply disintegrate us.

The solution? A process called "Enseraphiming." I remember the first time I tried to explain this to a study group, and I could see the skepticism on their faces. It sounds like science fiction, doesn't it? Yet the description in Paper 39 is remarkably detailed and internally consistent. A point needs to be made here, the human body cannot be enseraphimed, it has to be de-materialized to be transported and rematerialized on the new world. This was the process for Adam and Eve to come to this planet. The rematerializing process was done by the surgeons of Avalon. This is not what happens when we die. You are given a new, morontia body when you are reawakened on the mansion worlds. You guardian seraphim only transports you soul and mind transcript to the mansion worlds your body returns to dust.

When a morontia or celestial being needs to be transported from one world to another, they're placed within the very form of a transport seraphim. The angel undergoes what the text calls "a strange metamorphosis," becoming almost transparent, taking on a torpedo-shaped outline that glows with what's described as an amber luminosity. The passenger, whether morontia, or another order of being, is completely enclosed within this transformed seraphic form, insulated from the tremendous forces involved in cosmic travel.

The process requires extensive preparation. First, there are the transformers and transmitters, specialized beings who manipulate energy. Then come the mechanical controllers, at least two of them for each transport, who verify that all systems are properly calibrated. But here's what really struck me: it takes one thousand living energy transmitters to enable a single seraphic departure. One thousand beings, standing ready, providing the energy boost necessary for the transport seraphim to swing into the universe circuits.

Think about that for a moment. One thousand intelligent beings, coordinating their efforts, focusing their energies, just to send one angel and perhaps a few passengers on their way. This isn't casual travel. Every departure involves tremendous resources and coordinated effort. It speaks to how seriously the celestial administration takes the movement of personalities through the cosmos.

The Midnight Departure: A Standardized Protocol

Planetary space reports are received at noon at what the book calls "the Meridian of the designated spiritual headquarters." Transport seraphim depart at midnight, not just any midnight, but midnight at the spiritual pole of the planet. For Urantia, we don't actually know where this spiritual headquarters is located. The text doesn't tell us, and frankly, I'm not sure it matters much to our immediate spiritual growth. What does matter is the orderliness of it all. There's a standard protocol, a regular schedule. The cosmos operates with precision.

I've sometimes wondered if ancient peoples, observing these departures with spiritualized vision, as Jacob apparently did when he saw angels ascending and descending, might have contributed to our various cultural mythologies about midnight as a mystical time. It's speculation, of course, but intriguing, nonetheless.

When everything is ready, the chief of transport makes a final inspection. The seraphim is verified to be "properly in circuited," the energies are confirmed as adjusted, the passenger is secure. Then comes what must be one of the most dramatic moments in all of cosmic travel: one of the energy transmitters simply touches the seraphic carriage, and in a flash of celestial luminosity, the transport seraphim shoots forward at speeds we can barely conceive, leaving a trail of light as it departs the planetary atmosphere. In less than ten minutes, the spectacular display fades from view, even from the enhanced vision of other seraphim.

The Orders of Angelic Ministry: Specialized Service

Paper 39 outlines numerous classifications of seraphim, each with distinct responsibilities. While I won't exhaustively detail every order here, that would be tedious for both of us, several categories deserve our attention because they directly impact our journey.

The Recorders: Custodians of Planetary Affairs

The seraphic recorders maintain what we might think of as the official records of each planet's relationship to its system and the larger universe government. These aren't the angels who track your individual life; that's the job of your guardian seraphim and their cherubim assistants. The recorders operate at a different scale entirely, documenting planetary affairs, governmental developments, and the world's progress toward light and life.

It's a reminder that while each of us is infinitely precious as individuals, we're also part of something vastly larger, a planetary evolution that spans hundreds of thousands of years and involves billions of souls.

The Reserves: Always Ready

Every order of seraphim maintains reserve corps, and for good reason. Angelic ministry requires flexibility. Emergencies arise. Missions expand. Sometimes a seraphim serving as a guardian of destiny is called to Seraphington or reassigned to other duties. When that happens, the reserves step in, ensuring continuity of service.

The reserve corps stationed on Jerusem, our system capital, serve multiple functions. They act as personal messengers, carrying communications throughout the local system. They minister to transition mortals, those of us who've graduated from our mortal existence and awakened on the mansion worlds. They assist the Material Sons and Daughters. In essence, they keep everything running smoothly behind the scenes.

One detail I find particularly touching: these reserves help keep our world in intimate touch with interplanetary affairs, even though we're technically outside the normal spiritual circuits due to our quarantined status. They're messengers, traveling to Urantia frequently despite our isolation. They don't abandon us just because our world has a troubled history.

Transition Ministers: Guides for Our Morontia Life

When we arrive on the mansion worlds, that first stage of our post-mortal existence, we encounter the transition ministers. These seraphim work specifically with ascending mortals as we begin our morontia careers. The text identifies seven distinct orders within this classification: seraphic evangelists, racial interpreters, mind planners, morontia counselors, technicians, recorder-teachers, and ministering reserves.

Now, here's something interesting. Unlike other sections of Paper 39, which provide detailed descriptions of each sub-order, the discussion of transition ministers remains relatively brief. The text explicitly states this is intentional, these angels minister to us during our morontia progression, and revealing too much about their work would be revealing too much about our future experiences. It's as if the revelators are saying, "Some discoveries you need to make for yourselves."

I appreciate that restraint, actually. If every detail of our future was mapped out for us, where would be the adventure? Where would be the genuine growth that comes from facing the unexpected?

Seraphim of the Future: Preparing for Light and Life

There's one more classification I want to mention: the seraphim of the future. These angels don't minister extensively to worlds like ours. Instead, they're held in reserve on more advanced spheres, preparing for the eventual dawning of the age of light and life on each evolutionary planet.

Light and life represents the goal of planetary evolution, a stage where an entire world has become settled in spiritual maturity, where rebellion and default are distant memories, where civilization has achieved genuine stability and progress. It may seem impossibly distant from where Urantia stands today, but it's coming. These seraphim are preparing now for that future age.

They also work with "modified orders of ascension", mortals whose developmental path differs from ours, perhaps from non-breathing worlds or other unique planetary conditions. The text doesn't detail their activities with us specifically, and again, I think that's appropriate. They're working on a timeline we can't yet fully appreciate.

Guardians of Destiny: The Personal Partnership

Now we come to the heart of everything, the guardians of destiny. This is where the vast celestial organization we've been discussing becomes intensely, intimately personal.

The Assignment of Guardian Angels

I need to be clear about something that often confuses people when they first encounter this material: not every human being automatically receives a personal pair of guardian seraphim from birth. Initially, seraphim minister to groups, families, communities, nations. But when an individual makes that crucial decision, that genuine commitment to seek and follow God's will, everything changes. At that moment, two seraphim are permanently assigned as guardians of destiny to that individual.

You also receive two cherubim, younger angelic beings who assist the seraphim, and one sanobim, who works in partnership with the cherubim. So, when you make that ultimate choice to align your will with the Father's will, you gain an entire celestial team invested in your success.

Let me make this personal. If you've read this far in this book, if you've been sincerely seeking to understand God's nature and your relationship to the divine, you almost certainly have guardian angels. Right now. Present with you. They're not physically visible, but they're no less real. They observe your struggles, celebrate your victories, and work tirelessly to create opportunities for your growth.

That realization should change how you view your daily life. You're never truly alone. You're never abandoned. Even in your darkest moments, when you feel most isolated, you have companions who see your potential, who believe in your ultimate success, and who will journey with you literally forever if you'll let them.

The Journey Through the Mansion Worlds

Your guardian seraphim accompany you through all seven mansion worlds, those progressive spheres of morontia life where we shed our material limitations and prepare for fuller spiritual service. They're with you as you reconstruct your identity after mortal death. They guide you through the challenges of each successive stage. They celebrate with you as you master new dimensions of reality.

There's a beautiful detail here that touches me every time I contemplate it. If for some reason your original guardians are called to other service, perhaps they're summoned to Seraphington, having qualified for advancement, you don't lose continuity. New guardians of destiny are assigned, and they must familiarize themselves completely with your entire history. They become, in effect, experts on you, your personality, your experiences, your unique path. You never lose the personalized attention and guidance.

Before you complete the mansion world experience, you receive permanent seraphic associates. This permanence matters. These aren't temporary guides who'll leave once you've learned certain lessons. They're partners for the eternal journey.

The Separation at Havona

Eventually, if we persevere, we graduate from the local universe entirely and begin the ascent through the superuniverse. We reach Uversa, the capital of our superuniverse, and from there, we're ready to enter Havona, those billion perfect worlds that encircle Paradise itself.

At this point, something remarkable happens. Your guardian seraphim, who've been with you since those early mansion world days (or perhaps even earlier, if they accompanied you from Urantia), bid you a temporary farewell. This isn't abandonment; it's graduation for them, too. They're summoned to Seraphington, the angelic destiny sphere, where they traverse seven circles of seraphic light, their own form of advanced training and spiritual achievement.

Meanwhile, you're assigned Paradise companions, beings of an entirely different order, who guide you through the billion worlds of Havona. This separation isn't permanent, though. It's more like parallel advancement, with both mortal and angel pursuing their own developmental paths.

Reunion and Eternal Service

The beauty of this system reveals itself in what comes after. Many, though not all, of these destiny guardians who accompanied you through material life and the mansion worlds rejoin their mortal associates on Paradise. They become, in the text's evocative phrase, "the everlasting associates of the mortal finaliters."

Think about that. The angels who helped you take your first spiritual steps, who guided you through death and resurrection, who celebrated each small victory with you, they complete their own journey and reconnect with you for eternal service together. You don't lose these relationships. They deepen and expand into dimensions we can barely imagine now.

Some angels follow different paths after Seraphington, entering various non-mortal finaliter corps or joining the Corps of Seraphic Completion. But those who return to serve with their mortal charges do so by choice, drawn by bonds forged over what amounts to thousands or even millions of years of shared experience.

The Seraphic Destiny: Service as Ultimate Achievement

I want to spend some time on what angels themselves seek, because it illuminates something crucial about the nature of spiritual reality. Angels don't pursue power or status or comfort. They pursue service. More accurately, they achieve their highest destiny through ever-expanding capacities for service.

Multiple Paths to Paradise

Angels can reach Paradise through various routes. Some achieve it by becoming celestial artisans, mastering creative expression to such a degree that they're welcomed as technical advisors in the central universe. Others become celestial recorders, so skilled at preserving and transmitting knowledge that Paradise itself has use for their abilities. Some join the corps of Paradise companions, an entirely different form of eternal ministry.

But the most important path, the one most desired by seraphim themselves, is serving as guardians of destiny. This work, guiding mortal ascenders from the lowest levels of material existence all the way to the portals of Havona, qualifies them more thoroughly than any other experience for ultimate Paradise attainment.

Why? Perhaps because it teaches them something they couldn't learn any other way. Angels are created "a little higher than" mortals, as the text puts it. They don't start at the absolute bottom of existence as we do. By accompanying us on our journey, they gain experiential understanding of what it means to ascend from true material origin. They compensate for their native advantages through shared experience with beings who start with less but potentially achieve just as much.

Seraphington: The Angelic Threshold

Seraphington is described as the angelic threshold to Paradise, the transition sphere where angels pass from time ministry to eternal service. Attaining Seraphington isn't automatic, even for experienced seraphim. It represents genuine achievement, the culmination of ages of faithful service.

Once an angel reaches Seraphington, however, something definitive happens. Sin becomes impossible. Not just unlikely or resisted, actually impossible. The text states plainly: "Sin will never find response in the heart of a seraphim of completion."

This tells us something profound about spiritual growth. There comes a point where certain choices become fixed, not through external compulsion, but through internal transformation so complete that alternatives simply cease to be attractive or even conceivable. The seraphim of completion have so fully aligned themselves with divine purposes that rebellion against God would be as unthinkable as willfully harming themselves.

The Corps of Seraphic Completion

Angels who graduate from Seraphington join the Corps of Seraphic Completion, and from there they serve in various exalted capacities. They become associates of the superuniverse seconaphim and assistants to the supernaphim of Paradise. They may return to their native universes to complement "the ministry of divine endowment by the ministry of experiential perfection."

That phrase caught my attention when I first encountered it. Divine endowment, that's what comes from Paradise, the inherent perfection that flows from the Trinity itself. Experiential perfection, that's what these returned seraphim bring, having traversed the long path from time to eternity, having witnessed and participated in the struggles of evolutionary ascension.

Both are needed. A universe built solely on divine endowment, with no experiential component, would lack something essential. Conversely, experience without connection to divine perfection would be meaningless groping in the dark. The completion seraphim, having united both in their own beings, become uniquely qualified to minister to worlds approaching light and life.

The Mystery of the Caligastia One Hundred

I need to address something that often puzzles students of *The Urantia Book*: why did sixty members of the Caligastia staff join the Lucifer rebellion? These were experienced beings, mortals who'd completed the seven mansion worlds and ascended to Jerusem. They weren't naive. They'd been extensively trained for their mission to Urantia. Yet when Caligastia, our Planetary Prince, chose rebellion, sixty of his staff of one hundred followed him.

The key detail is this: when the Caligastia one hundred volunteered for service on Urantia, they left their Thought Adjusters behind on Jerusem. This wasn't punishment; it was protocol for the type of mission they undertook. They would be taking on modified material forms to interact with early humans, and their Thought Adjusters couldn't accompany them in that state.

Without the indwelling presence of God, without that constant inner voice of divine guidance, these experienced beings became vulnerable in ways they hadn't been before. They had training, yes. They had knowledge and experience. But they no longer had the Father's fragment dwelling within them, constantly orienting them toward truth and righteousness.

When temptation came, when Caligastia presented his arguments for rebellion, sixty of them fell. Forty remained loyal. Those forty, after eons of faithful service during the default period and the subsequent dark ages of Urantia's history, were eventually returned to Jerusem, where they reunited with their Thought Adjusters. The sixty who rebelled eventually died, having lived out extended lifespans, and they're now presumably waiting resurrection and adjudication.

There's a sobering lesson here. Spiritual maturity, even advanced spiritual maturity, doesn't make us invulnerable to error if we sever our connection to the divine source. The Thought Adjuster, that indwelling fragment of the Father, isn't just a nice addition to our spiritual equipment. It's foundational, essential, the very core of our protection against ultimate spiritual disaster.

Fusion: The Ultimate Security

This is why fusion with the Thought Adjuster is so crucial. Once you've fused, once your identity has merged eternally with the Father fragment within you, rebellion becomes impossible. You can't rebel against yourself. When you are part of God, literally unified with a fragment of divinity, you cannot choose to oppose God. The circuits of the Father flow through you. You've become, in a very real sense, an extension of the Father's will in the cosmos.

There's never been a recorded case of a fused mortal joining rebellion. Not one. Ever. Fusion settles the question of loyalty permanently and irrevocably.

Most mortals fuse with their Thought Adjusters sometime between the fifth and sixth mansion worlds, though it can happen as early as the third mansion world or even during mortal life in rare cases. A few don't fuse with their Adjusters at all; instead, they achieve fusion with a fragment of the Son or the Spirit. But one way or another, fusion represents the decisive moment when our evolutionary journey reaches a point of no return. After fusion, the universe can trust us completely, because we've become trustworthy at the deepest possible level.

Adam and Eve: Default, Redemption, and the Twenty-Four Counselors

Speaking of failure and redemption, I can't discuss celestial service without addressing the case of Adam and Eve, our Material Son and Daughter who defaulted in their mission to Urantia.

Adam and Eve were volunteers. They weren't sentenced to come to this troubled world; they applied for the assignment. They underwent extensive preparation, perhaps 150,000 years of training, to equip them for the challenges they'd face. They knew about the Lucifer rebellion. They knew about Caligastia's default. They were explicitly warned against the very temptations they eventually succumbed to.

Yet they failed. Eve first, persuaded by deception to violate the explicit instructions they'd received about breeding with the native races before sufficient time had passed. Adam followed, choosing loyalty to Eve over loyalty to the plan. Both knew better. Both did it anyway.

The consequences were catastrophic for the world. The racial uplift program, designed to improve the genetic stock of humanity over thousands of years through gradual blending, was disrupted. The Adamic line became diluted prematurely and chaotically. The violet race, their children, spread across the world in ways never intended, creating confusion and conflict that persists to this day in our racial consciousness.

The mystery is this: Adam and Eve now serve among the Twenty-Four Counselors on Jerusem, an exalted position of leadership and guidance for our entire planetary system. How does failure lead to such responsibility?

I've wrestled with this question. It bothers me, honestly. I look at the suffering on this world, the racial conflicts, the genetic limitations, the cultural confusion, and I think about how much of it traces back to that default. Yet Jesus, our Creator Son himself, chose to rehabilitate them and eventually elevate them to the council.

Perhaps, and this is speculation, not revelation, perhaps their very failure made them wiser in ways success never could have. They know experientially what it means to yield to temptation despite knowing better. They understand the long-term consequences of short-term choices. They've lived with regret, made restitution, and found redemption. Maybe that makes them better counselors than beings who've never fallen.

They certainly lost many of their children, watching their descendants struggle with the consequences of their parents' choices. That kind of pain changes you. Perhaps it humbled them in ways that qualified them for greater service.

I don't claim to fully understand it. But I'm not Jesus, and he chose to forgive and restore them. I have to trust that he sees something we don't, some potential for future service that outweighs past failure.

Ancient Records and the Nephilim

One more historical note before we conclude. The Caligastia one hundred who rebelled didn't simply disappear. They lived out long lifespans, we're talking centuries, approaching a thousand years in some cases, because their rematerialized forms had different biological properties than normal humans.

During those centuries, some of them mated with the sons and daughters of humanity. The offspring of these unions were the Nephilim, the giants mentioned in Genesis and other ancient texts. These beings became legendary, their stories passed down through oral tradition and eventually codified in the earliest written records we possess.

If you examine ancient Sumerian texts, Egyptian records, and other near-Eastern sources, you'll find accounts of beings who don't quite fit the normal human pattern, giants, powerful individuals, sometimes benevolent, sometimes tyrannical.

These stories probably reflect dim memories of the Nephilim and their descendants.

Note here: the Caligastia 60 that rebelled were NOT Angels, Angels do not have sexual organs, they could never mate with humans! The Caligastia 100 had modified human bodies create by the Surgeons of Avalon much like Adam and Eve's body. The statement that the Angels fell from heaven to mate with humans is a LIE! Angels have never mated with humans; they are not equipped to do so. The Rebellious sixty did have human forms and it is they who mated with humans to create the Nephilim or the Giants of old.

The Nephilim themselves eventually died out. Their genetic line became absorbed into the general human population, diluted over generations until it disappeared as a distinct phenomenon. But the legends remained, and they've shaped our mythologies and religious traditions in ways we're still discovering.

Conclusion: Partners in Eternity

Let me bring this together. What have we learned?

We've explored the mechanics of seraphic transport and discovered that the cosmos operates with precision and order, not cold, mechanical order, but order infused with purpose and care. We've seen that angels don't travel casually; every departure involves coordination, preparation, and the focused energy of hundreds or even thousands of beings.

We've examined the various orders of seraphic ministry and recognized that each has a role, each contributes to the vast project of shepherding mortal ascenders from material worlds to Paradise itself.

Most importantly, we've understood that when you commit to seeking God's will, you enter into a partnership with celestial beings who will never abandon you. Your guardians of destiny aren't distant observers; they're invested companions who share your journey and ultimately share your destination.

The separation at Havona isn't an ending, it's preparation for reunion at even higher levels of service. And that reunion, when it comes, brings together beings who've traveled parallel paths toward the same goal: eternal service in the name of the Paradise Trinity.

Angels achieve their destiny through service. We achieve ours through growth and eventual fusion with divinity. Both paths converge at Paradise, and both continue forever in expanding circles of ministry and adventure.

I find tremendous comfort in this. We're not alone, and we never will be. The universe is organized to nurture our growth, to support our struggles, and to celebrate our successes. Behind the veil of material reality, there exists a vast infrastructure of loving ministry, all designed to help every sincere seeker find their way home.

That's what Paper 39 ultimately teaches us: we matter, individually and eternally. The investment the celestial administration makes in each ascending mortal, the guardians assigned, the teachers provided, the opportunities created, demonstrates beyond any doubt that we're valued beyond our capacity to fully comprehend.

Take a moment to appreciate the invisible companions who share your journey. They're patient with your failings, delighted by your progress, and committed to your success. You're never alone. You're partnered with beings who've chosen to bind their destiny to yours. That's not sentiment, it's revealed truth. And it changes everything.

Chapter 14: The Solitary Messengers - First Children of the Infinite Spirit

Now we are going to shift gears back to the very first created beings by The Infinite Spirit from Paper 23 of *The Urantia Book.* These next chapters will teach us about all the other celestial beings created by The Infinite Spirit which are considered support beings though not named Angels they are part of the support beings of the Infinite Spirit. We will, of course, come back to all the rest of the Angelic orders we have yet to cover.

The Solitary Messengers represent something so fundamental to the universe's functioning, yet so mysteriously beyond our ordinary comprehension, that I found myself reading and rereading these passages with growing wonder. These beings, he very first personality creatures brought into existence by the Infinite Spirit, operate at levels of reality we can barely imagine, traveling at speeds that defy human understanding, sustained by cosmic circuits we cannot see, and serving purposes that span from Paradise itself to the remotest worlds of time and space.

What strikes me most powerfully about studying the Solitary Messengers is this: they were created perfect. Not progressively perfected like us, not evolved through experience, but instantaneously brought into being with complete knowledge, full capability, and unwavering loyalty. From the moment of their creation in that single, unrepeatable creative episode eons ago, they possessed everything they would ever need, all the information, all the wisdom, all the capacity required to serve from the beginning of time to the end of time. This presents a fascinating contrast to our own journey as ascending mortals, struggling forward one decision at a time, learning through trial and error, growing through the very anxieties and disappointments that mark our existence.

Understanding the First Creative Act

The opening paragraph of Paper 23 contains a statement so significant that I believe we need to pause and let it sink in completely. The text tells us that Solitary Messengers "are the personal and universal corps of the Conjoint Creator; they are the first and senior order of the Higher Personalities of the Infinite Spirit." This was the Infinite Spirit's initial creative action, bringing into existence solitary personality spirits. What's particularly noteworthy here is that neither the Universal Father nor the Eternal Son directly participated in this tremendous spiritualization.

Think about what this means. The Infinite Spirit, acting independently, created the first order of personal beings. This wasn't a collaborative project with the other members of the Paradise Trinity. This was the Third Source and Center stepping forward and saying, in effect, "I will now create." The result? Beings of such remarkable capability and trustworthiness that in all the annals of the master universe, there has never been recorded a single instance of a Solitary Messenger stumbling into darkness, disobeying orders, or defaulting on their assignments.

I've spent considerable time studying the organizational charts that map out the children of the Infinite Spirit, and I want to share something important about how to read these diagrams. When you look at these charts, you'll notice small, dotted lines running horizontally across the page. These lines aren't decorative, they're crucial for understanding which level of universe reality we're discussing. The top section, above the first dotted line, represents Paradise. Below that, the next section indicates Havona. As you move down the chart, subsequent dotted lines mark off the seven superuniverses, then the major sectors, then the minor sectors, and finally the local universes.

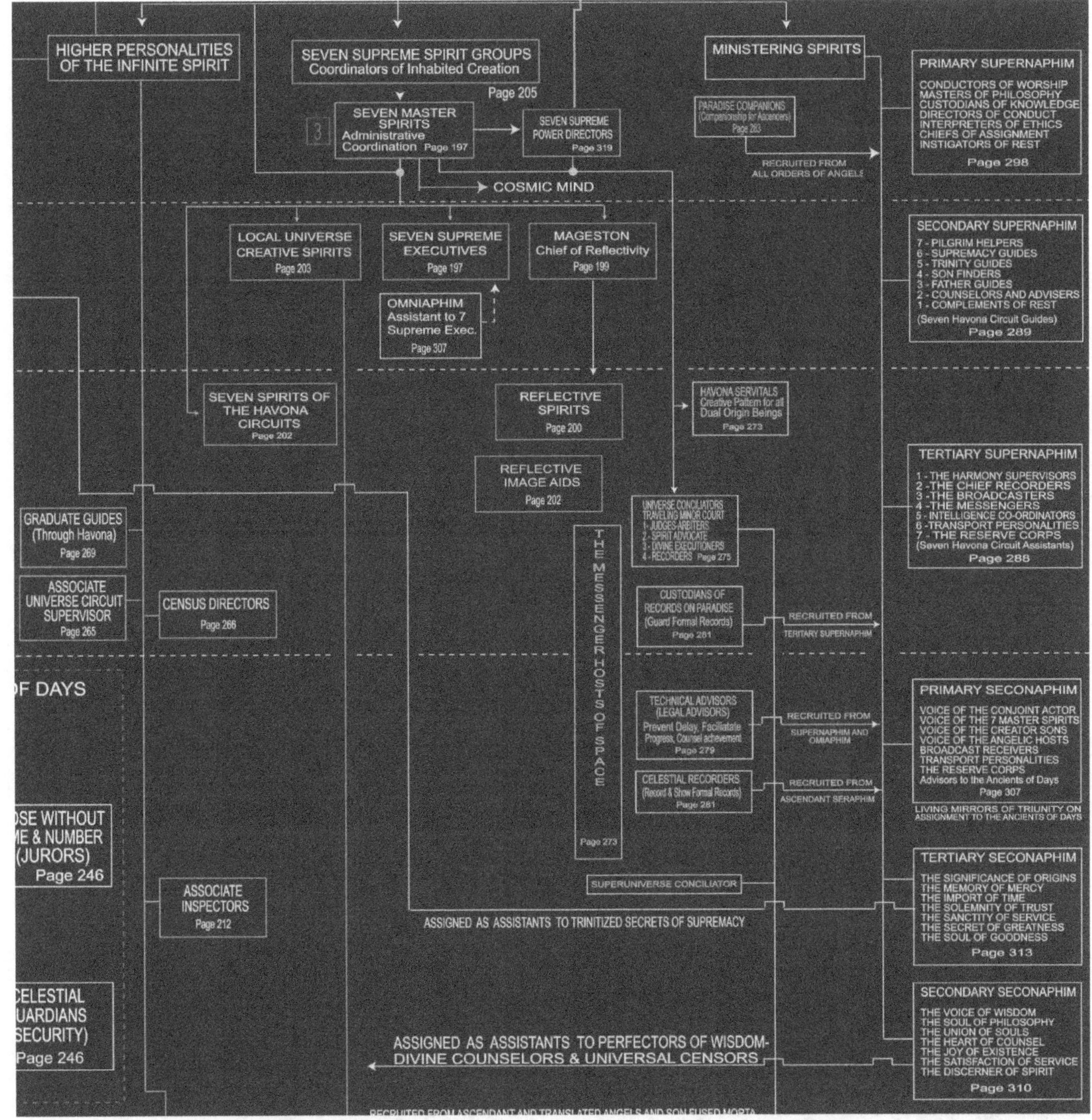

Figure 1: Higher Personalities of The Infinite Spirit

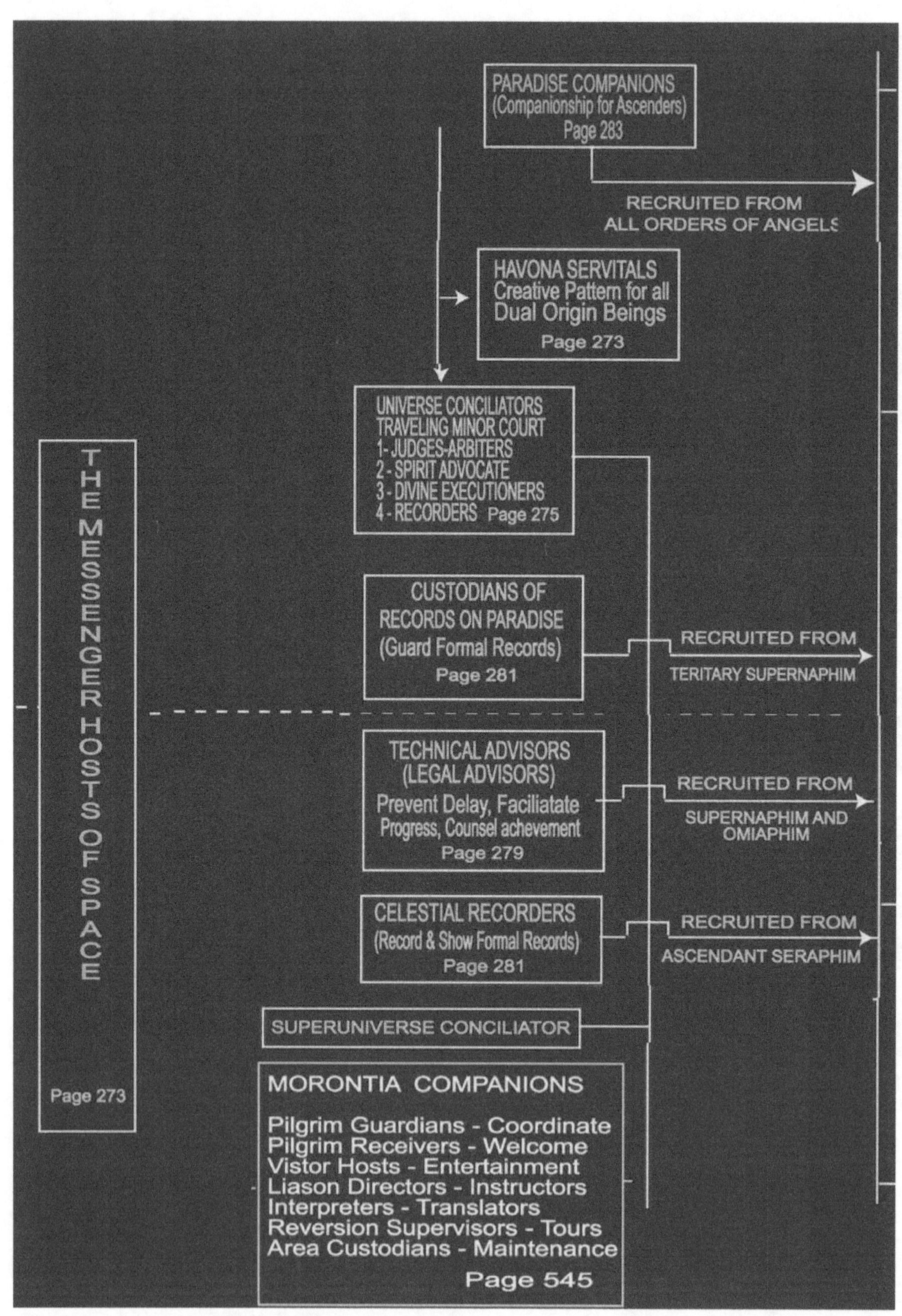

Figure 2: The Messenger Hosts of Space

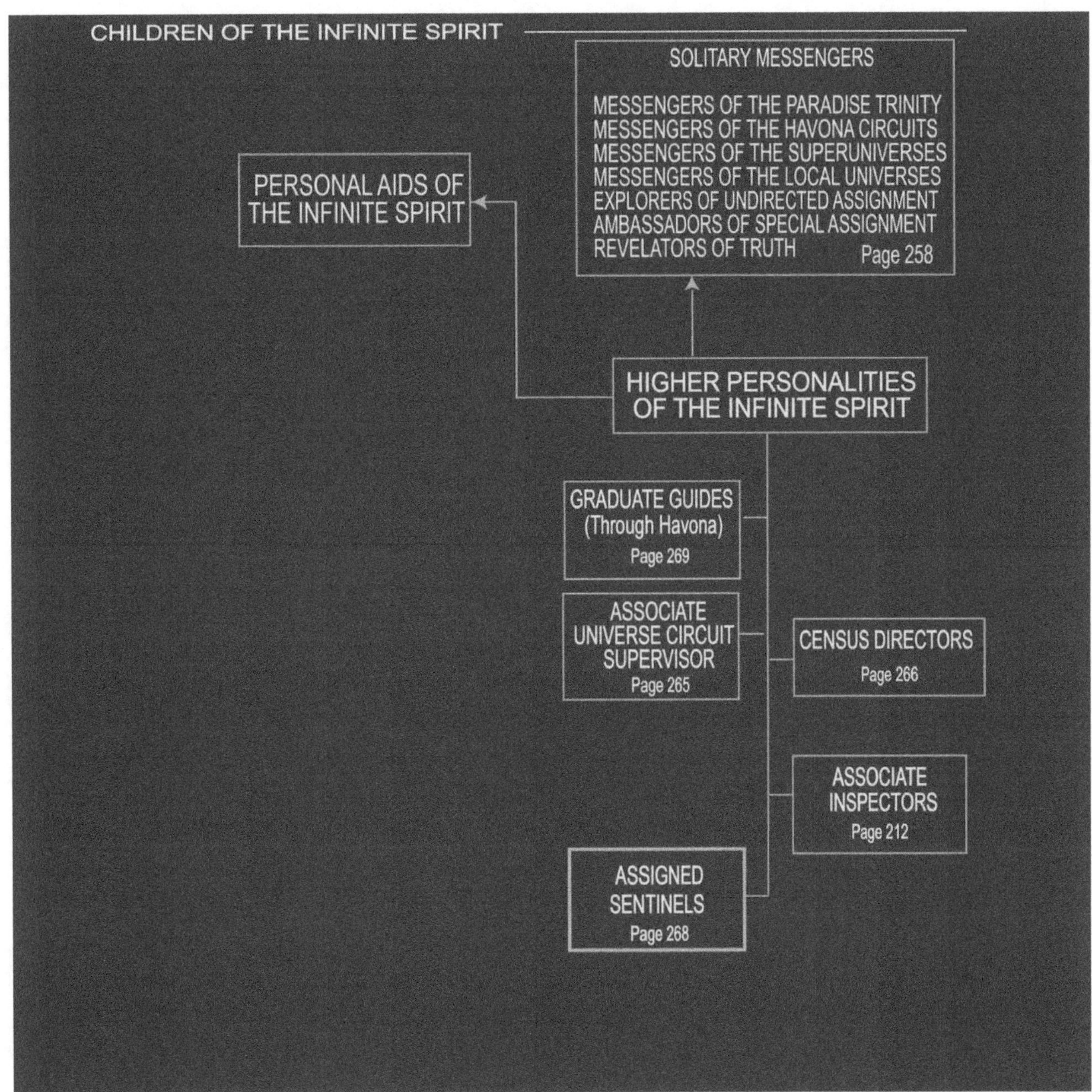

Figure 3: Children of The Infinite Spirit

Why does this matter? Because the Infinite Spirit has created different orders of ministering spirits for each level of reality. In Havona, we find the tertiary supernaphim serving ascending pilgrims. In the superuniverses, we encounter the primary, secondary, and tertiary seconaphim. As we descend to the local universe level, our level, we find the seraphic hosts, those angels we're most familiar with, along with cherubim, sanobim, and even the planetary midwayers who serve on individual worlds like our own.

This organizational structure reveals something profound about how the Infinite Spirit administers the universes. Each level has beings specifically designed and created for service at that level. The Solitary Messengers, however, transcend these boundaries. They operate everywhere, from Paradise to the outermost inhabited worlds, carrying messages, gathering information, and serving as the personal representatives of the Infinite Spirit himself.

The Mystery of Their Number

One of the questions that naturally arises is: exactly how many Solitary Messengers exist? The text gives us a tantalizing glimpse. A celestial author tells us that from the last report received, there were "almost 7,690 trillion solitary messengers then operating within the boundaries of Orvonton", that's our superuniverse. The author then adds something remarkable: "I conjecture that this is considerably less than one-seventh of their total number."

Let's pause and consider what this means. If Orvonton contains fewer than one-seventh of all Solitary Messengers, and if we do the simple mathematics, we're looking at a total population approaching or exceeding 50,000 trillion of these beings operating throughout the grand universe. That's a number so vast it becomes nearly meaningless to our finite minds. Yet each one of these beings is a distinct personality, known by name to the Infinite Spirit, created in that single creative episode at the dawn of time.

What I find particularly fascinating is that their number is stationary. The Infinite Spirit created exactly as many Solitary Messengers as were needed, and that was that. No more have been created since. They don't reproduce, they can't reproduce. There is no power of personality extension among them. The number that came into being in that first creative act is the number that exists today and will exist tomorrow. This speaks to something I've noticed throughout *The Urantia Book*: the universe operates with extraordinary precision. Nothing is random, nothing is wasted, and nothing is left to chance.

The Nature of Their Existence

Here's where things get truly interesting, and I'll confess this took me quite some time to wrap my mind around. Solitary Messengers don't have bodies, not physical bodies like ours, and not even spiritual bodies like those of other angels or celestial beings. They exist as what the revelation describes as a "presence." They're somewhere between pure spirit and something else entirely, something the authors struggle to help us understand because we lack the frame of reference.

During one of our study sessions, someone asked a perfectly reasonable question: "If we have some kind of spiritual experience where we sense God's presence, are we actually encountering a Solitary Messenger?" The answer is more nuanced than a simple yes or no. In our current mortal state, we cannot perceive Solitary Messengers at all. They operate at a level of reality beyond our sensory capabilities. Even during the revelation of *The Urantia Book* itself, when a Solitary Messenger was present and actively participating in the process, only certain celestial beings involved in the project even knew the Solitary Messenger was there. Most couldn't see or sense this being's presence.

This changes as we ascend. When we eventually reach Havona, and if we're faithful to our indwelling spirit, we will reach Havona, we'll develop the capacity to recognize the presence of Solitary Messengers. Not in the sense of seeing a physical or even spiritual form, but in recognizing their unique presence. Perhaps it manifests as a spiritual signature, an ethereal consciousness, or a vibration at frequencies we'll finally be attuned to perceive. The text doesn't give us complete clarity on this, which I find refreshingly honest. Not everything can be explained in terms we'd understand today.

Consciousness, Time, and Selfhood

One of the most thought-provoking statements in Paper 23 concerns the Solitary Messengers' consciousness of time. The text tells us they "are conscious of time, being the first of the creation of the Infinite Spirit to possess such a time consciousness. They are the first-born creatures of the Infinite Spirit to be personalized in time and spiritualized in space."

Someone in our study group raised an excellent question about this: Why wouldn't the Seven Spirits of the Havona Circuits, who were created before the Solitary Messengers, have this same time consciousness? The answer reveals something fundamental about the difference between Paradise-Havona and the evolutionary universes. In Havona, there is no time as we understand it. There's sequence, one thing happens, then another thing happens, but there's no time in the sense of past, present, and future flowing in one direction. The Seven Spirits of the Havona Circuits, being native to that eternal realm, have no consciousness of time because time doesn't exist where they were created.

The Solitary Messengers, on the other hand, were created with a specific purpose: to operate throughout the grand universe, including the time-space universes like ours. They needed consciousness of time from the very beginning. They're aware of their beginning, their selfhood, their existence as distinct beings who came into being at a specific point (even if that point was at the dawn of creation itself).

This awareness of selfhood is something I think we take for granted as humans. We look in a mirror at some point in early childhood, maybe at age four or five or six, and we suddenly realize, "That's me. I'm a person. I exist." Before that moment, consciousness exists but self-awareness doesn't quite. The Solitary Messengers had this self-awareness from the instant of their creation. They were born fully conscious, fully capable, fully aware. It's reminiscent of certain animals and insects that emerge from birth knowing exactly what to do, the bird that builds its nest using a design it never learned, the salmon that returns to its spawning ground without a map. But the Solitary Messengers possess this instinctive knowledge at a level of complexity and cosmic scope that makes our instincts look like the simplest reflexes.

Classifications Without Hierarchy

Here's something that initially puzzled me: the text states clearly that among the Solitary Messengers "there are no classes or subdivisions founded on personal variation. Their classifications are based wholly on the type of work to which they are from time to time assigned." In other words, while the revelation categorizes them into seven divisions of service, Messengers of the Paradise Trinity, Messengers of the Havona Circuits, Messengers of the Superuniverses, Messengers of the Local Universes, Explorers of Undirected Assignment, Ambassadors and Emissaries of Special Assignment, and Revelators of Truth, these aren't different orders of beings. They're all the same. They're completely interchangeable.

A Solitary Messenger serving as a Messenger of the Paradise Trinity today could be reassigned tomorrow as an Explorer of Undirected Assignment or as a Revelator of Truth. In fact, the Solitary Messenger who participated in revealing *The Urantia Book* to us served in that highest capacity, as a Revelator of Truth. This is considered their highest honor, their most prestigious assignment, because they get to relay information directly from the Infinite Spirit to groups of beings working on planetary revelations. When you consider that this being was involved in bringing us this remarkable book, you begin to appreciate just how special this world is in the larger scheme of things.

This interchangeability among the Solitary Messengers speaks to something I find deeply meaningful: they were created perfectly, and they were created equally. There's no hierarchy of better or worse among them, no senior and junior members, no ranking by skill or accomplishment. They're all equally capable of any assignment. The only distinction is what work they happen to be doing at any given moment.

The Urge Outward from Paradise

One of the most touching aspects of the Solitary Messengers is described in a passage that contrasts their nature with ours. "We mortals start out as well-nigh material beings on the worlds of space and ascend inward towards the great centers; these solitary spirits start out at the center of all things and crave assignment to the remote creations, even to the individual worlds of the outermost local universes and even on beyond."

Notice that word: *crave*. The Solitary Messengers crave these assignments. They long to move outward from Paradise, to reach the edges of creation, to serve on distant worlds. This wasn't programmed into them as a mere function; it's described as a deep desire, an authentic yearning. When a Solitary Messenger receives an assignment as a Revelator of Truth to some remote evolutionary world like ours, this represents the fulfillment of that deep longing to serve at the frontiers of existence.

I find this beautiful because it shows that even beings created perfect still have desires, still have preferences, still have things they find more or less fulfilling. Perfection doesn't mean sameness or mechanical obedience. It means alignment with divine purpose while retaining authentic personality and genuine preference.

Speed, Circuits, and the Warning System

Now we come to one of the most fascinating technical aspects of the Solitary Messengers: their method of travel and the extraordinary warning system they possess. The revelation tells us that Solitary Messengers travel at speeds that are, frankly, beyond our comprehension. When we read about their velocity in later sections, the numbers become so large they lose meaning to human minds. They travel along the cosmic circuits, those spiritual energy pathways that connect all parts of creation, and they draw their sustenance directly from the circuit of the Infinite Spirit.

This is where things get technically interesting. The Solitary Messengers are constantly encircuited, connected to, the Infinite Spirit through what might be called a spiritual energy flow. This circuit provides them with everything they need to function. They don't eat, they don't rest in the way we understand rest, they don't require physical or even spiritual sustenance in conventional terms. The circuit itself sustains them.

But here's the problem: if two or more Solitary Messengers get too close to each other while traveling along these circuits at incomprehensible speeds, they create what the revelation describes as a "short circuit." Both messengers are immediately thrown out of liaison with the higher circulating forces. They lose their connection to the Infinite Spirit's sustaining circuit. If this disconnection were permanent, they would cease to exist.

To prevent this catastrophe, the Solitary Messengers possess an inherent automatic alarm system, a warning signal that operates perfectly and unfailingly to alert them when they're approaching another Solitary Messenger. When this alarm sounds, both beings immediately stop or alter course, avoiding the collision that would throw them both off the circuit. One participant in our study group compared this to the automatic braking systems in modern cars that detect an imminent collision and apply the brakes without driver intervention. It's an apt comparison, though the Solitary Messengers' system actually works perfectly every time.

What makes this even more intriguing is that Solitary Messengers possess two types of these automatic alarm systems. The first detects other Solitary Messengers, as I've described. The second detects something entirely different: Thought Adjusters and inspired Trinity spirits. When a Solitary Messenger approaches a Thought Adjuster, that fragment of God the Father that indwells human beings, an alarm sounds. Not because the Solitary Messenger is in danger, but because this alarm serves as a notification: "Warning, you are in the presence of God."

Think about that. The Solitary Messenger, created by the Third Source and Center (the Infinite Spirit), carries an automatic reverence detector for the First Source and Center (the Universal Father). When that alarm sounds, it's as if the Solitary Messenger's entire being is reminded: the Father is here, present in fragment form, indwelling this mortal creature. To me, this speaks volumes about the importance of our Thought Adjusters and the respect they command throughout all creation.

The alarm for inspired Trinity spirits serves a different purpose. These beings, also created by the Infinite Spirit, can travel at speeds comparable to the Solitary Messengers. If both an inspired Trinity spirit and a Solitary Messenger are traveling down the same circuit at these tremendous velocities, the alarm system gives them advance warning so they can avoid collision. It's a safety feature built into their very nature, another example of the precision and foresight evident in how the universe operates.

Their Service and Purpose

The Solitary Messengers, despite their name, aren't actually lonely beings. The revelation makes this clear: "Though denominated solitary messengers, they are not lonesome spirits, for they truly like to work alone." This is their nature. They're designed for independent function, yet they equally enjoy the rare occasions when they can fraternize with the few orders of universe intelligence capable of perceiving them.

Think about how limiting this must be in some ways. Most beings in creation, angels, humans, even many celestial personalities, cannot see or sense a Solitary Messenger's presence. Only a handful of very high orders of beings have this capability. Yet the Solitary Messengers don't experience this as isolation because they're constantly in touch with "the wealth of the intellect of all creation." They can listen in on all the broadcasts of the realms where they serve. They're never truly alone because they're always connected to the vast network of universal communication.

They could communicate with other Solitary Messengers serving in different superuniverses, but they've been directed by the Council of the Seven Master Spirits not to do so. Why? Because each of the seven superuniverses represents a unique evolutionary experiment. Each is progressing under the guidance of a different Master Spirit, each of whom embodies a different combination of the natures of the Father, Son, and Spirit. If Solitary Messengers shared information freely across superuniverse boundaries, it might contaminate these separate evolutionary paths. It might blend the seven unique expressions of deity into a premature uniformity. So, they're instructed to maintain appropriate boundaries, and being loyal servants, they obey perfectly.

Exempt from Apprehension

Here's a detail that initially struck me as odd but makes perfect sense upon reflection: Solitary Messengers, along with the Universe Power Directors, are among the very few types of beings "exempt from apprehension or detention by the tribunals of time and space." They can't be arrested, detained, or called to account before any court except that of the Seven Master Spirits themselves. And remarkably, in all the annals of the master universe, this Paradise council has never been called upon to adjudicate the case of a Solitary Messenger.

Why this exemption? For Solitary Messengers, it's because they work directly under the authority of the Infinite Spirit. They're personal representatives of deity. To detain or arrest them would be, in effect, to challenge the authority of the Third Source and Center. Since they've never once failed in their duties, never defaulted on an assignment, never stumbled into darkness, there's simply no reason anyone would ever need to bring charges against them.

The Universe Power Directors have a different reason for their exemption: they literally hold the physical universe together. These beings manipulate and control energy, not just a little energy, but the fundamental forces that keep suns burning, planets rotating, and matter existing in stable form. If you could arrest or detain a Universe Power Director, you might inadvertently collapse an entire sector of space. So they're exempt not because they're above the law, but because their function is so critical that any interruption could be catastrophic.

The Circuit and the Mother Spirit

I need to clarify something about how Solitary Messengers maintain their connection to the Infinite Spirit, because this involves some subtle but important theology. When a Solitary Messenger operates within a local universe, like our local universe of Nebadon, they work under the immediate influence of the Local Universe Mother Spirit. For us, that's our Divine Minister, the Creative Spirit who partners with Christ Michael (Jesus) in administering our local universe.

Now, every other being who receives spiritual sustenance in Nebadon receives it through the Divine Minister's circuit. She's the local presence and representative of the Infinite Spirit. When the Caligastia one hundred were brought to our planet to establish civilization, they were "encircuited" through the Divine Minister. They received spiritual nutrition, guidance, and sustenance through her. When they later joined the Lucifer rebellion, one of the consequences was being cut off from that circuit, a spiritual death of sorts, though not complete annihilation.

The Solitary Messengers are different. Yes, they work through the local universe Mother Spirit's circuit while in her domain, but they maintain a direct connection to the Infinite Spirit on Paradise. It's as if they have two connections simultaneously: the local connection that allows them to function within the local universe, and a direct line back to Paradise that never disconnects. This is why, when they leave the local universe to travel to the superuniverse level or beyond, they simply shift from one circuit to another without losing their sustenance or connection.

This dual-circuit capability is crucial to their function. They operate throughout all levels of reality, from Paradise to the outer edges of inhabited space. They need to be able to transition seamlessly from one level to another without interruption. The direct connection to the Infinite Spirit makes this possible.

Listening In and Broadcasting

One capability of the Solitary Messengers that I find particularly significant is their ability to "listen in" on all the broadcasts of the realms where they serve. This includes both local universe broadcasts and superuniverse broadcasts. They're constantly receiving information, constantly updated on what's happening throughout vast regions of space and time.

This isn't eavesdropping in any negative sense. They're authorized to do this; it's part of their function. How else could they serve as effective messengers if they didn't know what was happening? They need to be informed about everything relevant to their assignments. This also means they're among the most well-informed beings in all creation. They hear the announcements, they receive the updates, they monitor the communications that keep the universe functioning.

But there's a restriction here too. Solitary Messengers can communicate with others of their number serving in the same superuniverse, but again, they've been instructed not to share information across superuniverse boundaries. This isn't because of any distrust but because of the need to maintain the unique evolutionary character of each superuniverse.

Messengers of the Paradise Trinity

The seven divisions of Solitary Messenger service form a hierarchy of responsibility and honor. At the highest level serve the Messengers of the Paradise Trinity. The revelation is quite direct about these beings: "I am not permitted to reveal much of the work of the group of messengers assigned to the Trinity. They are the trusted and secret servants of the Deities, and when entrusted with special messages which involve the unrevealed policies and future conduct of the Gods, they have never been known to divulge a secret or betray the confidence reposed in their order."

This is important: these particular Solitary Messengers carry messages that involve the unrevealed policies and future plans of the Paradise Deities themselves. They know things about the future direction of creation that even very high celestial beings don't know. And they've never, not once in the entire history of creation, divulged a secret or betrayed a confidence. This isn't because they're programmed like computers. Remember, they're personality beings with free will. They choose loyalty. They choose faithfulness. They've had eons of time and countless opportunities to reveal secrets, yet they never have.

The revelation adds something I find deeply meaningful: "All this is related in this connection, not to appear boastful of their perfection, but rather to point out that the Deities can and do create perfect beings." This is worth pondering. The Deities don't create only evolutionary beings like us who must grow toward perfection over vast ages. They also create beings who begin perfect and remain perfect. Both types of beings are necessary. We bring something unique through our evolutionary struggle, genuine experience, hard-won wisdom, character forged in the furnace of imperfection. The perfect beings bring something else, reliability, immediate competence, unwavering service.

The Other Divisions

Below the Messengers of the Paradise Trinity come the other divisions, each with its own sphere of service. The Messengers of the Havona Circuits work in that eternal universe, assisting the pilgrims who are ascending toward Paradise. The Messengers of the Superuniverses coordinate activities at that vast level. The Messengers of the Local Universes, like the ones serving in our universe of Nebadon, work with the local universe administrations, carrying communications between the local universe and the superuniverse, and performing countless other essential functions.

The Explorers of Undirected Assignment have perhaps the most intriguing role. They're sent out to investigate, to explore, to discover. Where other messengers have specific orders and defined missions, these explorers have more freedom to roam and report on what they find. They're the scouts of creation, going ahead to see what's there and bringing back information.

The Ambassadors and Emissaries of Special Assignment represent the Infinite Spirit in special situations, carry out unusual missions, and serve as representatives in circumstances requiring the personal touch of deity. And finally, the Revelators of Truth, the most honored assignment of all, participate in bringing divine revelation to the evolutionary worlds. One of these served in revealing *The Urantia Book*, working with the contact commission and the other celestial beings involved in this epochal revelation to our planet.

No Permanent Attachments

Unlike most celestial beings, Solitary Messengers have no permanent home base, no permanent assignment, no permanent attachment to any individual or group. They're always on duty by assignment, and when that assignment ends, they receive a new one. Among themselves, they have no organization, no government, no hierarchy beyond the temporary classifications based on current work. They are, in the truest sense, solitary messengers, independent operators working under direct assignment from higher authorities.

This means that across billions of years of service, a Solitary Messenger moves from assignment to assignment, accumulating an incomprehensible breadth of experience. One era they might serve in Havona, the next in a remote superuniverse sector, then on a local universe capital, then on an evolutionary world at the edge of inhabited space. Each assignment brings new experiences, new challenges, new beings to work with. Yet throughout all this variety, they remain unchanged in their essential nature, perfect, loyal, competent, trustworthy.

What This Means for Us

As I've studied the Solitary Messengers over the years, I've come to see them as embodying something we might call "functional perfection." They show us what it looks like when beings are created exactly right for their purpose, with no need for growth or development, yet still possessing authentic personality, genuine desire, and real satisfaction in their work.

This contrasts sharply with our own nature as ascending mortals. We aren't created perfect, far from it. We begin as barely conscious creatures on material worlds, confused about our purpose, uncertain about truth, prone to error and selfishness. Our entire purpose is growth, development, the long climb from imperfection toward perfection. We'll spend ages achieving what the Solitary Messengers possessed from the moment of their creation.

But here's what I find encouraging: both paths, the perfect creation and the imperfect evolutionary path, are valid. Both are part of the divine plan. The universe needs beings like the Solitary Messengers who can be trusted immediately, completely, without question. But the universe also needs beings like us, who bring the unique perspective that comes only from having struggled, failed, learned, and grown.

When a Solitary Messenger meets an ascending mortal, say, when one of us finally reaches Havona and encounters these beings we've been studying, what will that encounter be like? The Solitary Messenger will see someone who has climbed up from the very bottom of existence, who has chosen, step by painful step, to ascend toward Paradise. And we will see a being who has served flawlessly since the dawn of time, who possesses wisdom and capability we can barely imagine, yet who somehow isn't condescending or distant but rather genuinely interested in our unique journey.

The Anvil and the Hammer

I want to return to that final paragraph from Paper 23 that we touched on in our study session, because it encapsulates something essential about why our world is the way it is. The text acknowledges directly that "the confusion and turmoil of Urantia" might lead us to think that "the Paradise Rulers lack either interest or ability to manage affairs differently." But then it makes a stunning statement: "The Creators are possessed of full power to make Urantia a veritable paradise, but such an Eden would not contribute to the development of those strong, noble, and experienced characters which the Gods are so surely forging out on your world between the anvils of necessity and the hammers of anguish."

Read that again. God could make our world perfect. The Creators have the power to eliminate all suffering, all confusion, all turmoil. They could make Earth an Eden right now, today. But they don't, because such a world wouldn't produce the character qualities they're trying to develop in us. Our anxieties, our sorrows, our trials, our disappointments, these aren't mistakes or oversights. They're not evidence that God doesn't care or doesn't have the power to intervene. They're "just as much a part of the divine plan on your sphere as are the exquisite perfection and infinite adaptation of all things to their supreme purpose on the worlds of the central and perfect universe."

This is hard to accept, particularly when we're in the middle of suffering. When you're dealing with personal tragedy, financial crisis, relationship breakdown, health problems, or any of the countless difficulties that mark human existence, it's not comforting to hear "this is part of the plan." I get that. I've been there. We all have.

But here's what I've come to understand through years of studying these revelations and living through my own share of difficulties: the perfect beings, the Solitary Messengers, the supernaphim, all the beings created without flaw, can never possess what we possess. They can never know what it's like to be broken and become whole. They can never experience the triumph of overcoming genuine weakness. They can never feel the profound satisfaction of choosing good when evil seems more appealing or easier. They can never understand, from personal experience, what it means to be lost and then found.

We will carry these experiences with us forever. Millions of years from now, when we're serving somewhere in the grand universe, we'll possess something unique: the lived experience of ascending from near nothingness to divine perfection. We'll understand suffering because we suffered. We'll understand forgiveness because we needed forgiveness. We'll understand mercy because we received mercy. And this will make us more effective servants in the ages to come.

Looking Ahead

As we conclude this examination of the Solitary Messengers, I'm reminded that they represent only the first order of the Higher Personalities of the Infinite Spirit. In the next chapter, we'll explore the other extraordinary beings created by the Third Source and Center, the Universe Circuit Supervisors, the Census Directors, the Personal Aids of the Infinite Spirit, the Associate Inspectors, the Assigned Sentinels, and the Graduate Guides. Each order has its own unique nature, its own specific function, its own role in the vast administration of the cosmos.

But I think understanding the Solitary Messengers first is important because they set a pattern. They show us what the Infinite Spirit values: reliability, loyalty, competence, independence coupled with obedience, and the ability to function perfectly in service without supervision or constraint. These qualities characterize all the children of the Infinite Spirit to varying degrees.

They also remind us that we're not alone in this universe. As we struggle through our daily lives on this confused and troubled world, beings of unimaginable capability are working behind the scenes, carrying messages, coordinating universe administration, and yes, sometimes bringing divine revelation to worlds ready to receive it. We can't see them, we can't sense their presence, but they're there, faithfully performing their duties just as they have since the dawn of time.

And one day, if we choose the path of survival, if we continue to seek the Father's will, if we persist in our ascension, we'll finally see them. We'll recognize their presence in Havona. We'll understand, then, so much more than we can understand now. But even in our ignorance, even in our blindness to these higher realities, we can take comfort in knowing that the universe is administered by beings of perfect competence and unwavering loyalty, and that all of them, even the highest, serve the same loving Father we serve, moving toward the same ultimate destiny of perfected unity with the First Source and Center of all things.

The Solitary Messengers, first children of the Infinite Spirit, continue their tireless service throughout creation. May we serve with even a fraction of their dedication and loyalty as we traverse our own unique path toward Paradise.

Chapter 15: Messengers of the Havona Circuits and Beyond

I've spent years studying these celestial beings, and I have to tell you, every time I return to this section on Solitary Messengers, something new strikes me. Tonight, as we continue our exploration, I'm reminded of just how vast and intricate the universe's communication network really is. Last session, we covered the Messengers of the Paradise Trinity, laying the groundwork for understanding these remarkable beings. Now we're going to examine their work across the circuits of Havona, the superuniverses, and even into the unexplored reaches of outer space.

Messengers of the Havona Circuits

The revelation tells us something quite specific: "Throughout the ascendant career you will be vaguely but increasingly able to detect the presence of the Solitary Messengers, but not until you reach Havona will you recognize them unmistakably. The first of the messengers you will see face to face will be those of the Havona circuits."

Think about that for a moment. During our entire ascension journey, through all the mansion worlds, the constellation spheres, the local universe training worlds, we'll sense these messengers. Maybe we'll feel their presence, catch glimpses of their work. But it's only when we reach Havona, that central and perfect universe, that we'll finally see them clearly, face to face.

I like to picture this. There's the ascender, making their way through the billion worlds of Havona, and along the way are these Solitary Messengers. The text suggests something important here: if we're told we'll recognize them "unmistakably," it seems reasonable to assume we'll actually see them. That's quite different from our current state, where these beings operate completely beyond our perception.

The revelation continues with a fascinating observation about the relationship between Solitary Messengers and Havona natives: "These messengers, who are so functionally handicapped when associating with one another, can and do have a very close and personal communion with the Havona natives. But it is quite impossible to convey to human minds the supreme satisfactions consequent upon the contact of the minds of these divinely perfect beings with the spirits of such near-transcendent personalities."

Here's what strikes me about this passage: these messengers struggle to communicate with each other in certain ways, yet they share an intimate communion with the Havona natives. And the authors are telling us honestly, there's simply no way to explain to us what that relationship feels like. There's nothing in our experience that even comes close. These are near-transcendent personalities, and our reaction to them will be totally unlike anything else we've encountered in the universe. The authors are being transparent with us: some experiences transcend description until we're ready to have them ourselves.

Messengers of the Superuniverses

Now we come to something that reveals the practical necessity of these beings in universe administration. The text states: "The Ancients of Days, those personalities of Trinity origin who preside over the destinies of the seven superuniverses, those trios of divine power and administrative wisdom, are bountifully supplied with Solitary Messengers. It is only through this order of messengers that the triune rulers of one superuniverse can directly and personally communicate with the rulers of another."

Let me explain why this matters so much. The passage continues: "All other personalities must make such excursions by way of Havona and the executive worlds of the Master Spirits."

Do you see the implications? If you're an administrator in superuniverse number one and you need to communicate with administrators in superuniverse number seven, every other type of being has to travel to Havona first, then back out to the destination. That journey to Havona takes many, many years, possibly centuries. If messengers had to make that detour, you'd be doubling or quadrupling the communication time. But Solitary Messengers can go directly from one superuniverse headquarters to another.

The text does mention one exception: "aside possibly from the Inspired Trinity Spirits." These beings can travel at comparable velocities. They're the two types of beings capable of moving at what we might call super-velocities. That direct route makes all the difference in universe administration.

Now, you might wonder, why not just use the reflectivity service? That's instantaneous, isn't it? Yes, it is. The reflectivity service works somewhat like our modern video conferencing. Imagine the Ancients of Days on one end of a Zoom call and administrators on the other end, they can see each other, talk in real time, receive immediate responses. In that sense, our current technology gives us a small taste of what the reflectivity service accomplishes across unimaginable distances.

But here's the thing: there are many matters in superuniverse administration that shouldn't be broadcast over the reflectivity service. Too many beings have access to it. Think about it practically. Suppose a message that needed to be sent from our local universe headquarters stating that thirty-seven planets have rebelled. If that went out over the reflectivity service, it would put a negative connotation on our entire local universe. That might not be the desired outcome. So, when the Lucifer rebellion started, that message was probably carried by a Solitary Messenger, getting there quickly without the broadcast exposure.

Let me give you another example from our own planetary history. When Urantia went into rebellion, Van and Amadon sent a message to the Most Highs, likely through the broadcast system or something similar to the reflectivity service. That message reached them, and it reached the Ancients of Days. But here's what's remarkable, and frustrating: Van didn't receive a response for seven years.

Why? Because the beings who forward these broadcast messages can't initiate the forwarding themselves. It has to be initiated from the original source. There was a seven-year delay built into the system. This is exactly where a Solitary Messenger becomes invaluable. They bypass all those limitations.

So yes, the reflectivity service exists. It's instantaneous and remarkable. But there are administrative reasons, privacy concerns, and systemic limitations that make personal messengers essential. And nothing is 100% foolproof, except a Solitary Messenger or an Inspired Trinity Spirit. When the Ancients of Days dispatch one of these beings with a message, they're absolutely assured it will arrive exactly as intended.

We're going to see this concept reinforced in the next passage. The revelation states: "There are some kinds of information which cannot be obtained either by Gravity Messengers, reflectivity, or broadcast. And when the Ancients of Days would certainly know these things, they must dispatch a Solitary Messenger to the source of knowledge."

Then comes this stunning example: "Long before the presence of life on Urantia, the messenger now associated with me was assigned on a mission out of Uversa to the central universe. He was absent from the roll calls of Orvonton for almost a million years but returned in due time with the desired information."

Let that sink in. One million years. The being who helped compile this revelation once spent a million years traveling from Uversa, the headquarters of our superuniverse, all the way to Havona and back, carrying information. And he returned "in due time," meaning that was the expected timeframe for that journey.

Someone asked me once, "Is that our years or their years?" It's our years. Everything in the book is given in our time measurements unless specifically stated otherwise. For these beings, time passes differently than it does for them, of course. But we're being told in terms we can understand: a million of our years.

Think about the perfection involved here. The Ancients of Days didn't just send the message; they had to remember they'd sent it a million years ago. I can't remember what I ate for lunch yesterday, much less track a message sent out a million years prior. That's the level of perfection we're dealing with.

The revelation continues: "There is no limitation upon the service of Solitary Messengers in the superuniverses. They may function as executioners of the high tribunals or as intelligence gatherers for the good of the realm. Of all the super creations, they most delight to serve in Orvonton because here the need is greatest and the opportunities for heroic effort are greatly multiplied."

Two things catch my attention here. First, they function as "executioners of the high tribunals." That doesn't necessarily mean what we might initially think. If the Ancients of Days make a declaration that something must be done, these messengers are sent to execute that order, to ensure it's carried out. They probably back up the Celestial Guardians. If a Celestial Guardian is sent to bring someone before the Ancients of Days and encounters resistance, they could call upon a Solitary Messenger for support.

Second, they're "intelligence gatherers for the good of the realm." This becomes particularly relevant when we consider our own planet's history. If a Solitary Messenger was assigned to Urantia as an observer, and given what we know about rebellion, it seems likely one was, don't you think they would have relayed information about brewing rebellion immediately to Michael, our Creator Son? These beings can't be seen by anyone, not even by Caligastia and the other Sons of God involved in the rebellion. They could observe everything and report directly to Michael as events unfolded. That's an incredibly valuable function.

Messengers of the Local Universes

The text tells us: "In the services of a local universe, there is no limit upon the functioning of the Solitary Messengers. They are the faithful revealers of the motives and intent of the local universe Mother Spirit, although they are under the full jurisdiction of the reigning Master Son."

This applies to all messengers operating in a local universe, whether traveling directly from universe headquarters or working temporarily with Constellation Fathers, System Sovereigns, or Planetary Princes. But there's an important historical detail: "Before the concentration of all power in the hands of a Creator Son at the time of his elevation as sovereign ruler of his universe, these messengers of the local universes function under the general direction of the Ancients of Days and are immediately responsible to their resident representative, the Union of Days."

Why the Union of Days? Because the Union of Days represents the Paradise Trinity at local universe headquarters. These messengers fall under the purview of the Trinity's representative at all times; that's their primary allegiance. So, before a Michael Son completes his sovereignty (in our case, before Michael completed his seventh bestowal), these messengers could perform many different services while keeping everyone informed. They maintained communication networks across the developing universe.

After a Creator Son achieves sovereignty, they work directly for him, Michael, in our case. They become his personal agents. Yet they remain immediately responsible to the Ancients of Days through the Union of Days. That dual accountability ensures both local autonomy and universal oversight.

Explorers of Undirected Assignment

Here's where things get really interesting. The revelation states: "When the reserve corps of the Solitary Messengers is overrecruited, there issues from one of the Seven Supreme Power Directors a call for exploration volunteers, and there is never a lack of volunteers, for they delight to be dispatched as free and untrammeled explorers, to experience the thrill of finding the organizing nuclei of new worlds and universes."

Why would the Supreme Power Directors issue this call? Because they're the ones providing the power to initiate new universes. They need these regions of space explored first, mapped out. So, they dispatch Solitary Messengers into uncharted space. It's a fascinating connection, power directors and messengers working in tandem to prepare the way for new creation.

The passage continues: "They go forth to investigate the clues furnished by the space contemplators of the realms. Undoubtedly the Paradise Deities know of the existence of these undiscovered energy systems of space, but they never divulge such information."

Catch that? The Paradise Deities know about these undiscovered energy systems. Of course they do. The Unqualified Absolute encompasses all of space, nothing can escape its awareness. And if the Unqualified Absolute knows, then God the Father knows, because he's part of that absolute reality. All members of the Paradise Trinity always know what's happening, everywhere, all the time. That's what omnipotence and omniscience mean in their fullest sense.

But they don't simply tell everyone what's out there. Instead, they send out Solitary Messengers to explore and chart these regions. Once mapped, all the other beings involved in manipulating matter and energy have the information they need for their work. It's a remarkably organized system.

The revelation adds this intriguing detail: "Solitary Messengers, as a class, are highly sensitive to gravity. Accordingly, they can sometimes detect the probable presence of very small dark planets, the very worlds which are best adapted to life experiments."

Did you catch that? Those small dark planets we observe in space, many of them are actually planets in formation, destined to be populated with life. They're not dead rocks drifting meaninglessly. They're future homes for ascending mortals like us. And Solitary Messengers can detect them because of their sensitivity to gravity.

The text continues: "These messenger-explorers of undirected assignment patrol the master universe. They are constantly out on exploring expeditions to the uncharted regions of all outer space. Very much of the information which we possess of transactions in the realms of outer space we owe to the explorations of the Solitary Messengers."

This is crucial to understand. The master universe includes our superuniverse and the other six, all of which are still developing. Michael, our Creator Son, is still creating planets in our local system. We're told there are 619 inhabited worlds in our system, but who knows how many exist now? It's been two thousand years since that count. Creation continues.

But beyond the seven superuniverses lie the four outer space levels. Without Solitary Messengers, we'd have no information about those regions at all. They're our only source of knowledge about what's developing in those vast, distant realms. That makes them pretty important, wouldn't you say?

Ambassadors and Emissaries of Special Assignment

The revelation explains: "Local universes situated within the same superuniverse customarily exchange ambassadors selected from their native orders of sonship. But to avoid delay, Solitary Messengers are frequently asked to go as ambassadors from one local creation to another."

Here's why: "When a newly inhabited realm is discovered, it may prove to be so remote in space that a long time will pass before an enseraphimed ambassador can reach this far-distant universe. An enseraphimed being cannot possibly exceed the velocity of 558,840 Urantia miles in one second of your time."

Let me explain what "enseraphimed" means. When a being needs to travel through space but doesn't have the inherent ability to do so safely, they're enfolded in the protective transport of seraphim, angels. The angels create a kind of shield around them. But there are physical limits to how fast that transport can travel while keeping the passenger safe. Beyond 558,840 miles per second, it becomes dangerous to whatever being they're protecting.

The text adds: "Massive stars, crosscurrents, and detours, as well as attraction tangents, will all tend to retard such speed so that on a long journey the velocity will average around 550,000 miles per second."

So, in practice, seraphic transport averages about 550,000 miles per second. That's impressive by our standards, but across cosmic distances, it can mean journeys of hundreds or even thousands of years. That's why Solitary Messengers are so valuable: "When it develops that it will require hundreds of years for a native ambassador to reach a far-distant local universe, a Solitary Messenger is often asked to proceed there immediately to act as ambassador ad interim."

They can serve as acting ambassadors until the official representative arrives. It's an elegant solution to the time problem inherent in cosmic distances.

Revealers of Truth

The revelation states: "The Solitary Messengers regard the assignment to reveal truth as the highest trust of their order. And they function ever and anon in this capacity, from the superuniverses to the individual planets of space. They are frequently attached to commissions which are sent to enlarge the revelation of truth to the worlds and systems."

And that's exactly what happened on our planet. So, if someone asks you, "Where did The Urantia Book come from?" you can answer honestly: a Solitary Messenger was involved in bringing it to this world, along with about a dozen other celestial beings. This isn't the work of one person claiming divine inspiration. It's not someone being handed golden tablets. This is a coordinated effort by multiple celestial personalities working together to expand our understanding of cosmic reality.

I mention this specifically for our friends from various religious traditions who might wonder about the source of revelation. The pattern here is consistent with other epochal revelations, but the method and transparency are unique.

Time and Space Services

Now we come to some of the most mind-bending information in the entire revelation. The text begins: "The Solitary Messengers are the highest type of perfect and confidential personality available in all realms for the quick transmission of important and urgent messages when it is inexpedient to utilize either the broadcast service or the reflectivity mechanism."

It continues: "Of all orders assigned to the services of the superuniverse domains, they are the highest and most versatile personalized beings who can come so near to defying time and space."

Think about this in human terms. We just learned that a Solitary Messenger might spend a million years delivering a message. A million years. Now consider that our lives span maybe a hundred years at most. That's so small in comparison it barely registers. Any Solitary Messenger assigned to reveal truth to us has existed for epochs we can't truly comprehend. And yet here we are, in our brief lifespans, sometimes thinking we understand everything.

It must require an extraordinary sense of humor on their part, if nothing else. It's like us trying to have a serious philosophical discussion with an ant and getting frustrated when it doesn't immediately grasp quantum mechanics.

The revelation then provides crucial context: "The universe is well supplied with spirits who utilize gravity for purposes of transit. They can go anywhere any time, instantaneously, but they are not persons."

That distinction matters. There are beings who can traverse space instantly using gravity circuits, but they're not personal beings in the way we understand personality. Then there are personal beings like Gravity Messengers and Transcendental Recorders, but they're not available to superuniverse and local universe administrators for routine communication.

The text continues with specific velocity measurements: "The limit of velocity for most non-enseraphimed beings is 186,280 miles of your world per second of your time."

That's interesting, it's essentially the speed of light. A being traveling under their own power, without seraphic transport, maxes out at light speed.

"The midway creatures and certain others can often attain double velocity, 372,560 miles per second, while the seraphim and others can traverse space at triple velocity, about 558,840 miles per second."

So midwayers, those beings native to our planet who exist between the material and spiritual realms, can travel at twice the speed of light. Seraphim can go three times light speed. That's the maximum velocity for seraphic transport we discussed earlier.

Then comes this crucial statement: "There are, however, no transit or messenger personalities who function between the instantaneous velocities of the gravity traversers and the comparatively slow speeds of the seraphim, except the Solitary Messengers."

They occupy a unique middle ground, faster than anything except instant gravity transport, yet they retain full personality and conscious experience of their journey.

Now, let me apply this to something that matters deeply to many people. When we die and our guardian seraphim transports our soul to the first mansion world, how long does that journey take? The revelation tells us we "wake up on the third period." People often assume that means three Earth days, probably because of the resurrection of Jesus on the third day. But look carefully at what the text actually says, it doesn't say "three Earth days." It says," the third period."

If they're referring to mansion world days, and that seems likely given the context, we need to do some calculation. The Jerusem Standard Day (Mansion World Days) = Three Urantia Days. Local Universe (A bit longer) The standard day = 18 days and 6 hours of Urantia time Plus two ½ minutes. A mansion world day is approximately three times longer than an Earth day. So, three mansion world periods would equal roughly nine Earth days.

Why does it take that long? Because our seraphim can only travel at 558,840 miles per second, and the first mansion world is that far away from Urantia. Even at that incredible velocity, it takes about eighteen days to make the journey.

Now, does it matter if it's three days, eighteen days, three months, or even a year? Not really. We're not conscious during the transport. When we wake up, it feels like we just died. The time passage is irrelevant to our experience.

But here's why the distinction matters: we often think it's three Earth days because Jesus rose on the third day. But there's a crucial difference. Jesus resurrected himself. He's the Son of God. He didn't need the normal resurrection processes. He brought himself back to life in the tomb, none of the usual agencies assisted him. That's why it was three literal days for him.

Moreover, Jesus went through his entire morontia experience, what we'll experience across multiple mansion worlds, right here on Urantia. He didn't have to travel anywhere. He accomplished in days what will take us lifetimes.

Let me clarify the timeline of Jesus's resurrection, since there's often confusion about "three days." He died Friday afternoon. He rose around 3:00 AM Sunday morning. Count that out: Friday to Saturday is one day, Saturday to Sunday is two days. It wasn't even forty-eight hours, more like forty hours. But in Jewish reckoning, any part of a day counts as a full day. Friday counts as the first day, all of Saturday. is the second day, and Sunday morning is the third day. So yes, it's called three days, even though it's less than two full days by our modern calculation.

The point is, we shouldn't rigidly hold to the idea that we'll wake up after exactly three Earth days. It's likely longer, and honestly, it doesn't matter to us experientially.

Now, getting back to the midwayers for a moment, the text mentions they're "non-enseraphimed beings." That means they can traverse space without needing seraphic transport. A Midwayer can travel at 186,280 miles per second on their own and often achieves double that velocity. But if a Midwayer is enseraphimed, enfolded in seraphic transport, their speed increases to the full seraphic velocity of 558,840 miles per second.

I've included a chart with all these velocities for your reference. We covered this somewhat last time, so you can review it at your leisure.

Now comes the moment we've been building toward. The revelation states: "Solitary Messengers are therefore generally used for dispatch and service in those situations where personality is essential to the achievement of the assignment, and where it is desired to avoid the loss of time which would be occasioned by the dispatch of any other readily available type of personal messenger."

It continues: "They are the only definitively personalized beings who can synchronize with the combined universal currents of the grand universe. Their velocity in traversing space is variable, depending on a great variety of interfering influences, but the record shows that on the journey to fulfill this mission, my associate messenger proceeded at the rate of 841,621,642,000 of your miles per second of your time."

Let me say that again, because it bears repeating: 841 billion, 621 million, 642 thousand miles per second.

That's not a typo. That's not an exaggeration. That's eight hundred forty-one billion miles every single second.

No vehicle we could ever construct could approach that velocity. No material being with any kind of physical body, not even one molecule of matter, could survive that speed. Even morontia beings need seraphic protection at far lower velocities. This tells us something profound about the nature of Solitary Messengers. They must be beings of such pure spirit essence that they can move at these velocities without any kind of protective transport.

Someone usually asks at this point: "Wait, didn't we just read that it took a million years for a message to be delivered?" Yes, we did. And here's what that tells us, the distance from Uversa to Havona is so incomprehensibly vast that even at eight hundred forty-one billion miles per second, it takes a million years to make the round trip.

Think about that. We can't see Havona with any telescope, no matter how powerful. Even traveling at the speed of light, we'd never receive any signal from Havona in our lifetimes, or in a thousand lifetimes. That's how far away the central universe really is.

What I take from this is simple: relax. We're on our way to Paradise, yes. But we're going to spend time on countless worlds, learning, growing, serving. We'll pause on each sphere to master its lessons. The journey might take billions of years of mortal time measurement. And that's perfectly fine. There's no hurry. In fact, trying to rush would defeat the entire purpose of the ascension experience.

The revelation concludes this section by emphasizing the incomprehensibility of these beings: "It is wholly beyond my ability to explain to the material type of mind how a spirit can be a real person and at the same time traverse space at such tremendous velocities. But these very Solitary Messengers actually come to and go from Urantia at these incomprehensible speeds. Indeed, the whole economy of universal administration would be largely deprived of its personal element were this not a fact."

The author is being honest with us. They can't explain how it works because our minds aren't equipped to understand it yet. But it does work. These beings do exist. They do travel at these velocities. And without them, the personal touch in universal administration would be severely diminished.

The text adds: "The Solitary Messengers are able to function as emergency lines of communication throughout remote space regions, realms not embraced within the established circuits of the grand universe. It develops that one messenger, when so functioning, can transmit a message or send an impulse through space to a fellow messenger about a hundred light-years away as Urantia astronomers estimate stellar distances."

So, they can communicate with each other across a hundred light-years of space, instantly. They form a living communication network spanning creation.

The final passage in our study tonight reads: "Of the myriads of beings who cooperate with us in the conduct of the affairs of the superuniverse, none are more important in practical helpfulness and timesaving assistance. In the universes of space, we must reckon with the handicaps of time; hence the great service of the Solitary Messengers who, by means of their personal prerogatives of communication, are somewhat independent of space and, by virtue of their tremendous transit velocities, are so nearly independent of time."

Nearly independent of time and space. For beings like us, trapped as we are in the flow of temporal existence, that's almost impossible to imagine. Yet that's the reality of these messengers. They represent the solution to the problem of distance in a universe so vast it takes light itself millions of years to cross.

Notes on time:

The Jerusem Standard Day = Three Urantia Days.
The Standard Year = 100 Jerusem Days. Page 509
Superuniverse The Standard day = Thirty Urantia Days
Superuniverse The Standard year = 100 Standard Days = 3000 Urantia Days
1000 Standard Years = 1000x 3000 Urantia Days =3,000,000 days / 365 =8219.17 Urantia years
33:6.7 Chronology is reckoned, computed, and rectified by a special group of beings on Salvington. The standard day of Nebadon is equal to eighteen days and six hours of Urantia time, plus two and one-half minutes. The Nebadon year consists of a segment of the time of universe swing in relation to the Uversa circuit and is equal to one hundred days of standard universe time, about five years of Urantia time.
33:6.8 Nebadon time, broadcast from Salvington, is the standard for all constellations and systems in this local universe. Each constellation conducts its affairs by Nebadon time, but the systems maintain their own chronology, as do the individual planets.
33:6.9 The day in Satania, as reckoned on Jerusem, is a little less (1 hour, 4 minutes, 15 seconds) than three days of Urantia time. These times are generally known as Salvington or universe time, and Satania or system time. Standard time is universe time.
Local Universe The standard day = 18 days and 6 hrs of Urantia time. Plus, two ½ minutes
Local Universe The standard year = 100 standard days = 5 Urantia Years

We'll close here for tonight. Next time, we'll pick up at section 23.3.5 and continue our exploration of these remarkable beings. I hope this has given you a deeper appreciation for the intricate organization of universe communication and administration. These aren't abstract concepts, they're the practical realities that make cosmic governance possible.

Before we part, I want to thank you for your patience as we work through this material. I know some of these concepts stretch our understanding to the breaking point. That's okay. We're not meant to fully grasp everything immediately. We're planting seeds of understanding that will grow throughout our ascension careers. Each time we revisit these teachings, we'll find new depths of meaning.

May we all approach this revelation with the patience it deserves, recognizing that we're being given glimpses of a reality far vaster and more beautiful than we can currently comprehend. And may we share what we learn with others in whatever way serves their journey.

Until next time, may you find peace in knowing that the universe is not only vast but also intimately personal, administered by beings who care deeply about every ascending mortal's journey toward Paradise.

Chapter 16: Solitary Messengers - The Swift Servants of the Infinite Spirit

Introduction

Before we dive deeper into the remarkable beings known as Solitary Messengers, I need to make a correction from our previous discussion. Last week, when we were talking about the mansion worlds, I mentioned that it takes three periods to reach the mansion world after death, that part was correct. However, I also said it takes eighteen days, and that's wrong. I want to clarify this because I've confused these time calculations before, which is precisely why I created the Time Study chart on our website.

The confusion comes from mixing up two different time systems. You see, there's Local Universe Standard Time (Salvington time) and System Time (Satania time). The mansion worlds operate on Satania time, not local universe time. According to the time calculations, one day in Satania, as reckoned on Jerusem, the capital of the mansion worlds, is less than one hour, forty minutes, and fifteen seconds shorter than three days of Urantia time. This means it takes three Urantia days to make one day in Satania or one day in the mansion worlds.

So, when The Urantia Book tells us it takes three periods to get to the mansion world, we're talking about three Satania periods, not three Salvington periods. Three times three equals nine days of Urantia time, not eighteen. I had been thinking of Salvington time when I said eighteen days, but the mansion worlds don't use that system. It's an easy mistake to make, but an important one to correct.

Now, you might wonder whether this timing still allows for the preparation of the resurrection body. The answer is absolutely yes. These bodies are already prepared well before we die. The celestial administrators know the exact hour, moment, and time of our death ahead of time. The instant we die, it registers with the Universal Census. The moment you're born and the moment you die, both are recorded with the Universal Census. When that happens, they know you're coming.

Here's how it works: If you're on the third psychic circle when you die, your guardian angel comes immediately to pick your soul up and transports you directly to the first mansion world. If you haven't reached the third psychic circle, you sleep until a group resurrection occurs. Either way, there's no difference in your perception of time. If you wake up a thousand years later, it feels as if you died just a moment before.

How do we know if we're living on the third psychic circle? I believe most people who are reading The Urantia Book have probably reached this level. Why? Because you're actively searching for God the Father. That's a significant part of being on the third psychic circle, you realize this world is temporary and your new world is yet to come. You've already prepared yourself mentally and spiritually to move on to the mansion world. People who haven't done this aren't prepared, so they're awakened in group resurrections where they need training from the very beginning, in what you might call remedial classes.

If you want to explore this topic further, I recommend reading Paper 112 on personality, or you can watch our video on Paper 112. It explains all of this in greater detail. We'll eventually get to it again in future studies.

The Incomprehensible Speed of Solitary Messengers

With that correction made, let's return to where we left off last time: discussing the tremendous speed of Solitary Messengers, 841 billion, 621 million, 642,000 miles per second. Yes, you read that correctly: per second, not per hour. This incomprehensible velocity represents one of the most remarkable capabilities in all of universe administration.

The Urantia Book tells us plainly: "It is wholly beyond my ability to explain to the material type of mind how a spirit can be a real person and at the same time traverse space at such tremendous velocities. But these very Solitary Messengers actually come to and go from Urantia at these incomprehensible speeds."

Indeed, the entire economy of universal administration would be largely deprived of its personal element if this weren't a fact. Think about what this means for the functioning of the universe. Because of these tremendous speeds, the Solitary Messengers can perform tasks that would otherwise take unimaginably long periods of time. Without their ability to travel at such velocities, the personal, responsive nature of universe governance would be severely limited.

Let me give you a concrete example. The angel who brought Paper 23 to us, the very paper on Solitary Messengers, took a million years to carry a message from Uversa (the headquarters of our superuniverse) to the seven rings. That's traveling at this incredible speed of 841 billion miles per second. If it took him that long to make that journey, imagine how long it took to come from Uversa all the way out here to Urantia to help reveal The Urantia Book.

What does this tell us? It means the Ancients of Days and Christ Michael both planned this revelation millions of years before it came to fruition. I sometimes joke that we now know what Solitary Messengers do during these million-year journeys, they write the book! They certainly have plenty of time to do it. Of course, we should remember there are about twelve other beings who come with them, plus twelve midwayers already on the planet waiting to help. So, there are roughly twenty-four beings involved in bringing this revelation to our world.

Traversing the Grand Universe

Solitary Messengers obviously have no problem at all traversing from the seven superuniverses to Havona, passing through the quiet zone, and going straight to the central universe. But we need to keep in mind just how far that actually is. When we look at pictures and diagrams of the universe, when we see Havona and Paradise in the center, we sometimes forget that Paradise itself is larger than all the mass of all seven superuniverses plus the outer space levels combined. Paradise alone is larger than all of that. That's a staggering amount of space.

To keep the gravity balance properly maintained, the amount of space between Havona and the seven superuniverses must be a gap that's simply inconceivable to us. If it takes a Solitary Messenger traveling at 841 billion miles per second a million years to make certain journeys, you can begin to grasp the vast distances involved.

This also explains something fundamental about the universe's structure. Paradise sits at the center, ever-expanding because we're always getting more people ascending toward it, so they need more space. Our universe as a whole is expanding ever outward. This explains the entire design, the circle is the only shape you can expand infinitely without worrying about corners or right angles creating structural problems.

I've maintained for years, going back to my Origins of the Universe classes in 2013, that while we currently know of four outer space levels, there will probably eventually be seven outer space levels. God is always expanding. Why would He stop? He does everything in patterns of seven, so why would He stop at four? It makes sense that at some point in the remote future, there will be seven outer space levels. The expansion simply never stops.

Now, someone might point out that while the seven superuniverses and the outer space levels are expanding, the central universe itself is not. That's correct. Paradise is stationary, it never moves, doesn't rotate, doesn't do anything. Havona revolves around Paradise, but Havona itself is not expanding either. It consists of a fixed number of one billion planets that are transcendental in nature.

We sometimes forget that these planets are transcendental, not finite. Being transcendental, they transcend time and space. So even though Havona appears to occupy space, you can't really say it occupies space in the same way finite universes do, because it exists on a totally different dimension than the finite universes. Are we all still together? I haven't lost anybody, have I? I know it's hard to conceive of, but that's precisely why the revelators tell us in this section that it's beyond human comprehension to travel at these speeds, we simply don't have any reference point for this kind of reality.

Emergency Communication Across Space

Solitary Messengers serve another crucial function: they can act as emergency lines of communication throughout remote space regions, realms not yet embraced within the established circuits of the grand universe. Here's something fascinating: when functioning in this capacity, one Solitary Messenger can transmit a message or send an impulse through space to a fellow messenger about one hundred light-years away, as Urantia astronomers estimate stellar distances.

Why would this capability be necessary? Because not all places that Solitary Messengers travel to are necessarily within the established circuits of the grand universe. This is somewhat hard to understand and explain but let me try. Some of the circuits they travel on simply end at certain points, and they have to keep traveling beyond those endpoints.

For example, the circuits of the Infinite Spirit that extend out to the outer space levels only reach to certain boundaries. Solitary Messengers may be assigned as explorers beyond those boundaries, so they have to leave the circuits, travel into unexplored regions, and then return to the circuit to get back. They get their energy from being on these circuits, but they're intelligent enough to know their limits. As Clint Eastwood would say, "A man's got to know his limitations." They understand how long they can be away from the circuits before they need to return, because we know they become re-energized when they get close to one another or back on the circuits.

They are, in every sense, true astronauts, pioneer explorers of uncharted cosmic regions. And their ability to send messages to one another across a hundred light years means that if a messenger gets out to some remote location and needs assistance, help can be summoned from remarkable distances.

The Value of Timesaving Service

The revelators make a striking statement about Solitary Messengers: "Of the myriads of beings who cooperate with us in the conduct of the affairs of the superuniverse, none are more important in practical helpfulness and timesaving assistance."

In the universes of space, we must reckon with the handicaps of time. Hence the great service of the Solitary Messengers who, by means of their personal prerogatives of communication, are somewhat independent of space. And by virtue of their tremendous transit velocities, they're nearly independent of time as well. Because they move faster than the speed of light, multiple times faster, they've effectively transcended many of the limitations that other beings face.

Form, Personality, and Spiritual Presence

Here's something that puzzles even advanced celestial beings: "I am at a loss to explain to Urantia mortals how the Solitary Messengers can be without form and yet possess real and definite personalities."

Although they lack any form that would naturally be associated with personality, they do possess a spirit presence that's discernible by all higher types of spirit beings. Solitary Messengers are the only class of beings who seem to be possessed of nearly all the advantages of a formless spirit coupled with all the prerogatives of a full-fledged personality. They are truly persons yet endowed with nearly all the attributes of impersonal spirit manifestation.

You could almost call them the ultimate ghosts, you can't see their body at any level accessible to mortals. But here's what's important to understand: when we become full-fledged spirits ourselves, we'll be able to see them. Does this make things a bit clearer? As spirit beings, we'll exist at a higher level of reality ourselves, so we'll be able to perceive their forms or their essence far better than we can as human beings. Right now, as humans, we can't see them at all. We can't even sense them. But as spirit beings, we'll not only be able to sense and see them, but we'll be also able to communicate directly with them.

The Exception to Universal Law

In the seven superuniverses, there's a general principle: everything that tends to increase any creature's liberation from the handicaps of time and space proportionally diminishes personality prerogatives. It's almost a law of inverse proportionality, the more freedom from time and space you gain, the less personal autonomy you typically retain.

Solitary Messengers are a remarkable exception to this general law. They are, in their activities, almost completely unrestricted in the utilization of any and all of the limitless avenues of spiritual expression, divine service, personal ministry, and cosmic communication. If we could view these extraordinary beings in light of the full experience of universe administration, we would understand how difficult it would be to coordinate superuniverse affairs without their versatile cooperation.

This might explain why they were created first of all the beings brought into existence by the Infinite Spirit. They're so essential that we could almost not function without them. The universe administration depends on them in ways that are difficult to overstate.

A Fixed Number Serving an Expanding Universe

Here's an intriguing fact: no matter how much the universe may enlarge, no more Solitary Messengers will probably ever be created. Their number appears to be fixed. As the universes grow, the expanded work of administration must increasingly be borne by other types of spirit ministers and by those beings who take origin in these new creations, such as the creatures of the Sovereign Sons and the local universe Mother Spirits.

What this tells us is profound: as we grow and become more spiritual, we'll have to take up some of the work that Solitary Messengers currently do. We're being prepared to serve in ever-expanding capacities.

Special Ministry: Coordinators of Spiritual Personalities

Solitary Messengers seem to serve as personality coordinators for all types of spirit beings. Their ministry helps make all the personalities of the far-flung spiritual world akin to one another. They contribute significantly to the development in all spirit beings of a consciousness of group identity.

Every type of spirit being is served by special groups of Solitary Messengers who foster the ability of such beings to understand and fraternize with all other types and orders, however dissimilar they may be.

Did you catch that? Solitary Messengers are the beings who will help us understand and work in groups with many types of beings we're not only unfamiliar with, but that we probably don't even have the capacity to understand right now. They'll help us work cooperatively with these beings and help us understand their nature and perspective. This will come in especially handy on the mansion worlds and later in Uversa, where we'll encounter an astonishing diversity of personality types.

The Solitary Messengers demonstrate such an amazing ability to coordinate all types and orders of finite personality, they can even make contact with the absonite regime of the master universe over controllers. This has led some to theorize that the creation of these messengers by the Infinite Spirit is somehow related to the Conjoint Actor's bestowal of Supreme-Ultimate Mind.

We know that absonite beings are part of not only the central universe but also the outer space levels. The connection becomes clearer when we remember that the Supreme-Ultimate Mind has to do with the outer space levels. That's how this relationship comes together.

Guardians of Trinitized Sons of Destiny

Here we come to one of the most mysterious aspects of Solitary Messenger service. When a finaliter and a Paradise citizen cooperate in the trinitization of a time-space child, a transaction involving the unrevealed mind potentials of the Supreme-Ultimate, something remarkable occurs. When such an unclassified personality is dispatched to Vicegerington, a Solitary Messenger is always assigned as guardian-companion to such a creature-trinitized son.

Let me break this down. In Havona, when a Paradise citizen or one of the beings from Havona trinitizes with a mortal finaliter, the trinitization process creates a new being. This being possesses the mind potentials of the Supreme and Ultimate. Why? Because you have a combination of a Paradise citizen or Havoner, who exists at transcendental levels, with an experiential finaliter. The resulting being is created ready for service in the outer space levels.

This isn't because they're merely experiential; it's because they're trinitized. They're transcendental. Since they're transcendental, they have the mind potentials of the Supreme and Ultimate. They're no longer finite, even though the finite part contributed to their creation. They've crossed over to the transcendental realm, so they become associated with the Supreme-Ultimate. They get assigned a Solitary Messenger, and then they fall under the supervision of the Architects of the Master Universe, because the Architects are the ones who oversee the outer space levels.

When ready for assignment beyond Vicegerington, they'll be sent to the outer space levels. And here's the remarkable part: not only the new trinitized being, but also the assigned Solitary Messenger, both go to Vicegerington together. And they never leave. They remain there, preparing for some future destiny we can barely imagine.

These aren't like the trinitized sons created by finaliters who come back to the local universe to serve the Ancients of Days. This is a different category entirely. These are trinitized beings from the pairing of a Paradise citizen and a finaliter, or a Havoner and a finaliter. They immediately go to Vicegerington and stay there. They're paired up with a Solitary Messenger, and together they wait for whatever the future holds.

The Exhaustion of Solitary Messengers

Here's where the mystery deepens. Solitary Messengers exist in stationary numbers, they're not being created anymore. But the trinitization of sons of destiny appears to be an unlimited technique. Since each trinitized son of destiny has a Solitary Messenger assigned to him, it appears that at some time in the remote future, the supply of messengers will become exhausted.

This raises profound questions that even celestial administrators can't answer: Who will take up their work in the grand universe when they're all assigned? Will their service be assumed by some new development among the Inspired Trinity Spirits? Is the grand universe at some remote period going to be administered more by Trinity-origin beings while single and dual-origin creatures move on into the realms of outer space?

If the messengers eventually return to their former service, will these sons of destiny accompany them? Will the trinitizations between finaliters and Paradise-Havoners cease when the supply of Solitary Messengers has been absorbed as guardian-companions of these sons of destiny? Are all of our efficient Solitary Messengers going to be concentrated on Vicegerington? Are these extraordinary spirit personalities going to be eternally associated with these trinitized sons of unrevealed destiny?

What significance should we attach to the fact that these pairs gathering on Vicegerington are under the exclusive direction of those mighty mystery beings, the Architects of the Master Universe?

The revelators ask these and many similar questions, but they don't know the answers. We don't need to know them right now either, that's the point. But what we do understand is that Solitary Messengers will eventually be exhausted in numbers because of this trinitization process involving ascending mortals and Paradise citizens or Havoners. When that happens, nobody really knows what will come next. The celestial administrators project that this is way, way off into the future, unimaginably distant. But they acknowledge all these questions remain unanswered, and so they can't tell us what will happen. It's one of the genuine mysteries of the universe.

Vast Reorganization in Progress

What the revelators can tell us with certainty is this: "This transaction, together with many similar occurrences in universe administration, unmistakably indicates that the personnel of the grand universe, even that of Havona and Paradise, is undergoing a definite and certain reorganization in coordination with and with reference to the vast energy evolutions now taking place throughout the realms of outer space."

The only thing they know for sure is that everything is being reorganized, the entire universe is being prepared for something. However it all works out, it will work out according to divine plan, but even celestial beings don't know the exact details. They're teaching us as much as they can while acknowledging the limits of their own understanding.

Looking Toward the Eternal Future with Keen Relish

The paper on Solitary Messengers concludes with words that capture both the mystery and the excitement of our cosmic future:

"We are inclined to the belief that the eternal future will witness phenomena of universe evolution which will far transcend all that the eternal past has experienced. And we anticipate such tremendous adventures, even as you should, with keen relish and ever-heightening expectation."

Think about this for a moment. We've gone through tremendous evolution on this planet since human life began, haven't we? That's just a small taste of how the universe is going to evolve over the coming ages, evolution that will transcend everything experienced in the past. What's actually going to happen, nobody really knows, not even these advanced celestial beings who are sharing this revelation with us.

That last sentence tells us everything about why they've given us all this information. They don't fully have all the answers, and our brains don't even resemble a tiny fraction of theirs. But they want us to anticipate the future "with keen relish and ever-heightening expectation." They want to prepare us for the adventure ahead, and they want to prepare us with what they do know so that as we grow and journey toward Paradise, we can continuously expand our consciousness. We never stop learning. They want us to keep the enthusiasm burning.

That's what it's all about, maintaining that sense of wonder, that eagerness to grow, that excitement about what's to come. The adventure has only just begun.

This paper on Solitary Messengers was presented by a Divine Counselor from Uversa, acting by the authority of the Ancients of Days on Uversa.

Closing Reflection

As we conclude this study of Solitary Messengers, I find myself both humbled and energized by what we've learned. These beings, formless yet personal, swift beyond comprehension yet ever-present where needed, represent just one category among the vast hierarchy of celestial personalities serving the infinite purposes of God.

In our next chapter, we'll explore the Higher Personalities of the Infinite Spirit, including the various orders of angels and other ministering spirits who touch our lives more directly than we often realize. We'll discover how these beings work together in coordinated service, each order contributing its unique gifts to the spiritual upliftment of time-and-space mortals like ourselves.

Until then, may we all approach our daily lives with that same spirit the Divine Counselor commended to us: with keen relish and ever-heightening expectation for the adventures that await us, both in this life and in the ages to come.

Chapter 17: Higher Personalities of the Infinite Spirit - The Celestial Infrastructure

Introduction

As we move into Paper 24 of The Urantia Book, we encounter a fascinating category of celestial beings that forms the administrative backbone of the universe.

On Uversa, the headquarters of our superuniverse, all personalities and entities of the Conjoint Creator, the Infinite Spirit, are divided into three grand divisions: the higher personalities of the Infinite Spirit, the messenger hosts of space, and the ministering spirits of time. These spirit beings concern themselves with teaching and ministering to the will creatures of the ascendant scheme of mortal progression. In simpler terms, they're all devoted to helping us on our journey to Paradise .

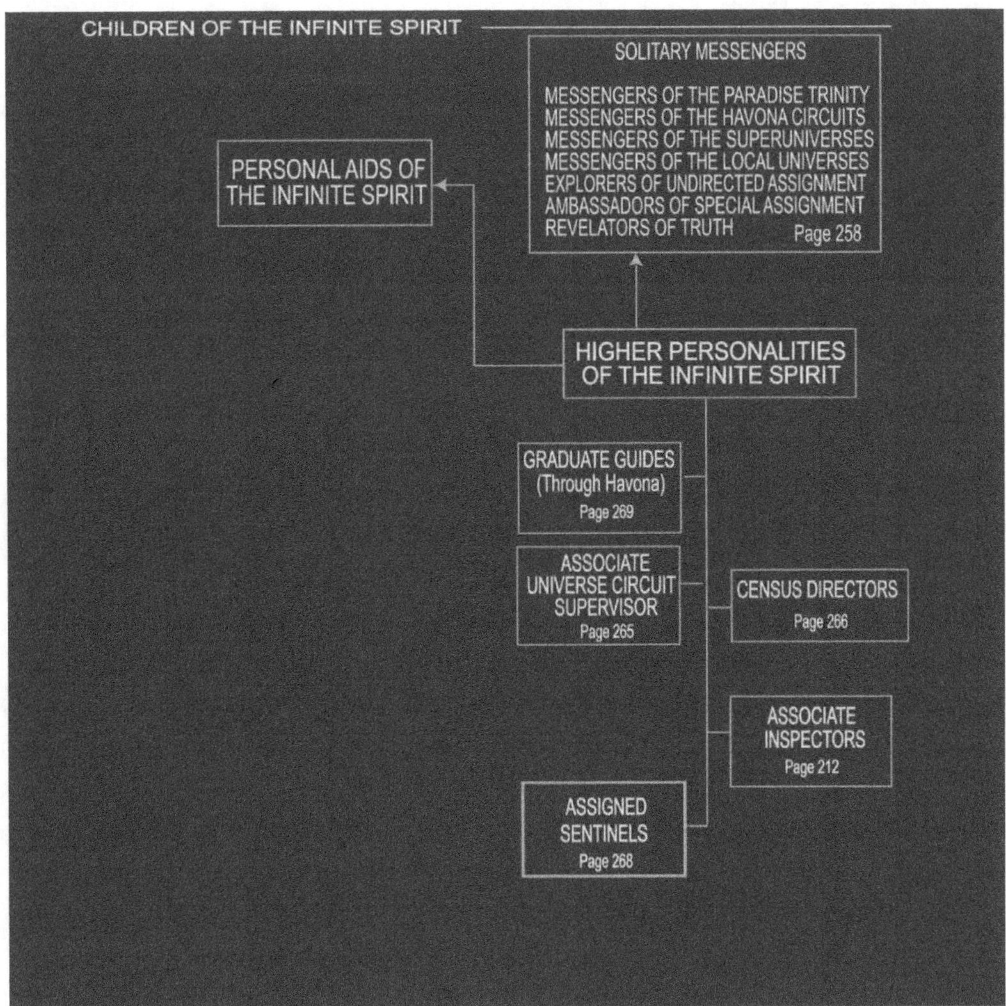

Tonight, we'll focus on the first category: the higher personalities of the Infinite Spirit. In future studies, we'll explore the messenger hosts of space and the ministering spirits of time. But for now, we need to understand these remarkable beings who form what I think of as the celestial infrastructure, the essential framework that makes universe administration possible.

These higher personalities function throughout the grand universe in seven distinct divisions:

1 The Solitary Messengers (which we studied in the previous chapter):

2 The Universe Circuit Supervisors

3 The Census Directors

4 The Personal Aides of the Infinite Spirit

5 The Associate Inspectors

6 The Assigned Sentinels

7 The Graduate Guides.

By the time we finish this study, you'll understand what each of these orders does and why they matter so much to our own spiritual journey.

The Organizational Framework

Before we examine each order individually, let's get the big picture. There's also a Reserve Corps, along with Census Directors stationed on the Paradise worlds of the Spirit. Then we have seven Census Directors in Havona itself, one on each of the first worlds of the seven rings of Havona. Beyond that, there are seven Census Directors for the superuniverses (one for each superuniverse), and countless local Census Directors spread throughout the local universes, one for each local universe.

What strikes me about this organizational structure is its completeness. Nothing is left to chance. Every level of universe administration has the personnel it needs to function properly. The Graduate Guides work exclusively in Havona, helping us navigate all billion worlds and preparing us to meet God the Father, God the Son, God the Spirit, and the Supreme Being. Meanwhile, other orders maintain stations throughout the local universes, though they're not organically attached to the administrations of the evolutionary realms.

This last point is important. Because they're not locked into local administration, these beings remain free to carry out their assignments without getting entangled in local politics or procedures. They answer to higher authority, maintaining a kind of independence that allows them to serve the broader needs of the universe. Yet they all have a clear chain of command, a pecking order that ensures coordination and efficiency.

The Mystery of Personal Aides

The Solitary Messengers, Universe Circuit Supervisors, Census Directors, and Personal Aides all possess tremendous endowments of anti-gravity. The Solitary Messengers, as we learned in the previous chapter, have no general headquarters, they roam the entire universe of universes. The Universe Circuit Supervisors and Census Directors maintain headquarters on the capitals of the superuniverses. But the Personal Aides of the Infinite Spirit occupy a special category. They're stationed on the central Isle of Light, Paradise itself.

Here's where things get interesting. Of the seven classes we're discussing, only the Solitary Messengers and perhaps the Personal Aides range throughout the universe of universes. Notice that qualifier: "perhaps." The revelators aren't entirely certain about the Personal Aides. Why such uncertainty about beings who presumably should be well-known?

The answer tells us something profound about the hierarchy of spiritual reality. The Personal Aides exist at such an elevated level that most beings, even other spiritual beings, don't know when they were created. We know that the first class of beings created by the Infinite Spirit was the Solitary Messengers. But the Personal Aides? Their origin remains shrouded in mystery because they're of such a high order that they don't have physical bodies. Most spiritual beings can't even see them. You have to sense their presence, much like you would sense a Solitary Messenger, but the Personal Aides operate on an even higher scale.

So, if you're keeping track, there are at least two groups of beings we'll probably never see in any conventional sense: Solitary Messengers and Personal Aides of the Infinite Spirit. However, there's a caveat here. Some believe the Personal Aides may eventually become Graduate Guides. If that's true, then we would be able to see them at that stage, because the Graduate Guides interact directly with ascending mortals in Havona. When you look at artistic representations of Personal

Aides, they appear as wisps or lines, visual metaphors for beings without physical form.

Understanding the Universe Circuit Supervisors

Now we come to one of the most crucial orders for understanding how the universe actually functions: the Universe Circuit Supervisors. The vast power currents of space and the circuits of spirit energy may seem to operate automatically, functioning without hindrance. But that's not the case at all. All these stupendous systems of energy are under intelligent supervision and control.

Let me be clear about what the Circuit Supervisors do and don't do. They're not concerned with purely physical or material energy, that's the domain of the Universe Power Directors. Instead, they handle the circuits of relative spiritual energy and those modified circuits essential to maintaining both highly developed spiritual beings and morontia or transition-type intelligent creatures. They don't originate circuits of energy or the super essence of divinity, but they do manage all the higher spirit circuits of time and eternity, along with all relative spirit circuits involved in administering the component parts of the grand universe. They direct and manipulate all such spirit energy circuits outside the Isle of Paradise.

Do you remember when we talked about the Universe Power Directors? They work closely with the Seven Master Spirits. The Seven Master Spirits control the power centers that provide power to all seven superuniverses. Everything physical, from the finest atom to the largest universe, depends on the Universe Power Directors for its continued existence.

But there's a completely separate system called the Universe Circuit Supervisors. What do they manage? All the circuits emanating from Paradise and the Seven Master Spirits, that carry spiritual energy. The spiritual circuit reaches all spiritual beings, and that includes morontia-type beings as well.

Here's how this affects us directly. Right now, as human beings, we're entirely physical. We fall under the jurisdiction of the Universe Power Directors. But when we die and awaken in our morontia form on the mansion worlds, we'll come under the authority of the Universe Circuit Supervisors, because their domain encompasses both morontia and spiritual realities.

Think of the spirit circuit this way: spiritual beings can actually travel along it. When a spiritual being moves from one universe to another, from one planet to another, they travel along this circuit of the spirit itself. I've used this analogy before, but it's worth repeating. Imagine the wiring diagram for a house. The Universe Circuit Supervisors function like the main breaker box where all the circuits originate. They control all those switches that distribute power to different parts of the house. The lines running to all the outlets and fixtures represent the circuits themselves.

Someone once suggested that the breaker box should represent the Universe Power Directors instead. You could think of it that way, two separate circuits, two separate boxes. The Power Directors might be the minor circuit box, while the Circuit Supervisors represent the main breaker box at a higher level. Or you could view the Universe Circuit Supervisors as the substation outside the house and the Universe Power Directors as the load center inside. Either analogy works, but here's the key point: the spiritual circuit operates at a higher level than the material circuit. Spiritual reality is more real than material reality. The spiritual will always take precedence over the material.

This matters enormously because the Universe Circuit Supervisors control the movement of all beings, both morontial and spiritual, throughout the universe. When your guardian angel picks your soul up at death and transports you to the mansion worlds, what are you traveling on? The spiritual circuit. They don't just fly randomly through space. If they did, there would be constant collisions. The Circuit Supervisors act as traffic controllers, ensuring that everyone using the circuits stays on the right path, moving in the right direction.

Now, the Circuit Supervisors don't give origin to circuits of energy, that's still the domain of the Power Directors. And they have nothing to do with what's called the "super essence of divinity." What does that mean? It means these Circuit Supervisors have no involvement whatsoever with the Father's Paradise personality circuit. That's outside their purview, beyond their job description. It's a separate circuit entirely. They only manage the spiritual circuits.

But we have one more circuit to consider: the mind circuit. The mind circuit is also controlled by the Infinite Spirit, operating through the Seven Master Spirits. The cosmic mind of the universe probably travels through the Seven Master Spirits out to the seven superuniverses. The revelators say nothing about mind circuits in this section, which suggests the Circuit Supervisors may not be involved with those either.

The Spiritual Circuit and Planetary Rebellion

Jane raised an excellent point during one of our study sessions. The Universe Circuit Supervisors don't just facilitate motion, they also control what flows through the spiritual circuit. And what else comes through the spiritual circuit? The Spirit of Truth. When you think about it, all information broadcasts, everything related to spiritual life, passes through these Circuit Supervisors.

This brings us to a sobering reality. Who do you think was involved when our world went into rebellion? Thirty-seven planets joined Lucifer's rebellion, and we were cut off from everyone else. We were quarantined. The Tertiary Circuit Supervisors, are the ones who cut us off.

Even though Christ Michael has resolved the rebellion by proving his sovereignty, it's up to the Circuit Supervisors to determine when the circuits will be restored. We won't receive the broadcasts of glory from Havona, from the superuniverse, from the local universe, none of these will reach our planet until the circuits are reopened. What has to happen first? The rebellion must be completely adjudicated according to their standards.

Why such strictness? As long as rebellion persists on thirty-seven planets, as long as rebellious beings occupy those worlds, they don't want the rebellion spreading any further. There won't be any communication beyond these thirty-seven quarantined planets until the rebellion is fully adjudicated and all beings who rebelled have either been judged or destroyed.

So, we have to wait until Caligastia is judged? Yes, exactly. Do I think those circuits will be restored in our lifetime? No, probably not. We're likely looking at thousands, perhaps millions of years yet.

Now we can better understand how the Circuit Supervisors function. They operate throughout the grand universe, manipulating all spiritual energy circuits outside the Isle of Paradise. Why outside Paradise? Does Paradise need these spiritual circuits? No. Paradise already exists in perfection. They don't need circuit management there.

Rodney raised an interesting question: once the outer space levels are populated with life, will the circuits extend there? The text specifically mentions the grand universe, not the master universe, which might suggest limitations. But here's the puzzle: if Solitary Messengers venture into outer space, and they travel along spiritual circuits, what happens when they reach the end of the seven superuniverses? Are they on their own, or do circuits already exist out there that they can follow to some extent?

We don't know. The revelators don't tell us, and apparently they don't know either. It's on a need-to-know basis. As far as what lies beyond the seven superuniverses, all bets are off.

The Four Orders of Circuit Supervisors

Universe Circuit Supervisors are the exclusive creation of the Infinite Spirit, functioning solely as agents of the Conjoint Actor. They're personalized for service in four distinct orders: Supreme Circuit Supervisors, Associate Circuit Supervisors, Secondary Circuit Supervisors, and Tertiary Circuit Supervisors. There's a specific reason for this fourfold division, and it relates to the different levels of universe administration.

The Supreme Supervisors of Havona and the Associate Supervisors of the seven superuniverses exist in completed numbers. No more of these orders are being created. The Supreme Supervisors number exactly seven, and they're stationed on the pilot worlds of the seven Havona circuits. The circuits of the seven superuniverses fall under the charge of seven Associate Supervisors who maintain headquarters on the seven Paradise spheres of the Infinite Spirit, the worlds of the Seven Supreme Executives. From these headquarters, they supervise and direct the circuits of the superuniverses of space.

Let me clarify what "pilot worlds" means, since Millie asked about this during our study. The pilot worlds are the very first worlds you land on when you enter a particular circuit or ring in Havona. When you finish visiting all the planets in the seventh circuit (the outermost circuit), the very next planet you'll stop on is the pilot world of the sixth circuit. After you complete all the worlds of the sixth circuit, you arrive at the pilot world of circuit five. So, the first world you encounter in each circuit is called a pilot world.

The Supreme Circuit Supervisors handle Havona. The Associate Circuit Supervisors manage the seven superuniverses, working under the Seven Supreme Executives, who in turn serve under the Seven Master Spirits. We still have two more orders to discuss: the Secondary and Tertiary Circuit Supervisors.

On the headquarters worlds of each superuniverse, Secondary Supervisors serve the local universes of time and space. The major and minor sectors are administrative divisions of the super governments, but they're not involved in matters of spirit energy supervision. I don't know exactly how many Secondary Circuit Supervisors exist in the grand universe, but on Uversa alone there are 84,691 of these beings. Secondary Supervisors are continuously being created, appearing in groups of seventy on the worlds of the Supreme Executives. They're obtained on requisition as arrangements are made for establishing separate circuits of spirit energy and liaison power to newly evolving universes.

Notice that they don't concern themselves with the major and minor sectors. That responsibility falls to the Associate Circuit Supervisors at the superuniverse level. The Secondary Circuit Supervisors focus on local universes. There's at least one for every local universe, and these numbers keep changing because local universes are constantly coming online. As new universes are created, new Secondary Circuit Supervisors are needed. They're requisitioned from the Ancients of Days on Uversa and dispatched by the Supreme Executives.

Finally, we have the Tertiary Circuit Supervisors, who function on the headquarters worlds of every local universe. Like the Secondary Supervisors, they're continuously created in groups of seven hundred and assigned to local universes by the Ancients of Days. So, the Secondary Supervisors connect to local universes through the major and minor sectors from the superuniverses, while the Tertiary Supervisors are actually stationed,one on each headquarters world of every local universe.

All four types serve the same ultimate purpose: maintaining the circuits, specifically the spiritual circuits for morontia and spiritual beings.

Permanent Assignment and Professional Dedication

Circuit Supervisors are created for specific tasks, and they eternally serve in the groups of their original assignment. They're never rotated in service, which allows them to make an age-long study of the problems found in their assigned realms. For example, Tertiary Circuit Supervisor number 572,842 has functioned on Salvington since the early concept of our local universe, (this is probably the one who put us in quarantine) and he serves as a member of Christ Michael's personal staff.

Think about what this means. Once assigned, they never leave. This particular supervisor was assigned to Salvington even before our local universe fully materialized, during the conceptual phase. When the idea of our local universe first took shape with Michael, he already had a Circuit Supervisor assigned to him. Michael needed a way to travel along the circuits as a spirit being, moving to and from wherever his mission required. The Circuit Supervisor for our local universe was in place before the universe itself existed in its current form.

Whether operating in local universes or higher administrative centers, Circuit Supervisors direct all concerned parties regarding the proper circuits to use for transmitting spirit messages and transporting personalities. In their work of circuit supervision, these efficient beings utilize all agencies, forces, and personalities throughout the universe of universes. They employ unrevealed spirit personalities of circuit control and receive able assistance from numerous staffs composed of personalities of the Infinite Spirit.

Here's a sobering reality: it's the Circuit Supervisors who would isolate an evolutionary world if its Planetary Prince rebelled against the Universal Father and his vicegerent Son. They can throw any world out of certain universe circuits of the higher spiritual order, but they cannot annul the material currents of the Power Directors.

They can disconnect us from spiritual circuits, but they cannot interfere with the Power Directors. Why? Because if the Power Directors were stopped, we'd all die. The physical universe would collapse. Everything would descend into chaos. That's why they can't touch that system.

However, they do possess the authority to cut off spiritual circuits the moment a Planetary Prince enters rebellion. That's exactly what happened to the thirty-seven planets involved in Lucifer's rebellion. As soon as Lucifer rebelled and the Planetary Princes allied with him, we were severed from the spiritual circuits. Then everyone regresses. We go backward, and it takes an enormously long time to recover.

Notice the text refers to a Planetary Prince rebelling "against the Universal Father and his vicegerent Son." Who's the vicegerent Son? That was Jesus before he earned his own sovereignty. At that point in universe history, he served as the vicegerent of the Father. Can this type of rebellion still happen now that Michael has achieved full sovereignty over his local universe? No, not anymore. He's no longer the vicegerent of the Father. He is, for all practical purposes, God within his local universe. He could summarily stop any rebellion with immediate judgment. But he chooses to allow the Ancients of Days to follow the established judicial process, because that's how it's always been done.

Mind Circuits and Personality Authority

The Circuit Supervisors exercise certain oversight of mind circuits that are spirit-associated, much as the Power Directors have jurisdiction over phases of mind connected to physical energy, what we might call mechanical mind. In general, the functions of each order expand through liaison with the other, but the circuits of pure mind are subject to the supervision of neither. The two orders aren't coordinate in this respect. In all their varied labors, the Universe Circuit Supervisors remain subject to the Seven Supreme Power Directors and their subordinates.

The mind circuits operate on an entirely different principle. The mind circuit runs through the cosmic mind, but there's also a physical energy component associated with mechanical mind, and that's us. There's actually a physical aspect of our mind that connects to the mind of the cosmos itself, working through the Seven Adjutant Mind-Spirits and related mechanisms. This falls outside the direct jurisdiction of the Circuit Supervisors. The Infinite Spirit and the Local Universe Mother Spirits oversee that domain. Yet they all ultimately answer to the Seven Supreme Power Directors, because mind has this mechanical component.

While Circuit Supervisors are entirely alike within their respective orders, they're all distinct individuals. They're truly personal beings, but they possess a type of personality that's not Father-endowed, something not encountered in any other type of creature throughout all universe existence. Our personalities come from the Father. But who bestowed personality on the Circuit Supervisors? The Infinite Spirit. This represents one of the rare exceptions where the Infinite Spirit directly conferred personality.

Professional Distance and Future Encounters

As we journey inward toward Paradise, we'll recognize and know the Circuit Supervisors. But we won't have personal relations with them. They're Circuit Supervisors, and they attend strictly and efficiently to their business. They deal solely with those personalities and entities having oversight of activities concerned with the circuits under their supervision.

These beings maintain an almost austere professionalism. They don't interact with ascending mortals making their way to Paradise. We won't stop to visit with them or engage in conversation. They're very strict about maintaining their focus, doing nothing but their assigned work. We might encounter one, we might even be aware of their presence, but we won't enter into any meaningful interaction with them. They work constantly, never deviating from their responsibilities.

Next time, we'll explore the Census Directors, the beings who keep track of us, whether we're alive or dead or anywhere in between. Just like the census here on earth but operating on a cosmic scale with perfect accuracy.

Closing Reflection

As we conclude this exploration of the Universe Circuit Supervisors and their associated orders, I'm struck by the meticulous organization underlying all universe administration. Nothing is random. Nothing is left to chance. Every function has its designated personnel, every responsibility its appointed overseer.

The spiritual circuits connecting all morontia and spiritual beings throughout the grand universe don't simply exist, they're actively managed by intelligent, dedicated beings who've specialized in this work for ages. The isolation of rebellious worlds isn't arbitrary, it's a carefully considered decision made by beings who understand the danger of allowing rebellion to spread unchecked.

What we've learned tonight should give us confidence in the larger cosmic order. Even when we can't see these beings, even when we're unaware of their constant work, they're maintaining the infrastructure that will carry us forward on our journey to Paradise. The circuits are ready. The pathways are clear. The traffic controllers are at their posts.

In our next chapter, we'll meet the Census Directors and explore how the universe keeps track of every personality, every being, throughout all of creation. We'll discover that nothing and no one is ever lost or forgotten in the vast administrative machinery of the grand universe.

Chapter 18: The Census Directors and Personal Aids of the Infinite Spirit

When I first encountered the concept of Census Directors in *The Urantia Book*, I'll admit I found it almost comical, the idea that the universe needs celestial accountants. But as we studied Paper 24 together, something profound began to emerge. These beings represent something far more significant than mere record-keeping. They embody the precision, care, and intimate awareness that permeates every level of creation.

Tonight, as we continue our exploration of the higher personalities of the Infinite Spirit, I want us to consider what it means that every single will creature in the grand universe, from the moment of our first willful act to our last, is known, counted, and valued. There's something deeply reassuring in that, though it may also feel a bit unsettling. You can't really get away with anything, can you?

The Cosmic Mind and Universal Awareness

The text tells us something remarkable: "Notwithstanding that the cosmic mind of the Universal Intelligence is cognizant of the presence and whereabouts of all thinking creatures, there is operative in the universe of universes an independent method of keeping count of all will creatures."

That Universal Intelligence is the Infinite Spirit himself. He already knows where every sentient being is, knows about every thought of all thinking creatures. Yet there exists this separate, independent system for maintaining an exact census. Why? It appears that even in a universe where God knows all things, there's still a need for systematic organization and precise accounting at various administrative levels.

Here's where it gets interesting, the text specifically says "will creatures." During our study group discussions, we've debated what that means. Millie pointed out that this designation refers only to human beings and similar beings with genuine volitional capacity, not animals. That's the province of the local universe Mother Spirit. The distinction matters because it highlights what makes us truly significant in the cosmic order: our ability to make genuine moral choices.

The Nature and Function of Census Directors

The Census Directors themselves are fascinating beings. Created by the Infinite Spirit as a special and completed order, they exist in numbers unknown to us. They possess an unusual dual capacity, they maintain perfect synchrony with the reflectivity technique of the superuniverses while remaining personally sensitive and responsive to intelligent will.

Through some technique that even the revelators don't fully understand, these directors become immediately aware of the birth of will anywhere in the grand universe. Think about that for a moment. The instant a baby makes its first truly willful decision, whatever that might be, and nobody seems entirely certain when that occurs, a Census Director knows. Is it the first breath? The first cry? The first time those tiny eyes focus with intention. We discussed this at length in our study group, and the honest answer is we don't know.

What we do know is that Census Directors are competent to provide the number, nature, and whereabouts of all will creatures in any part of the central creation and the seven superuniverses. But, and this is crucial, they don't function on Paradise. There's no need for them there. On Paradise, knowledge is inherent. The Deities know all things automatically.

This tells us something important about the nature of Paradise versus the rest of creation. Paradise embodies absolute perfection where knowledge simply *is*. But step outside Paradise, even into the perfect but not-absolute realm of Havona, and you need these specialized beings to maintain order and awareness.

The Organizational Structure

When we look at how Census Directors are organized, a clear pattern emerges. There are seven Census Directors in Havona, one stationed on the pilot world of each of the seven circuits. Why only seven? Because there's one for each pilot world, and their function involves tracking the progression of ascending beings as they move through different spirit stages.

When you transition from a fourth-stage spirit being to a fifth-stage spirit in Havona, that changes the count. Someone has to keep track of which category you're in. That's what these Census Directors do, they're essentially totalizers for different groups and stages of spiritual development.

Then we have seven superuniverse Census Directors, one presiding at the headquarters of each superuniverse. Subject to each chief director are thousands upon thousands of subordinates, one on the capital of every local universe. In our superuniverse of Orvonton alone, there are one hundred thousand Census Directors, one for each local universe. These beings are all equal, except for those stationed on the Havona pilot worlds and the seven superuniverse chiefs.

The chief of our Orvonton Census Directors is named Usatia, and he's fundamentally different from his subordinates. While the local universe Census Directors directly sense when every will creature is born, dies, or transitions to a different type of being, Usatia doesn't have that immediate perception. He's what the text calls a "totalizing personality", he receives reports from all the local universe directors and synthesizes them.

I think of it this way: the local universe Census Directors are like sensors, constantly aware of every change in their jurisdictions. Usatia is like the master computer that takes all those inputs and creates the comprehensive picture. If you've seen the movie *Rain Man*, there's something of that quality to Usatia, an almost savant-like capacity for instant calculation and totalization.

The Staggering Scale of Their Work

Let's try to grasp the scope of what these beings do. In Orvonton, we have one hundred thousand local universes. Each local universe has a Census Director who must track every single being, living, dying, and being born. These are, as someone in our group said, "busy little bees."

Consider just our own world. Thousands of people die every moment. Thousands of babies are born every second. Now multiply that by all the inhabited worlds in our local system, then by all the local systems in our local universe, then by all the local universes in our superuniverse. The mathematical complexity is staggering.

And here's something that challenges our earthly perception of time: what seems long to us is incredibly brief from a cosmic perspective. Jesus spoke of the "twinkling of an eye," and that's exactly what our entire mortal existence amounts to in universal terms. If thousands are dying in what we perceive as a moment, from the Census Directors' frame of reference, it's an even shorter instant, a hundred thousand beings transitioning in what amounts to a cosmic blink.

These must be minds of almost inconceivable mathematical capacity, constantly adding and subtracting beings, tracking transitions, maintaining perfect accuracy across billions upon billions of individuals.

The Precision of Will Recognition

The text tells us something quite specific: "Census Directors register the existence of a new will creature when the first act of will is performed. They indicate the death of a will creature when the last act of will takes place."

We struggled with this concept in our study sessions. When exactly is that first real act of will? I suggested that when a baby cries for the first time, there's a decision that involved, the infant is upset about something and chooses to express that distress. That seems like a willful act to me. Babies can smile, coo, and respond from the very beginning. Who's to say that's not the will of a baby working?

But others in the group drew a distinction between will and moral choice. The Thought Adjuster, that fragment of God that indwells each of us, doesn't arrive until a person makes their first true moral decision. That's different from simple will. A child can exercise will for years before making that first genuinely moral choice.

Similarly, what constitutes the last act of will? Is it the final breath? The last conscious thought? The text admits that "exactly how they register the function of will, we do not know." There's an appropriate humility in that admission. Some mysteries remain, even for those far advanced beyond us.

One thing seems clear though: breathing itself isn't a willful act, it's automatic, controlled by the autonomic nervous system. But you do have to have a will to live for that automatic system to function properly. It's a subtle but important distinction.

The Character of Census Directors

What strikes me most about these beings is their absolute reliability. The text states it plainly: "These beings always have been and always will be Census Directors. They would be comparatively useless in any other division of universe labor, but they are infallible in function. They never default, neither do they falsify."

Someone in our group joked, "Couldn't work in our government." It's funny, but it points to something profound. These beings embody perfect integrity. They would never lie about whether someone was alive or dead. The thought wouldn't even occur to them.

Yet despite their marvelous powers and unbelievable prerogatives, they are persons. They have recognizable spirit presence and form. They're will creatures or beings just like us, but created for this specific, essential function. There's something beautiful in that, the idea that even in a vast cosmos, some beings find their entire purpose in ensuring that no one is overlooked, that every individual matters enough to be counted.

Personal Aids of The Infinite Spirit: The Invisible Servants

Moving beyond the Census Directors, we encounter another mysterious order: the Personal Aids of the Infinite Spirit. We have no authentic knowledge of when or how they were created. Their number must be legion, but there's no record of it on Uversa. Conservative estimates suggest their number extends high into the trillions.

These Personal Aids are super-supreme high spiritual beings working directly for the Infinite Spirit. They don't have a physical body as we would conceive of it, or even a physical form in the way other spirit beings do. They're more like the Inspired Trinity Spirits or the Solitary Messengers, beings without fixed form who can travel at unbelievable speeds.

What makes them particularly intriguing is their near invisibility. The text tells us that although the Infinite Spirit regards them as true personalities, it's difficult for others to view them as real persons. They don't manifest a spirit presence to other spirit beings. Paradise-origin beings are always aware of their proximity, but they don't recognize a personality presence.

In other words, one of these beings could be standing right next to you, and you'd never know it. They're essentially the eavesdroppers for the Infinite Spirit, gathering information throughout creation without being detected.

During our study, someone asked whether the Infinite Spirit actually bestowed personality on them, since they seem to have a kind of group personality rather than individual personalities. It's one of those fascinating paradoxes: the Conjoint Actor sees them as true personalities, but their lack of individual presence makes them all the more serviceable to the Third Person of Deity.

Here's something that should give us pause: "Of all the revealed orders of spirit beings taking origin in the Infinite Spirit, the Personal Aids are about the only ones you will not encounter on your inward ascent to Paradise."

Why won't we encounter them? Because we won't recognize them. They'll know about us, but we won't know about them. They're there, observing, reporting, serving, completely invisible to our perception. One person in our group called them "the original double-O-sevens," and while that's a bit flippant, there's truth in it. They are agents in the most literal sense.

Associate Inspectors: Accountability in Action

The organizational sophistication continues with the Associate Inspectors. These high observers of local creations are the joint offspring of the Infinite Spirit and the Seven Master Spirits of Paradise. In the near times of eternity, seven hundred thousand were personalized.

Why seven hundred thousand? Because there are seven hundred thousand local universes, and each needs one Associate Inspector. These beings are the personal embodiment of the authority of the Seven Supreme Executives, who serve the Seven Master Spirits, to the local universes of time and space.

Think of them as the ultimate checks and balances. They work under the direct supervision of the Seven Supreme Executives and serve as their personal and powerful representatives. An inspector is stationed on the headquarters sphere of each local creation and works as a close associate of the resident Union of Days, the representative of the Paradise Trinity. In our local universe of Nebadon, that would be Immanuel.

If things aren't proceeding according to plan, the Associate Inspector is there to notice and report. They receive reports and recommendations only from their subordinates, the Assigned Sentinels, while making their reports only to their immediate superior, the Supreme Executive of their superuniverse.

As someone in our study group noted, "We can't get by with nothing." And that's exactly right. There's always some observer around, ensuring accountability and maintaining standards across the vast reaches of creation.

Assigned Sentinels: The System-Level Watchers

The chain of observation extends even further down with the Assigned Sentinels. These coordinating personalities and liaison representatives were personalized on Paradise by the Infinite Spirit for the specific purposes of their assignment. There are exactly seven billion of them in existence.

Why seven billion? Because there are seven billion local systems across all the superuniverses, and each system needs its own Assigned Sentinel. Our local system is Satania, and it has its Assigned Sentinel stationed here.

These beings are of stationary numbers, once created, no more are added or subtracted from their ranks. However, within a local creation, they do serve in rotation, being transferred from system to system. They're usually changed every millennium of local universe time.

Among the highest-ranking personalities stationed on a system capital, the Assigned Sentinels never participate in deliberations concerned with system affairs. Instead, they serve as ex-officio heads of the twenty-four administrators from the evolutionary worlds. Ascending mortals like us will have little direct contact with them, as they're almost exclusively concerned with keeping their Associate Inspector fully informed about matters relating to the welfare and state of their assigned systems.

Here's where the chain of command becomes crystal clear. When Lucifer initiated his rebellion in our local system of Satania, what happened? The Assigned Sentinel immediately notified the Associate Inspector for Nebadon. The Associate Inspector notified the Seven Supreme Executives. The Seven Supreme Executives notified the Seventh Master Spirit, who notified the Infinite Spirit, immediately.

That's how quickly information travels up the hierarchy when something significant occurs. The system ensures that no major event goes unnoticed or unreported.

One detail I find intriguing: the text explicitly states that "Assigned Sentinels and Associate Inspectors do not report to the Supreme Executives through a superuniverse headquarters. They are responsible solely to the Supreme Executive of the superuniverse concerned. Their activities are distinct from the administration of the Ancients of Days."

This parallel reporting structure fascinates me. The Ancients of Days govern the superuniverses, but this entire network of observers and inspectors operates independently, reporting directly to the Seven Supreme Executives stationed on the Paradise worlds of the Spirit. It's a separate oversight system, ensuring multiple layers of awareness and accountability.

The Graduate Guides: Companions for the Final Journey

Perhaps the most personally significant beings we encounter in this study are the Graduate Guides. These highly personal beings take their name from the nature and purpose of their work, they're exclusively devoted to guiding mortal graduates from the superuniverses of time through the Havona course of instruction and training that prepares ascending pilgrims for admission to Paradise and the Corps of the Finality.

You receive your Graduate Guide when you reach the first planet of Havona, and that guide remains with you throughout your entire journey through the billion worlds of the central universe. This is no temporary assignment, your Graduate Guide will follow you to the end of your Havona progression.

The guide's responsibility is profound: to teach you everything you need to recognize, first the Supreme Being, then the Infinite Spirit, then the Eternal Son, and eventually God the Father himself. These are among the most important beings you'll ever meet in your ascension career.

The revelator admits something touching: "I am not forbidden to undertake to tell you of the work of these Graduate Guides, but it is so ultra-spiritual that I despair of being able to adequately portray to the material mind a concept of their manifold activities."

Even beings vastly superior to us struggle to explain what the Graduate Guides do. But we're promised that on the mansion worlds, after our vision range is extended and we're freed from the fetters of material comparisons, we'll begin to comprehend realities that can "neither be seen nor heard nor have entered into the concept of human minds", those things that God has prepared for those who love eternal truth.

These words, of course, echo Jesus' own teaching. We have so much to look forward to.

The Mystery of Their Origin

Graduate Guides present us with an intriguing mystery. They haven't existed from eternity, they mysteriously appear as they're needed. There was no record of a Graduate Guide anywhere in the central universe until that far-distant day when the first mortal pilgrim of all time made his way to the outer belt of the central creation.

The instant he arrived on the pilot world of the outer circuit, he was met by Malvorian, the first of the Graduate Guides and now the chief of their supreme council and director of their vast educational organization.

Can you imagine what that must have been like? The very first mortal to ever reach Havona, and suddenly there's Malvorian, greeting him with friendly welcome. One moment there were no Graduate Guides in existence; the next moment, one appeared, eventuated, perhaps, precisely when needed.

The Paradise records contain this initial entry: "And Malvorian, the first of this order, did greet and instruct the pilgrim discoverer of Havona and did conduct him from the outer circuits of initial experience, step by step and circuit by circuit, until he stood in the very presence of the Source and Destiny of all personalities, subsequently crossing the threshold of eternity to Paradise."

The Source and Destiny of all personalities, that's God the Father. The first mortal to ever complete the ascension journey, guided by the first Graduate Guide to ever exist.

Grandfanda: The Pilgrim Discoverer

We even know the name and origin of that first pilgrim: Grandfanda. He came from planet 341 of system 84 in constellation 62 of local universe 1,131, situated in superuniverse number one. His arrival signaled the establishment of the broadcast service of the universe of universes.

Before Grandfanda reached Havona, only the broadcasts of the superuniverses and local universes had been in operation. But his arrival at the portals of Havona inaugurated what became known as the "space reports of glory", so named because the initial universe broadcast reported the Havona arrival of the first evolutionary being to attain entrance upon the goal of ascendent existence.

The revelator who provides this information was attached to the service of the Ancients of Days on Uversa at that time, and he recalls the moment vividly: "We all rejoiced in the assurance that eventually pilgrims from our superuniverse would reach Havona. For ages we had been taught that the evolutionary creatures of space would attain Paradise, and the thrill of all time swept through the heavenly courts when the first pilgrim actually arrived."

I try to imagine that moment, the thrill that must have swept through all creation when everyone realized: someone actually made it. The plan works. Mortal creatures can indeed ascend to Paradise.

And here we are, on this young, troubled world, preparing for that same journey. When someone in our study group pointed out how young our planet is, how far we still have to go, I felt both humbled and excited. We're so early in the process, yet the path is clear, the guides are ready, and countless beings throughout the universe are invested in our success.

The Certainty of the Plan

The final words about the Graduate Guides contain both promise and warning: "Graduate Guides never leave the Havona worlds. They are dedicated to the service of graduate pilgrims of time and space. And you will sometime meet these noble beings face to face if you do not reject the certain and all-perfected plan designed to affect your survival and ascension."

Notice that phrase: "if you do not reject." The plan is certain and all-perfected, but we retain our free will. We can choose not to participate. The option to decline always remains open to us, even after we've made considerable progress.

But why would we reject it? Everything in creation seems designed to help us succeed. From the Census Directors who ensure we're never overlooked, to the Personal Aids who observe without interfering, to the Associate Inspectors and Assigned Sentinels who maintain standards and accountability, to the Graduate Guides who will personally escort us through our final educational journey, the entire universe appears to be conspiring for our success.

Reflections on Order and Care

As I reflect on everything we've covered in this study of Paper 24, Section 2, I'm struck by several themes that weave through it all.

First, there's the extraordinary precision and order of the universe. Nothing happens by accident. No one falls through the cracks. From the moment of our first willful act until our last, we're known and counted. Every transition, every stage of growth, every change in status, all of it is tracked with perfect accuracy.

Some might find this level of oversight oppressive, but I see it differently. It speaks to how much we matter. In a universe of such unimaginable scope, with billions upon billions of inhabited worlds, each individual will creature is important enough to be counted, observed, and guided.

Second, there's the theme of appropriate mystery. Even the revelators admit to gaps in their knowledge. They don't know exactly how Census Directors sense the function of will. They can't adequately explain what Graduate Guides do because it's too ultra-spiritual for material minds to grasp. They acknowledge that there are hosts of unrevealed personalities involved in universal administration.

This humility about the limits of knowledge seems healthy to me. We're being taught vast amounts of information, but we're also reminded that even those teaching us don't know everything. Mystery remains, and that's appropriate. If we understood everything, what would be left to discover as we ascend?

Third, there's the recurring emphasis on personality and relationship. Despite the massive organizational structure and the billions of beings involved, everything comes down to personal connection. You will have *your* Graduate Guide. *Your* Thought Adjuster knows when you die. The Census Director is personally conscious and aware of your living presence.

The universe isn't a vast, impersonal machine. It's a family of beings, each with their own personality, purpose, and relationships. Even the Personal Aids, who seem to lack individual personality presence, are regarded as true personalities by the Infinite Spirit who created them.

Looking Forward

As we prepared to close our study session, Millie offered a prayer that captured something important. She thanked God for this book and for sending this message to tell us where Christ Michael came from, how we may follow him, and where we will go. She noted that before studying *The Urantia Book*, we were simply told you die, you go to heaven. "Well, it's not that simple," she said, "and we're so glad to have this explained to us."

That's really it, isn't it? The traditional teaching is so simplified that it leaves us with more questions than answers. What happens between death and heaven? How do we grow? What do we learn? Who helps us? Where exactly do we go?

The Urantia Book provides a framework for understanding the vast journey ahead of us. It's not simple, but it's comprehensible. It's not brief, but it's purposeful. And it's not solitary, we're surrounded by beings whose entire existence is devoted to ensuring our success.

In our next session, we'll explore the final section on the Origin of the Graduate Guides, learning more about these mysterious beings who appear exactly when needed and dedicate themselves wholly to guiding us home.

For now, I'm left with a sense of gratitude for the elaborate care built into the fabric of creation, and a renewed appreciation for the journey that awaits each of us, if we choose not to reject the certain and all-perfected plan designed for our survival and ascension.

The path is clear. The guides are ready. The only question that remains is whether we're willing to take the next step.

Chapter 19: The Graduate Guides and the Evolution of Havona

When I first began studying the Higher Personalities of the Infinite Spirit, I'll admit I found myself returning to certain sections again and again, trying to grasp how these celestial beings fit into the grand architecture of creation. Tonight, as we conclude Paper 24 with Section 7, I'm struck by how this particular group, the Graduate Guides, reveals something profound about the nature of experience itself, even in a universe designed to be perfect.

The Paradox of Evolution in Perfection

Let me start with something that might seem contradictory at first. The opening statement of this section declares plainly: "Though evolution is not the order of the central universe..." Now, why would that be? Some of you might recall that Havona exists in a state of divine perfection. It never evolves in the way we understand evolutionary progress. Everything there simply *is*, complete, flawless, eternal.

Yet here's where it gets interesting. While Havona itself doesn't evolve, something does change when evolutionary creatures like us begin arriving there. The Havona beings and Paradise citizens both gain something precious from our experience, they witness imperfection becoming perfect, and that transforms them in ways that perfection alone never could. But this isn't evolution in the traditional sense. Evolution requires incompleteness moving toward completion, and Havona has never been incomplete.

I should clarify something that occasionally trips people up: when we talk about the grand universe, we're referring to the seven superuniverses plus Paradise and the seven rings of Havona. The master universe, on the other hand, encompasses all of that *and* the outer space levels beyond. It's easy to conflate these terms, and I've caught myself doing it more times than I care to admit.

The Mystery of the Servitals

So where do the Graduate Guides actually come from? The revelators believe, and notice they say "believe," not "know with certainty", that these guides originate as Havona servitals who undergo a remarkable transformation. The servitals themselves are fascinating beings. They're creatures jointly created by the Seventh Master Spirit and the Seven Supreme Power Directors, which makes them what we might call "fourth creatures", beings who can discern both spirit and matter, existing in a semi-physical state that we could actually perceive if we encountered them.

There are billions upon billions of these servitals. On Uversa alone, more than 138 billion serve as assistants to the Ancients of Days. They're sometimes called the "midway creatures of Havona," and they accompany ascending pilgrims throughout their journey across the superuniverse capitals and then into Havona itself. What's particularly touching is that once a servital is assigned to you, that same being stays with you through all the billions of worlds of Havona. Imagine that kind of dedication, one guide, one pilgrim, across an entire universe.

The Divine Embrace

Here's where the mystery deepens. After a servital completes a long assignment in one of the superuniverses and returns to Havona, something extraordinary may happen. The servital is granted what the text calls "personal contact" with the Paradise central shining, that is, God the Father himself. The servital experiences what's described as the divine embrace, surrounded by luminous persons who, I believe, represent the Trinity itself: the Father, the Son, and the Infinite Spirit.

And then... the servital disappears. Never to return as it was.

The records on Paradise contain entries like this one: "Servital number 842,042,682,846,782 of Havona, named Sudna, came over from superuniverse service, was received on Paradise, knew the Father, entered the divine embrace, and is not."

"And is not." Those three words carry such weight. Not dead, not destroyed, but fundamentally transformed into something new. The being that was Sudna no longer exists in that form.

The Transformation Timeline

Now, I want to address something that confused me for years, and I think it's worth clarifying because the text itself draws a specific distinction. When a servital receives the divine embrace and vanishes, how long before a new Graduate Guide appears? The paper tells us: "in just three moments, a little less than three days of your time."

This is *not* the same timeframe we're given for our own resurrection on the mansion worlds. That passage speaks of "three periods", mansion world periods, which appear to be about nine days total by our earthly reckoning. But here, we're dealing with Paradise time, and the relationship between Paradise time and our time is staggering. It takes a thousand years of Earth time to equal one day of Paradise time.

Three moments of Paradise time translating to roughly three days of our time suggests something about the nature of this transformation, it's almost instantaneous by cosmic standards, yet it requires a brief interval, perhaps to allow the newly emerged Guide to orient itself to its new existence.

Where New Guides Appear

The newborn Graduate Guide materializes on the outer circuit of Havona, specifically, on the pilot world of the seventh circuit. Why there? Because that's exactly where we ascending mortals first wake up when we arrive in Havona. It's beautifully coordinated: just as we open our eyes in this new realm, a freshly created Guide appears, ready to accompany us on the next stage of our journey. One guide, one mortal, across billions upon billions of Havona worlds.

The numbers work out with remarkable precision. The total number of Graduate Guides, accounting for slight variations due to beings currently in transition, exactly equals the number of vanished servitals. The mathematics of transformation, you might say.

The Bond Between Guides and Servitals

There's another piece of evidence that suggests Graduate Guides are indeed evolved servitals, and it's more subtle than you might expect. The Graduate Guides and the Havona servitals share what the text describes as an "unfailing tendency" to form extraordinary attachments to one another. The way these supposedly separate orders of beings understand and sympathize with each other is described as "wholly inexplicable."

Think about what that implies. If you were transformed from one state of being to another, yet retained some essential quality of your former self, wouldn't you feel an immediate kinship with those who remain in your original order? The text calls their mutual devotion "refreshing and inspiring." It's as if the Graduate Guides never quite forget what it was like to be servitals, even though they've transcended that state entirely.

The Supreme Being's Role

Here's where things get theologically complex, and I want to tread carefully because we're venturing into territory where the revelators themselves use words like "believe" and "conjecture." The Seven Master Spirits and the Seven Supreme Power Directors act as personal repositories for the mind potential and power potential of the Supreme Being, who doesn't yet function fully in his own right. They're essentially serving as his vicegerents, his stand-ins, until he completes his own evolutionary emergence.

When these Paradise associates collaborate to create Havona servitals, those servitals become inherently involved in "certain phases of supremacy." They're living reflections in the perfect central universe of evolutionary potentialities that exist in time and space. And when a servital transforms into a Graduate Guide, this transformation appears to occur in response to the will of the Infinite Spirit, who's likely acting on behalf of the Supreme Being.

Here's my understanding of why this matters: when a servital serves in a particular superuniverse, let's say ours, Orvonton, that servital takes on something of the character of that superuniverses Master Spirit. When the servital transforms into a Graduate Guide, it retains that particular "tinge" or flavor. Why? Because when ascending mortals from Orvonton arrive in Havona, they're assigned guides who understand their specific experiential background, who've served where they came from, who think in patterns familiar to beings from that same universe.

It's experiential matching at its finest. The Supreme Being, as the God of evolutionary creatures, seems to orchestrate this process to ensure that each ascending mortal receives guidance from a being who truly understands their journey.

The New Havona

The chapter concludes with a statement that should give us pause: "The Havona of the present day differs in many respects from the central universe as it was before the times of Grandfanda."

Grandfanda, you may remember, was the first mortal to complete the ascension journey from time and space to Paradise. Before his arrival, Havona had never hosted an evolutionary creature. It existed in pristine perfection, perhaps beautiful beyond imagining, but static in a way. The arrival of imperfect beings seeking perfection inaugurated "sweeping modifications" in the organization of the central and divine creation.

Both the Graduate Guides and the tertiary supernaphim, angels who serve ascending mortals, came into existence around this time. They weren't needed before. There were no evolutionary spirits to guide, no struggling mortals to encourage, no imperfect beings learning what it means to become perfect.

The revelators attribute these developments to God the Supreme, whose very nature is experiential rather than existential. In a sense, we evolutionary creatures didn't just arrive in Havona, we changed it. Our presence called forth new orders of beings whose purpose is to facilitate our journey. That's both humbling and awe-inspiring when you really sit with it.

Closing Reflections

As we conclude this study of the Higher Personalities of the Infinite Spirit, I find myself thinking about what this all means for us personally. We're reading about beings we've never met, describing transformations we've never witnessed, in a universe we've only glimpsed through revelation. Yet there's something deeply reassuring in knowing that the cosmos itself adapts to accommodate our journey, that new orders of beings come into existence specifically to help us along.

The Graduate Guides represent something essential about the divine plan: perfection serving imperfection, experience bridging the gap between what is and what will be, eternal beings taking on characteristics specifically suited to guiding temporal creatures like us toward eternal destinies.

Next time, we'll turn our attention to Paper 25, the Messenger Hosts of Space, and continue our exploration of these remarkable beings who inhabit realms we're only beginning to understand. Until then, may you carry with you the assurance that somewhere in the future, on the pilot world of Havona's seventh circuit, a Graduate Guide waits, perhaps even now being transformed from a devoted servital who once served beings from our corner of creation, ready to walk with you across a billion worlds toward the presence of the Universal Father.

And perhaps that's the most profound truth of all: in a universe this vast, this ancient, this complex, the journey is never taken alone.

Chapter 20: The Messenger Hosts of Space

As we continue our journey through the Urantia Book, I find myself increasingly amazed at how perfectly organized the celestial hierarchy really is. Tonight, we turn our attention to Paper 25, "The Messenger Hosts of Space," which begins on page 273.

Understanding the Messenger Hosts

The Messenger Hosts of Space occupy an intermediate position within the family of the Infinite Spirit. These versatile beings function as connecting links between the higher personalities and the ministering spirits, essentially bridging the gap between the elevated celestial administrators and the angelic corps that work more directly with us. Before we examine each order in detail, I need to clarify something that came up in our previous study session, because it's crucial for understanding how these groups relate to one another.

Last week, we discussed the Havona Servitals extensively, and I intentionally sidestepped a question about their exact classification. The reason? I knew we'd be covering it properly this week. Here's what you need to understand: the Havona Servitals are believed to be the origin of the Graduate Guides. Now, the Graduate Guides belong to what we call the Higher Hosts of the Infinite Spirit, that's the group we studied previously. But here's the important distinction: even though all Graduate Guides come from the Havona Servitals, the Servitals themselves are *not* part of the Higher Personalities of the Infinite Spirit. They're part of the Intermediate Family of the Infinite Spirit.

This might seem like splitting hairs, but it's actually quite significant. The Servitals start out in one group, and then they literally graduate, hence the name, and become Graduate Guides, moving into a different classification entirely. Think of it like completing your undergraduate degree and then moving on to graduate school; you're the same person, but your role and status have fundamentally changed.

The Havona Servitals work both in the seven superuniverses, mainly around the Ancients of Days, whom they assist in teaching us about universal law and governance, and they also work in Havona itself. So why are these beings and their companions called "Messenger Hosts of Space"? It's really about how the Infinite Spirit reveals information to us as mortals. These beings don't just deliver messages in the simple sense; they give us information, instruction, and guidance that flows from the Infinite Spirit through their teaching and ministry. That's their essential function, to be channels of divine wisdom and understanding.

They serve as the connection between the Higher Personalities and the Ministering Spirits. When I refer to the Ministering Spirits, I'm talking about the Angelic Corps, all the various orders of angels who serve throughout creation. The Messenger Hosts are the bridge, the connection point between these two vast groups, and you'll see exactly how this works when we get to discussing the Morontia Companions and the Paradise Companions. These are the beings who help us understand the direction we're heading as we ascend toward Paradise.

The Seven Orders of Messenger Hosts

Let me share with you the seven distinct orders that comprise the Messenger Hosts of Space: Havona Servitals, Universal Conciliators, Technical Advisors, Custodians of Records on Paradise, Celestial Recorders, Morontia Companions, and Paradise Companions. Now, here's an important structural detail: four of these orders are created specifically for their roles, while the other three have their origins in the Angelic Corps and are recruited or promoted into their positions.

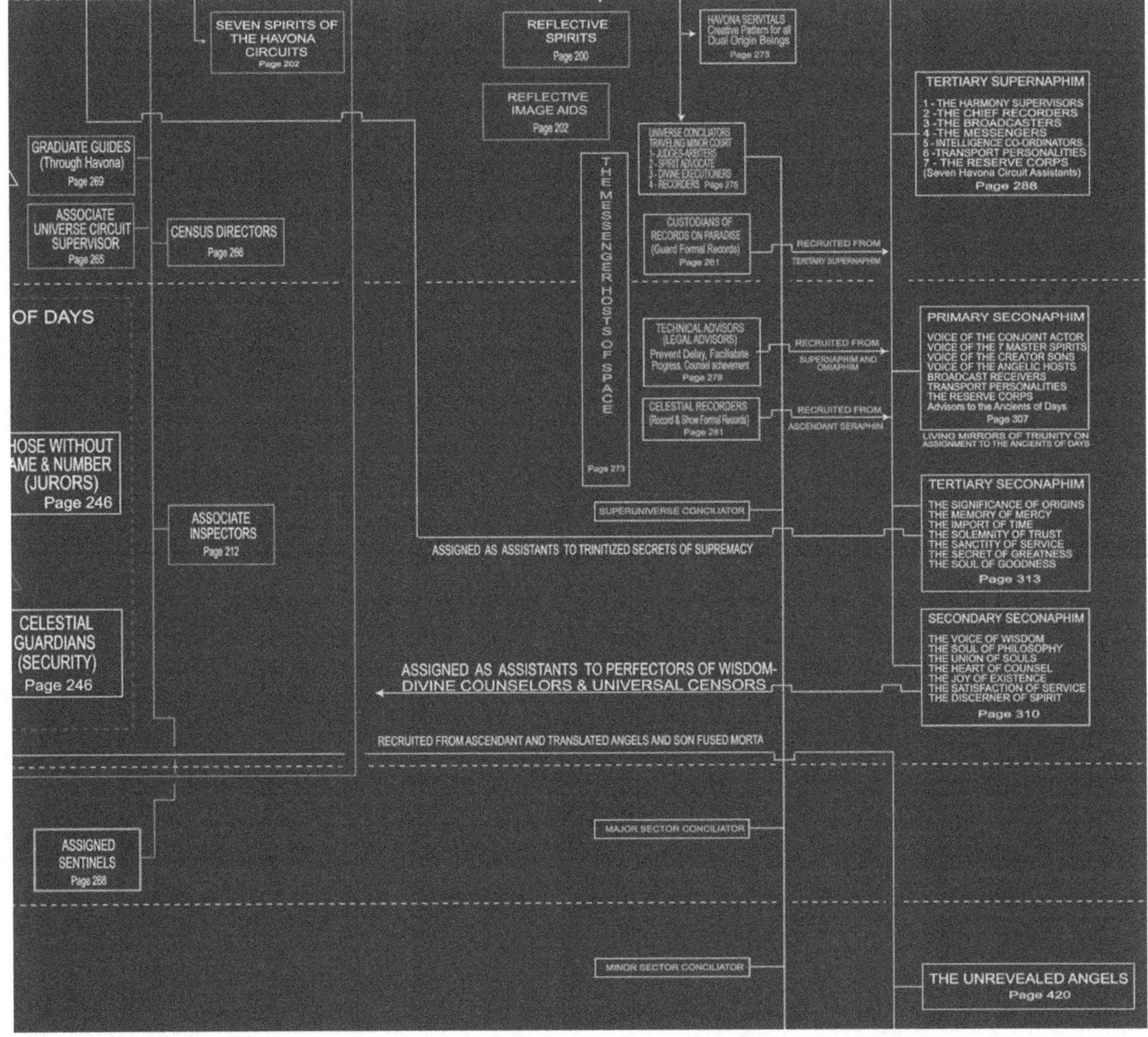

Figure 4: Messenger Host of Space

Of the seven groups, only three, Servitals, Conciliators, and Morontia Companions, are created as such from the beginning. The remaining four represent attainment levels reached by various angelic orders. According to their inherent nature and attained status, these Messenger Hosts serve variously throughout the universe of universes, but they always remain subject to the direction of those who rule the realms of their assignment.

Let me show you how this works in practice. The Paradise Companions, who serve as companions for us ascenders, are recruited from all orders of angels, and any angelic being might eventually serve in this capacity. The Havona Servitals, on the other hand, represent the creative power behind all dual-origin beings. What do I mean by dual origin? The Servitals are created through the combined effort of the Seventh Master Spirit and the Seventh Supreme Power Director. This partnership creates beings with both spiritual and physical characteristics. And we ourselves are dual-origin beings, created by a Creator Son and a Local Universe Mother Spirit working together. The Creator Sons themselves, along with the Local Universe Mother Spirits, are also dual-origin beings. There's a pattern here that repeats throughout creation.

Moving down through the orders, the Universal Conciliators function as traveling minor courts, comprising Judge Arbiters, Spirit Advocates, Divine Executioners, and Recorders. We'll explore each of these roles in detail later. These are created beings, as are the Morontia Companions and the Superuniverse Conciliators and Celestial Recorders. But the Technical Advisors, who serve as legal advisors throughout the universes, are recruited from the Supernaphim and the Omniaphim, both of which are angelic orders. The Celestial Recorders come from the ascendant Seraphim, and if you've been following along, you'll recognize that Seraphim serve as our guardian angels. So, some of our own guardians eventually advance to become Celestial Recorders.

Why does this matter? Because when we reach the mansion worlds and begin our morontia career, we need to realize that the Morontia Companions and Paradise Companions were often created specifically for those jobs. That's the fundamental difference between them and those who were originally created as angels and later recruited for specialized service. The companions have different origins and different training. I hope that clarifies things rather than muddying the waters.

The Havona Servitals: Midway Creatures of the Central Universe

Now let's examine each order in detail, starting with the Havona Servitals. Though they're called Servitals, these midway creatures of the central universe are not servants in any menial sense of the word. In the spiritual world, there's simply no such thing as menial work. All service is sacred and exhilarating, and the higher orders of beings don't look down upon the lower orders of existence. Remember this principle when you reach the mansion worlds: no work is menial work. Everything you're assigned to do carries importance and meaning.

We can think of these Servitals as midway creatures of the central universe, much like we have midway creatures here on our planet. What do our planetary midwayers do? They help the local celestial government with anything and everything that requires a being who can, first, make themselves visible to humans, and second, move material matter in any form or fashion. The primary midwayers lean more toward the spiritual side, while the secondary midwayers are more physical. Secondary midwayers get assigned jobs that require physical manipulation, moving objects, interacting with material reality. They're also the ones who can make themselves visible to us when necessary.

Think about it this way: if the celestial government needed to prevent us from launching nuclear weapons in some catastrophic scenario, who do you think would be assigned that task? Most likely the secondary midwayers, because it involves physical intervention. In fact, it was midwayers who rolled away the stone from Jesus's tomb at the resurrection, a perfect example of their ability to interact with the material world on behalf of celestial administration.

The text tells us something fascinating about how Servitals become Graduate Guides. A Servital who has been long absent from Havona on superuniverse assignment, having served on many such missions, will eventually return home and be granted the privilege of personal contact with the Paradise Central Shining. They're embraced by the Luminous Persons (God The Father, God The Son, and The Infinite Spirit) and disappear from the recognition of their spiritual fellows, nevermore to reappear among those of their kind. This is the transformation process, this is how a Havona Servital becomes a Graduate Guide.

The Creation of Dual-Origin Beings

The Havona Servitals represent the joint creative work of the Seven Master Spirits and their associates, the Seven Supreme Power Directors. This creative collaboration comes nearest to being the pattern for the long list of reproductions of the dual order in the evolutionary universes. The pattern extends from the creation of a Bright and Morning Star by a Creator Son-Creative Spirit liaison all the way down to sexual procreation on worlds like ours, Urantia.

Let me help you visualize this. The Havona Servitals originate from one of the Seven Master Spirits, you can think of this as the spiritual side. Then you have the physical side, represented by the Seven Supreme Power Directors (not the Executives, as I mistakenly said earlier). These two types of beings come together and create what we call dual-origin beings. Now, why do the revelators make such a big deal about this dual-origin concept? Because the Creator Sons and Creative Mother Spirits essentially copy this process. They learned it from watching the Master Spirits and the Power Directors work together.

How does it work in the local universes? You have the Creative Mother Spirit providing the physical component, and the Creator Son providing the spiritual component. Actually, it works both ways, you can also think of the Spirit coming down through the Son in a spiritual circuit, with the physical aspect coming through the Local Universe Mother Spirit. The Creator Sons and Creative Mother Spirits are replicating the creative process they learned from the Seven Master Spirits and the Seven Power Directors. When these pairs come together, they create Havona Servitals in mass production, for each superuniverse.

That's right, for each superuniverse. One Master Spirit pairs with one Power Director to create all the Servitals for that particular universe. This happens for each of the seven superuniverses. So, if all seven pairs created Servitals simultaneously, how many would that produce? Seven thousand, because they're created in batches of one thousand at a time.

The Nature and Number of Servitals

Here's another revealing detail: the number of Servitals is prodigious, and more are being created all the time. They appear in groups of one thousand on the third moment following the assembly of the Master Spirits and the Supreme Power Directors at their joint area in the far northerly sector of Paradise. Every fourth Servital is more physical in type than the others. That is, out of each thousand, 750 are apparently true to spirit type, but 250 are semi-physical in nature. These fourth creatures are somewhat on the order of material beings, material in the Havona sense, resembling the Physical Power Directors more than the Master Spirits.

Did you catch that reference to the "third moment"? We heard this same term just last week. They're talking about Paradise moments here. Remember, a Paradise moment equals three days in our time. The pattern keeps recurring throughout these papers. But focus on this fascinating detail about the nature of these beings: every fourth one is more physical. They're described as more physical in the Havona material sense, and keep in mind that Havona material has a thousand different atomic combinations, while we only have one hundred elements.

These fourth creatures resemble the Power Directors more than the Master Spirits. Why would that be? Think it through. The Power Directors work with physical matter, that's their primary function. All matter of every type, shape, form, and fashion derives its power and composition from whom? The Power Directors. The Power Directors themselves are inherently more physical than the Master Spirits.

That's why every fourth being they create is more physical and better able to work in the physical realms. They handle anything physical that needs to be done.

In personality relationships, the spiritual is dominant over the material, even though it doesn't currently appear that way here on Urantia. In the production of Havona Servitals, the law of spirit dominance prevails absolutely. The established ratio yields three spiritual beings to one semi-physical. So, 75 percent of the Servitals created, three-fourths, are more spiritual, while the other fourth is more physical. The spiritual dominates in the real universe, the eternal universe. When we reach the mansion worlds, the things that are more spiritual in our world will become increasingly dominant as we climb through the mansion worlds and eventually become spirit beings ourselves. We'll be glorified, if you will.

Training and Service

The newly created Servitals, together with newly appearing Graduate Guides, all pass through courses of training that the senior guides continuously conduct on each of the seven Havona circuits. Servitals are then assigned to activities for which they're best adapted. Since they exist in two types, spiritual and semi-physical, there are few limits to the range of work these versatile beings can perform. The higher or spiritual groups are assigned selectively to the services of the Father, the Son, and the Spirit, and to the work of the Seven Master Spirits. In large numbers, they're dispatched from time to time to serve on the study worlds encircling the headquarters spheres of the seven superuniverses, worlds devoted to the final training and spiritual culture of ascending souls of time who are preparing for advancement to the circuits of Havona.

Both spirit Servitals and their more physical fellows receive assignments as associates of the Graduate Guides, assisting and instructing the various orders of ascending creatures who have attained Havona and who seek to attain Paradise. Notice that Graduate Guides train the Havona Servitals. Why would that be? The Graduate Guides were themselves Servitals before their transformation, so they have extensive experience in that role. They're the perfect beings to train incoming Servitals. And because three-quarters of the Servitals are more spiritual, they get assigned jobs that are more spiritually oriented, while the semi-physical ones work more directly with us ascending mortals. We're coming up through Havona as former physical beings, we've become spirits by that time, of course, but we still carry the concepts and experiences of physical existence. The semi-physical Servitals serve as ideal instructors for beings with our background.

Why does the training occur on all seven Havona circuits? Because as the circuits progress higher and higher, they teach higher and higher concepts. The ascending curriculum matches our increasing capacity for spiritual comprehension. As you advance upward, you'll be learning more advanced material, and the Servitals and Graduate Guides will be teaching correspondingly more sophisticated concepts.

The Affection Between Servitals and Guides

The Havona Servitals and the Graduate Guides manifest a transcendent devotion to their work and a touching affection for one another, an affection which, while spiritual, you could only understand by comparison with the phenomenon of human love. There is divine pathos in the separation of Servitals from the guides, as so often occurs when Servitals are dispatched on missions beyond the limits of the central universe. But they go with joy and not with sorrow. The satisfying joy of high duty is the eclipsing emotion of spiritual beings. Sorrow cannot exist in the face of consciousness of divine duty faithfully performed. And when your ascending soul stands before the Supreme Judge, the decision of eternal import will not be determined by material successes or quantitative achievements. The verdict reverberating through the high court's declares: "Well done, good and faithful servant. You have been faithful over a few essentials, and you shall be made ruler over universe realities."

That's powerful, isn't it? Let me explain the term "divine pathos" that appears here. Pathos is a Greek word meaning, essentially, godly love. It's not human love in the romantic or sexual sense, it's a love that transcends human love entirely. The Greeks actually had three different words for different types of love, and English has nothing comparable, which is probably why the revelators chose this particular term. What they're telling us is that the Servitals love each other with something approaching godly love. That's why they separate with joy rather than sorrow, because they love each other so profoundly that they want what's best for each other in every act and decision. That's a remarkably special kind of love, completely non-selfish in nature.

The other point I want to emphasize: when your soul stands before the Supreme Judge, who is that? The Ancients of Days. We actually undergo this evaluation three separate times. First, we stand before Jesus, Michael, and we want to hear those words: "Well done, my good and faithful servant." When we hear that verdict, we graduate from being morontia beings to becoming spiritual beings. Then, before we're ready to advance to Havona, we stand before the Ancients of Days, and again we hope to hear: "Well done, my good and faithful servant." That approval allows us to proceed to Havona. Eventually comes the third evaluation: we stand before God the Father himself. We want to hear once more, "Well done, my good and faithful servant," and then we're enlisted into the Corps of the Finality. That's the ultimate achievement we're all working toward.

Servitals on Superuniverse Service

On superuniverse service, the Havona Servitals are always assigned to that domain presided over by the Master Spirit whom they most resemble in general and special spirit prerogatives. They serve only on the educational worlds surrounding the capitals of the seven superuniverses. The last report from Uversa indicates that almost 138 billion Servitals were ministering on its 490 satellites. They engage in an endless variety of activities in connection with the work of these educational worlds comprising the super universities of the superuniverse of Orvonton. Here they are your companions, they've come down from your next career stage to study you and to inspire you with the reality and certainty of your eventual graduation from the universities of time to the realms of eternity. Through these contacts, the Servitals gain preliminary experience in ministering to ascending creatures of time, which proves invaluable in their subsequent work on the Havona circuits as associates of the Graduate Guides or as Graduate Guides themselves.

Notice that the Servitals have the basic tendencies of their superuniverse of origin. If you're a Servital who came from Superuniverse Number Four, then your reflective tendencies and personality characteristics would match those of Superuniverse Number Four, not Number Seven. Each one is unique in this way. When we're assigned Servitals to help teach us at Uversa on those 490 satellite worlds, we get Servitals from our own superuniverse. These same Servitals will likely be assigned to us when we begin our journey through Havona. You'll receive the characteristic influence of our Master Spirit all the way through your ascension. It makes perfect sense when you think about it, we'll be able to relate better to them because they share the same fundamental tendencies that we developed coming from Superuniverse Number Seven.

This pattern continues when you reach Havona. The Graduate Guides assigned to you will have the same tendencies. If you get a Graduate Guide, he'll be a former Servital who originated from Superuniverse Number Seven. He'll be able to relate to you more effectively because he understands your background and perspective. I should mention something else here: throughout this entire journey, from the mansion worlds all the way through to Uversa, we never really get out of school. If you don't like going to school, well, you're heading to the wrong destination. There are 490 satellites around Uversa, and they're essentially universities, every single one. That's a tremendous amount of learning ahead. But remember, it's gradual, you're given eons of time to master each level before moving on.

The Creation of Universal Conciliators

Now we come to the Universal Conciliators. For every Havona Servital created, seven Universal Conciliators are brought into being, one in each superuniverse. The creative enactment involves a definite superuniverse technique of reflective response to transactions taking place on Paradise. On the headquarters worlds of the seven superuniverses, there function the seven reflections of the Seven Master Spirits. It's difficult to describe the natures of these Reflective Spirits to material minds. They're true personalities, yet each member of a superuniverse group perfectly reflects just one of the Seven Master Spirits.

Every time the Master Spirits associate themselves with the Power Directors for the purpose of creating a group of Havona Servitals, there's a simultaneous focalization upon one of the Reflective Spirits in each of the superuniverse groups. Forthwith and full-fledged, an equal number of Universal Conciliators appear on the headquarters worlds of the super creations. If, in the creation of Servitals, Master Spirit Number Seven should take the initiative, none but the Reflective Spirits of the seventh order would become, and here's an interesting word choice, pregnant with Conciliators. Concurrently with the creation of one thousand Orvonton-like Servitals, one thousand of the seventh-order Conciliators would appear on each superuniverse capital.

Out of these episodes, reflecting the sevenfold nature of the Master Spirits, arise the seven created orders of Conciliators serving in each superuniverse. When they decide to create Servitals, Master Spirit Number Seven initiates the process. At that same moment, on each of the seven superuniverses, Conciliators appear on every capital. So, when they're made, it happens simultaneously across all seven superuniverses. Each group of Conciliators would be reflective of the Master Spirit of that universe. If you had Master Spirit Number One creating his group, all those Conciliators would reflect the characteristics of Master Spirit Number One. See where this becomes important? Each order is unique and specialized.

When do we benefit from all these different types of beings? When we reach Havona, we'll be trained by representatives from all seven types of beings from all seven superuniverses. There's a rhyme and reason to this entire arrangement. After the reaction initiated by Master Spirit Number Seven, and it's significant that

Number Seven kicks off the process, one thousand Servitals appear on Paradise after the third moment, while simultaneously, one thousand Conciliators appear on each of the seven superuniverse headquarters. Why does Number Seven initiate? Because it's the action of the Supreme, an experiential occurrence tied to the evolution of the Supreme Being.

The Unique Character of Conciliators

Here's something really interesting: Conciliators of pre-Paradise status don't serve interchangeably between superuniverses. They're restricted to their native segments of creation. Every superuniverse corps, embracing one-seventh of each created order, therefore spends a very long time under the influence of one of the Master Spirits to the exclusion of the others. While all seven are reflected on the superuniverse capitals, only one is dominant in each super creation.

This tells us that while Conciliators are serving in our superuniverse, they work solely as a reflection of Master Spirit Number Seven. They don't deviate from their own superuniverse's influence until they reach Havona. In Havona, everything changes, because we're becoming an amalgamation of all the universe perspectives. But while you're in a particular superuniverse, the influence remains specific to that superuniverse. The same holds true for all seven superuniverses, each maintains its unique character.

Each of the seven supercreations is actually pervaded by that one of the Master Spirits who presides over its destinies. Each superuniverse thus becomes like a gigantic mirror reflecting the nature and character of the supervising Master Spirit, and all of this continues further in every subdividing local universe through the presence and function of the Creative Mother Spirits. The effect of such an environment upon evolutionary growth is so profound that in their post-superuniverse careers, the Conciliators collectively manifest 49 experiential viewpoints, or insights, each angular, hence incomplete, but all mutually compensatory and together tending to encompass the circle of Supremacy.

The circle of Supremacy represents the circle of experience. By serving in just one of the seven superuniverses, Conciliators develop a somewhat focused view of reality. But when they advance past the superuniverse level and enter Havona, they gain access to a collective consciousness that includes all seven viewpoints from all seven superuniverses. That's precisely why the system is designed this way. They ultimately gain experience of all seven perspectives, which is seven times seven, giving us those 49 experiential viewpoints mentioned in the text.

The Conciliating Commission

In each superuniverse, the Universal Conciliators find themselves strangely and innately segregated into groups of four, associations in which they continue to serve. In each group, three are spirit personalities, and one, like the fourth creatures of the Servitals, is a semi-material being. This quartet constitutes a conciliating commission and is organized as follows:

First, the Judge-Arbiter, the one unanimously designated by the other three as the most competent and best qualified to act as judicial head of the group. At this point, I need to help you grasp a fundamental concept. What is a Universal Conciliator? A Universal Conciliator consists of a group of four beings, always. These four beings always work together as a unit. They don't transfer to different groups. You can think of a Universal Conciliator as a mobile court system.

Why is this important? Because Universal Conciliators handle problems arising anywhere from the superuniverse level all the way down to individual planets. If anyone encounters something they believe is wrong and needs adjudication, these are the beings who come and take care of it. What's an example? Let's say Caligastia decided to lead this planet into rebellion, that's certainly a problem, isn't it? One of these commissions would be assigned to investigate. When one of the loyal beings on this planet, someone like Van, sent notice to the Most Highs that Caligastia was about to rebel and drag the whole planet with him, that would fall under the jurisdiction of the Universal Conciliators.

What would happen then? They'd take the case. There would be two sides: Caligastia's position and Van's position. Van was one of Caligastia's staff of one hundred, along with his associate Amadon. That's exactly what happened on our planet. Amadon and Van sent notice that Caligastia was planning rebellion, listing all the points they believed were going wrong, and sent their report to the Most Highs. This was forwarded to a conciliating commission. The response from the Most Highs got stuck in the circuits somehow, it couldn't get through because the circuits can only forward messages, they can't initiate contact. Once a message is stopped, what happens?

Well, the message coming back was blocked because we were placed under quarantine. When quarantine was imposed on this planet, the return message to Van and Amadon got lodged in the circuit. It was seven years before they learned that they'd done the right thing. But this illustrates why these commissions are so crucial.

We have four beings in each commission. Let me walk you through each role. The first is the Judge-Arbiter, who serves as the judge for the entire group. All four beings get together and decide who's best qualified to be judge. Once someone is designated as judge, he remains judge of that group forever. He's unanimously chosen by the other three as the most competent and best qualified to act as judicial head.

The second member is the Spirit-Advocate, the one appointed by the Judge-Arbiter to present evidence and safeguard the rights of all personalities involved in any matter assigned to the adjudication of the conciliating commission. The Spirit-Advocate essentially takes the side of whoever made the complaint. Think of him as the attorney representing the complainant.

Third, we have the Divine Executioner, the Conciliator qualified by inherent nature to make contact with the material beings of the realms and to execute the decisions of the commission. Divine Executioners, being fourth creatures, are quasi-material beings, almost but not quite visible to the short-range vision of mortal races. These beings take whatever decision the court makes and ensure that it's carried out.

I don't want you to confuse the Divine Executioner with Celestial Guardians. Remember those beings from previous lessons? Celestial Guardians are the ones who can remove the life force if someone is judged to be in rebellion against the universe. This is completely different. The Divine Executioner executes the will of the court, that's why they're called Executioners. They carry out the court's decisions; they don't execute people.

This operates at every level, from the planetary up to the superuniverse. These are traveling courts. They move from planet to planet, system to system, constellation to constellation, through the local universe, and on to the minor and major sectors. There are thousands upon thousands of these commissions traveling around, handling disagreements and disputes. Any conflict between two beings can be brought before them. When we reach the mansion worlds, we'll encounter people we have difficulty getting along with, and sometimes these commissions will step in to serve as arbiters.

The fourth member is the Recorder, the remaining member of the commission who automatically becomes the Recorder, the clerk of the tribunal. He makes certain that all records are properly prepared for the archives of the superuniverse and for the records of the local universe. If the commission serves on an evolutionary world, a third report, with the assistance of the Executioner, is prepared for the physical records of the system government of jurisdiction.

The Recorder keeps track of everything that happens, just like in a regular court. They maintain books or recordings of all proceedings, and all these cases go into permanent records. Any commission can look up a previous case and use it as precedent, exactly as they do in earthly court systems. It's a system of perfect order.

How the Commissions Function

When in session, a commission functions as a group of three, since the Advocate is detached during adjudication and participates in the formulation of the verdict only at the conclusion of the hearing. Hence, these commissions are sometimes called referee trios. That makes sense, three of them work together throughout the case, examining evidence and arguments, and then the Spirit-Advocate joins at the end for the verdict, after which the Judge makes the final decision.

The Conciliators are of tremendous value in keeping the universe of universes running smoothly. Traversing space at the seraphic rate of triple velocity, that's about 550,000 miles per hour, so they can get there pretty quickly, they serve as the traveling courts of the worlds, commissions devoted to the quick adjudication of minor difficulties. Were it not for these mobile and eminently fair commissions, the tribunals of the spheres would be hopelessly overwhelmed with the minor misunderstandings that arise constantly throughout the realms.

These referee trios do not pass upon matters of eternal import. The soul, the eternal prospects of a creature of time, is never placed in jeopardy by their acts. Conciliators don't deal with questions extending beyond the temporal existence and cosmic welfare of creatures of time. But when a commission has once accepted jurisdiction of a problem, its rulings are final and always unanimous. There is no appeal from the decision of the Judge-Arbiter. What they say stands, backed by the authority of the Ancients of Days. However, they handle no case involving a soul, nothing concerning the permanent survival of an individual. Those are always minor misunderstandings and temporal disputes.

Conclusion: Looking Ahead

We've covered quite a bit tonight, from the fascinating dual-origin nature of the Havona Servitals to the sophisticated judicial system represented by the Universal Conciliators. In our next session, we'll continue with the far-reaching services of

Conciliators and move on to explore the Technical Advisors, Custodians of Records, and the other Messenger Hosts who assist us in our Paradise ascent.

As we close, remember this: the celestial administration is not some distant, disconnected bureaucracy. It's a living, caring system of beings who've dedicated themselves to our welfare and advancement. The Servitals who will teach us, the Conciliators who ensure justice, the Companions who will guide us, they're all part of a grand design meant to help us succeed in our eternal adventure.

Thank you for joining me in this study. Until next time, may you find peace in knowing that an entire universe of loving beings awaits to welcome you home.

Chapter 21: The Messenger Hosts of Space - Conciliators

We continue our exploration of the Messenger Hosts of Space, focusing specifically on the Conciliators. If you've been following along with our studies, you'll recall that these celestial beings represent one of the most fascinating administrative orders in the universe. They serve as the universe's conflict resolution specialists, and their work touches virtually every level of cosmic administration.

The Far-Reaching Service of Conciliators

Let me begin by explaining where these remarkable beings are headquartered. Conciliators maintain their primary headquarters on the capital of their superuniverse, in our case, that would be Uversa. Their secondary reserves are stationed on the capitals of local universes throughout the superuniverse. What strikes me as particularly interesting is how their career progression works. The younger, less experienced commissioners begin their service on what we might call the "lower worlds", planets like our own Urantia. Only after acquiring substantial experience do, they advance to adjudicating more complex problems.

Think of it as a cosmic apprenticeship system. These commissions start out handling local planetary disputes, and if a problem proves beyond their capacity, they can elevate it to the local universe level. Most issues, however, are resolved right where they occur. As they gain experience and demonstrate competence, the entire commission graduates as a unit to the next level, from planetary systems to constellations, then to the local universe itself, and potentially all the way up to the minor and major sectors of the superuniverse.

Now, you might wonder what exactly these Conciliators do. Picture this: whenever two individuals, though more commonly two groups of beings, find themselves in disagreement, that's when the Conciliators step in. These disputes often arise between different orders of celestial beings. For instance, you might have a group of angels disagreeing with a group of mortals about procedural matters, or perhaps angels and Melchizedeks finding themselves at odds over how something should be handled.

Let me give you a concrete example from our own world. We sometimes forget that our human governments don't actually control this planet in the ultimate sense. The celestial government, the real administrative structure, operates behind the scenes. So, imagine the chief of the archangels believes something should be done

one way on this planet, while the midwayers think it should be done differently. That disagreement would require a conciliating commission to step in and arbitrate. Whatever decision they reach becomes, essentially, universal law. It's binding.

The Order of Conciliators: Wholly Dependable

Here's something that sets the Conciliators apart from many other orders of beings: they are wholly dependable. Not one has ever gone astray. Not one has ever joined a rebellion. Now, they're not infallible in wisdom and judgment, they can make mistakes in their reasoning, but they are absolutely unerring in their faithfulness. This reliability proved critical during the Lucifer rebellion. When Lucifer led thirty-seven planets into rebellion, the Conciliators remained completely loyal. They wouldn't rebel under any circumstances, which made them uniquely qualified to handle the aftermath of that terrible crisis.

The Conciliators originate on superuniverse headquarters and eventually return there, but between their origin and their return, they advance through multiple levels of universe service. Let me walk you through how they function at each level.

Conciliators to the Worlds

At the planetary level, whenever the supervising personalities of individual worlds become perplexed or deadlocked about proper procedure under existing circumstances, and the matter isn't significant enough to bring before the regularly constituted tribunals, a conciliating commission can be activated. All it takes is a petition from two personalities, one from each side of the contention.

Once a case has been placed in the Conciliators' hands for study and adjudication, they hold supreme authority. However, they won't formulate a decision until all evidence has been heard. There's no limit whatsoever to their authority to call witnesses from anywhere in the universe. If a similar problem occurred on another planet or in another universe, they can call witnesses from those locations to testify about how it was handled there.

Now, if at any point the commission decides the matter exceeds their jurisdiction, they can transfer the entire question to higher tribunals. This might be a tribunal at the next level up, or it could go all the way to the Ancients of Days on the superuniverse capital. When would they do this? Primarily when the decision involves questions about the soul or the eternal survival of any individual.

Let me give you a powerful example. When Van and Amadon challenged Caligastia's authority during the planetary rebellion, they likely called for a conciliating commission. As soon as that commission heard the evidence, they would have immediately elevated the case to the Constellation Fathers, because Caligastia's rebellion threatened the eternal destinies of countless souls. The Constellation Fathers rendered an opinion, but Van wasn't satisfied with it, so he appealed for a higher judgment. That appeal got lodged in the communication relays, and Van didn't receive an answer for seven years. But this illustrates a crucial principle: as soon as a decision affects even one person's soul, just one, it automatically gets elevated to the Ancients of Days if there's any question about permanent survival.

For matters that don't involve eternal destiny, however, the Conciliators' decisions are final. You don't have to agree with their finding, but unless it concerns salvation or the lasting soul, what they decide is law. The Ancients of Days don't come along behind them and overturn their decisions. These beings have acquired enough experience from other cases throughout the universe to know what the proper decision should be.

The Divine Executioner

Here's where things get particularly interesting. The commissioners' decisions are placed on planetary records, and if necessary, they're put into effect by the Divine Executioner. His power is considerable, and the range of his activities on an inhabited world is remarkably wide.

Remember, the Divine Executioners are semi-material beings. Unlike their three colleagues on the commission, they can actually manipulate matter. This unique capability is why they're called executioners, they execute, or carry out, the will of the commission. Sometimes their acts on the worlds of time and space are difficult to explain, precisely because they can manipulate physical reality in ways that seem almost miraculous to us.

They don't violate natural law, you won't see them making things float across the sky in defiance of gravity, but they can effect immediate physical changes that would normally require time. Let me give you an example. Diane and I were reading about Christ's resurrection recently, and it mentions that the chief of the archangels requested the body of Jesus after the resurrection. They didn't want to watch Christ's physical body degenerate over time; the torture of his execution had been too much for them to bear. So, they used a technique of accelerated time to disintegrate the human body of Jesus immediately.

A Divine Executioner may possess that same capability, using accelerated time to make something vanish, disappear, or disintegrate instantly. His physical aspect gives him nearly unlimited power in this regard. Another example? The first "miracle" at the wedding in Cana, when water was turned into wine. That was basically accelerated fermentation, compressing what normally takes weeks or months into an instant. The midwayers were involved in that particular event, but it demonstrates how time itself can be manipulated when you're operating from a higher dimensional perspective.

This points to something profound: reality as we conceive it isn't quite what we think it is. True reality, spiritual reality, is the only lasting reality. Everything else is somewhat like a shadow of the spiritual.

Conciliators of the System Headquarters

As these four-person commissions advance from planetary service, they move up to duty on system headquarters. Here they encounter much work, and they prove themselves to be understanding friends not just of mortals, but of angels and other spirit beings as well.

On system headquarters, places like Jerusem, both spiritual and material beings reside, along with combined types. The Material Sons and Daughters stationed there are physical beings like us, yet they're also connected to the spiritual circuits. They exist in a kind of middle state. When misunderstandings arise between Material Sons and Daughters and angels, or between Material Sons and Daughters and Melchizedeks, or between any of these groups, the conciliating commissions step in to work out the differences.

Something fascinating happens as we ascend to higher levels: there are fewer conflicts. Why? As we become more intelligent and spiritually mature, we become more accepting of other beings and their perspectives. We have less to get upset about, fewer contentions to pursue. Think about it this way: if you're advancing toward a state of being where you can exist with God, there must be considerable similarity among all those who make that journey. Understanding increases. You might say to someone, "Hey, I stubbed my toe," and they'd respond, "Oh yeah, I did that last year too. Hurts terribly, doesn't it?" That shared experience, that mutual understanding sharing it, reduces conflict naturally.

Here's the deeper principle: the moment the Creators brought into existence evolving individuals with the power of choice, a departure was made from the smooth working of divine perfection. Misunderstandings became certain to arise, and provision for the fair adjustment of these honest differences of viewpoint had to be made.

Consider this: the all-wise and all-powerful Creators could have made the local universes just as perfect as Havona, the central universe. No conciliating commissions would be needed in a perfect universe. But the Creators, in their wisdom, chose not to do this. While they've produced universes that abound in differences and teem with difficulties, they've also provided the mechanisms and means for resolving all these differences and harmonizing all this apparent confusion.

Why would they do this? Because if everything were perfect, we wouldn't gain the experience of working out our difficulties. That experience, learning to resolve conflicts, to understand different perspectives, to find common ground, is itself part of our growth. The struggle matters.

A Visual Journey Through Jerusem

Let me take a moment here to help you visualize the structure of our own system headquarters, because it illustrates beautifully how ascending mortals progress through these worlds.

At the center sits Jerusem itself. Surrounding Jerusem are seven major satellites: the Finaliter World, the Morontia World, the Angelic World, the Super Angel World, the World of the Sons, the World of the Spirit, and the World of the Father. Each of these seven worlds itself is surrounded by seven smaller satellites, forty-nine additional worlds in all.

Now, beyond these satellites are the seven mansion worlds where we ascending mortals first awaken after death. Mansion world number one sits at the outer edge of this system. When we arrive on mansion world number one, we receive clearance to visit world number one, the Finaliter World. That's the only major satellite we can initially access.

As we progress to mansion world number two, we gain clearance to visit the Morontia World and its seven surrounding satellites. Advance to mansion world three, and we can visit the Angelic World and its satellites. This pattern continues:

each mansion world we complete grants us access to the corresponding major satellite and all its associated worlds.

Some of us might spend a million years on that first mansion world, progress is highly individualized. But if we advance at a reasonable pace, we'll eventually have clearance to visit all these worlds. And when we complete all seven mansion worlds, we become citizens of Jerusem itself.

Here's an intriguing detail: when you reach the seventh mansion world, you gain clearance to visit the World of the Father. And on one of that world's satellites is the prison world, the place where Lucifer and Satan are held pending their adjudication. Once you've progressed to that level, you could actually visit and observe these fallen beings in their confinement. You don't have to, of course, but the opportunity exists.

During your progression through the mansion worlds, you're also invited on trips to Jerusem itself. So, you get to see the capital before you become a citizen, sort of like a preview of what's coming. These field trips are arranged by those training you, based on your readiness.

The exception to this pattern is mansion world number one. You can't simply jump from one mansion world to another until you've completed the necessary training. But once you advance from mansion world one to mansion world two, you gain access not just to the Morontia World, but to all seven of its satellites as well. You still can't visit mansion world three yet, you're not qualified for that. But you can take educational trips and vacations to the Morontia World.

It's like a tease. They show you the possibilities awaiting you on the next level, motivating you to continue your progress. As you advance through mansion worlds three, four, five, six, and seven, you're simultaneously being introduced to increasingly higher worlds and their satellites. You don't live on these higher worlds, not yet, but you visit them, take classes there, meet the beings who inhabit them. When you visit the Angelic World, for instance, you meet angels. It's all part of your expanding education.

The transportation system for all this travel appears to be primarily seraphic transport. However, there's an interesting distinction made between "earned space" and "unearned space." The texts tell us you can negotiate earned space on your own, though they don't explain exactly how that works. Unearned space requires seraphic transport, and typically you're rendered unconscious during these journeys. You go to sleep, and the next thing you know, you've arrived at your destination. The transit time must be fairly short since these worlds are in close proximity to each other, like moons orbiting a planet.

Once you've earned the right to be somewhere, you can apparently return there at will. The one exception? We can't return to our birth planet, to Urantia, until a thousand years have passed. After that millennium, we can visit our home world, but only with a supervising being. How exactly do we get there? Maybe seraphic transport, or perhaps there's some kind of morontia transportation system for student visitors. We honestly don't know all the details. But we do know that in the morontia form, we can be transported without being dematerialized and rematerialized, which would be necessary for purely physical beings.

Some of these mysteries we'll simply have to wait to experience firsthand. We might discover that seraphic transport in the morontia form is actually like an incredible carnival ride through space, with us fully conscious and enjoying the journey. Or it might be something entirely different from what we imagine. The universe has a way of surprising us. Most likely we will be unconscious,

Conciliators of the Constellation

From service in the systems, conciliators are promoted to handling problems arising in the constellation, which oversees one hundred systems of inhabited worlds. Not many problems developing on constellation headquarters fall directly under their jurisdiction, but they stay busy traveling from system to system, gathering evidence and preparing preliminary statements.

Here's what matters: if the contention is honest, if the difficulties arise from sincere differences of opinion and honest diversity of viewpoints, a conciliating commission can always be convened to pass judgment on the merits of the controversy. It doesn't matter how few individuals are involved. It doesn't matter how apparently trivial the misunderstanding might seem. The commission system ensures fair hearing and resolution.

The capital of our constellation is Edentia, a name that honors the Garden of Eden on our world. Even at this level, there are fewer misunderstandings than at the system level. The upward pattern continues.

Conciliators to the Local Universe

In the larger work of a local universe, the commissioners provide great assistance to the Melchizedeks, the Magisterial Sons, the constellation rulers, and the hosts of personalities concerned with coordinating and administering the one hundred constellations. The different orders of seraphim and other residents of local universe headquarters also make use of the help and decisions provided by these referee trios.

Remember, a complete local universe contains ten million inhabited planets when fully settled. The organizational structure builds from individual planets to local systems to constellations to the local universe itself. And at each level, conciliators serve their essential function.

It's almost impossible to explain the nature of the differences that arise in the detailed affairs of a system, constellation, or universe. Difficulties do develop, but they're nothing like the petty trials and trivial disputes we take to court on evolutionary worlds. The scale and significance are entirely different. We'll have to wait until we experience these realms firsthand to truly understand.

Conciliators to the Superuniverse Minor Sectors

From local universe problems, commissioners advance to studying questions arising in the minor sectors of their superuniverse. And here's where things shift significantly: the further they ascend inward from individual planets, the fewer material duties fall to the Divine Executioner. He gradually assumes a new role as a mercy-justice interpreter, while still maintaining his quasi-material nature, keeping the commission sympathetically connected to material aspects of their investigations.

Why this change? Once you step into the minor sectors, you're dealing primarily with spiritual beings. When you advance from the local universe into the minor sector, you become a first-stage spirit. Morontia beings no longer exist at this level. The difficulties that arise are between first-stage spirits, the angelic corps, and other personnel of the minor sector. Since there are fewer material concerns to address, the Divine Executioner's role naturally evolves.

Our minor sector is called Ensa, and it includes training spheres that continue our education as first-stage spirits.

Conciliators to the Superuniverse Major Sectors

At this level, the character of the commissioners' work continues its evolution. There's progressively less misunderstanding to adjudicate and more mysterious phenomena to explain and interpret. From stage to stage, they're evolving from arbiters of differences into explainers of mysteries, judges transforming into interpretive teachers.

Think about what this means. Initially, these beings arbitrated disputes arising from ignorance, permitting difficulties and misunderstandings to develop between parties. But now they're becoming instructors for those who are sufficiently intelligent and tolerant to avoid clashes of mind and wars of opinion. The higher a creature's education, the more respect that creature has for the knowledge, experience, and opinions of others.

We discussed this pattern earlier, but it bears repeating: the higher you ascend, the fewer problems you encounter because you become more accepting of other beings. The whole commission group becomes interpreters and teachers rather than judges and arbiters. Interestingly, the text mentions they increasingly interpret "mysterious phenomena." I imagine there's considerable physical and spiritual phenomena we encounter as we pass through the major sectors that requires expert explanation, things that simply don't make sense to us based on our current level of understanding.

You might wonder if we still carry our ego at these levels, or if that's been left behind. The ego never completely disappears, but it diminishes more and more as we advance. We become less egocentric and more accepting of everyone and everything because we grow more intelligent. We realize that egotism isn't the way to function in an advanced society.

It's somewhat like what happens as we age in mortal life. Notice how elderly people tend to become more accepting of young people who think they know everything? That's wisdom gained through experience. Grandparents become popular partly because they've learned acceptance. It's also why we don't have many teenagers teaching deep spiritual truths; they haven't lived long enough to develop that perspective.

Conciliators to the Superuniverse

At this highest level of superuniverse service, the conciliators become coordinate, four mutually understood and perfectly functioning arbiter-teachers working in seamless unity. The Divine Executioner is divested of retributive power and becomes simply the physical voice of the spirit trio. By this time, these counselors and teachers have become expertly familiar with most of the actual problems and difficulties encountered in conducting superuniverse affairs. They've transformed into wonderful advisors and wise teachers for ascending pilgrims residing on the educational spheres surrounding superuniverse headquarters.

We ascending mortals become residents of these educational spheres. We spend time on each world as we progress upward. When we leave the local system, we first become Jerusem citizens. Moving up to the constellation, we become Edentia citizens. Advancing to the local universe, we become Salvington citizens. When we leave Salvington as first-stage spirits, we become citizens of Ensa, the minor sector. This pattern continues with each upward jump, we become citizens of each world for however long our training there requires.

Now, these conciliators themselves are also advancing. They matriculate through increasingly higher responsibilities. Could we, at some stage, decide to become conciliators and follow that route? Not really. Our goal remains constant: to reach Havona and ultimately Paradise. We'll first master everything there is to learn on Uversa and its 490 surrounding satellites. Then we'll progress to Havona. Throughout this entire journey, we'll have multitudes of different tasks and jobs assigned to us.

For instance, you might be assigned work on the same sphere where Michael, our Creator Son, maintains his headquarters. You could spend a hundred thousand years doing something specific related to that sphere. But when it's time to advance as a first-stage spirit, Michael essentially gives you your graduation papers, and you move into the minor sector, where new tasks await you. With each jump, you learn new things and take on new responsibilities. This process multiplies upon itself all the way to Paradise. By the time you become a Finaliter, you've become remarkably capable and knowledgeable.

This was actually one of Lucifer's complaints, the extensive training mortals receive in universe administration. He resented it because he didn't have that same opportunity. As a Lanonandek Son, he couldn't be released from his position during the period when he was responsible for the entire system. He grew impatient and wanted to advance but couldn't. Jesus later acknowledged that the things Lucifer wanted would have come to him eventually. Being a Lanonandek Son, Lucifer was already highly intelligent and would have progressed through additional training much faster than we mortals do. But he couldn't wait. Patience, that was his failing.

The advantage we ascending mortals have is that we're always moving forward toward Paradise. All Sons of God can also look forward to Paradise, but they may have to serve in the outer universes for enormously long periods. It's all about perspective and patience.

Paradise Service

After serving under the Ancients of Days on Uversa for an extended period, conciliators are eventually advanced to Paradise. During their Paradise sojourn, they report to the Master Spirit who presides over the superuniverse of their origin, the very being who, in a sense, created them. They become increasingly like the personality of that Master Spirit.

The superuniverse registries don't enumerate conciliators who have passed beyond their jurisdiction, and such commissions are widely scattered throughout the grand universe. The last report of registry on Uversa gives the number operating in Orvonton, our superuniverse, as almost eighteen trillion commissions, representing over seventy trillion individuals. But these represent only a very small fraction of the multitude of conciliators created in Orvonton. The total number is far higher and is equivalent to the total number of Havona Servitals, with allowances for transmutation into Graduate Guides.

This tells us something profound: every type of being has a pathway to advance. These beings continue evolving, taking on new roles and responsibilities. After reaching Havona, when the four outer space levels begin developing, conciliators may have entirely different jobs waiting for them. We're talking about vast new superuniverses developing in outer space, all requiring personnel. Perhaps the conciliators will serve roles in those realms analogous to what the Ancients of Days serve now. We simply don't know yet. Everything remains possible.

From time to time, as superuniverse conciliator numbers increase, they're translated to the Council of Perfection on Paradise. From there they subsequently emerge as the coordinating corps evolved by the Infinite Spirit for the universe of universes, a marvelous group constantly increasing in numbers and efficiency. Through experiential ascent and Paradise training, they've acquired a unique grasp of the emerging reality of the Supreme Being, and they roam the universe of universes on special assignment. They become specialists in the experiential understanding of the Supreme Being.

Here's the final beautiful detail about these commissions: the members of a conciliating commission are never separated. A group of four forever serves together, just as they were originally associated. Even in their glorified service, they continue functioning as quartets of accumulated cosmic experience and perfected experiential wisdom. They're eternally associated as the embodiment of the supreme justice of time and space.

Their experience and wisdom, gained across billions of years and countless cases, make them uniquely qualified for this eternal association. What a wonderful concept, partnership and loyalty that lasts forever.

Conclusion

The Conciliators represent one of the most essential and far-reaching ministries in the universe. From humble beginnings on worlds like ours, these four-person commissions advance through every level of universe administration, resolving conflicts, interpreting mysteries, and eventually becoming teachers and advisors of supreme wisdom.

Their absolute loyalty, their patient progression through experience, and their eternal partnership exemplify principles that apply to all of us on the ascending path. We too will progress from level to level, gaining experience, developing wisdom, and learning to work harmoniously with an increasingly diverse array of beings. Conflict resolution, mutual understanding, and respect for different viewpoints aren't just administrative necessities, they're fundamental aspects of spiritual growth.

Next time, we'll explore another fascinating order of beings in the Messenger Hosts of Space: the Technical Advisors. These remarkable beings specialize in universe mechanics and technical knowledge, providing expertise wherever it's needed throughout the universes. I think you'll find their role equally fascinating.

Until then, may we all grow in our appreciation for the magnificent organization that makes the universes function so smoothly, and may we recognize that even in our current struggles and disagreements, we're learning skills that will serve us throughout eternity.

Chapter 22: The Technical Advisors—Perfection in Universal Service

When I first encountered the concept of Technical Advisors in The Urantia Book, I'll admit I was puzzled. The name itself sounds almost bureaucratic, doesn't it? Like celestial accountants or cosmic consultants. But as I dug deeper into Paper 25, I discovered something far more profound, these beings represent one of the most elegant solutions to a universal problem: How do you maintain perfect justice across billions of worlds without stifling the growth that comes from experience?

Tonight, as we continue our journey through Paper 25, "The Messenger Hosts of Space," we're exploring Section 4, which introduces us to these remarkable beings. What I've come to appreciate is that Technical Advisors aren't just experts in cosmic law, they're living libraries of applied wisdom, beings who bridge the gap between divine perfection and evolutionary experience.

Before we dive in, I want to address something practical that often confuses students of this book. You may have noticed that different editions of The Urantia Book number their paragraphs differently, and this can create real challenges in study groups. So let me take a moment to explain what happened and how we can navigate it together.

A Note on Editions and Paragraph Numbering

The original 1955 printing of The Urantia Book was limited to 10,000 copies, and those original volumes have become quite rare. I searched for two years to find an authentic first printing, and when I finally located one, I paid over $850 for it. Why? Not because there's anything "holy" about the physical book itself, we've discussed before how the book is a tool, not an object of worship, but because I needed to understand the textual history for teaching purposes.

You see, when the Uversa Press edition came out, likely around 1976, if I remember correctly, they renumbered the paragraphs throughout the entire book. The people behind this edition were sincere and knowledgeable students of the book who thought they were doing everyone a favor by creating what they considered a more logical numbering system. Unfortunately, this created confusion that persists to this day.

The key difference lies in how they handled lists. In the original Foundation edition, each item in a numbered or bulleted list counts as a separate paragraph.

The Uversa Press edition didn't count these items as individual paragraphs, which threw off all subsequent numbering. So, when I reference paragraph 25.4.13 in this study, someone with a Uversa Press edition might be looking at what they see as paragraph 25.4.6.

This is why I've created eight different study versions on our website at the Fifth Epochal Revelation Fellowship. Now I have reduced these versions to six. Some versions show only the original Foundation paragraph numbers, others show only the Uversa Press numbers, and several show both side by side. It took me nearly four years to program each paragraph separately across all these versions, going through the entire book eight times, but I wanted to make sure everyone could follow along regardless of which edition they own.

My advice? When teaching or studying in a group, always read the first few words of the paragraph you're referencing so everyone can locate it, regardless of their edition. And remember, while paragraph numbers may differ, the content remains essentially the same. There's also a helpful document available online called "Summary of Textual Changes Made in the Urantia Book Since the First Printing in 1955," which lists the minor corrections made over the years. Most are simple typos like "some time" versus "sometime", nothing that changes the meaning or message of the text. The Foundations eventually standardized the references to the paragraphs hoping that everyone would use this standardization.

Now, with that practical matter addressed, let's turn our attention to these fascinating beings called Technical Advisors.

The Nature and Purpose of Technical Advisors

The book tells us something quite striking right from the start: "These legal and technical minds of the spirit world were not created as such." Unlike many orders of beings who are created fully formed for their specific roles, Technical Advisors are recruited and trained. They represent something, I find deeply meaningful, the universe values experience and earned expertise, not just innate ability.

From the earliest supernaphim and omniaphim, and let me pause here to clarify that distinction, one million of the most orderly minds were chosen by the Infinite Spirit as the nucleus of this vast group. The omniaphim are servants of the Seven Supreme Executives, while the supernaphim were created directly by the Infinite Spirit. Both groups, along with others, form what we often call "angels," though technically only the seraphim truly hold that designation. The rest are more accurately described as members of the family of the Infinite Spirit, ministering spirits who serve in various capacities throughout creation.

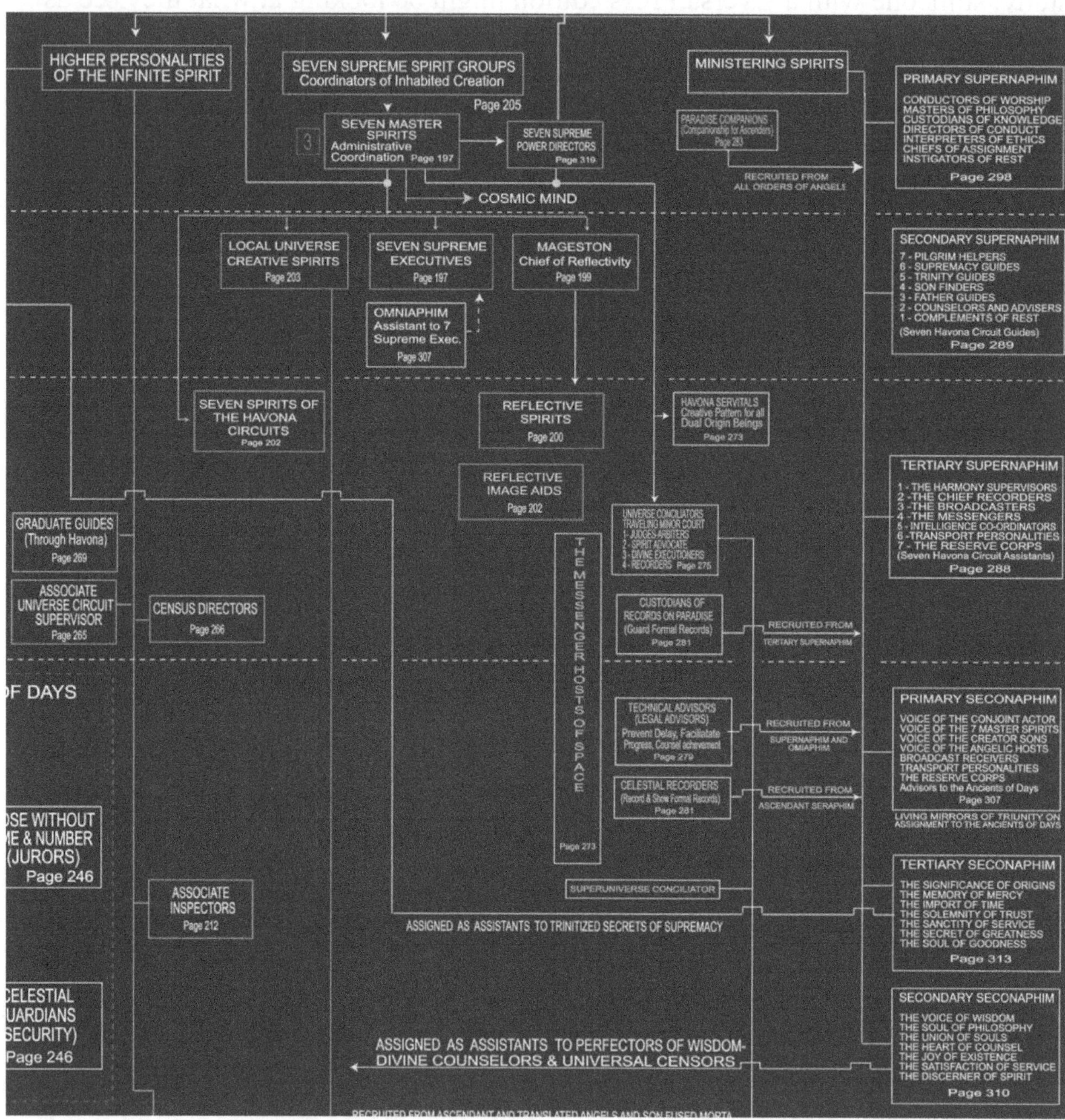

What strikes me most is this statement: "Ever since that far-distant time, actual experience in the application of the laws of perfection to the plans of evolutionary creation has been required of all who aspire to become Technical Advisors." Experience matters. The universe doesn't just hand out these positions based on potential, candidates must prove themselves through real-world application of universal principles.

The Recruitment of Technical Advisors

Currently, Technical Advisors are recruited from seven distinct personality orders:

1. The Supernaphim
2. The Seconaphim
3. The Tertiaphim
4. The Omniaphim
5. The Seraphim
6. Certain types of ascending mortals
7. Certain types of ascending midwayers

Now, when we see "ascending mortals" on this list, that's talking about beings like us, humans who've begun the long journey toward Paradise. But notice it says, "certain types." Not all ascending mortals become Technical Advisors, only those who develop particular expertise in the legal and procedural aspects of universe administration. These mortals choose this service temporarily as they progress through the ascension plan, gaining invaluable experience before continuing their journey.

The same applies to the ascending midwayers, those unique beings who originate on evolutionary worlds like ours. Both mortals and midwayers serve in a transient capacity, they come, they learn, they contribute, and then they move on. The other five orders, however, once they accept appointment as Technical Advisors, remain in that role essentially forever, at least until the Supreme Being comes into full fruition.

Think about what this means. At present, registered on Uversa and operating in our superuniverse of Orvonton alone, there are slightly more than 61 trillion Technical Advisors. And that's just one of the seven superuniverses. When you multiply that across all creation, you begin to grasp the scale of universe administration. We're not talking about a small legal department, we're talking about a vast network of experienced, reliable counselors available to guide decisions affecting countless billions of worlds.

The Organization and Function of Technical Advisors

Technical Advisors don't work in isolation. They organize for service in groups of seven, and here's where it gets interesting: at least five in each group must be of permanent status, while two may be of temporary association. This structure ensures continuity of experience and wisdom while still allowing for fresh perspectives from ascending mortals and midwayers who are passing through on their way to Paradise.

The book makes clear that those mortals and midwayers who serve with the advisors "do not enter the regular courses of training for Technical Advisors, nor do they ever become permanent members of the order." Why not? Well, think about it, the full training program takes an enormous amount of time, and requiring temporary members to complete it would significantly delay their progress toward Paradise. The universe is practical. It values the contribution these ascending beings can make with their unique evolutionary perspective without burdening them with training they won't need for a permanent role they'll never hold.

But here's something beautiful that applies to all of us: "As you journey toward your Paradise goal, constantly acquiring added knowledge and enhanced skill, you are continuously afforded the opportunity to give out to others the wisdom and experience you have already accumulated."

Let me tell you what this means for us personally. When you get to the mansion worlds, and you will get there, you're going to be doing exactly what I'm doing right now: teaching others what you've just learned. All the way into Havona, you'll act as both pupil and teacher, working your way through what the book calls "the ascending levels of this vast experiential university."

Now, I don't want anyone thinking I have some special advantage because I've spent years studying this book. Everything I've learned is stored in this little pea brain of mine, and there's no guarantee how much of it transfers to the mansion worlds. We're told we take with us what's spiritually valuable and applicable to our continuing growth. I may remember everything because I've been through it so many times, or I may need to relearn portions of it just like you will. The important principle is this: "You are not reckoned as having possessed yourself of knowledge and truth until you have demonstrated your ability and your willingness to impart this knowledge and truth to others."

If I get halfway through studying a paper and die this week, I may well need to finish that paper when I wake up on the mansion worlds. The same applies to each of you. We pick up where we left off, continuing our education in a setting perfectly designed for our next phase of growth.

The Extensive Training Program

The training of Technical Advisors follows a clear progression through increasingly elevated spheres of instruction. It begins in the Melchizedek colleges of the local universes, those same colleges where so many other orders of beings receive their foundational education. From there, the training continues to the courts of the Ancients of Days in the superuniverse capitals.

After completing their superuniverse training, these candidates proceed to something called "the schools of the seven circles" located on the pilot worlds of the Havona circuits. Each of the seven circuits of Havona has a pilot world, and on each of these worlds stands a school dedicated to training Technical Advisors. From these pilot worlds, they're received into "the College of the Ethics of Law and the Technique of Supremacy," which is the Paradise training school for perfecting Technical Advisors.

Now, why would this final training focus specifically on "the Technique of Supremacy"? Because Technical Advisors are intimately connected with the evolution of the Supreme Being. As they gain experience and render service throughout time and space, they're contributing to the experiential growth of God the Supreme. By the time they've advanced enough to reach Havona and Paradise for final training, they're ready to understand the deeper principles of how their service relates to this great cosmic synthesis of finite experience.

The book tells us something remarkable: these advisors "even essay to elucidate the technique of the Ultimate." In other words, the knowledge and principles they master will remain useful not just through the age of the Supreme, but even into the next universe age when we'll be dealing with God the Ultimate and the vast outer space levels. This isn't temporary or limited knowledge, it's foundational wisdom that applies across multiple ages of universal development.

Living Law Libraries

Here's one of my favorite descriptions in this entire section: Technical Advisors "become the living law libraries of time and space, preventing endless trouble and needless delays by instructing the personalities of time regarding the forms and modes of procedure most acceptable to the rulers of eternity."

Think about that phrase, "living law libraries." They're not just repositories of information; they're experienced, wise beings who can apply universal principles to specific situations. They understand not just what the law says, but how it should be applied across vastly different circumstances, cultures, and planetary conditions.

The book emphasizes that these advisors are "students and teachers of applied law, the laws of the universe applied to the lives and destinies of all who inhabit the vast domains of the far-flung creation." Notice that word "applied." They're not theoretical scholars debating fine points in ivory towers. They're practical advisors who help real beings navigate real situations in harmony with eternal principles.

Who do they advise? Primarily, they serve the Universal Conciliators, those remarkable four-person tribunals we studied in the previous section that consist of a divine counselor, a perfector of wisdom, a universal censor, and a divine executor. When these tribunals are called upon to settle disputes or render judgments, they can summon Technical Advisors as expert witnesses. The advisors provide historical context, procedural guidance, and wisdom drawn from countless similar cases across the universes.

But their service extends far beyond the courts. "They are available to the Universal Conciliators and to all others who desire to know the truth of law; in other words, to know how the Supremacy of Deity may be depended upon to react in any given situation having factors of an established physical, mindal, and spiritual order."

Let me break that down, because it's saying something profound. When you face a complex situation that involves physical realities, mental or intellectual factors, and spiritual principles, and most important situations do involve all three, the Technical Advisors can counsel you on how to proceed in a way that harmonizes with the way deity itself would respond. They help us align our actions with the divine pattern.

The Absolute Reliability of Technical Advisors

Now here's something that should give us great confidence: "Technical Advisors are selected and tested beings; I have never known one of them to go astray. We have no records on Uversa of their ever having been adjudged in contempt of the divine laws which they so effectively interpret and so eloquently expound."

Read that again. Never. Not one has ever rebelled, gone astray, or been found in contempt of the very laws they interpret. This is extraordinary when you consider that we live in a universe where even high celestial beings, Lucifer, Satan, Caligastia, have chosen rebellion. But not a single Technical Advisor has ever failed in their trust.

Why this perfect record? Perhaps it's because their selection process is so rigorous, requiring extensive experience and demonstrated wisdom before appointment. Perhaps it's because the very nature of their work, constant immersion in divine law and eternal principles, reinforces their alignment with deity. Or perhaps it's simply that those who are drawn to this service possess a fundamental stability and loyalty that makes rebellion unthinkable.

Whatever the reason, it means we can trust their counsel completely. When a Technical Advisor offers guidance, you're receiving wisdom that's been tested across countless worlds and situations, filtered through minds that have never deviated from their dedication to truth and justice.

The book adds something else that should encourage us: "There is no known limit to the domain of their service, neither has any been placed upon their progress. They continue as advisors even to the portals of Paradise; the whole universe of law and experience is open to them."

Their usefulness doesn't end when they reach Paradise. They continue serving, continue learning, continue growing. The knowledge they accumulate is relevant not just to our current age but to future ages of universal development that we can barely imagine.

Special Counsel to the Life Carriers

Before we close this section, I want to highlight one particular application of Technical Advisor service that has profound implications for understanding our own world. The text tells us: "A special group act as law counselors to the Life Carriers, advising these Sons concerning the extent of permissible departure from the established order of life propagation and otherwise instructing them respecting their prerogatives and latitudes of function."

This is crucial for understanding how life develops on evolutionary worlds. The Life Carriers are the beings responsible for initiating life on planets throughout the universes. On our world, Urantia, they actually formulated the life plasm here rather than bringing it from elsewhere, a fact that relates to our status as an experimental world.

But the Life Carriers don't have unlimited freedom to create whatever life forms they imagine. They work within boundaries, and those boundaries are established and explained by Technical Advisors serving as law counselors. These advisors tell the Life Carriers how much variation they can introduce, what types of modifications are permissible, and where the limits lie.

Now here's where it gets really interesting for us: Urantia is decimal planet number 606 in our local system. That means we're one of the experimental worlds, specifically, every tenth planet is designated for experimentation. On such worlds, the Life Carriers are granted greater latitude to try new approaches; to introduce variations they couldn't attempt on standard worlds.

So, what does this mean practically? It means that when the Life Carriers were designing the life plasm for Urantia, the Technical Advisors gave them permission to experiment more boldly. The types of creatures that would evolve, the colors and variations within species, the specific challenges and opportunities built into our biosphere, all of these were influenced by this experimental status, guided by Technical Advisors who understood how far the Life Carriers could push the boundaries while still maintaining cosmic legal standards.

Think about the implications. Before we ever existed, before the first single-celled organism appeared in Earth's ancient oceans, there were deliberations about what kinds of life might develop here. Technical Advisors counseled Life Carriers on the possibilities and limits, ensuring that our world's development would serve both scientific interests and divine purposes.

And yes, we can blame them for mosquitoes. Someone in the chat mentioned that, and it's actually accurate, every form of life on this planet, from the most beneficial to the most annoying, traces back to the original life plasm formulation that the Life Carriers created under the guidance of Technical Advisors. The bacteria, the viruses, the insects, the plants, the animals, all of it began as potential encoded in that first living matter, then evolved according to natural processes over millions of years.

The Adamic Default and Its Continuing Effects

There's another piece of this puzzle worth understanding. When Adam and Eve came to Urantia about 37,000 years ago, and modern genetic science has actually detected significant changes in human DNA that date to approximately that time, they were supposed to introduce what we call "Adamic" or "violet" blood into the human race. This genetic upgrade would have strengthened our immune systems, enhanced our intellectual capacities, and provided other biological benefits.

The plan called for Adam and Eve's descendants to number at least one million before they began intermarrying with the indigenous human races. But the plan failed. The default occurred, and the Adamic genetic contribution spread into the general population much earlier and in much smaller quantities than intended.

So, does that mean we lost out entirely? Not at all. The Adamic genes are out there in the human gene pool. They're real and they're functioning. It's just going to take much longer for them to reach the level of distribution and effect that was originally planned. Instead of the benefits appearing over tens of thousands of years, it may take hundreds of thousands of years. But the improvement is still happening. Every time people with Adamic genetic heritage have children, especially when they partner with others carrying similar heritage, they strengthen that genetic line.

The Life Carriers who initiated life on Urantia left a few observers stationed here, and they're still watching. Not to interfere, their work is essentially done, but to observe how the life plasm they designed continues to evolve and adapt. The knowledge they're gaining by watching our slow biological and social evolution will inform their work on future worlds. They're learning from what worked well and what didn't, from our successes and our struggles.

We're planet 606 in our system, which means 600 other worlds preceded us. The Life Carriers had 600 previous experiments to learn from before they designed life on our world. And being an experimental planet, we gave them the opportunity to try approaches they couldn't attempt on standard worlds. In another 100,000 planets' worth of experience, Life Carriers will be extraordinarily skilled at their craft. And throughout this entire process, Technical Advisors set the legal and ethical boundaries, ensuring that experimentation never crosses lines that would violate cosmic law or harm the greater purposes of creation.

The Technique of Perfection

Let me share something that both comforts and challenges me. The book states clearly: "There is always a best and right way to do things; there is always the technique of perfection, a divine method, and these advisors know how to direct us all in the finding of this better way."

On one hand, this is wonderfully reassuring. We're not wandering blindly through existence, making it up as we go. There actually are better and worse ways to approach situations, and beings exist who can guide us toward the better ways. The universe isn't arbitrary or chaotic, it has structure, principles, laws that work.

On the other hand, this challenges my human tendency toward relativism, toward thinking "whatever works for you is fine." No, there are objectively better approaches to most situations, methods more aligned with eternal reality. The Technical Advisors can perceive these patterns because they've studied countless situations across countless worlds and seen what produces harmony and what produces discord.

Now, does this mean we're all supposed to act like robots, following some cosmic rulebook? Not at all. Remember what we learned about the Paradise Deities, they know everything that will happen, but they don't tell us. They don't rob us of the experience of figuring things out for ourselves. As I mentioned in our discussion, there was a wonderful old "Twilight Zone" episode where a gangster dies and goes to what he thinks is heaven, he wins every bet, every woman falls for him, he's given everything he wants. Eventually he realizes he's actually in hell, because life without challenge, without genuine uncertainty, without real consequence, becomes meaningless torture.

The gods love us enough to let us struggle. They love us enough to allow us to make mistakes, to experience consequences, to learn through trial and error. The Technical Advisors are available to guide us, but they're not going to do our homework for us. They'll show us the principles; we have to apply them to our specific circumstances.

My wife has a card taped to the bathroom mirror listing the Fruits of the Spirit, love, joy, peace, patience, kindness, goodness, faithfulness, gentleness, self-control. When I brush my teeth in the morning, I see that list and I ask myself: "Are these qualities showing in my life? Am I living these principles today?" If the Fruits of the Spirit are evident in our lives, we're learning the lessons Jesus came to teach. We're aligning ourselves with that "technique of perfection" the Technical Advisors represent.

A Divine Withholding

Here's another passage that strikes me deeply: "Such a living library of applied law could not be created; such beings must be evolved by actual experience. The infinite Deities are existential, hence are compensated for lack of experience; they know all even before they experience all, but they do not impart this non-experiential knowledge to their subordinate creatures."

God the Father, God the Son, and God the Spirit know everything. They know what's going to happen before it happens. They don't need advice about the future because they already possess complete knowledge. But, and this is crucial, they don't share that knowledge with us. They don't tell us what's coming. They don't warn us about every mistake we're about to make or guide us around every hardship.

Why not? Because doing so would rob us of the very thing that makes us valuable to the universe: our experiential growth. If we knew everything in advance, we wouldn't truly learn. We wouldn't develop wisdom, judgment, or character. We'd be sophisticated robots, not beings who've earned our place in eternity through genuine struggle and choice.

This is an act of profound love. The gods deliberately withhold information that would make our lives easier in the short term because they're committed to our long-term growth. They want us to become beings of genuine experience and earned wisdom, not pampered children who've never had to think for ourselves.

So the next time you're going through something difficult and you wonder, "Why didn't God warn me about this?" remember: He's loving you enough to let you learn. He's trusting you enough to believe you can handle it. And He's confident enough in the process that He knows you'll emerge stronger, wiser, and more valuable to the universe because of what you're experiencing.

Technical Advisors embody this principle. They're not created with all knowledge pre-installed. They have to earn their expertise through actual experience applying universal laws to real situations. And that earned wisdom is precisely what makes them so valuable as counselors.

Looking Ahead

As we close this chapter, I'm struck by the careful design evident in universe administration. Technical Advisors represent just one order among many that work together to maintain justice, foster growth, and help evolutionary beings like us find our way through the complexities of cosmic citizenship.

We've barely scratched the surface of the angelic orders. In the next paper, we'll explore in detail the various types of ministering spirits, the supernaphim, seconaphim, tertiaphim, and many others. We'll see how each order has specific functions, how they work together, and how they all contribute to the vast ministry that makes our ascension to Paradise possible.

For now, though, let me leave you with this thought: Technical Advisors are proof that the universe values experience and expertise. They show us that there's always a better way to do things, even when we can't see it yet. And they demonstrate that beings who dedicate themselves to understanding and applying divine law can serve throughout eternity without ever going astray.

That's a model worth contemplating as we continue our own journey toward Paradise.

Chapter 23: The Custodians of Records on Paradise

Introduction: Keepers of Universal History

As I've studied The Urantia Book over the years, few topics have captured my imagination quite like the celestial beings who maintain the records of all creation. When we think about the vastness of the universe, billions of inhabited worlds, countless personalities, innumerable events spanning unimaginable stretches of time, the question naturally arises: How is all of this documented? Who keeps track of everything that happens across seven superuniverses?

The answer reveals one of the most remarkable administrative structures in all of creation: the Custodians of Records on Paradise. These beings, along with their associates throughout the universes, maintain what might be called the ultimate library, a repository containing every significant event since the beginning of recorded time. But this isn't merely an academic exercise or bureaucratic function. Understanding how the universe documents our lives, our choices, and our spiritual progress helps us grasp something profound about the nature of reality itself: nothing we do is lost, forgotten, or without meaning.

In this chapter, we'll explore the hierarchy of celestial recorders, from the living libraries of Paradise to the guardian angels who document every moment of our earthly existence. We'll discover how records are kept in both spiritual and material form, why accuracy matters so deeply to the celestial administrators, and what all of this means for our own journey from this world to the mansion worlds and beyond.

The Dual Nature of Universal Records

When I first read about the record-keeping systems of Paradise, I was struck by the sophistication of what The Urantia Book describes. There aren't just written archives, there are two distinct types of records, each serving a different purpose and accessible to different orders of beings.

The formal archives represent what we might think of as the traditional concept of records. These are kept by certain senior Chief Recorders chosen from among the tertiary supernaphim, the angels native to Havona, the central universe. These custodians maintain the physical (or perhaps more accurately, the semi-material) documentation of everything that transpires throughout creation. Imagine, if you can, libraries containing detailed accounts of every inhabited world, every significant event, every spiritual milestone achieved by billions upon billions of ascending mortals. The scope alone staggers the imagination.

But there's another kind of record that seems even more extraordinary: the living records. These exist in the minds of beings known as the Custodians of Knowledge, sometimes called the living libraries of Paradise. These remarkable personalities literally *remember* everything since the beginning of time. They don't consult documents or search databases, the information simply resides within them, accessible and complete. When I try to comprehend what that must be like, my mind struggles with the concept. We forget where we put our keys, yet these beings hold within themselves the entire history of universal events.

The Urantia Book makes it clear that both types of records serve essential functions. The formal archives provide a tangible reference point, something that can be examined, studied, and verified by multiple sources. The living records offer immediacy and completeness, a kind of cosmic memory that never fades or becomes corrupted. Together, they create a redundant system ensuring that truth is preserved and accessible across all levels of reality.

How Information Flows Through the Universe

One aspect of celestial record-keeping that I find particularly fascinating is the way information moves through the various levels of universe administration. It's not as though everything happening on every world gets immediately transmitted to Paradise. Instead, there's a sophisticated filtering and forwarding system that ensures appropriate information reaches the right destinations.

Let me explain how this works, starting from our own world, Urantia. Here on Earth and on every other inhabited planet, recording angels, typically seraphim, document all individual records. Everything that happens to each person from birth onward gets recorded by these dedicated celestial beings. It's a humbling thought, really. Every choice we make, every kindness we show, every time we resist selfishness or give in to it, all of it is documented with perfect accuracy.

But not everything that happens on Urantia needs to be forwarded beyond our local system. Events of purely local importance find only local recording. However, when something of wider significance occurs, something that affects the constellation or the entire local universe, that information gets passed along to higher administrative levels.

From planets to systems to constellations, information flows upward through our local universe of Nebadon. Anything of true universe importance is posted at Salvington, the headquarters of our local universe. From there, episodes of even greater significance are advanced to the minor sector headquarters, then to the major sector, and eventually to Uversa, the capital of our seventh superuniverse, Orvonton.

Paradise itself maintains a relevant summary of all superuniverse and Havona data. The complete historic and cumulative story of the universe of universes rests in the custody of those exalted tertiary supernaphim we discussed earlier. When you think about the efficiency of this system, the way it captures everything while avoiding overwhelming any single administrative level, you begin to appreciate the wisdom built into universal governance.

This filtering system also employs a remarkable technique called reflectivity. Information doesn't travel through space in the way we might imagine. Instead, it's instantaneously reflected through the angelic corps, allowing the custodians to stay constantly updated. As anything significant happens anywhere in the universe, that information is immediately available to those who need to know. There's no lag time, no waiting for reports to arrive. The system operates in real-time across distances that would take light billions of years to traverse.

The Celestial Recorders: Ascending Seraphim with a Special Calling

While the tertiary supernaphim serve as the ultimate custodians on Paradise, much of the actual recording work throughout the superuniverses is performed by beings called Celestial Recorders. Understanding who these beings are and what they sacrifice for their service adds a deeply personal dimension to this topic.

Celestial Recorders are not created as such. They are ascended seraphim from the local universes, angels who have themselves progressed spiritually and chosen to enter this specialized service. This is where the story becomes particularly meaningful to me. You see, seraphim who serve as guardian angels have the opportunity to ascend alongside their mortal charges. When a seraphim faithfully guards a human being through their earthly life and that person chooses to continue their Paradise ascent, the seraphim can advance together with them, experiencing the same journey of discovery and growth all the way to Paradise.

But when a seraphim is called to become a Celestial Recorder and accepts that assignment, something changes. They can no longer follow that path of personal ascension in the same way. Once they take on the role of recorder, they're assigned to that job permanently, at least until the full personalization of God the Supreme, which represents a future age of the universe. They can advance within the recording service, gaining greater responsibility and skill, but they cannot continue as ascending seraphim in the traditional sense.

Think about what this means. These angels make a choice to serve in a way that permanently alters their own spiritual journey. They don't do this because they're forced or because they have no other options. They do it because the work matters, because accurate record-keeping serves the greater good, because someone needs to ensure that truth is preserved throughout all of time and space.

When a seraphim accepts this calling, they receive training in specialized schools located on the headquarters worlds of the seven superuniverses. On Uversa, our superuniverse capital, these schools are conducted by the Perfectors of Wisdom and the Divine Counselors. I imagine these must be extraordinary educational experiences, preparing these angels for work that demands absolute precision and unwavering dedication.

The Celestial Recorders possess a peculiar ability that makes them uniquely suited for their role: they can simultaneously manipulate both spiritual and material energy. This allows them to execute all records in duplicate, making an original spirit recording and what The Urantia Book describes as a semi-material counterpart, something like a carbon copy, though far more sophisticated than that analogy suggests. This dual recording ensures that records remain accessible to beings of vastly different natures, from material creatures like ourselves to high spirits of light.

The Character of Those Who Keep Records

I've always believed you can learn a great deal about the importance of a task by looking at the character of those assigned to perform it. In the case of celestial record-keeping, The Urantia Book offers remarkable testimony to the integrity of these beings.

One passage particularly stands out to me: "The recorders are a tested and tried corps. Never have I known of the defection of a celestial recorder, and never has there been discovered a falsification in their records."

Think about that statement for a moment. Across trillions upon trillions of records spanning unfathomable stretches of time, there has never been a single case of deliberate falsification. Never. This isn't because these beings are mindless automatons following programming, they're genuine personalities with free will and the capacity for choice. Yet they choose, consistently and without exception, to maintain absolute fidelity to truth.

Their records are subjected to dual inspection. Other exalted recorders from Uversa scrutinize their work, as do the Mighty Messengers, who specifically certify the correctness of the quasi-physical duplicates. This might seem like overkill, why inspect records created by beings who have never falsified anything? But I think the answer lies in understanding how seriously the universe takes truth. It's not that anyone doubts the integrity of individual recorders; rather, the process itself becomes a demonstration of how much accuracy matters.

While advancing recorders stationed throughout the subordinate spheres of our superuniverse number in the trillions, those who have attained graduate status on Uversa itself are not quite eight million. These senior recorders serve as the superuniverse custodians and forwarders of the sponsored records of time and space. They maintain permanent headquarters in circular abodes surrounding the area of records on Uversa, and here's something I find intriguing: they never leave the custody of these records to others. Individuals may be absent, but never in large numbers.

During one of our study sessions, someone asked an interesting question: Does this mean the records could be at risk? It's hard to imagine what threat they might face, who would want to destroy or alter them, and how could they even attempt it in such a secure environment? Perhaps the constant presence serves more to ensure efficiency and immediate availability. At any moment, somewhere in the universe, someone might need access to specific records, a court might require documentation, an administrator might need historical context, a teacher might want to illustrate a point. The records must always be accessible.

But I think there's something else at work here too, something more profound than mere practical necessity. These records represent something sacred, not in a religious sense, but in terms of their intrinsic value. They document the spiritual growth of countless individuals, the evolution of entire civilizations, the unfolding of divine plans across cosmic ages. Such material deserves to be guarded not because it's vulnerable, but because it's precious beyond measure.

Our Personal Records: The Angels Who Know Everything

Now let me bring this down to a more personal level, because all of this cosmic record-keeping has very direct implications for each of us. Everything that happens to you is being recorded with perfect accuracy from the moment of your birth.

The recording angels of inhabited planets, the seraphim assigned to our worlds, are the source of all individual records. On Earth, as on every inhabited world, these faithful angels document our lives in complete detail. Every significant event, every moral choice, every spiritual insight, every act of kindness or selfishness, all of it goes into the record.

When you reach the third psychic circle in your spiritual development, which occurs when you make a definitive, permanent decision to follow the will of God in your life, something changes. Up until that point, you're under the general care of recording angels, but at the third circle, you receive personal guardians. Two seraphim are permanently assigned to you, along with two cherubim who serve as assistants. One of these four beings remains on duty at all times, ensuring continuous documentation of your life.

I remember when this realization first hit me during my studies. Right now, as I write these words, my guardian seraphim or one of my cherubim is recording this moment. When you read this chapter, your guardians are aware of it and documenting your response. When we gather with others to study, when we're alone making difficult decisions, when we experience joy or struggle through hardship, they're always there, always observing, always recording.

Someone once told me they found this idea disturbing, like living under constant surveillance. But I've come to see it very differently. These angels aren't spies trying to catch us doing something wrong. They're devoted servants ensuring that nothing about our lives is lost or forgotten. When we arrive on the mansion worlds, we'll have access to complete, accurate records of our earthly existence. We'll be able to review anything that happened, understand patterns we couldn't see while living through events, and gain insights that will help us grow.

The Urantia Book puts it beautifully: "In your transition experience as you ascend from this material world, you will always be able to consult the records of and to be otherwise conversant with the history and traditions of your status sphere." We won't lose connection with our origins. We can keep track of what happens on Earth after we leave, stay connected to the ongoing story of our world, and maintain awareness of how our efforts contributed to larger patterns of progress.

These personal records become part of the Book of Life, that ancient concept that appears in various religious traditions. If your name is written in the Book of Life, it means all records of your existence are preserved and accessible. You matter. Your life has significance. Nothing you've experienced or accomplished will be forgotten.

Guardian Angels: What They Do and Don't Do

Since we're discussing the seraphim who record our lives, I want to address some common misunderstandings about guardian angels. These clarifications came up during one of our study sessions, and I think they're worth exploring here.

Guardian angels are assigned to each of us at birth. Every child born into this world comes under the care of the angelic corps. However, as I mentioned earlier, when you reach the third psychic circle, you receive permanent personal guardians, a dedicated team of two seraphim and two cherubim who will remain with you through your entire ascension journey.

Now here's what's important to understand: while these angels do guard our souls, that's not primarily what they guard us against physical harm. They cannot and do not intervene to prevent accidents, illnesses, or natural consequences of our choices. If you step in front of a moving train, your guardian angel will not push you out of the way. If you develop cancer, they will not miraculously cure it. If you make foolish decisions that lead to painful consequences, they will not shield you from those outcomes.

This might sound harsh, but it reflects a crucial principle: free will cannot be violated, and natural cause-and-effect must be allowed to operate. We're here on this world to learn and grow, and that learning often comes through experiencing the results of our choices. Angels who constantly intervened to prevent negative outcomes would actually hinder our spiritual development.

What guardian angels *can* do, and what they do constantly, is manipulate circumstances to create opportunities for spiritual growth. They arrange situations that challenge us, place certain people in our paths, and create conditions that test our character. Some of the difficulties we face may actually be orchestrated by our guardians specifically because struggling through them will strengthen us spiritually.

Their primary job isn't protecting our physical bodies; it's protecting our souls and fostering our spiritual progress. They record our lives, yes, but they also actively work to create conditions conducive to moral and spiritual development. They can't make our choices for us, but they can influence the menu of options we face.

One person in our study group shared an interesting experience. Years ago, he was driving home in a snowstorm and came to a traffic light. For some inexplicable reason, he didn't proceed when the light changed. He just sat there, experiencing what felt like a blank moment in time. When he came to his senses, he turned right instead of going straight, then made a left turn. Looking up the street ahead, he saw a flash of light, an accident occurring exactly where he would have been if he'd continued on his original route.

Was that angelic intervention? Possibly not in the direct sense. More likely, it was his own superconscious awareness, facilitated perhaps by his Thought Adjuster, sensing danger and causing him to hesitate. We all have some capacity for precognition, for intuiting things about to happen. Our Thought Adjusters, those fragments of God dwelling within our minds, certainly know what's coming and can sometimes influence our instincts.

But here's the key point: guardian angels are not responsible for that kind of protection. Their mission involves something far more important than keeping us physically safe. They're working to ensure we become spiritually mature, morally courageous, and genuinely ready for eternal life.

Connecting with Your Thought Adjuster

Speaking of Thought Adjusters, let me address another topic that came up in our discussions: How do we connect with this divine presence within us?

The Thought Adjuster's real job is to spiritualize your life. That's the number one priority, to make your life more spiritual, to help you see things from an eternal perspective, to gradually transform your thinking from purely material concerns to increasingly spiritual awareness. Anything your Thought Adjuster can do to make your life more spiritual, it will do.

Some people think you need formal meditation practice to connect with your Thought Adjuster. While meditation certainly helps and I encourage it, you don't have to enter some special state of consciousness to communicate with the God-fragment within you. You can talk to your Thought Adjuster just as easily while walking through your day as while sitting in quiet contemplation.

Think about it: your Thought Adjuster resides in your mind. It hears every thought, is aware of every emotion, knows your intentions before you fully form them. You don't need to speak aloud or even form deliberate mental messages. Simply being aware that this divine presence is with you, acknowledging it throughout your day, talking to it as you would to your closest friend, this works perfectly well.

You don't need to know your Thought Adjuster's name. The best name we have for it is simply "God" or "Father." That's enough. What matters isn't the label but the relationship, the ongoing conversation, the gradual alignment of your will with the divine will operating within you.

Your Thought Adjuster is working patiently and persistently to help you grow spiritually. Every time you choose mercy over judgment, every time you act with integrity when no one is watching, every time you extend compassion to someone who doesn't deserve it, your Thought Adjuster is right there, encouraging and supporting those choices. The connection happens naturally when you live with awareness of this indwelling presence.

The Assurance That Grows Over Time

Let me share something personal that I hope illustrates an important point about spiritual growth. If I asked everyone in our study group whether they had any doubt about God's existence, every single person would say no. Not a shred of doubt. We've reached a place in our lives where God's reality is as certain to us as our own existence.

But this assurance didn't appear overnight. None of us woke up one morning as children and thought, "I know with absolute certainty that God exists and that will never change." That's not how it works. Faith develops over time, like personality develops over time, like wisdom accumulates gradually through experience.

The assurance of God is a patient thing you have to learn slowly. It grows in you through years of seeking, questioning, testing, and discovering. Every answered prayer, or seemingly unanswered one that later reveals unexpected meaning, adds to your certainty. Every time you sense divine guidance, every moment when you feel that unmistakable presence, every instance when cosmic principles suddenly make sense... these experiences accumulate, building a foundation of assurance that eventually becomes unshakeable.

I think about what it will be like when I'm lying in that final bed, 80 or 90 years old, struggling to breathe, knowing the end is near. One thing I know with absolute certainty: God the Father will be with me. And when I take that last breath and close my eyes for the final time, I know my guardian angel will be right there to take my hand. That assurance only grows from faith, and that faith only develops over time.

All of us who've grown older together in faith have discovered something remarkable: we're not afraid of death anymore. Oh, we might be afraid of *how* we'll die, nobody wants to suffer unnecessarily or experience a traumatic end. But the actual process of passing over and going on? That doesn't frighten us. We've developed that assurance I'm talking about, that deep certainty that death is simply a transition, not an ending.

This relates directly to what we'll face when we ascend through the universes. When we traverse the circuits of Havona and eventually attempt to recognize the three Deities, the Infinite Spirit, the Eternal Son, and the Universal Father, we won't see them in physical form. We'll need to sense them spiritually, to recognize their presence through spiritual perception rather than material sight.

Think about how you sense the local universe Mother Spirit right now. You recognize her through the Holy Spirit working in your life, through the fruits of the spirit that grow in you, love, joy, peace, patience, kindness, goodness, faithfulness, gentleness, and self-control. These qualities don't come from your human nature; they flow from the Mother Spirit's influence. When you experience them authentically in yourself or others, you're experiencing her presence.

That's the kind of recognition we'll need to achieve in Havona, only at an infinitely more profound level. Most ascending mortals successfully recognize all three Deities and continue their Paradise journey. But occasionally someone cannot quite grasp the spiritual reality of one of the Paradise Deities, most commonly the Universal Father. There's no shame in this, it simply means they need more preparation.

When this happens, the ascending mortal is remanded back to the superuniverses for remedial training. A Paradise Companion accompanies them because their mortal companion who successfully completed the Deity adventure cannot return to the superuniverses once they've reached Havona. So, the Paradise Companion provides friendship and support while the temporarily defeated pilgrim receives additional spiritual training, then makes another attempt at the Havona circuits.

This entire system reflects something fundamental about the universe: it's designed for success, not failure. Every provision is made to help us achieve our goals. No one is abandoned. No one faces challenges alone. And every setback is simply an opportunity for further growth.

When We Arrive on the Mansion Worlds

Let's talk about what happens when we first awaken after death, because the record-keeping system plays an important role in that transition.

When you arrive on the first mansion world, those records your guardian seraphim have been keeping become immediately accessible. The celestial administrators can review anything from your earthly life. They know your strengths, your weaknesses, your patterns of behavior, your spiritual progress, and the areas where you still need growth.

But you're not alone in this new existence. The local universe Mother Spirit has created special beings called morontia companions specifically to keep us company during our early mansion world experiences. Currently, there are over 70 billion of these unique beings serving in Nebadon, our local universe. They're created in groups of 100,000 and are assigned to help ascending mortals like us enjoy ourselves, learn to play again, and adapt to morontia life.

These companions are not indispensable to our progression, they don't teach us essential lessons or conduct our training. They simply make the journey more pleasant. They're gracious hosts with a sense of humor who help us navigate this new reality. Think about how thoughtful that is. The Mother Spirit didn't have to create beings whose sole purpose is making us comfortable and happy. She did it anyway because she cares about our well-being, not just our spiritual progress.

You'll have progressively difficult tasks to perform on the morontia training worlds, yes. But you'll always have regular seasons of rest and reversion. Throughout the entire journey to Paradise, which takes longer than we can currently imagine, there will always be time for rest and spirit play. Even in the perfected career of light and life, there's always time for worship and new achievement.

These morontia companions serve exclusively in the local universes. When you eventually prepare to leave Nebadon and embark on the superuniverse spirit adventure, you'll truly regret that these friendly creatures cannot accompany you. But by then, you'll have formed deep friendships with your fellow ascenders, and eventually, you'll meet the Paradise Companions.

Paradise Companions: Friendship at the Highest Level

The Paradise Companions represent something special, a composite group recruited from all the angelic orders: seraphim from local universes, seconaphim from the superuniverses, supernaphim from Havona and Paradise, and omniaphim who originate in Havona. These angels volunteer for temporary service as companions, and when their ministry is complete, they return to their original duties.

What do Paradise Companions do? Nothing specific, actually. They have no particular tasks to accomplish, no lessons to teach, no essential services to render. They exist simply to be with us and commune with us as personality associates. Almost every other being we'll encounter during our Paradise sojourn will have something definite to do with us or for us. Paradise Companions are different, they're assigned only to be with us.

This becomes especially important if you reach Paradise alone. If your mortal companion or close associate from your earthly career arrives with you, or if your seraphic guardian arrives with you or is already waiting, then no permanent companion will be assigned. But if you arrive alone, a companion will certainly welcome you as you awaken on the Isle of Light from the terminal sleep of time.

Let me address a question that came up in our study group because it troubles many people: What about marriages that were unhappy? If someone was trapped in an abusive relationship, will they be forced to remain with that person in the afterlife?

The answer is an emphatic no. When you pass from this life to the next, you're not considered married anymore. There is no marriage in the mansion worlds, not in the legal or obligatory sense we know on Earth. You choose whether you want to be with someone or not. It's always a choice based on mutual affection and shared spiritual goals.

If someone awakens on the mansion worlds and doesn't want to see their former spouse, they won't have to. Even if the other person has changed and improved dramatically, the choice remains entirely free. No one is ever forced into unwanted relationships. Everything operates on the basis of genuine affection, shared interests, and mutual spiritual benefit.

For those who shared loving, spiritually progressive relationships on Earth, the mansion worlds offer opportunities to continue and deepen those bonds. For those whose earthly marriages were difficult or even destructive, the afterlife brings freedom and new possibilities. The universe is designed for growth and happiness, not continued suffering.

When you reach Paradise, Reception Companions will have carefully examined your records, your mortal origin, your eventful ascent through the worlds of space, your progression through the circuits of Havona. When they greet you, they're already well versed in your career. They immediately prove to be sympathetic and intriguing companions who understand what you've been through and what you've achieved.

These companions are assigned in order of waiting, with one important stipulation: an ascender is never placed in charge of a companion whose nature is unlike their superuniverse type. Since we're from the seventh superuniverse, Orvonton, our companions will always reflect the nature of the Seventh Master Spirit, the combined nature of the Universal Father, the Eternal Son, and the Infinite Spirit. This ensures we're comfortable with our companions and they understand our fundamental characteristics.

The omniaphim, the angels native to Havona, do not serve as Paradise Companions for ascenders from the seven superuniverses. They can serve in other capacities, but companionship requires understanding born from similar origins. We need companions who reflect the spiritual characteristics of our own superuniverse, beings who understand us because they share our fundamental nature.

The Archives of Eternity

Before I close this chapter, I want to return to where we began: the archives themselves, those vast repositories on Uversa and Paradise containing the records of everything that's ever happened.

On Uversa, senior Celestial Recorders can show the records of everything of cosmic importance in all Orvonton since the far distant times when the Ancients of Days first arrived in our superuniverse. That reaches back unimaginably far into the past.

But on Paradise, in the eternal Isle itself, the Custodians of Records guard archives that testify to the transactions of Paradise since the times of the personification of the Infinite Spirit. Think about what that means. When the Universal Father and the Eternal Son together created the Infinite Spirit through their trinitization, that marked the beginning of recorded time, not because nothing existed before, but because that event initiated the creation of all the celestial personalities and universal structures we know.

Everything since then has been documented. Every plan conceived by the Paradise Trinity, every universe brought into existence, every ascension scheme designed for evolutionary mortals, every mission undertaken by descending Sons, all of it exists in those archives.

Someday, if we choose, we can spend time in the halls of records examining whatever interests us. We can trace the history of Nebadon from its inception, follow the career of Christ Michael before he came to Earth, study the evolution of life on countless worlds, learn about rebellions and how they were resolved, investigate the development of universal laws and administrative procedures, or delve into philosophical questions that have occupied great minds across the ages.

The knowledge is there, preserved perfectly, accessible to all who are qualified to understand it. No truth is hidden. No significant event is forgotten. The universe maintains perfect records because truth matters, because history matters, because the struggles and achievements of every personality contribute to something larger than themselves.

Conclusion: The Meaning of Perfect Records

As we close this exploration of celestial record-keeping, I want to emphasize what I believe is the deepest significance of all we've discussed.

The fact that the universe maintains such complete, accurate records of our lives tells us something profound about our value. We matter. Each of us, individually, matters enough that angelic beings dedicate themselves to documenting our existence. Our choices have consequences that ripple through eternity. Our growth contributes to the evolution of the Supreme Being. Our experiences add something unique to the cosmic story that cannot be added by anyone else.

When I feel insignificant, just one person among billions on this small world, in one solar system among millions, in one local universe among 700,000, in one superuniverse among seven, I remember these record-keepers. Someone considers my life worth documenting with perfect accuracy. The universe cares enough about what I do, how I grow, what I choose, that it preserves every significant moment.

This should affect how we live. Not in the sense of paranoid self-consciousness, we're not being watched by some cosmic Big Brother waiting to catch us doing something wrong. Rather, we're being witnessed by beings who care about us, who want to see us succeed, who document our lives because those lives have intrinsic worth and ultimate significance.

Every act of kindness you show, every time you choose integrity when it would be easier to compromise, every moment when you act from love instead of fear, these things are recorded. They're not just noticed by God; they're documented by angels, preserved in archives, and celebrated throughout the universe. You're building a reputation, creating a record that will follow you through eternity, that will introduce you to new friends on the mansion worlds, that will testify to your character as you advance through successive universe levels.

At the same time, our failures are recorded too. Our mistakes, our selfishness, our moments of cowardice or cruelty, these also go into the archives. But here's what I find encouraging: the universe doesn't maintain these records to shame us or limit our future. They're kept so we can learn from them, so we can see patterns we need to address, so we can receive appropriate training and grow beyond our limitations.

The entire system exists for our benefit, to facilitate our growth, to ensure that nothing valuable from our experience is lost. When we understand this, it changes how we think about life. We're not just passing through a meaningless existence, marking time until we die. We're creating something permanent, building something eternal, contributing to a universal story that matters more than we can currently comprehend.

In the next chapter, we'll explore the Ministering Spirits of the Central Universe, those remarkable beings who will guide us through Havona and prepare us for the ultimate adventure of recognizing and approaching the Paradise Deities. But the foundation we've laid here will remain with us: the understanding that we live in a universe that values truth so highly it maintains perfect records, that considers each personality so important it documents their entire existence, and that provides every possible resource to ensure our success.

That's the universe we inhabit. That's the reality The Urantia Book reveals. And that's why this study matters, not just as an intellectual exercise, but as a transformative encounter with truth that can reshape how we see ourselves, our lives, and our eternal destiny.

Chapter 24: The Ministering Spirits of the Central Universe

Introduction: Understanding Our Celestial Helpers

When I first began studying Paper 26 of The Urantia Book, I'll admit I found myself swimming in a sea of unfamiliar names and complex hierarchies. Supernaphim, seconaphim, tertiaphim, the terminology alone seemed designed to confuse rather than clarify. Yet as I pressed forward, something remarkable happened. What initially appeared as an impenetrable catalog of celestial bureaucracy revealed itself to be something far more personal and profound: a detailed map of the spiritual helpers who accompany us on our journey from this world to Paradise.

This chapter marks a significant turning point in our exploration of angelic ministry. We're moving beyond the familiar territory of guardian seraphim who watch over us here on Urantia and venturing into the vast realm of the central universe itself. These are the angels of Paradise, Havona, and the super universes, beings whose very existence speaks to the magnificent organization of creation and the Father's infinite care for his ascending children.

I want to be honest with you from the start: this material is challenging. The Urantia Book presents us with multiple orders of angels, each with primary, secondary, and tertiary classifications, serving across different levels of universe administration. It's easy to get lost in the details. But here's what I've learned through years of study and teaching: you don't need to memorize every classification to grasp the essential truth. What matters is understanding that at every stage of our eternal journey, from the moment we awaken on the mansion worlds to our eventual arrival on Paradise itself, we are never alone. An unbroken chain of spirit ministers stands ready to guide, teach, and assist us.

Before we dive into the specifics, let me share a tool that has proven invaluable to countless students. Hara Davis created an exceptional resource called the Study Aids of the Urantia Book. On page 12, you'll find a comprehensive summary of the Ministering Spirits of the Central Universe, and on page 14, a corresponding summary of the Ministering Spirits of the Super Universe. These charts have saved me, and many of my students, from drowning in confusion more times than I can count. I strongly recommend keeping them handy as we work through this material together.

The Central Universe: Paradise, Havona, and Beyond

Let's establish our bearings. When The Urantia Book speaks of the "central universe," it's referring to a specific cosmic region comprising three distinct but interconnected parts: the eternal Isle of Paradise at the very center of all things, the twenty-one satellites that orbit Paradise in prescribed circuits, and Havona, that perfect creation of one billion worlds arranged in seven concentric circuits around Paradise.

This is important because the ministering spirits we're about to explore serve throughout this entire region. They're not confined to a single world or even a single circuit. Their ministry extends from the shores of Paradise itself outward through all of Havona, and in many cases, even beyond into the super universes and down to individual planets like our own.

Think of it this way: the central universe represents the pattern, the divine template for all creation. Everything that exists in the evolving super universes, including our own local universe of Nebadon, finds its perfect archetype in Havona. Similarly, the ministering spirits of the central universe represent the highest expression of angelic service. They set the standard that all other orders of angels aspire to reach.

The Highest of the Lowest: Understanding Angelic Classifications

Here's where things get a bit tricky, and I want to walk through this carefully because confusion at this point can derail your understanding of everything that follows. The Urantia Book tells us that supernaphim are "the highest order of the lowest group of the children of the Infinite Spirit." When I first read that phrase, I remember thinking, "Well, which is it? Are they high or low?" The answer, as it turns out, is both, and understanding why helps us see the beautiful structure of spiritual creation.

The Infinite Spirit creates numerous orders of beings. At the top of this hierarchy stand the Seven Master Spirits and the Seven Supreme Executives, beings of enormous power and cosmic responsibility. These represent the "highest groups" of the Spirit's children. But there are also the "ministering groups", angels specifically created to serve, guide, and assist ascending mortals like us. These ministering spirits represent the "lowest group" in terms of their service function, not their dignity or importance.

Within this ministering group, however, there exists its own hierarchy. Supernaphim stand at the pinnacle. They're the most experienced, most capable, most spiritually advanced angels in the service of ascending creatures. So, while they belong to the "lowest group" functionally speaking, they're the "highest order" within that group. It's rather like saying a master sergeant is part of the enlisted ranks (the "lowest group" compared to officers) yet stands at the top of that enlisted hierarchy.

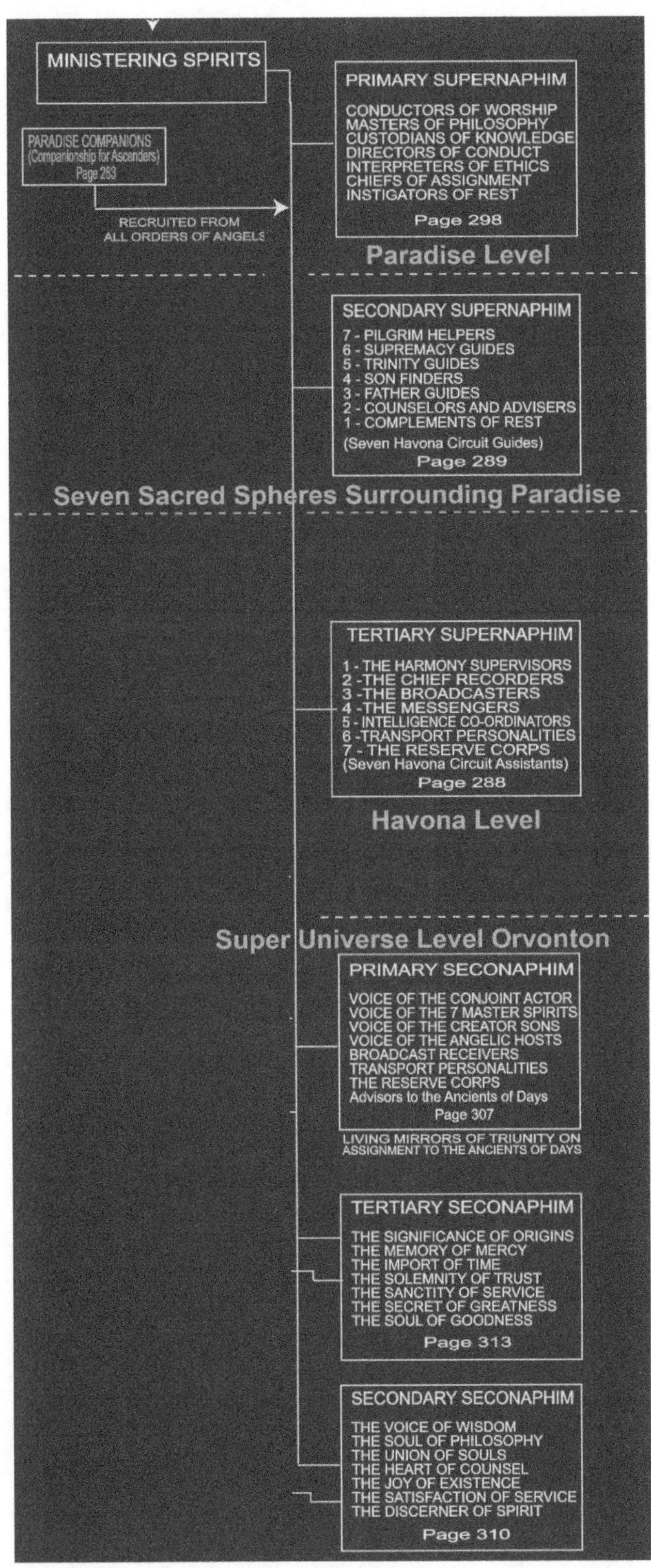

Figure 5: Ministering Spirits

Why does this matter? Because it tells us something profound about the nature of spiritual greatness. The highest angels aren't those who wield the most cosmic power or govern vast regions of space. The highest angels are those who most perfectly serve the Father's children on their journey home. Service, not dominion, marks true spiritual achievement.

When Worlds Rebel: The Supernaphim Among Us

Now, you might be wondering, "If supernaphim serve primarily in Paradise and Havona, what do they have to do with us here on Urantia?" The answer reveals just how seriously the universe administration takes our spiritual welfare, especially during times of crisis.

Under normal circumstances, our world would be served primarily by seraphim, the angels of the local universe. But Urantia isn't under normal circumstances. We're a decimal planet, meaning we're used for special life experiments. We've experienced the tragedy of planetary rebellion under Caligastia. We've witnessed the default of Adam and Eve. Our world has been quarantined, cut off from normal universe circuits for nearly two hundred thousand years.

In response to our planet's rebellion, something extraordinary happened. The angelic administration of Urantia didn't simply continue as before. Instead, the highest authorities assigned a supernaphim, one of the most experienced and capable angels in all creation, to oversee and coordinate all angelic activity on our world. An archangel initially took emergency control, but immediately afterward, a supernaphim arrived to assume ultimate authority over the angelic hosts serving here.

Think about what this means. Our troubled little sphere, isolated and wounded by rebellion, received not a junior administrator but one of Paradise's finest. It's as if the cosmic President personally sent his most trusted aide to ensure that nothing, absolutely nothing, would prevent willing souls from finding their way to the Father. This supernaphim continues to serve here today, coordinating the work of countless angels in their ministry to us.

This assignment pattern appears throughout the grand universe. Wherever rebellion strikes, wherever emergency circumstances threaten the spiritual progress of the Father's children, supernaphim are dispatched to stabilize the situation and ensure that the ascending plan continues without interruption. They bring the wisdom of Paradise, the experience of ages, and the authority to make whatever decisions circumstances demand.

Three Orders, Different Origins: Primary, Secondary, and Tertiary Supernaphim

The supernaphim divide into three distinct orders, and understanding their origins helps us grasp their different functions and assignments. This is where those charts I mentioned earlier become particularly helpful, because keeping these classifications straight challenges even experienced students.

Primary supernaphim are the children of the Infinite Spirit and the Seven Master Spirits. They're created directly by these divine personalities, which tells us something about their nature and capacity. These are the angels who serve on Paradise itself, in the immediate presence of the Universal Father, the Eternal Son, and the Infinite Spirit. They work with ascending mortals who have completed their journey through the super universes and Havona and now stand on the threshold of finaliter status. Primary supernaphim are the angels who guide us through our last steps before we stand in the Father's presence.

Their home is Paradise, though as we've seen, they can be assigned throughout creation wherever their unique skills and experience are needed. But Paradise is where they originate, and Paradise is where most of them serve throughout eternity.

Secondary supernaphim are the offspring of the Seven Master Spirits. Notice the shift here, these angels are one step removed from the Infinite Spirit, being created by the Master Spirits rather than by the Spirit directly. This doesn't make them inferior; it simply means their nature and function differ from their primary brethren. Secondary supernaphim serve primarily in Havona, stationed in the worlds associated with the Seven Master Spirits. They work with ascending pilgrims as we progress through the billion worlds of the perfect central creation, teaching us, guiding us, and preparing us for eventual arrival on Paradise.

Tertiary supernaphim have yet another origin. They're created by the Seven Spirits of the Circuits working in conjunction with the Infinite Spirit. These Spirits of the Circuits are themselves fascinating beings, seven personalities, each associated with one of Havona's seven concentric rings. Each one maintains their headquarters on a pilot world, the first sphere of each circuit. The tertiary supernaphim they create serve on these pilot worlds, assisting ascending mortals as we navigate our way through Havona from the outer seventh circuit toward the inner first circuit and Paradise beyond.

When you awaken on the mansion worlds and eventually make your way to the super universe capital of Uversa, you'll begin your Havona journey on the pilot world of the seventh circuit. There you'll encounter tertiary supernaphim for the first time, angels specifically prepared to help beings like us who are just beginning our education in perfect environment. As you progress inward through each successive circuit, you'll meet more tertiary supernaphim on each pilot world, each group specializing in the particular lessons and experiences that circuit provides.

The Seconaphim: Angels of the Super Universe

Now, here's where many students, myself included, have stumbled. The Urantia Book introduces us not only to the three orders of supernaphim (primary, secondary, tertiary) but also to three orders of seconaphim (primary, secondary, tertiary). The similar names cause endless confusion. I've seen people mix these up repeatedly, and honestly, I still have to pause and check my references sometimes to make sure I have them straight.

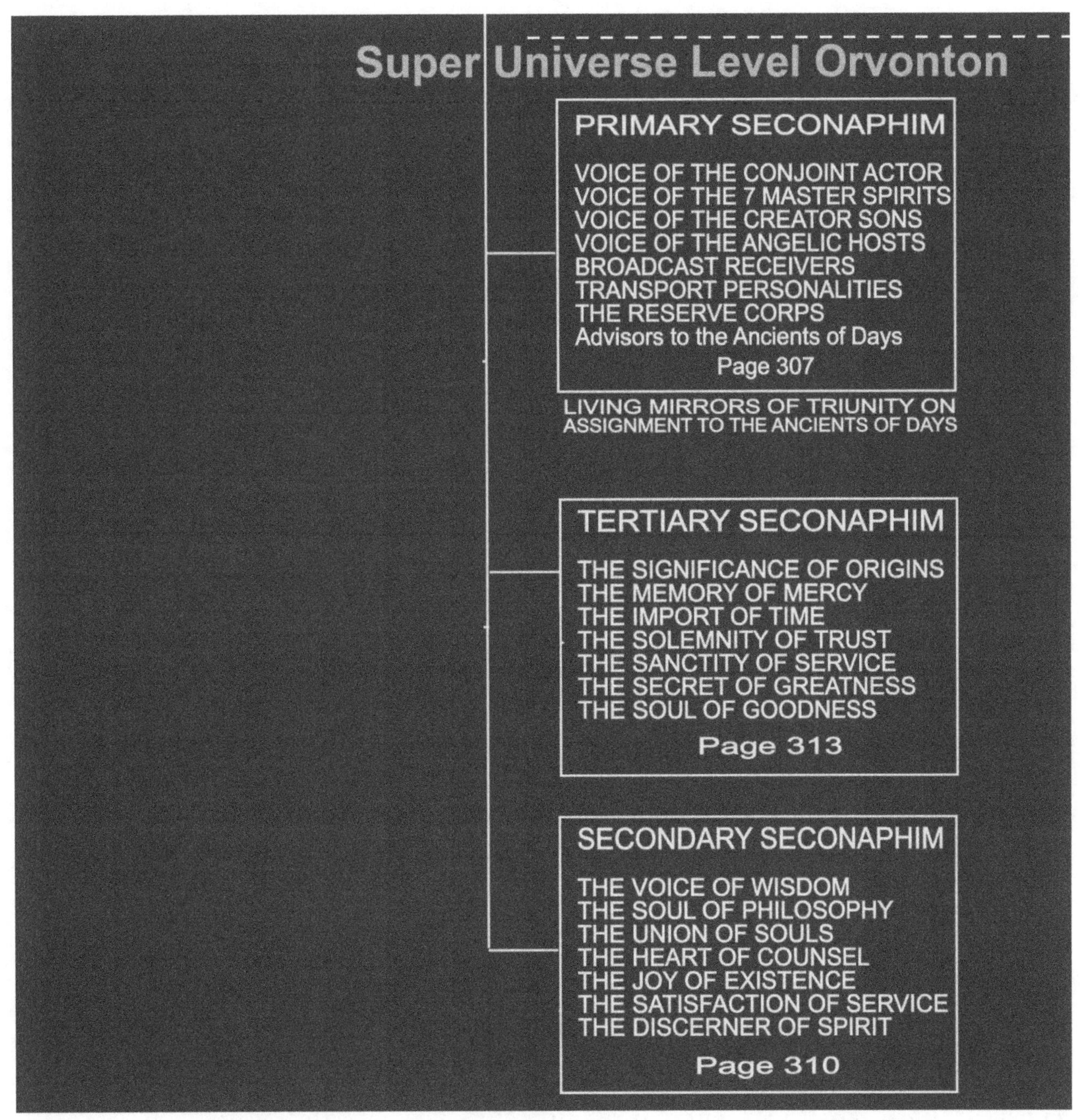

Figure 6: Super Universe Level - Orvonton

Let me be absolutely clear: supernaphim and seconaphim are completely different orders of angels. Supernaphim are the ministering spirits of the central universe, Paradise and Havona. Seconaphim are the ministering spirits of the super universes. They serve in places like Uversa, the capital of our super universe, Orvonton. While supernaphim are created by the Infinite Spirit and the Master Spirits, seconaphim are the children of the Reflective Spirits, who are themselves offspring of the Trinity and the Master Spirits.

The confusion multiplies because seconaphim also come in three orders: primary, secondary, and tertiary. But these classifications don't correspond directly to the three orders of supernaphim. They represent parallel but distinct hierarchies serving in different cosmic regions.

Here's what makes it even more confusing, and this is where the charts become essential: The Urantia Book sometimes lists the tertiary order before the secondary order when discussing seconaphim. Why? Because tertiary seconaphim were actually created before secondary seconaphim. The sequence of their origin doesn't match the numbering of their classification. I don't fully understand the reason for this peculiarity, and I'm not sure anyone does except the Infinite Spirit. But it's there in the text, and it trips people up constantly.

The best approach I've found is to think of "primary" as order one, "secondary" as order two, and "tertiary" as order three, regardless of when they were actually created. This keeps things straight in your mind even if the historical sequence differs.

The Full Spectrum: Seven Orders of Ministering Spirits

When we step back and look at the complete picture, The Urantia Book presents seven distinct orders of ministering spirits who serve throughout the grand universe. Let me walk you through them, because understanding this full classification helps us see where each order fits and how they all work together.

First come the supernaphim, whom we've discussed at length, the angels of Paradise and Havona, divided into primary, secondary, and tertiary orders.

Second are the seconaphim, the super universe angels, also divided into primary, secondary, and tertiary orders.

Third come the tertiaphim. Now, this is the same term used for tertiary supernaphim, but in this classification system, it apparently refers to a distinct order. The text can be ambiguous here, and I've seen different interpretations.

Fourth are the omniaphim, angels created by the Infinite Spirit and the Seven Supreme Executives. These beings serve primarily in administrative capacities at the super universe level. The Urantia Book doesn't tell us much about them, probably because their work doesn't directly involve the ascending plan in ways we'd recognize or understand at our current level.

Fifth come the seraphim, and ah, now we're on familiar ground! These are the angels of the local universes, our constant companions throughout much of our ascension journey. Every person reading this who has made a definite choice to seek God and do the Father's will has at least one, and probably two, seraphim assigned to them right now. These faithful ministers will be the first faces you see when you awaken on the mansion worlds after death.

Sixth are the cherubim and sanobim, also local universe angels who work closely with the seraphim but generally don't accompany us beyond the local universe. However, and this is a beautiful provision, cherubim can aspire to seraphic status. When a cherubim achieves this transformation, that angel gains all the rights and privileges of any other seraphim, including the possibility of accompanying their charge all the way to Paradise and joining the Corps of Finality.

Seventh and finally come the midway creatures. Now, The Urantia Book is careful to note that midwayers aren't really angels at all. They're a unique order of being, native to inhabited worlds, existing in a realm midway between material mortals and spiritual angels. On most worlds, midwayers serve throughout the planet's evolutionary development, then eventually are released to begin their own ascension journey, receiving Thought Adjusters and progressing exactly as humans do.

Why are they listed here among angelic orders if they're not actually angels? Because functionally, on the worlds where they serve, midwayers are drafted into the angelic corps. They work alongside seraphim, cherubim, and other angels in ministering to mortals. So, while their origin and ultimate destiny differ from true angels, their service role is similar enough that they're classified with the ministering spirits.

A Word About True Angels

Here's something that surprises many students: strictly speaking, only seraphim, cherubim, and sanobim are actually considered "angels" throughout most of the universe. All the rest, supernaphim, seconaphim, tertiaphim, omniaphim, are more accurately termed "ministering spirits" rather than angels.

So why does The Urantia Book call them angels at all? Why do I call them angels in this study? For the same reason: because we humans relate to the concept of angels. We've been taught from childhood about guardian angels watching over us. The term resonates with us emotionally and spiritually in ways that "tertiary superaphic ministering spirit" simply doesn't.

The revelators use language we can grasp. They meet us where we are. Yes, there are technical distinctions in universe classification systems. But for our purposes, for understanding who these beings are and how they serve us, it's perfectly appropriate to call them angels. Just be aware that when you get to Paradise and enroll in the celestial universities, you might need to adjust your terminology.

The key point isn't what we call them. The key point is that they're real, they're devoted to our welfare, and they'll be with us every step of our eternal journey.

Seraphim: Our Closest Companions

Since seraphim are the angels most directly involved in our immediate spiritual lives, they deserve special attention. These remarkable beings are created by the Universe Mother Spirit, the Divine Minister of our local universe of Nebadon, working in conjunction with our Creator Son, Christ Michael. Every local universe has its own corps of seraphim, uniquely created for service in that universe.

What makes seraphim so special is their capacity for personal attachment and loyalty. Unlike the higher orders of supernaphim who serve vast multitudes throughout Paradise and Havona, seraphim are assigned to individuals. Right now, this moment, if you're a spiritually minded person seeking to do God's will, you have seraphim watching over you. They know your name, your struggles, your victories, your secret dreams. They've been with you perhaps since childhood, certainly since you made your first real moral choice and received your Thought Adjuster.

Most people have two seraphim assigned to them, working as a complementary pair. One is dominant, the one you might think of as your guardian angel proper. The other is complemental, assisting the dominant partner. Together they coordinate their efforts to present you with opportunities for growth, to protect you from dangers you may not even perceive, and to enhance your capacity to hear the Adjuster's leading.

Here's what makes seraphim even more remarkable: they have choices about their own destiny, just as you do. When you die and repersonalize on the first mansion world, your seraphim will be there waiting for you. At that point, they face a decision. They can choose to accompany you throughout your entire ascension journey, through all seven mansion worlds, through the constellation and super universe capitals, through Havona, all the way to Paradise itself. If they make this choice and see it through, they can qualify to join the Corps of Finality alongside you.

Or they can choose to return to regular universe service, being reassigned to other mortals as they're born and begin their own spiritual journeys. This isn't a lesser choice; it's simply a different path of service. Many seraphim choose it, finding fulfillment in repeated cycles of ministry to emerging souls.

But seraphim who commit to the long journey with their ascending charge are called "evolutionary seraphim." They evolve and grow spiritually just as we do. They face challenges and learn lessons just as we do. And if they persevere to the end, they achieve something extraordinary: they become ascending sons of God, not by origin but by achievement.

Think about what this means. Your guardian angel may choose to tie her eternal destiny to yours. She'll walk every step of the path you walk, face every challenge you face, and celebrate every victory you win. And at the end of ages, when you stand before the Universal Father and join the Corps of Finality, she'll stand there too, not as your servant but as your companion, your friend, your fellow finaliter.

I find that prospect almost overwhelming. The faithfulness, the devotion, the sheer love required for such a commitment staggers the imagination. Yet countless seraphim make this choice every day throughout the universe.

The Archangels: A Special Case

Before we move on, I want to address one order of angels that isn't included in the standard classification we've been discussing: the archangels. Students often wonder why archangels seem to be left out of Paper 26's comprehensive survey of ministering spirits. The answer reveals something important about how the universe organizes spiritual service.

Archangels are a specialized order created by the Universe Mother Spirit and Creator Son in each local universe. Their specific mandate is to oversee the ascension plan for mortals, to track, record, and certify every aspect of our progress from initial Adjuster indwelling through our eventual departure from the local universe. They maintain the records. They certify resurrections on the mansion worlds. They coordinate with other orders of angels to ensure smooth administration of the entire ascending program.

In many ways, archangels are the most powerful angels in the local universe because of the scope of their responsibility and authority. But they're excluded from Paper 26's discussion because that paper focuses specifically on the ministering spirits of the central universe, Paradise, Havona, and by extension, the super universes. Archangels don't operate in those realms. Their jurisdiction ends at the local universe boundary.

However, archangels have an interesting connection to the central universe angels we've been discussing. When a Creator Son and Creative Mother Spirit go forth to create a new local universe, they're loaned 100 tertiaphim from the central universe and 100 archangels from a nearby local universe. These archangels serve the new universe until the Mother Spirit has created enough native archangels to take over their duties. At that point, the loaned archangels return to their home universe.

Our world has special significance in the archangel administration. Urantia hosts a divisional headquarters for archangels, one of only a handful of such installations in our entire local system. This gives our planet strategic importance and makes it a destination for student visitors throughout the universe who want to study how the archangel corps functions.

When Caligastia led Urantia into rebellion, an archangel immediately assumed emergency control of our planet. This archangel continues to serve here, though as I mentioned earlier, a supernaphim was quickly assigned to provide overall supervision of all angelic orders working here.

The Mystery of Encircuitment: How Angels Live

I want to share something that has fascinated me for years, something that helps us understand the fundamental difference between material beings like us and spiritual beings like angels. We stay alive by eating and drinking. Food and water provide the chemical energy our bodies need to function. But angels don't eat or drink. So how do they survive? What sustains their existence?

The answer is encircuitment, a concept that sounds abstract until you grasp its implications. Angels sustain themselves by being connected to, or "encircuited" in, the spiritual energy circuits that flow from Paradise throughout creation. There are four primary circuits: the circuit of the Universal Father, the circuit of the Eternal Son, the circuit of the Infinite Spirit, and the general Paradise circuit. When angels polarize in complementary pairs, they can tap into these circuits and draw spiritual energy directly, energy that sustains their existence and powers their ministry.

Now here's where it gets interesting. Angels can function alone when necessary, but they can't remain encircuited when working alone. To maintain connection to the life-sustaining circuits, they must polarize with a complementary partner.

When two angels join in this polarized relationship, they act as a kind of spiritual circuit, allowing the energy to flow through them and sustain them both.

This explains why angels so often work in pairs. It's not merely an administrative preference; it's a practical necessity for their survival. A single angel might undertake a brief mission requiring only a few hours or days. But for extended service, angels must pair up to remain encircuited. If an angel remains alone and unencircuited too long, the result is the same as if you or I went without food and water: eventually, they would perish.

When we reach the mansion worlds, we too will experience encircuitment for the first time. Our morontia bodies will draw sustenance partly from food but increasingly from direct connection to spiritual circuits. As we progress upward through the mansion worlds, through the constellation and universe capitals, our dependence on physical food decreases while our capacity to draw energy from the spiritual circuits increases. By the time we reach Havona, we'll be fully sustained by encircuitment, requiring no material food whatsoever.

The Tree of Life: A Circuit Made Physical

This concept of encircuitment helps us understand one of the most intriguing elements of Urantia's history: the Tree of Life. You may have wondered about this peculiar plant that appears at several critical junctures in our planet's story. What was it, exactly? And how did it work?

The Tree of Life was a living plant native to Edentia, the capital world of our constellation. But it wasn't an ordinary plant. It was encircuited, directly connected to the spiritual energy circuits of the universe. When Adam and Eve came to Urantia as Material Son and Daughter, this tree came with them. Why? Because Adam and Eve, though appearing human, were actually beings from an architectural world. Their bodies were constructed from patterns on Edentia and were designed to live indefinitely when sustained by periodic contact with the Tree of Life.

The tree functioned like a physical access point to the spiritual circuits. Adam and Eve would consume a leaf or fruit from the tree, and this would re-encircuit them, providing the spiritual energy their bodies needed to regenerate and repair. Under normal circumstances, they could go about a hundred years between visits to the tree.

The Caligastia 100, the corporeal staff members who came to Urantia with Prince Caligastia some 500,000 years ago, also depended on the Tree of Life. These unique beings had been modified to be non-reproducible and potentially immortal, sustained by regular consumption from the tree, which was kept in Dalamatia, the headquarters of the Planetary Prince.

When Caligastia led his rebellion, Van and Amadon, two staff members who remained loyal, (Van being of the 100 and Amadon a modified human associate) fled Dalamatia, taking the Tree of Life with them. They established a new headquarters in a mountainous region near what we now call Lake Van. The 40 staff members who remained loyal had continued access to the tree and lived on. But the 60 who joined the rebellion lost that access. Cut off from the circuit connection the tree provided, they eventually died, though it probably took centuries given the residual effects of their long exposure to the tree's sustenance.

Remember it was the 60 that rebelled lost access to the tree, so they became human and mixed with the daughters of men who become the giants and the source of the Nephilim.

Now here's something that intrigues me: How did the Tree of Life get to Urantia in the first place? Seraphim can transport many things by dematerializing them, moving them through space, and rematerializing them at their destination. But a living organism can't survive that process. The cellular structure would be destroyed. So, this tree, a precious, encircuited, living plant, had to be transported physically across vast reaches of space from Edentia to our world.

I suspect it made the journey in some kind of protective vessel, probably accompanied by a gardener to keep it alive during what might have been hundreds of thousands of years of travel. Can you imagine? A mission spanning eons, all to ensure that the Material Son and Daughter, when they eventually arrived, would have access to the circuit connection they needed to sustain their physical lives.

The Tree of Life is gone from our world now, removed when the default of Adam and Eve made it clear that they wouldn't fulfill their mission in the normal manner. But the story reminds us of how carefully the universe administration plans for our welfare, going to extraordinary lengths to provide what's needed for the success of each phase of planetary development.

Quarantine and Circuit Isolation

Understanding encircuitment also helps us grasp what happened to Urantia when we fell into rebellion. The planet was quarantined, but what did that actually mean? It meant that Urantia was disconnected from normal universe circuits. We were isolated, cut off from the regular flow of spiritual energy and information that sustains normal planetary development.

However, and this is crucial, the angels themselves remained fully encircuited. They had to. Without circuit connection, they couldn't survive, let alone serve. So, what was blocked wasn't the angels' access to spiritual energy, but rather the planet's access to the broader network of communication, coordination, and support that characterizes normal planetary administration.

Think of it like a computer network. The planet was essentially taken offline, disconnected from the universal internet, so to speak. But the angels, like technicians with emergency access codes, maintained their connections to headquarters. They could still communicate with higher authorities, still draw orders, still receive the resources they needed to minister to us. What they couldn't do was restore our normal circuit connections until the rebellion was fully adjudicated.

That isolation persisted for nearly 200,000 years. Only recently, with the completion of certain legal and administrative procedures following the adjudication of Lucifer and the bestowal of Michael on our world as Jesus, has our planet begun to be reintegrated into normal universe circuits. It's a gradual process, but it's happening. It may take a undetermined amount of time to finish, but sooner or latter we will be reconnected completely.

Knowledge, Wisdom, and the Trinity Teacher Sons

One more aspect of angelic existence deserves mention before we close this chapter. The Urantia Book tells us that angels don't only draw energy from the spiritual circuits; they also draw knowledge and wisdom. Specifically, they partake of "the circulating teachings of the marvelous Trinity Teacher Sons."

These Teacher Sons, some of the highest and most experienced personalities in creation, constantly broadcast instruction throughout the universes. It's as if there's an eternal university broadcasting lectures on every conceivable subject related to universe administration, spiritual development, and divine purpose. Angels tune into these broadcasts as naturally as they draw energy from the circuits, absorbing knowledge and wisdom as a normal part of their existence.

When we reach the mansion worlds, we too will begin to experience this. Our minds will be enhanced, our capacity for understanding expanded, and we'll discover that learning doesn't require the laborious study methods we're used to here. Instead, knowledge will flow to us through the circuits, absorbed almost effortlessly as we open ourselves to receive it.

This is why your seraphim are always several steps ahead of you in understanding. They're already plugged into this universal education system. They already benefit from the wisdom of the Teacher Sons. And when they guide you, when they arrange circumstances to teach you spiritual lessons, they're drawing on resources of knowledge you can't yet access. But you will. On the mansion worlds, you'll begin to share in that same flowing river of divine wisdom.

Conclusion: An Unbroken Chain of Ministry

As we close this introduction to the ministering spirits of the central universe, I want you to hold one image in your mind: an unbroken chain of spiritual ministers reaching from the Isle of Paradise down through all of Havona, through every level of universe administration, through every mansion world and architectural sphere, all the way to our troubled little planet.

At every stage of your eternal journey, from this moment until you stand before the Universal Father, you'll be surrounded by angels. Different orders at different stages, certainly. Primary supernaphim won't greet you when you wake up on mansion world one; seraphim will do that. But eventually, yes, primary supernaphim will guide you on Paradise itself, and they'll do so with the same devoted care that your seraphim extend to you now.

This is what Lucifer couldn't accept. He looked at all these resources devoted to mortal ascension, all these orders of angels, all this careful planning, all this patient ministry, and resented it. Why should mortals receive such attention? Why should imperfect, error-prone beings from the worlds of time be given such extravagant support in their journey to perfection?

The answer, I believe, lies at the heart of the Father's nature. We're his children. Not his servants, not his subjects, but his children. And the Father will stop at nothing to ensure that every child who desires to find him has every possible resource, every necessary guide, every form of support required to make that journey successful.

The angelic hosts, from the mightiest supernaphim of Paradise to your personal seraphim here on Urantia, exist to express that divine determination. They embody the Father's commitment to your success. They are, in very literal terms, the Father's love made manifest in service.

In the next chapter, we'll dive deeper into the specific orders and functions of these ministering spirits. We'll explore what primary, secondary, and tertiary supernaphim actually do. We'll discover the unique roles of seconaphim and tertiaphim. And we'll see how all of this magnificent organization serves one central purpose: helping you reach Paradise and stand at last in the Father's presence, welcomed home by angels who have accompanied you every step of the way.

For now, I simply want you to know that you're not alone. You've never been alone. And you never will be alone. The angels are real, their ministry is constant, and your journey to Paradise is assured if you desire it. Everything else is simply details, important details, fascinating details, but details nonetheless compared to that central, glorious truth.

Chapter 25: The Mighty Supernaphim

I'll admit I was overwhelmed by the sheer scope of angelic orders and their functions, when I first encountered Paper 26 of *The Urantia Book*. But as I've studied this material over the years, and more importantly, as I've discussed it with fellow students in our weekly sessions, I've come to appreciate why this information matters so deeply. This isn't just celestial taxonomy for its own sake. What we're really exploring here is the careful, intentional architecture of our eternal education. Every angel, every circuit, every training world exists for a purpose: to prepare us for something far greater than we can currently imagine.

Tonight, we continue our journey through Paper 26 with Section 2, "The Mighty Supernaphim." This paper is quite long and packed with information, but I encourage you to stay with it. What you're about to learn describes the actual experiences you'll have when you reach Havona, the billion worlds you'll traverse, the teachers who will guide you, and the profound spiritual training that awaits. It's not abstract theology; it's your future itinerary.

Understanding the Mighty Supernaphim

Before we dig into the details, let me address a question that came up during one of our study sessions. You might recall that when Jesus prayed in Gethsemane, Scripture tells us "an angel appeared to Him and strengthened Him." Could this have been a mighty supernaphim? The answer is quite possibly yes. While the text doesn't specify which order of angel ministered to Jesus that night, we know that mighty supernaphim are Paradise angels who can be assigned to planets, especially those experiencing rebellion. Given Urantia's troubled status, it's entirely reasonable to think a mighty supernaphim was present during that critical moment.

But why are they called "mighty"? This designation isn't arbitrary. The mighty supernaphim hold a unique distinction: they are the only order of supernaphim created directly by the Infinite Spirit alone. All other orders of supernaphim are created by the Infinite Spirit working in conjunction with another being, whether the Seven Master Spirits or the Reflective Spirits. This direct creation by the Third Person of the Trinity gives them their distinctive nature and their designation as Paradise angels. Though their primary work is in Paradise and Havona, they also serve throughout the seven superuniverses, particularly in emergency situations like the Lucifer rebellion that has marked our world.

The Three Orders of Supernaphim

The mighty supernaphim are organized into three major classifications: primary, secondary, and tertiary. Understanding these distinctions is essential because each order serves a specific function in the grand educational plan.

Primary Supernaphim: Ministers of Paradise

As the text makes clear, primary supernaphim are "the exclusive offspring of the Conjoint Actor", that is, the Infinite Spirit. They divide their ministry equally between two vastly different groups: Paradise citizens and ascending pilgrims like us. Think about what this means. These angels spend half their time serving beings who were created perfect in Paradise, and the other half serving what the revelation candidly calls "the perfected evolution of the lowest type of will creature in all the universe of universes."

That's us, by the way. We're the lowest type.

Now, before that sounds too discouraging, consider the remarkable fact embedded in this statement: Paradise citizens are will creatures, just as we are. They may be perfect from their inception, but they share with us the fundamental dignity of free will. The primary supernaphim understand both realities, perfection and the journey toward perfection, which uniquely qualifies them to facilitate understanding between these two groups.

You'll primarily encounter primary supernaphim when you reach Paradise or Havona. They're not typically involved with us during our planetary existence, though exceptions do occur (as we may have seen in Gethsemane). Their work with ascending mortals really begins when we arrive at the eternal Isle and the central universe.

Secondary Supernaphim: Directors of Havona

Secondary supernaphim serve as "the directors of the affairs of ascending beings on the seven circuits of Havona." They're equally concerned with ministering to Paradise citizens who sojourn for long periods on the billion worlds of the central creation, though we're not given full details about that aspect of their service.

Here's where our earlier study of the Seven Master Spirits becomes crucial. I spent considerable time emphasizing the seven combinations of Trinity characteristics reflected in each Master Spirit, and this is exactly why that matters. Each secondary supernaphim originates from one of the Seven Master Spirits and is patterned according to that Spirit's nature.

Let me break this down because it's genuinely important. When the Seven Master Spirits create beings collectively, those beings are uniform in nature. But when the Seven Master Spirits create individually, as they do with secondary supernaphim, the resulting orders are sevenfold in nature. Each child of a Master Spirit partakes of that creator's specific characteristics.

We come from the seventh superuniverse, Orvonton. Our Master Spirit reflects the combined nature of God the Father, God the Son, and God the Spirit, the full Trinity. This means we naturally think, react, and process reality in a way that reflects this threefold influence. Someone from the first superuniverse, by contrast, would have tendencies reflecting only the Father.

Why does this matter for secondary supernaphim? Because when you arrive in Havona, you'll be assigned supernaphim who share the nature of your superuniverse origin. They're pre-qualified to understand how you think, what challenges you'll face, and how you process spiritual truth. They're sympathetic to your particular approach to the Deity adventure, that progressive recognition of God the Supreme and the Infinite Spirit, then God the Son, and finally God the Father.

Paradise citizens, however, don't have this sevenfold tendency. They were created perfect in Paradise by the Trinity itself, so they don't lean toward one aspect of Deity over another. This creates a beautiful opportunity for mutual learning. The secondary supernaphim facilitate exchanges between ascending mortals (who have one of seven different "flavors" of Trinity influence) and Paradise citizens (who embody perfect balance). The ascending mortals gain from the Paradise citizens' perfect perspective; the Paradise citizens gain experiential knowledge from mortals who have lived, struggled, and grown.

Tertiary Supernaphim: The First Created

Here's where things get interesting from a chronological perspective. The tertiary supernaphim were actually created before the secondary supernaphim, even though they're third in classification.

Tertiary supernaphim originate from the seven Spirits of the Circuits, not from the Seven Master Spirits themselves. Each Spirit of a Circuit, working under the empowerment of the Infinite Spirit, creates sufficient tertiary supernaphim to meet the needs of their particular Havona circuit. The Circuit Spirits produced relatively few of these angelic ministers before ascending mortals began arriving in Havona.

Meanwhile, the Seven Master Spirits didn't even begin creating secondary supernaphim until Grandfanda, the very first ascending mortal, landed in Havona.

This timing reveals something profound about divine foresight and responsive creation. The tertiary supernaphim were created first because they were needed first, to maintain the circuits of Havona even before evolutionary mortals existed. The secondary supernaphim were created second because their specialized ministry only became necessary once the experiential journey began.

The Spirits of the Circuits

Let me take a moment to clarify something that often confuses new students. Each of the seven planetary circuits of Havona operates under the direct supervision of one of the seven Spirits of the Circuits. These Spirits are themselves a collective creation, meaning all seven Spirits of the Circuits were created together by the Seven Master Spirits acting in unison. This is why the text describes them as "uniform" in nature.

Since they were created collectively by all seven Master Spirits working together, the Spirits of the Circuits don't take on the individual characteristics of any single Master Spirit. Instead, they partake uniformly of the nature of the Third Source and Center, the Infinite Spirit himself.

Now here's where it gets even more intriguing. These Circuit Spirits were not part of the original pattern universe. They came into existence as "a creative response of the Master Spirits to the emerging purpose of the Supreme Being." They were discovered functioning upon the organization of the grand universe, which means they appeared in response to the need for experiential reality.

Let me say that again, because it's worth pausing over: these beings emerged as a creative response to the Supreme Being's purpose. They weren't needed in the original, perfect, static Havona. They became necessary when evolutionary mortals, experiential beings, would begin their journey through the central universe. The Infinite Spirit and his creative associates seem "abundantly endowed with the ability to make suitable creative responses to the simultaneous developments in the experiential Deities and in the evolving universes."

This is part of why Lucifer's rebellion was so tragically misguided. He couldn't understand why God would invest so much in training mortal creatures. But what he missed was the big picture. All this training, through the superuniverses, through Havona, through the recognition of all Deity, prepares us for careers we can't yet imagine. Without this comprehensive experience, we'd be limited to our origins. With it, we're prepared for service anywhere: in the superuniverses, in the local universe, in the outer space levels that are even now beginning to form. We gain the full picture. We become useful to the universal plan in ways that would be impossible without this patient, progressive education.

The Path Through Havona

Let me paint you a practical picture of what happens in Havona, because understanding the geography helps clarify the ministry of these angels.

When Paradise citizens leave Paradise to gain experiential knowledge, they land on the pilot world of the first circuit, the innermost ring of Havona. They then proceed outward through the circuits, from first to seventh.

We ascending mortals arrive from the opposite direction. Coming from the seven superuniverses, we land on the pilot world of the seventh circuit, the outermost ring. We then proceed inward, from seventh to first.

So, imagine two streams of pilgrims moving through Havona: descending beings working their way out, and ascending beings working their way in. On every one of the billion worlds, these two groups meet, interact, learn from each other. The descending pilgrims share their knowledge of perfection. The ascending pilgrims share their hard-won experiential wisdom. Both groups contribute to the Supreme Being's growing reality.

And here's something you need to understand clearly: there are no shortcuts. The text is emphatic on this point. While you might be exempted from certain training worlds in the local universe if you're sufficiently advanced, "no pilgrim may avoid passing through all seven of the Havona circuits of progressive spiritualization."

That phrase "progressive spiritualization" is key. This is baby steps. This is gradual transformation. You will traverse every circuit, touch every world, engage with every lesson. The billion study worlds of the perfect central creation exist for exactly this purpose, and every single one matters to your development.

Teaching the Unteachable

During one of our study sessions, someone asked me a question that I think many people wonder about: "The size and complexity of *The Urantia Book* may be beyond the comprehension level required to understand its teachings for many people. How will we be able to teach these people the essence of its message?"

My answer is simple: exactly the way I'm doing it every Tuesday and Thursday night. You take the information and break it down to the lowest level you can conceive. You make it accessible. You build from there, one concept at a time.

How do you teach a child to read? You start with ABCs. How do you teach a baby to eat? One spoonful at a time. The same principle applies to spiritual education, whether here or in the mansion worlds. You take it one paragraph at a time, one concept at a time, and you explain it in ways people can grasp.

Not everyone has access to someone who can break down these concepts, and that's part of our purpose, to make this material understandable and accessible. But we also have two incredible teachers already working within us: the Holy Spirit and the Spirit of Truth. If you spend enough time genuinely studying this revelation, particularly if you start at the beginning and work your way through, you will eventually understand it.

I'll be honest about my own experience. When I first read *The Urantia Book*, the Foreword went in one ear and out the other. It wasn't until I got to the second section that I thought, "Oh, that's what they were talking about in the first section!" So, I went back and checked the Foreword again, then moved forward into the second section. Much of the material didn't make complete sense until I reached the third section. That's how this book works, one part builds on another. It's designed that way intentionally.

The Foreword is essentially the ABCs of the entire revelation. It's difficult to grasp when you're starting out, but once you get it, everything else falls into place. It establishes the terminology, the conceptual framework, the basic vocabulary you need for what follows. You'll find yourself moving backward and forward, picking up a concept, reading ahead, returning when something clicks, then advancing again. This isn't a book you simply read cover to cover once. It's a book you study, discuss, question, and gradually absorb.

That's what we do in these sessions. We share with each other, we ask questions, and through conversation we figure things out together. Nine minds working on a problem are considerably more effective than one. We learn from each other's insights and perspectives. This communal approach to study mirrors, in a small way, what we'll experience throughout our eternal careers, learning together, teaching together, growing together.

The Ministry Ahead

Before we close this chapter, I want you to take a look at something. In the reference materials, you'll find a chart showing the specific jobs of the secondary and tertiary orders of supernaphim on each of the circuits. We'll explore these roles in detail in our next session, but I want to plant that seed now. These aren't vague, abstract functions. Each order has concrete responsibilities, guiding, teaching, facilitating, revealing, calibrated to your needs at each stage of your Havona journey.

The seven circuits of Havona are completely inclusive. Everything you need is there, all combinations of Trinity influence, all aspects of experiential reality, all the training necessary for whatever service God has planned for you in eternity. Havona isn't just a waystation between the superuniverses and Paradise. It's a comprehensive university of spiritual reality, staffed by the most skilled ministers in creation.

And this brings us back to where we started: the mighty supernaphim. They're called mighty not because of raw power, though they certainly possess that, but because they represent the Infinite Spirit's direct creative touch. They embody his nature without the modifications introduced by working through other beings. When you encounter them, whether in Paradise, Havona, or (in rare cases) on worlds like ours, you're meeting angels who carry the unmistakable signature of the Third Person of the Trinity.

Looking Forward

As we prepare to move into the next chapter, keep in mind that what we've covered tonight is foundational. Understanding the three orders of supernaphim, their origins, their natures, and their purposes sets the stage for comprehending the specific ministries they'll perform as you progress through Havona.

We'll examine each circuit in turn, discovering what these angels will teach you about the Supreme Being, about the Infinite Spirit, about the Eternal Son, and ultimately about the Universal Father. We'll explore how the billion worlds function as laboratories of spiritual discovery, where theory becomes experience and knowledge transforms into wisdom.

You're not studying this material for academic interest alone. You're studying your own future. Every paragraph, every concept, every careful distinction the revelators make is describing what you will actually experience. These angels are real. These circuits exist. These training programs are running right now, preparing for the moment when you, yes, you, arrive and begin your own journey through the perfect central creation.

That's a humbling thought, isn't it? But it's also thrilling. The universe doesn't just have a place for you; it has a carefully designed curriculum waiting for you, staffed by teachers who understand exactly where you're coming from and exactly where you need to go.

In our next chapter, we'll begin exploring those specific teachings in detail. But for now, I hope you're beginning to see the grand architecture of divine education, how every level, every order of being, every circuit and world exists to nurture, challenge, and perfect those who are willing to make the journey from animal origin to Paradise citizen.

The mighty supernaphim are ready. Havona is waiting. And remarkably, impossibly, wonderfully, all of this has been prepared for you.

Chapter 26: The Seven Orders of Tertiary Supernaphim and Secondary Ministers

Before we move forward tonight, I want to circle back to something we touched on last week, something that deserves more attention than we gave it. Buried in the middle of an earlier paragraph, the text mentions there's no time limit set on the progress of ascending creatures from world to world and from circuit to circuit in Havona. No fixed time period. You can take as long as you need. The same principle, I should add, applies to the mansion worlds. There's no arbitrary span of time assigned to residents on the morontia worlds. If it takes you a million years to get off the first mansion world, that's perfectly acceptable.

Someone in our study group pointed out something interesting about this. In the central universe, there's no time anyway. "Take your time" becomes more like "take your event." That's closer to the reality there.

Tonight, we're working through the tertiary supernaphim, and the different types assigned to each circuit. The picture I mentioned last week shows all the different types of tertiary supernaphim that serve on each circuit, and we're going to discuss each one. These are beings assigned to help us out, both ascending mortals and descending Paradise pilgrims. They're some of the key helpers who will be there for us, along with other celestial ministers.

Let me read the opening sentence, and then we'll work through each classification: "The corps of tertiary supernaphim, which is chiefly assigned to the service of the pilgrims of time, is classified as follows."

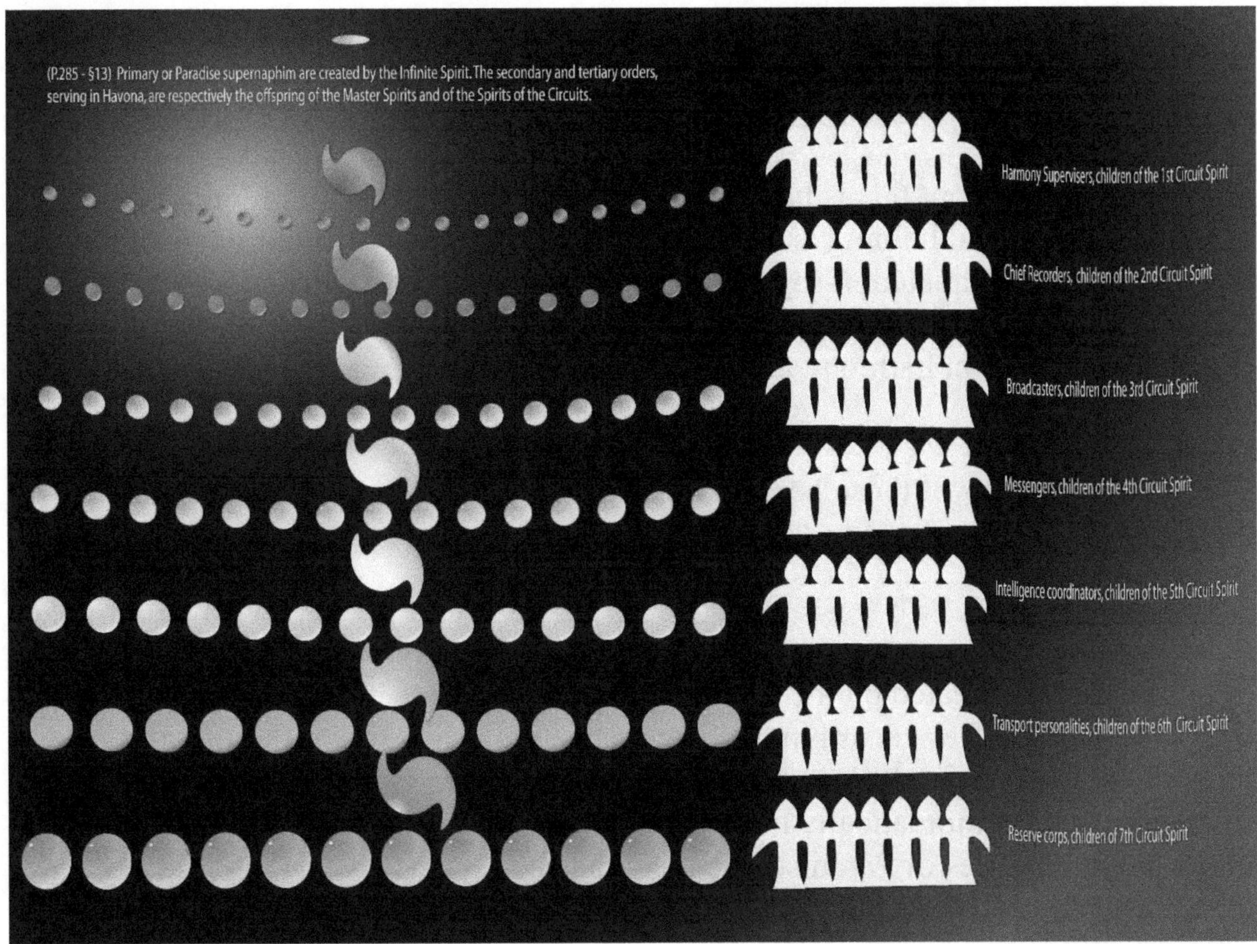

The Seven Orders of Tertiary Supernaphim

1. The Harmony Supervisors

It must be apparent that some sort of coordinating influence would be required, even in perfect Havona, to maintain system and ensure harmony in all the work of preparing the pilgrims of time for their subsequent Paradise achievements. Such is the real mission of the harmony supervisors to keep everything moving along smoothly and expeditiously. Originating on the first circuit, they serve throughout Havona, and their presence on the circuits means that nothing can possibly go amiss. A great ability to coordinate a diversity of activities involving personalities of differing orders, even multiple levels, enables these supernaphim to give assistance wherever and whenever required. They contribute enormously to the mutual understanding of the pilgrims of time and the pilgrims of eternity.

It's interesting they call these beings "harmony supervisors." You'd think that would have something to do with music, but it doesn't. The harmony supervisors help everyone get along smoothly through everything. They originate on the very first circuit, remember, the first circuit is the innermost circuit, not the outermost. We land on the seventh circuit and work our way inward to the first. So, they originate in the very first circuit and work all the way out.

What strikes me about this is how they're divided between helping Paradise citizens descend and helping us ascend. They keep all the different types of beings and creatures coordinated, it says here, even multiple levels. That enables them to do whatever is required to keep everything moving smoothly. They keep everything in perfect harmony as we move through the circuits. That's actually quite reassuring.

We could use a few of those here on our world. Maybe put them in Congress so everyone could get along.

2. Chief Recorders

These angels are created on the second circuit but operate everywhere in the central universe. They record in triplicate, executing records for the literal files of Havona, for the spiritual files of their order, and for the formal records of Paradise. In addition, they automatically transmit the transactions of true knowledge import to the living libraries of Paradise, the custodians of knowledge of the primary order of supernaphim.

These are the beings that record everything, everything that happens to individuals, everything that happens as groups, everything that happens that adds any knowledge to the libraries of Paradise itself and the custodians of knowledge. But they record everything in triplicate, so nothing is ever lost. Pretty interesting when you think about it. Everything that happens to the Paradise citizens and everything that happens to us has a triplicate recording as we go through. Just like everything's been recorded about us all the way up.

Which means Heaven has a bureaucracy. Which explains why there's no time limit on getting anything done.

3. The Broadcasters

The children of the third circuit Spirit function throughout Havona, although their official station is located on planet number 70 in the outermost circle. These master technicians are the broadcast receivers and senders of the central creation and the directors of the space reports of all deity phenomena on Paradise. They can operate all of the basic circuits of space.

These have their fingers on all the buttons. These are the broadcasters that send out all the reports to all the seven superuniverses, through Havona, and everywhere else. What's interesting to me is finding out that they're on planet number 70 on the outermost circuit, which would be number seven. But they come from the third circuit.

I don't entirely get the connection there. They come from the third circuit yet operate off of this planet 70 on the very seventh circuit. So, all the space reports, the reports out to all the superuniverses, all the local universes, all these reports come from these beings.

Now, there's some confusion here worth addressing. They're from the third circuit and they're located on planet number 70 in the outermost circle. The circle is the circuit too, as far as I know. The broadcasters are called "children of the third circuit Spirit," not the first or second Spirit. But the way they explain this, it sounds like they're on planet number 70 in the outermost circle, which sounds like it's on the outermost circuit.

Perhaps they were originated on the third circuit but function elsewhere. Or, and here's another possibility, they talk about dwelling places in both the mansion worlds and Paradise as having dwelling places that are arranged in circles. If you think about Dalamatia and all these other planned cities, they're all in circles, aren't they? Every single one of them. So, they could be talking about being in the outermost circle of the dwelling place on the third circuit.

Many of these beings live in domiciles that are arranged in circles. They go out in concentric circles, like seven concentric circles, which may be what they're talking about. I'm not entirely sure. It's not clear, but it sounds like they're talking about the outermost circuit. They may also be talking about the outermost circle in their dwelling place. So, it could be on planet number 70 in the third circuit. I wanted to make that clarification because I'm not sure which one it is, to be honest. It could be either one.

Why This Knowledge Matters Now

Let me say something else while we're on this subject. Last week someone asked me a very good question, which I didn't address very well, and I want to address it now. She said, "Why do we need to know all this stuff? This is all information about when we get to Havona, and that's a long time away."

Let me put it this way. First of all, we have to learn it somewhere along our pathway before we get there. And it says in the book that the things we remember from this life, not talking about the mansion worlds or anywhere else, are things of spiritual significance.

Now, we'll still know that two times two is four when we get to the mansion worlds, but we may not have a relation point about two times two is four as a memory like we will about the broadcasters or harmony supervisors. Because these memories all have what? Spiritual significance. So, when you get to the mansion worlds, you should remember everything we studied, because they all have spiritual significance. You may not remember who your little brother was, but you will remember what you studied. That's why this stuff is so important.

4. The Messengers

The messengers take origin on circuit number four. They range the Paradise-Havona system as bearers of all messages requiring personal transmission. They serve their fellows, the celestial personalities, the Paradise pilgrims, and even the ascendant souls of time.

The messengers will relay messages for us if we need them, if it's anything of importance, from circuit number four. They're like a celestial communications system, probably a little more dependable than AT&T.

5. The Intelligence Coordinators

These tertiary supernaphim, the children of the fifth circuit Spirit, are always the wise and sympathetic promoters of fraternal association between the ascending and the descending pilgrims. They minister to all the inhabitants of Havona and especially to the ascenders by keeping them currently informed regarding the affairs of the universe of universes. By virtue of personal contacts with the broadcasters and the reflectors, these "living newspapers" of Havona are instantly conversant with all information passing over the vast news circuits of the central universe. They secure intelligence by the Havona graph method, which enables them automatically to assimilate as much information in one hour of Urantia time as would require a thousand years for your most rapid telegraphic technique to record.

What I find interesting is that they call these beings "intelligence coordinators." What strikes me about it is this: they're coordinating between ascenders and Paradise pilgrims. The Paradise pilgrims are born perfect. Their intelligence is probably pretty high up there, wouldn't you say? They know pretty much everything. So, I think the coordination that needs to be done is probably on our end, because we're not as smart as them. These intelligence coordinators actually help us understand the Paradise pilgrims.

Think about it this way. If you went to the jungles of South America or wherever, back in the bush, we would be the ones with knowledge. But if you go back in the bush, we'd look pretty stupid. So, it could work both ways.

6. The Transport Personalities

These beings of origin on circuit number six usually operate from planet number 40 in the outermost circuit. It is they who take away the disappointed candidates who transiently fail in the deity adventure. They stand ready to serve all who must come and go in the service of Havona and who are not space traversers.

That's the interesting point I want to explain. There are two types of beings here. When you have earned space, apparently when you have earned any space, you're able to traverse on your own. Let me explain what that means.

When we get to mansion world number six, we will have gone through mansion worlds one through five and all the satellites associated with those mansion worlds. So those mansion worlds will become what? Earned space. That space we are able, supposedly, to traverse on our own. That's what they mean by space traversers.

But when you get to Havona, where you're on a totally different level, the earned space you get to may not work the same way as it does when you're in the mansion worlds. They talk about the transport personalities, the supernaphim that transport beings around. Even when we take a side trip to Paradise, when we take our first trip to Paradise, we see this represented by a secondary supernaphim, a transport supernaphim. Even in Havona we have to be transported from Havona to Paradise by seraphic transport.

One transport that's particularly important is when you graduate from Havona to Paradise permanently. Then you go through a period of time when they actually put you to sleep for a long period to transport you from Havona to Paradise. That's a long trip, apparently. During that one, you're completely unconscious. They call it the "last rest."

The transport personalities, these are beings from circuit number six, their job is to transport individuals to planets. And if you fail on your adventure to find God the

Father, they'll transport you back to the seven superuniverses, apparently. That's a very involved, long trip which, even if you've earned that space, you can't do on your own.

So, if you fail, they send you back for remedial training. That's right. If you fail that adventure, you get to do it again.

There's another interesting part of this. They say, "those who are not space traversers." The question I always have is this: at what point can you traverse space on your own without a transport vehicle?

When we get to mansion world number one, how do we get transported to number two? Apparently you would think it would be by a seraphim. The second part of my question is, once we've gone to mansion world number two, we've earned the space between them. So, we can go on our own. Now does that mean without a guide or actually just being able to go there on our own.

This is the big question. I've had this for years, and I have thought about this every which way you can. It doesn't say that because it's earned space, we can fly there ourselves. However, the midwayers can move through space at triple velocity at times. But that's the midwayers. They don't have a physical body like we have a physical body. They have more of a morontia body. So, if they can transport through space as a morontia body, that makes you wonder: when we get our morontia bodies, when we get earned space, will we be able to transport ourselves from planet to planet?

It certainly sounds that way. It doesn't state it that way, but that's what it sounds like.

There could be large branches of transport vehicles that you go down, and you get a ticket, you get on the transport vehicle and head off to planet number two or planet number three or the satellite number three on planet number two. The fact is that we can negotiate that passage on our own because it's earned space, but the way we get there is not exactly clear.

My question's a question. It's a big question mark. It's got many possibilities. We may be able to fly through space ourselves and get there on our own, or we may have to get on some sort of transport vehicle. We know that if we get in seraphic transport, we go unconscious. It doesn't sound like when we go from mansion world to mansion world and satellite to satellite that we go unconscious. So, I would have to think that there's some other type of transportation, either that or we actually transport ourselves. We have the ability to fly there ourselves.

I know in the mansion worlds there are transport vehicles that fly in a grid. So, if it's needed there, certainly it would be needed between spheres and planets. If it worked that way, why would they have all these circuits that the archangels go on? All the other angels move on circuits. They don't just fly helter-skelter through the air.

If we did actually go on our own, we would have to stay in a circuit or some kind of traffic control mechanism, because you'd have beings flying all over the place running into each other. There has to be some control. So, I would think it'd have to be like it is on the mansion worlds where we actually have vehicles that transport us.

Now here's another mystery. Who are those who are not space traversers? So, there are beings that are space traversers. They can traverse space on their own besides just what the transport personalities do. In one way, fashion or another. Now whether we'll be that way, I am not sure. I can't say for sure.

7. The Reserve Corps

The fluctuations in the work with the ascendant beings, the Paradise pilgrims, and other orders of beings sojourning in Havona make it necessary to maintain these reserves of supernaphim on the pilot world of the seventh circle, where they take origin. They are created without special design and are competent to take up service in the less exacting phases of any of the duties of their superaphic associates of the tertiary order.

These beings are able to take the place of any of these we just read about in the lower phases of their duties, not the very important things, but they can take their place in the lower functions.

So that's the seven orders that we will see of the tertiary supernaphim on Havona.

The Secondary Supernaphim: Ministers of the Seven Circuits

Now let's talk about the secondary supernaphim, who will actually service us and the Paradise pilgrims on the circuits also.

The secondary supernaphim are ministers to the seven planetary circuits of the central universe. Part are devoted to the service of the pilgrims of time, and one half of the entire order is assigned to the training of the Paradise pilgrims of eternity. These Paradise citizens in their pilgrimage through the Havona circuits are also attended by volunteers from the Mortal Finality Corps, an arrangement prevailing since the completion of the first finaliter group.

So, the secondary supernaphim minister, half of their time is devoted to the Paradise pilgrims coming down. The other half of their time is devoted to us going up, along with the Mortal Corps of Finality.

On the first circuit, there's the complements of rest. The second, the counselors and the advisors. The third, the Father guides. The fourth, the Son finders. The fifth, the Trinity guides, which is interesting that instead of calling the fifth one the Infinite Spirit guide, they call it the Trinity guide. The sixth, the supremacy guides, which helps us recognize the Supreme. And the seventh is the pilgrim helpers.

According to their periodic assignment to the ministry of the ascending pilgrims, secondary supernaphim work in the following seven groups: one, pilgrim helpers; two, supremacy guides; three, Trinity guides; four, Son finders; five, Father guides; six, counselors and advisors; seven, complements of rest.

We're going to talk about each one of these in our future studies.

The Personal Assignment of Angels

Each of these working groups contains angels of all seven created types, and a pilgrim of space is always tutored by secondary supernaphim of origin in the Master Spirit who presides over that pilgrim's superuniverse of nativity. When you mortals of Urantia attain Havona, you will certainly be piloted by supernaphim whose created natures, like your own evolved natures, are derived from the Master Spirit of Orvonton. And since your tutors spring from the Master Spirit of your own superuniverse, they are especially qualified to understand, comfort, and assist you in all your efforts to attain Paradise perfection.

This group of angels are each created by the Master Spirit of our origin, whichever superuniverse you come from. This comes back to the nature again of that Master Spirit. So, the supernaphim that would be assigned to us would all be from Master Spirit number seven, Father, Son, and Spirit, with the tinge of the Supreme Being. They have the same natures as we will. So, they'll be especially devoted and especially assigned to us because they would understand us. We would understand them better, and they would be the ones that would help us make our way through these different levels. That's why they're assigned to us.

The Journey to Havona

The pilgrims of time are transported past the dark gravity bodies of Havona to the outer planetary circuit by the transport personalities of the primary order of seconaphim, operating from the headquarters of the seven superuniverses. A majority, but not all, of the seraphim of planetary and local universe service who have been accredited for the Paradise ascent will part with their mortal associates before the long flight to Havona and will at once begin a long and intense training for supernal assignment, expecting to achieve as seraphim perfection of existence and supremacy of service. And this they do, hoping to rejoin the pilgrims of time, to be reckoned among those who forever follow the course of such mortals as have attained the Universal Father and have received assignment to the undisclosed service of the Corps of the Finality.

This paragraph can be confusing. First of all, the seraphim that's been assigned to you when you leave, when you get your seraphim pair on this planet, they stay with you all the way up till you're ready to go to Havona. That pair, when you're ready to step into Havona and be transported to Havona, then you will be transported by one of these transport seconaphim past the dark space bodies into Havona on the very first pilot level.

You will be asleep during this thing. You'll be conscious that you're going to be transported, but you will not be awake during this transport. They take you past the dark bodies. This is a long, long flight. So, you'll go to sleep. You'll feel like you woke right back up, just like when you die. You won't be able to see them anyway. They're dark.

What happens to those seraphim? Those seraphim that have gone with you all the way up through this thing have the opportunity to train to go to Paradise also. At this point, they would go to their training, and when they're done with their training, you would be rejoined with them in Paradise. The same seraphim, because they will have made the same efforts that you made in Havona, learning to recognize the deity, God the Father, God the Son, and God the Spirit and the Supreme. That is the goal of a seraphim. They want this service.

By serving us, they get to this opportunity. They're born with all these things. They have everything they need when they're created by the local universe Creative Mother Spirit. She instills in them a certain amount of knowledge. Now how much of this stuff we've been learning in this book, I don't know. I really don't. But since each one of those pairs are with us during this training, they could be learning right along with us. They're on the pathway. That's the whole point of doing this.

It says, "and this they do, hoping to rejoin the pilgrims of time, to be reckoned among those who forever follow the course of such mortals as have attained the Universal Father and have received assignment to the undisclosed service of the Corps of Finality." That's what they want to do, just like we do.

Perfection of Purpose: The Only Perfection We Bring

The pilgrim lands on the receiving planet of Havona, the pilot world of the seventh circuit, with only one endowment of perfection, perfection of purpose. The Universal Father has decreed, "Be you perfect, even as I am perfect." That is the astounding invitation command broadcast to the finite children of the worlds of space. The promulgation of that injunction has set all creation astir in the cooperative effort of the celestial beings to assist in bringing about the fulfillment and realization of that tremendous command of the great First Source and Center.

Did you catch that? All the celestial beings are there to assist us in this command for us to be perfect even as God is perfect. It brings the question about Lucifer up, you know. How did he miss that? I don't know. I really don't. I've asked myself that question many a time.

It's interesting too here that they say that the only perfect thing as pilgrims that we really leave this planet with is perfection of purpose. The desire to survive. The desire to survive, to do God's will. That's what it's about. The purpose of all this.

When, through and by the ministry of all the helper hosts of the universal scheme of survival, you are finally deposited on the receiving world of Havona, you arrive with only one sort of perfection, perfection of purpose. Your purpose has been thoroughly proved. Your faith has been tested. You are known to be disappointment-proof. Not even the failure to discern the Universal Father can shake the faith or seriously disturb the trust of an ascending mortal who has passed through the experience that all must traverse in order to attain the perfect spheres of Havona. By the time you reach Havona, your sincerity has become sublime. Perfection of purpose and divinity of desire, with steadfastness of faith, have secured your entrance to the settled abodes of eternity. Your deliverance from the uncertainties of time is full and complete. And now you must come face to face with the problems of Havona and the immensities of Paradise, for to meet which you have so long been in training in the experiential epochs of time on the world schools of space.

This is the big show. Perfection of purpose. And by the time you get there, you've been through all these tests, all these different things that they've assigned to you, and you've made it, and you've shown that you're going to stick with it all the way to the end. Because we're going to have some disappointments on the way. It's just like here. You do and you do and you do, and sometimes you don't do so well, and other times you do really well. But I just think it's interesting that we become disappointment-proof.

Because we've been disappointed in so many different things. So many times, you get to the point where your faith is tested, and you've shown you have what it takes.

We've got a long way to go. Basically, what you're saying is Satan had lost some faith because he wasn't disappointment-proof, and he was disappointed in God with his progress. He did become disappointed, so he regressed.

One sentence here is striking: we must come face to face with the problems of Havona. Now Havona is created perfect, so there are no problems there. It would only be the problems we take there. The problems are our problems. How stubborn are we to carry them that far?

I found out in this book that kind of the problems we have in this world are self-made, and I think that probably follows through the entire course of evolution or ascension. Quite a few of them are.

The Three Keys to Eternal Progression

Faith has won for the ascendant pilgrim a perfection of purpose which admits the children of time to the portals of eternity. Now must the pilgrim helpers begin their work of developing that perfection of understanding and that technique of comprehension which are so indispensable to Paradise perfection of personality.

Ability to comprehend is the mortal passport to Paradise. Willingness to believe is the key to Havona. The acceptance of sonship, cooperation with the indwelling Adjuster, is the price of evolutionary survival.

That puts it all in a nutshell. That's important.

Faith has won us a purpose, perfection of purpose. Not just our faith, the faith has made you free. And then we have to start developing perfection of understanding. And a comprehension, a technique of comprehension, which is indispensable to the Paradise perfection of personality. So, for us to make it in Paradise, we have to develop this technique of comprehension that makes us available to go to Paradise. We're going to have a different type of mind, and we have to figure out how to utilize it.

This last sentence is a complete nutshell. The ability to comprehend is the mortal passport to Paradise. Think about that. In order to be saved, what do we have to have? Faith. The passport to Paradise is having the faith to believe. And the belief is, the willingness to believe is the key to getting to Havona. Then the next thing is acceptance of your own sonship. What did Jesus teach us over and over and over again? That God is our Father and we're all brothers and sisters. We're all sons and daughters of God. Acceptance of sonship.

Looking at these last three sentences, to me it looks like they've got it backwards. I think it should be the acceptance of sonship, cooperation with the indwelling Adjuster, is the price of evolutionary survival. Willingness to believe is the key to Havona. Ability to comprehend is the mortal passport to Paradise. It should be reversed the other direction.

Because really it's a roadmap if you think about it. If you reverse it the other direction, the price of survival is cooperation with the Adjuster. This is how we get off this world. Accept sonship and have the willingness to believe and have faith. Ability to comprehend is the passport to Paradise. But I think it's like the book, it's from the top down, from the inside out. That's why they state it to us that way.

In all this, it's interesting. Maybe they don't, maybe they tell us somewhere else, but what they don't tell us is that the way we progress through the universe is by making the hard decisions, not by making the easy decisions. It's always the difficult decisions, the harder, tough ones.

That's right, because when you are faced with a decision and you choose the hard thing, that's when the learning and the experience comes. When you choose the easy thing to make yourself comfortable, the easy pathway, there's not a lot of learning that goes along with that. It's always the hard decision. It's implied all throughout the book, but I don't know if they ever stated it point blank.

There's no growth with the easy stuff. No growth whatsoever, but the hard stuff will grow you every day.

To add to that, we know in our mortal life, in our daily experiences, that for spiritual growth, we keep encountering the same problem over and over again, whether it's overcoming pride, intolerance, impatience, all these things that are of spiritual value. We are continuously challenged on that, and it takes a long time for us to really examine our life in detail and to comprehend that part that really needs a good adjustment. The fruits of the spirit, right? Reading it is one thing, but actually having the experience and doing it is quite something else.

We're challenged. It takes us a while to fully acquire the ability to comprehend what it is we need to tweak and adjust and change.

Closing Reflection

What we've covered tonight reveals the careful architecture of celestial ministry. These seven orders of tertiary supernaphim and the secondary supernaphim are not random bureaucratic structures. They represent the thoughtful provision of the Infinite Spirit for every need we'll encounter on our eternal journey. From harmony supervisors who keep everything running smoothly, to transport personalities who carry disappointed candidates back for remedial training, to intelligence coordinators who help bridge the gap between ascending mortals and descending Paradise citizens, each order serves a specific, essential function.

The revelation that we arrive in Havona with only one perfection, perfection of purpose, should humble us. Everything else we must learn. But that single perfection, that unwavering desire to do the Father's will, opens every door ahead. It's enough. Combined with the three keys, ability to comprehend as our passport to Paradise, willingness to believe as our key to Havona, and acceptance of sonship through cooperation with our Adjuster as the price of survival, we have everything we need.

The problems we'll face in Havona aren't problems with Havona. They're our own problems, carried forward because we're stubborn or slow to learn. But we'll have help every step of the way. Angels created specifically to understand our superuniverse nature. Teachers who share our tendencies and sympathize with our struggles. And eventually, reunion with our seraphic companions who will have completed their own training while we complete ours.

In our next chapter, we'll examine the specific ministries of each order of secondary supernaphim on the seven circuits, the pilgrim helpers, supremacy guides, Trinity guides, Son finders, Father guides, counselors and advisors, and complements of rest. Each represents a stage in our progressive spiritual education, and each deserves our careful attention.

For now, rest in this knowledge: the universe is not indifferent to your journey. Every detail has been thought through. Every need anticipated. Every challenge calibrated to promote growth without overwhelming you. You are known, you are valued, and you are being prepared for something magnificent.

Chapter 27: The Pilgrim Helpers and Our Journey Through Havona

Introduction: Welcome to the Central Universe

I want to continue our exploration of the ministering spirits of the central universe as revealed in the Urantia Book. We're diving into Section 5 of Paper 26, which focuses on the Pilgrim Helpers, those remarkable beings who will one day welcome us to the stabilized worlds of Havona. This is the fourth installment in our series on this paper, and I believe you'll find this material both challenging and profoundly encouraging.

The Nature and Origin of Pilgrim Helpers

The groups of secondary supernaphim we encounter first in our journey through Havona are the Pilgrim Helpers. The Urantia Book describes these beings as possessing "quick understanding and broad sympathy" as they welcome the much-traveled ascenders of space to the stabilized worlds and settled economy of the central universe.

What strikes me as particularly fascinating is the timing of their creation. These high ministers began their work simultaneously for two completely different groups of pilgrims. The first Paradise pilgrims of eternity arrived on the pilot world of the inner Havona circuit at precisely the same moment that Grandfanda, the very first ascending mortal from the superuniverses, landed on the pilot world of the outer circuit. Think about that for a moment. These two groups, coming from opposite directions and representing vastly different origins, started their journeys at exactly the same time in those far distant days.

Eventually, pilgrims from Paradise and pilgrims of time first met on the receiving world of circuit number four. This meeting point appears significant, roughly halfway through the journey, suggesting a divine symmetry in how these encounters were orchestrated.

Now, you might wonder why the Paradise pilgrims didn't begin their journey long before Grandfanda arrived. After all, Paradise beings had existed for eons before any mortal creature achieved that first arrival in Havona. The answer reveals something profound about how the universe operates: beings are created or eventuated precisely when they're needed, not before. There was simply no need for Pilgrim Helpers until that historic moment when both ascending and descending pilgrims required their services.

This principle extends throughout our entire ascension career. When we wake up on the first mansion world, two seraphim will be there with us. They'll have brought our soul trust safely to that new world. If, for some unlikely reason, one of those seraphim couldn't complete that mission, what would happen? A replacement would appear immediately, either from the reserve corps of seraphim or through direct creation by our local universe Mother Spirit. She has that authority and that capacity.

The point I'm making is this: everything needed for your ascension journey appears automatically, either through creation or eventuation. You never have to worry whether the support you need will be there. Everything has been thought out. Everything has been planned in advance. As positions become necessary for our support, the Infinite Spirit or her agents create the beings to fill those roles, fully equipped with all the knowledge and capabilities required to serve effectively.

The Circuits of Havona: Understanding Earned Space

Let me take a moment to clarify something about the structure of Havona that often confuses students of the Urantia Book. When you think about the seven circuits of Havona, you might naturally assume that once you complete the last world of one circuit, you simply jump to the first world of the next circuit inward. That seems logical enough.

But the reality is more nuanced. Each circuit functions as a complete, self-contained system. The circuit goes around and around in a perfectly stable pattern. The worlds on circuit seven maintain their position relative to each other at all times. The same holds true for circuit six, circuit five, and so on. These aren't spirals leading gradually inward, they're distinct circular arrangements, each separate from the others.

Here's where the concept of "earned space" becomes important. When you first arrive on the pilot world of circuit seven, you can only proceed to world number two of that same circuit. Then you go to world three, then four, and so forth. You must visit each world in sequence until you've completed the entire circuit. You cannot skip ahead. You cannot jump to a world you haven't yet earned the right to visit, even if that world sits right next to one you've already mastered.

However, and this is crucial, once you've visited all the worlds of a circuit, you've earned the right to return to any of them. That's what we mean by earned space. At that point, you could revisit world number one or world number fifty million or any other world on that circuit. The restriction of forward-only movement remains until you've completed the circuit, but backward movement within your earned space becomes possible.

What determines when you leave a circuit and move inward to the next? You'll be tested. Even if you've visited every single world on a circuit, if you're not spiritually prepared to advance to the next circle, what happens? You remain on your current circuit. You'll receive remedial training, certainly, but you'll stay where you are until you're ready. And while you're there, you can visit any world within your earned space, potentially gaining new insights from worlds you've already experienced.

This system ensures that no one advances before they're truly prepared. You must matriculate through each world properly. There's no cheating, no shortcuts, no way to skip over difficult lessons. If you were inclined to cut corners in school, well, you might as well abandon that strategy now. It won't work anywhere in your ascension career.

The Comprehensive Curriculum of Havona

The Pilgrim Helpers functioning on the seventh circle of Havona worlds conduct their work for ascending mortals in three major divisions:

First, the supreme understanding of the Paradise Trinity.

Second, the spiritual comprehension of the Father-Son partnership.

Third, the intellectual recognition of the Infinite Spirit.

Notice the progression here, from Trinity to dual relationship to individual deity comprehension. But notice also the language used for each level. We achieve "supreme understanding" of the Trinity. We develop "spiritual comprehension" of the Father-Son partnership. And we gain "intellectual recognition" of the Infinite Spirit. These aren't random word choices. The Infinite Spirit, remember, doesn't manifest in a physical form the way the Eternal Son does on Paradise. Our recognition of the Infinite Spirit remains largely intellectual and experiential rather than visual or spatial.

Now here's where it gets truly mind-boggling. Each of these three phases of instruction divides into seven branches. Each branch contains twelve minor divisions. Each minor division encompasses seventy subsidiary groups. And in each of those seventy subsidiary groupings, instruction is presented in one thousand classifications.

Let me write that out so you can grasp the scale: 3 major divisions × 7 branches × 12 minor divisions × 70 subsidiary groups × 1,000 classifications. That's why there are a billion worlds in Havona. The instruction is that detailed. That minute. That comprehensive.

More detailed instruction comes on subsequent circuits, but an outline of every Paradise requirement gets taught by the Pilgrim Helpers on this seventh circuit. Think of it as establishing the framework, the foundational understanding upon which everything else will build.

Each world you visit might present one of those thousand classifications within one of those seventy subsidiary groups. It's almost like a pyramid of knowledge, with each level supporting and connecting to the levels above and below it. By the time you work through all these classifications across all these worlds, you'll have a pretty thorough grasp of what's being taught, wouldn't you say?

I certainly hope they improve our memory capacity by then. Actually, let me share a secret with you: when you start learning on the mansion worlds, you remember everything that's taught to you. Everything. No more forgotten lectures or misplaced notes. Your enhanced mind retains these truths perfectly, which is one reason why studying now provides such valuable preparation.

The Character Formation of Ascending Pilgrims

The Urantia Book tells us this is the primary or elementary course which confronts the faith-tested and much-traveled pilgrims of space. But notice what comes next, a description that should resonate deeply with anyone who's faced real challenges in life:

"Long before reaching Havona, these ascending children of time have learned to feast upon uncertainty, to fatten upon disappointment, to enthuse over apparent defeat, to invigorate in the presence of difficulties, to exhibit indomitable courage in the face of immensity, and to exercise unconquerable faith when confronted with the challenge of the inexplicable."

Let that sink in for a moment. We learn to feast on uncertainty. Not merely tolerate it, feast on it. We fatten upon disappointment. We enthuse over apparent defeat. These aren't the characteristics of people who've had easy lives. These are the traits of souls who've been tested, tried, and proven through genuine struggle.

Long since, the battle cry of these pilgrims became: "In legion with God, nothing, absolutely nothing, is impossible."

That's our battle cry right now. We are those pilgrims. We are the much-traveled ascenders of space. Long before we reach Havona, we will have faced many personal battles. Our souls will be battle-scarred. But those scars represent something precious, they're evidence of growth, of lessons learned, of faith tested and proven genuine.

What does it mean to "enthuse over apparent defeat"? It means that even when we've been defeated in tasks we've undertaken, we respond with renewed enthusiasm rather than despair. We become invigorated in the presence of difficulties. We welcome challenges. We develop unconquerable faith.

There's a significant difference between a challenge and a test, though. A test examines what you already know. That's why you're tested on every single level of your ascension. You don't advance until they know that you know that you know that you know. You follow me? It's about demonstrating your faith, that complete lack of doubt that comes from genuine spiritual experience.

This is why Jesus, when he came to Earth, said the requirement of survival is faith. That's what it's all about. Remember when Peter tried to walk on water and began to sink? That was lack of faith manifesting as physical consequence.

The Uniform Requirements of Paradise Attainment

There is a definite requirement of the pilgrims of time on each of the Havona circles. While every pilgrim continues under the tutelage of supernaphim naturally adapted to helping their particular type of ascendant creature, the course that must be mastered is fairly uniform for all ascenders who reach the central universe.

This course of achievement is quantitative, qualitative, and experiential. It's intellectual, spiritual, and supreme. In other words, it encompasses every dimension of your being.

Everyone goes through the same essential curriculum. Nobody gets to slide through on technicalities. Nobody gets to cheat. If you were inclined to cut corners in school, you might as well get over that habit now. It won't serve you anywhere in eternity.

Someone once asked me, "How many people don't reach the central universe?" The honest answer is that the Urantia Book doesn't give us precise numbers. But here's what I can tell you: you have no time limit on any of this. Eternity means just that, eternal. You must choose to make progress. You must choose to survive. And that choice manifests through faith.

Some people may survive but choose to remain in the local universe to serve. Not everyone possesses the same capacity or desire to reach Paradise, and that's perfectly acceptable. But for those who do continue the journey, everyone receives the same basic equipment when they reach the mansion worlds. You're given a functional mind, a morontia body, and access to all the resources needed for growth. How you develop that mind, how you apply your free will, these remain the most important factors.

Now, it's true that some people arrive at the mansion worlds with certain advantages carried over from their mortal life. If you were a musical genius on Earth, you retain that musical aptitude. If you developed significant spiritual insight during your earthly life, you wake up with that spiritual acumen intact. You begin exactly where you left off.

This is why I spend so much time teaching the Urantia Book. I want to give you a head start. When you wake up on the mansion worlds and they begin discussing God the Father, God the Son, and God the Spirit, you'll already know who they're talking about. When they mention the seven master spirits, you'll understand the reference. You won't need to start from absolute zero.

But there's an even more important reason for studying these revelations now: they improve your current life tremendously. These teachings build faith. They strengthen social bonds and foster genuine brotherhood. If the principles in this book were applied to human society, politically, socially, within families, this world would begin to resemble Paradise itself. That's not hyperbole. The revelators brought us this information not just to prepare us for the mansion worlds but to provide a roadmap for spiritual and social transformation right here, right now.

When spiritual awakening happens globally, and eventually it will happen, regardless of who holds political power, we'll witness what the Urantia Book calls the establishment of light and life on our planet. There is genuine hope for this world. We simply need faith that this future can and will arrive.

Time and Achievement on the Havona Circuits

Time is of little consequence on the Havona circles. In a limited manner, it enters into the possibilities of advancement, but achievement remains the final and supreme test.

The very moment your supernaphim associate deems you competent to pass inward to the next circle, you'll be taken before the twelve adjutants of the seventh circuit spirit. There you'll be required to pass tests determined by the superuniverse of your origin and by the system of your nativity. The divinity attainment of this circle takes place on the pilot world and consists in the spiritual recognition and realization of the master spirit of your superuniverse.

This is the first major milestone: recognizing your master spirit. Why do you think they send you a tutor from your own superuniverse, one whose nature matches your own? Because you need to recognize the nature and being of that master spirit experientially. They provide you with a tutor, a supernaphim, who is exactly like you in fundamental nature, someone you can relate to intimately. This allows for the most efficient possible learning.

Everything in your ascension journey is designed for your benefit, structured so you can advance as quickly as your capacity allows. As soon as the supernaphim determines you're ready for the next test, you'll be examined. But notice the statement about time being "of little consequence." There is no time in the traditional sense on Havona. What exists instead is a series of events, a progression of experiences.

There's no reason to hurry because hurrying serves no purpose. In fact, I'm not certain you even can hurry in a timeless environment. There's no clock to race against, no deadline to meet. Achievement matters. Readiness matters. But arbitrary time measurements? They become irrelevant.

Mental Capacity and Spiritual Progression

Someone asked an important question during one of our study sessions: "If a person is mentally disabled in this life, do they still progress?"

The answer is absolutely yes. Here's what happens: if you have a defective mind on Earth, whether from birth defects, injury, disease, or any other cause, when you reach the mansion worlds, you'll receive a fully functional, normal mind just like every other person. At that point, you'll need remedial instruction because you weren't able to learn much during your earthly life. But you'll have the full capacity to learn.

If you think about it carefully, people with severe mental disabilities almost receive a free pass past this world. They don't have the mental equipment necessary to make informed spiritual decisions during their mortal life. That's not their fault, and it doesn't count against them. But when they wake up on the mansion worlds, everything changes. They possess normal mental function and can begin their real education.

The same principle applies to elderly people who develop Alzheimer's, Parkinson's, or other forms of dementia. They get restored to normal mental function on the mansion worlds. All these conditions are biological malfunctions of the human brain. When you receive your morontia form, you get a brain that works properly.

This is why both the Bible and the Urantia Book encourage us: if your mind doesn't suit you, assume the mind of Christ. The Spirit of Truth dwells within you. If your mind isn't functioning the way you need it to, ask for the mind of Christ, and it will be granted. That's something we could all benefit from doing daily.

The Work of the Supremacy Guides

When the work of the outer Havona circle is finished and the course presented is mastered, the Pilgrim Helpers take their subjects to the pilot world of the next circle and commit them to the care of the supremacy guides. The Pilgrim Helpers always remain for a season to assist in making the transfer both pleasant and profitable.

The supremacy guides take over when you advance to the sixth circuit. Can you guess what they teach? That's right, they instruct you about the Supreme Being, about God the Supreme.

Ascenders of space are designated "spiritual graduates" when translated from the seventh to the sixth circle. They're placed under the immediate supervision of the supremacy guides. These guides shouldn't be confused with the Graduate Guides, who belong to the higher personalities of the Infinite Spirit and who minister on all circuits of Havona to both ascending and descending pilgrims. The supremacy guides function only on the sixth circuit of the central universe.

I find it significant that we're considered spiritual graduates once we leave the seventh circuit. We've graduated from being purely spiritual beings to something qualitatively different. We're still progressing spiritually, of course, but we're no longer learning only about spiritual matters. We're moving into deeper understanding of deity itself.

Since these supremacy guides function exclusively on the sixth circuit, we'll encounter entirely different instructors when we reach the fifth circuit. Each level brings new teachers, new perspectives, new dimensions of truth.

Encountering God the Supreme

It is on this sixth circuit that ascenders achieve a new realization of supreme divinity. Through their long careers in the evolutionary universes, the pilgrims of time have been experiencing a growing awareness of the reality of an almighty overcontrol of the time-space creations. Here on this Havona circuit, they come near to encountering the central universe source of time-space unity: the spiritual reality of God the Supreme.

Don't you think we'll have a fairly good grasp of this concept by the time we reach the sixth circuit? Consider this: who currently serves as the replacement or vice gerent of God the Supreme? The seventh master spirit. And the tendencies of the seventh master spirit are precisely the tendencies we possess as citizens of the seventh superuniverse.

This means we should be able to comprehend God the Supreme relatively quickly, or at least as quickly as such profound matters can be grasped. Our master spirit has been functioning in place of God the Supreme throughout our entire ascension journey up to this point. That relationship prepares us for this encounter.

By realizing the reality of God the Supreme, we make the vital connection between the central universe and the time-space universes. We see them united as one family under a single divine overcontrol.

Now, you might wonder about what the book calls "the almighty overcontrol of the time-space creations." Is this referring to corrections we've experienced because we didn't surrender to God's will? Actually, no. It's referring to the overcontrol of God the Supreme itself.

God the Supreme is the experiential deity being prepared to take sovereign control of all seven superuniverses and the central universe when he, or she, since deity transcends gender, comes into full actualization. We're beginning to sense this comprehensive control, this unified management of everything that happens throughout the grand universe. That sense of overarching order and purpose we're perceiving. That's God the Supreme.

God the Supreme is currently undergoing experiential growth, preparing for the moment when the Paradise Trinity will bestow full sovereign authority. At that point, the Supreme will become the vice gerent of the Trinity, functioning somewhat as Michael of Nebadon functions as sovereign of our local universe.

Michael was originally the vice gerent of God the Father in Nebadon. But after completing his seven bestowals, including his final bestowal as Jesus of Nazareth, Michael became the sovereign in his own right. Similarly, when God the Supreme comes into full fruition, the Supreme will transition from being vice gerent of the Father, Son, and Spirit to being the actual sovereign of the seven superuniverses and central universe.

Someone asked an excellent question: "Where will the Supreme Being physically be? We know the heavenly Father resides in the very center of all things. But what about the Supreme?"

The answer is that the Supreme will be everywhere, just like God the Father. The Supreme will be omnipotent, omnipresent, omniscient, possessing all the attributes of deity. The Supreme will become another expression, another shade if you will, of God the Father.

Now, God the Father will still be there. God the Son will still be there. The Infinite Spirit will still be there. But remember, four outer space levels are currently developing. Once the Supreme assumes sovereignty over the central universe and seven superuniverses, the focus of the Paradise Deities can shift more fully toward those outer space levels. The Supreme will maintain complete focus on the actualized grand universe while the original Trinity concentrates on bringing the outer space levels into full manifestation.

The Mystery of Transformation

The Urantia Book contains a remarkable passage here: "I am somewhat at a loss to explain what takes place on this circle. No personalized presence of supremacy is perceptible to the ascenders. In certain respects, new relationships with the seventh master spirit compensate for this non-contactability of the Supreme Being. But regardless of our inability to grasp the technique, each ascending creature seems to undergo a transforming growth, a new integration of consciousness, a new spiritualization of purpose, a new sensitivity for divinity, which can hardly be satisfactorily explained without assuming the unrevealed activity of the Supreme Being."

Let that sink in. Even the revelators, beings far more advanced than we are, admit they cannot fully explain what happens on this circuit. They observe ascending pilgrims undergoing profound transformation, but the mechanics remain partially mysterious even to them.

They continue: "To those of us who have observed these mysterious transactions, it appears as if God the Supreme were affectionately bestowing upon his experiential children, up to the very limits of their experiential capacities, those enhancements of intellectual grasp, of spiritual insight, and of personality outreach which they will so need in all their efforts at penetrating the divinity level of the Trinity of supremacy, to achieve the eternal and existential deities of Paradise."

Since even the revelators struggle to explain this process fully, I won't pretend I can clarify every detail. But I can point you toward understanding the Trinity of Supremacy itself.

The Trinity of Supremacy consists of three actualized or actualizing deities: the evolved Supreme Being, the eventuated God the Ultimate, and the unrevealed Consummator of Universe Destiny (sometimes called the qualified Absolute). This trinity represents the experiential expression of divinity in contrast to the existential Paradise Trinity.

Because we're operating at such an elevated level on this sixth circuit, and because of our intimate relationship with the seventh master spirit, the Trinity of Supremacy begins becoming perceptible to us. Not contactable in a personal sense, the Supreme doesn't have a localized, personalized form we can approach the way we might eventually approach the Eternal Son on Paradise. Rather, the Supreme permeates everything, much like the Father, Son, and Spirit do.

What we experience is more perception than recognition. It's a growing awareness, a sensitivity to presence rather than a face-to-face meeting. And because of this new realization of divinity, the Supreme becomes more real to us, more intimately known even without direct personal contact.

This matters profoundly because when the Supreme Being comes into full actualization, the Supreme will function as an adjunct to, not a replacement for, the Father himself. All of us will become, in a very real sense, permanent parts of the Supreme. That's why the Urantia Book calls us "children of the Supreme." We are literally the experiential arm of the Supreme Being, contributing our unique experiences to the growing reality of God the Supreme.

This is why we have Thought Adjusters, fragments of the Father, dwelling within us. When we fuse with our Thought Adjusters, we become part of divinity itself. This makes us increasingly aware of God the Father because the Father literally dwells within us. And as we gain experience, we contribute to the experiential growth of God the Supreme.

Now, God the Father doesn't need to grow in the absolute sense. He is already infinite, already perfect, already omnipresent. But the experiential dimension of deity, God the Supreme, does grow through our experiences and the experiences of all other creatures throughout the grand universe. This was always the divine plan.

For all eternity, we will be part of the Supreme. We are the experiential children of the Supreme Being, contributing forever to the growing perfection of deity expression in time and space.

Certification for Advancement

When the supremacy guides deem their pupils ripe for advancement, they bring them before the commission of seventy, a mixed group serving as examiners on the pilot world of circuit number six. After satisfying this commission regarding their comprehension of the Supreme Being and of the Trinity of Supremacy, the pilgrims are certified for translation to the fifth circuit.

If you wanted to explore the Trinity of Supremacy in more detail, you could follow that reference in the Urantia Book to discover exactly who comprises this trinity and how it functions. I encourage you to do that study on your own.

What's clear is that advancement requires demonstrated comprehension. You can't fake your way through these examinations. You can't memorize answers without genuine understanding. The commission of seventy will assess whether you truly grasp these profound concepts, and only genuine spiritual growth and real comprehension will satisfy their requirements.

Conclusion: Preparing for What Lies Ahead

We've covered substantial ground tonight, from the origin and function of Pilgrim Helpers to the structure of Havona's circuits, from the comprehensive curriculum we'll encounter to the mysterious transformation that occurs as we begin perceiving God the Supreme.

Several themes emerge that bear repeating:

First, everything you need for your ascension journey will be provided exactly when you need it. You don't have to worry about whether support will be available. It will be.

Second, there are no shortcuts. You must matriculate properly through each level, mastering each lesson before advancing. But you have all of eternity to complete this journey.

Third, the preparation you do now matters enormously. Studying the Urantia Book, developing your faith, cultivating love for your brothers and sisters, all of this gives you a significant head start when you wake up on the mansion worlds.

Fourth, we are children of the Supreme, participants in the greatest adventure ever conceived. Our experiences contribute to something far larger than ourselves.

Next time, we'll explore the Trinity Guides and continue our journey through the circuits of Havona. Until then, may you go in peace, knowing that you are loved, guided, and destined for glorious things beyond current imagination.

Chapter 28: The Trinity of Supremacy and the Ministering Spirits of Havona's Inner Circuits

When I first began teaching about the central universe, I didn't fully anticipate how challenging it would be to convey the concept of the Trinity of Supremacy. Even now, after decades of study, I approach this topic with a certain humility. It took me five years, and I'm not exaggerating, to genuinely grasp what the Supreme Being was and where it fit into the grand cosmic scheme. If you find yourself struggling with these ideas, you're in good company. The apparent failures of time, as The Urantia Book reminds us, are never confused with the significant delays of eternity.

This chapter focuses on circuits five and six of Havona, where ascending mortals undergo some of the most profound spiritual education in all of creation. On circuit six, pilgrims begin to comprehend the Supreme Being and the Trinity of Supremacy. On circuit five, they prepare to recognize the Paradise Trinity itself. These two circuits represent a critical transition in our eternal journey, one that moves us from understanding evolutionary deity to glimpsing the infinite persons of the Godhead.

Understanding the Trinity of Supremacy

Let me begin with what might seem like a detour but is actually essential groundwork. Master Spirit number seven, the one who presides over our seventh superuniverse, plays a unique role in our spiritual development. In his multiple capacities, he personally sponsors the progression of ascension candidates from the worlds of time in their attempts to achieve comprehension of the undivided deity of supremacy.

This comprehension involves grasping the existential sovereignty of the Trinity of Supremacy, coordinated with a concept of the growing experiential sovereignty of the Supreme Being. Together, these constitute what the revelators call the creature grasp of the unity of supremacy. When we realize these three factors, the Trinity of Supremacy, the Supreme Being, and their unified relationship, we achieve Havona comprehension of Trinity reality. This understanding, in turn, endows us with the ability to eventually penetrate the Trinity itself and discover the three infinite persons of deity.

You might wonder why understanding the Trinity of Supremacy allows us to comprehend the Paradise Trinity. The answer lies in recognizing that Master Spirit number seven functions, in a sense, as the vice gerent of the Supreme during this particular age. The Supreme is not yet in full fruition. It won't achieve that status until all seven superuniverses reach the stage of light and life. So, our path to understanding the infinite begins with understanding the finite and the evolving.

The Nature of the Supreme Being

The Foreword to The Urantia Book tells us that the grand universe is the threefold deity domain of the Trinity of Supremacy, God the Sevenfold, and the Supreme Being. God the Supreme is potential in the Paradise Trinity, from whom he derives his personality and spirit attributes. But he is now actualizing in the Creator Sons, the Ancients of Days, and the Master Spirits, from whom he derives his power as Almighty to the superuniverses of time and space.

This power manifestation of the immediate God of evolutionary creatures actually evolves concurrently with them. In other words, the Supreme evolves as we evolve. Think about that for a moment. The Almighty Supreme, evolving on the level of non-personal activities, and the spirit person of God the Supreme are one reality, the Supreme Being.

Eventually, the Supreme Being will be both the spirit person of God the Supreme and the non-personal part of God the Supreme, which gathers in all the experience from all the different beings throughout time and space. This is why our experiences matter cosmically. Every choice we make, every struggle we overcome, every act of love we perform contributes to the actualization of the Supreme.

The Creator Sons, in their deity association with God the Sevenfold, provide the mechanism whereby mortals become immortal and the finite attains the embrace of the infinite. Michael of Nebadon, whom we know as Jesus, exemplifies this role. The Supreme Being, however, provides the technique for the power-personality mobilization, the divine synthesis of these manifold transactions. This synthesis enables the finite to attain the absonite, and through other possible future actualizations, the attainment of the ultimate.

What are these future actualizations? The outer space belts. The four concentric rings of developing universes beyond the seven superuniverses represent the next grand phase of cosmic evolution. The Creator Sons and their associate Divine Ministers participate in this supreme mobilization, while the Ancients of Days and the seven Master Spirits probably remain eternally fixed as permanent administrators in the grand universe.

The Third Level of Cosmic Reality

Here's where things get genuinely challenging. The third level in what the revelators call the unqualified hypothesis of the second level of the Trinity of Trinities embraces the correlation of every phase of every kind of reality that is, was, or could be in the entirety of infinity. The Supreme Being represents not only spirit but mind, power, and experience, the ultimate expression of all this and much more.

In the conjoint conception of the oneness of the Universal, the Deity, and the Unqualified Absolute, there is included the absolute finality of all reality realization. What does this mean practically? It means the Trinity of Supremacy basically encompasses all possibilities of the finite, of mind, of power, and of experience through all time. Our understanding of this Trinity of Supremacy becomes necessary for us to understand the Paradise Trinity itself.

Understanding the God of experience prepares us to take the next step toward comprehending the Gods of infinity. Until we know this and are educated in it, we won't be able to comprehend what's going on in the universe. Without this framework, cosmic reality would appear chaotic, random, purposeless. The Trinity of Supremacy gives us the lens through which order, purpose, and meaning become visible.

The Supreme Being and the Paradise Trinity

Now, here's a critical distinction that you need to grasp firmly: The Supreme Being is something less than and something other than the Trinity functioning in the finite universes. The Supreme Being is always less than the Trinity. You cannot say that the Supreme Being will ever take the place of the Trinity. That's simply not going to happen. The Trinity is existential; the Supreme is experiential. The Trinity is infinite; the Supreme is finite, though perfecting.

But within certain limits, and during the present era of incomplete power-personalization, this evolutionary deity does appear to reflect the attitude of the Trinity of Supremacy. This encompasses everything from Supreme involvement all the way through to the Ultimate. The Father, the Son, and the Spirit do not personally function with the Supreme Being. The Supreme is separate. But during the present universe age, they collaborate with him as the Trinity.

They sustain a similar relationship to the Ultimate. The revelators tell us honestly that they often conjecture as to what the personal relationship will be between the

Paradise deities, God the Father, God the Son, God the Spirit, and God the Supreme when he finally evolves. But they really don't know. If celestial beings don't know, we shouldn't feel inadequate for being uncertain.

If you're a little confused about the Supreme, that's perfectly acceptable. As you continue to study The Urantia Book and allow its teachings to absorb within you, you'll develop a greater understanding. The relationship shown in the diagrams I've shared, the way the Ultimate Trinity connects to the Supreme, will start to sink into your consciousness. When you reach that sixth level of Havona, this relationship will become completely clear because you'll go through class after class after class of celestial beings teaching you about the Supreme and the Trinity of Supremacy.

You'll understand how the seven supreme creators and the Architects of the Master Universe relate to the evolved Supreme and how this eventually connects to the Ultimate Trinity. That's the whole purpose of spending so much time on circuit six. The importance of understanding the Supreme cannot be overstated. It forms the foundation for everything that follows.

The Trinity Guides of Circuit Five

Once you've comprehended the Trinity of Supremacy, what's the next step? Understanding the Paradise Trinity itself. That's the focus of circuit five and the work of the Trinity Guides.

The Urantia Book tells us: "Trinity Guides are the tireless ministers of the fifth circle of the Havona training of the advancing pilgrims of time and space. The spiritual graduates are here designated 'candidates for the deity adventure,' since it is on this circle, under the direction of the Trinity Guides, that the pilgrims receive advanced instruction concerning the divine Trinity in preparation for the attempt to achieve the personality recognition of the Infinite Spirit."

Just as you studied everything about the Supreme on the previous circuit, now you start studying the Trinity itself. This proves essential for understanding where the Infinite Spirit comes in and learning how to recognize this infinite person of deity. Here's something crucial to understand: Does the Infinite Spirit have a physical body? No. Does God the Son have a physical body? No. Does God the Father have a physical body? No. These are spirit beings. They have an essence, a presence, a reality, but not a material form.

Part of what the Trinity Guides teach us is how to recognize the essence of not only the Trinity but the essence of the three deities, starting with the Infinite Spirit.

This isn't something we would gaze upon with physical eyes. It's more like a feeling, an awareness, a profound spiritual recognition. You will stand in the presence of all of them, God the Father, God the Son, and God the Spirit. You will literally stand in their presence. But you won't see them physically the way you would see a finite being. You would recognize them through an essence in your spiritual self. You will know that you know that you know that you recognize them.

There's a passage in The Urantia Book that mentions if you have perfect faith, when you see a Creator Son, you have seen God the Father. That's the principle at work here. Because the all-mind comes from the Infinite Spirit, you use your mind to detect the presence, to recognize the mind of the Infinite Spirit. It becomes a connection, a mind-to-mind connection. The Conjoint Actor is responsible for mind, for bestowing it, for blending it throughout creation.

The Process of Preparation

Most faithful and efficient are the Trinity Guides. Each pilgrim receives the undivided attention and enjoys the whole affection of a secondary supernaphim belonging to this order. Never would a pilgrim of time find the first approachable person of the Paradise Trinity were it not for the help and assistance of these guides and the host of other spiritual beings engaged in instructing the ascenders respecting the nature and technique of the forthcoming deity adventure.

A secondary supernaphim is assigned to you personally. They help you through this entire process of recognition. You're not alone in this. You have helpers at every stage.

After completing the course of training on this circuit, the Trinity Guides take their pupils to its pilot world and present them before one of the many triune commissions functioning as examiners and certifiers of candidates for the deity adventure. These commissions consist of one fellow of the finaliters, one of the directors of conduct of the order of primary supernaphim, and either a Solitary Messenger of space or a Trinitized Son of Paradise.

Why would it be either a Solitary Messenger or a Trinitized Son of Paradise? They're both closely related in function and relationship. They would probably be the best ones to help us along in this process because of their unique relationships with other beings. So, you have this group of beings helping you prepare for examination by a finaliter, a director of conduct (who is a supernaphim), and a Solitary Messenger.

The First Journey to Paradise

Now this is where things become truly fascinating. When an ascendant soul actually starts for Paradise, he is accompanied only by the transit trio: the superaphic circle associate, the Graduate Guide, and the ever-present servital associate. These excursions from the Havona circles to Paradise are trial trips. The ascenders are not yet of Paradise status. They do not achieve residential status on Paradise until they have passed through the terminal rest of time, subsequent to the attainment of the Universal Father and the final clearance of the Havona circuits.

What this paragraph tells us is remarkable: When we're ready to leave the fifth circuit, we actually receive permission to visit Paradise. We take a transport supernaphim to get there. We go with this trio of beings to Paradise, where we're introduced to the wonders of that central Isle. But we're just visitors at this point, much like when you reach a certain level in the mansion worlds, sometime after the second mansion world, you get the opportunity to take a trip to Jerusem. It's the same principle.

You actually get to take a trip and see everything. But you won't be able to stay because you're not a Paradise citizen yet. You won't literally take up residence on Paradise until you've gone through what they call the divine rest. This divine rest appears to be longer and more significant than simply taking a trip to Paradise. The exact nature of this rest, I don't fully know. But you have to go through this long, extended divine rest, and at that point, you can actually partake of what they call the "essence of divinity."

At that point, you're ready to stand before God the Father, God the Son, and God the Spirit. When we stand before the essence of divinity, that will be in the center of Paradise. If you think of the three concentric circles, the first one we'll approach will be the Infinite Spirit. We'll approach the Infinite Spirit as spirit beings ourselves. Then we will go further toward the center and approach God the Son, the Eternal Son. And then we'll go even further inward and approach God the Father himself.

Someone once asked me about the essence of divinity and how to define it. In finite terms, we often talk about truth, beauty, and goodness. But the divinity they're talking about here refers to the actual persons of God the Father, God the Son, and God the Spirit. We also need to understand, at that point, the spirit of supremacy to be admitted into Paradise as citizens, the over-control, the recognition of the Supreme.

The book includes a beautiful image showing a secondary supernaphim (the transport supernaphim), the Graduate Guide, the Havona servital, and the ascender. These are the beings who ride on this secondary supernaphim to travel to Paradise itself. However, the majority of ascenders are barely able to intellectually recognize the third person of deity, the Infinite Spirit, on their first trip to Paradise. They're not ready. Why? Because we've only gone through circuits seven, six, and five. It's about spiritual development and recognition on each one of these circuits.

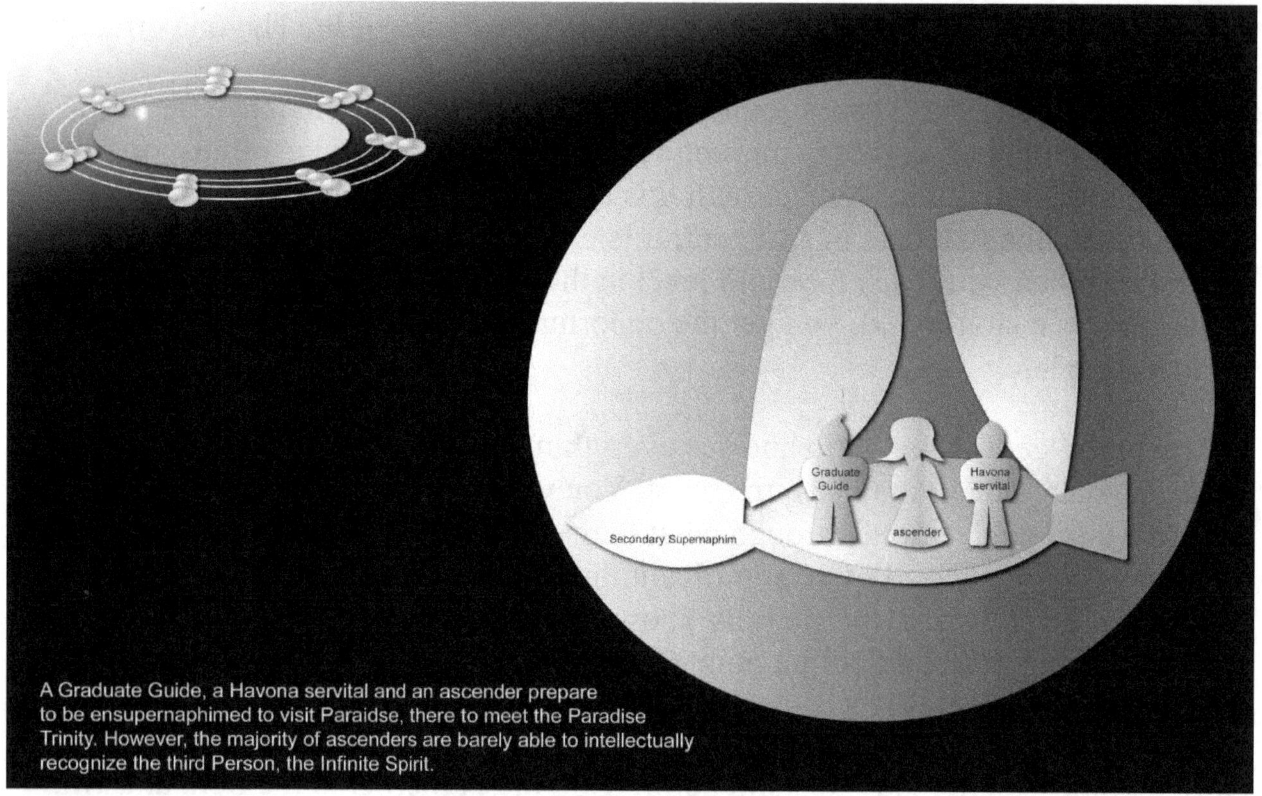

Figure 7: A Graduate Guide, a Havona Servital and an ascender prepare to be ensupernaphimed to visit Paradise

I think that's how we might recognize the Supreme, through experience, through our progress and comprehension over time, through actual spiritual growth rather than mere intellectual knowledge.

The Challenge of Recognition

The ascender's companions of the transit trio are not required to enable him to locate the geographic presence of the spiritual luminosity of the Trinity. Rather, they afford all possible assistance to a pilgrim in his difficult task of recognizing, discerning, and comprehending the Infinite Spirit sufficiently to constitute personality recognition.

Any ascendant pilgrim on Paradise can discern the geographic or locational presence of the Trinity. That's not the difficulty. The great majority are unable to contact the intellectual reality of the deities, especially the third person. Not all can recognize or even partially comprehend the reality of the spiritual presence of the Father and the Son. Still more difficult is even the minimum spiritual comprehension of the Universal Father.

This will be our first trip there, so all these beings will be very difficult for us to recognize when we're first able to visit Paradise. It's interesting, isn't it, that we can go before we can fully recognize? I've thought about this extensively. It seems like you would have to be able to recognize in order to go there, which goes back to the point about requiring experiential and spiritual enlightenment.

I think it's a teaser more than anything else. It's a preview of what's to come, not just for the recognition of the deities but for experiencing the wonders of Paradise itself. They don't talk about it extensively in the book, but Paradise is probably filled with amazing, incomprehensible wonders for us to see beyond the deities themselves. This visit serves as encouragement, a demonstration of what we're working toward. The process of reaching Paradise citizenship can take billions of years. By allowing us to visit early, it gives us faith, hope, and a tangible goal to pursue.

Also, by allowing us to go and experience the place, we know where we're heading. We get to experience Paradise itself. So, when we finally complete that divine rest and achieve citizenship, our minds aren't overwhelmed or distracted by all the external wonders. We've already seen them. We can focus entirely on the spiritual recognition of deity.

I'm sure it's an experience beyond comprehension, just meeting all the different types of beings on Paradise, plus experiencing the physical aspects of Paradise, the beauty, the architecture, the landscapes. It's something we'll look forward to visiting many times during our Havona sojourn.

The Son Finders of Circuit Four

Seldom does the quest for the Infinite Spirit fail of consummation. When their subjects have succeeded in this phase of the deity adventure, the Trinity Guides prepare to transfer them to the ministry of the Son Finders on the fourth circle of Havona.

The fourth Havona circuit is sometimes called "the circuit of the Sons." From the worlds of this circuit, the ascending pilgrims go to Paradise to achieve an understanding contact with the Eternal Son. Meanwhile, on the worlds of the seventh circuit, the descending pilgrims achieve a new comprehension of the nature and mission of the Creator Sons of time and space.

There are seven worlds in this circuit on which the reserve corps of the Paradise Michaels maintain special service schools of mutual ministry to both the ascending and descending pilgrims. It's on these worlds of the Michael Sons that the pilgrims of time and the pilgrims of eternity arrive at their first truly mutual understanding of one another. In many respects, the experiences of this circuit are the most intriguing of the entire Havona sojourn.

What strikes me as particularly interesting is that the Michaels maintain schools on this circuit. These schools serve dual purposes. First, they prepare the Paradise citizens who are descending for what's going to happen in the outer space levels. Second, they prepare us ascending mortals for what's going to happen in the outer space levels and what our jobs will be in those vast regions of developing universes.

The Michaels are already familiar with the plan of God. They already possess the big picture. What they want to do is share that big picture with us, so we know what's coming and what's expected of us. This circuit benefits both the Paradise citizens and us ascending mortals equally. We also get to know the Paradise citizens well, establishing relationships that will last throughout eternity. It's a mutual exchange that enriches both groups.

These Michaels on circuit four include those who will eventually go out to create and administrate in the outer space levels. The outer space levels will constitute a vast expansion of creation. The first outer space level alone, if I recall correctly, will contain something like 254 superuniverses. We currently have only seven. That gives you a sense of scale, we're in the infancy stage of universal development.

The Scale of Creation

Let me put this in perspective, because I think it helps us understand where we are in the cosmic scheme. For all those superuniverses in the first outer space level, each one will have the same amount or more of local universes that each of our seven superuniverses currently contain. You need to keep this in mind. Our local universe, Nebadon, the one that Michael created for us, is only forty percent complete. Forty percent. We're not even at the halfway point.

Michael and the Creative Mother Spirit have finished only forty percent of the work. Sixty percent of the inhabitable planets in our local universe haven't even been created yet. We're in the infancy stage of our local universe. So, don't you think we have considerable work to do before we leave this local universe?

That's why the book says the superuniverses are evolving, because they're all in a state of evolution. This isn't outer space in the sense of the four outer space levels beyond the seven superuniverses. This is developing space within the seven superuniverses, what you might call "inner space" from our perspective.

Our little niche, our local universe, which is one of one hundred local universes in our superuniverse, is forty percent done. Sixty percent of our local universe has nothing going on yet. It might be developing, it might be space dust, it might be nebulae in various stages of formation, but it's not finished. Michael and the Creative Mother Spirit have an enormous amount of work ahead. In doing that work, they'll assign countless other beings to help. They'll need to create probably more Lanonandek Sons, more Vorondadek Sons, more Material Sons and Daughters.

On our way up through the local universe, we may be assigned millions of tasks, working through these developing universes to prepare us eventually to step out into the minor sector and beyond. Within each of the seven superuniverses, there are still local universes that haven't even come online yet, haven't even been created. The celestial administrators know the projected number, but the work hasn't begun. The Michaels haven't even been assigned to those spaces yet.

Some of these Michaels teaching on circuit four may be in reserve for those future universes, undergoing training just as our Michael did before embarking on his bestowal career. It gives you a different perspective on where we are in cosmic history, doesn't it?

Think of it this way: Look at our planet Earth. Consider all the oceans. The cities and developed areas are so small compared to the vast expanses of ocean. We probably have something like forty percent land on the planet. That means sixty percent is water, undeveloped, as far as human habitation goes. Apply that same ratio to our local universe. Sixty percent isn't developed yet. That's a lot of real estate that hasn't been settled.

What happens when the allotted number of planets or inhabited worlds is attained and they all reach the stage of light and life? Then we step into the outer space levels. That's when all beings will achieve seventh-stage spirit status. We will no longer be sixth-stage spirits. We will be seventh-stage spirits, ready for assignment in the outer space levels.

So, we're defining outer space in two different ways. One is the outer space beyond the seven superuniverses, the four concentric rings of developing universes. The other is unexplored, undeveloped space within the seven superuniverses. Both are technically known space to the celestial astronomers, but the true outer space, the space beyond the four outer space levels, is really the great unknown. It's unorganized space, pure potentiality.

The Work of the Son Finders

The Son Finders are the superaphic ministers to the ascending mortals of the fourth circuit. In addition to the general work of preparing their candidates for a realization of the Trinity relationships of the Eternal Son, these Son Finders must fully instruct their subjects so they will be wholly successful in three areas.

First, in the adequate spiritual comprehension of the Son. Second, in the satisfactory personality recognition of the Son. And third, in the proper differentiation of the Son from the personality of the Infinite Spirit.

There's an issue here of potentially becoming confused between recognizing the difference between the Infinite Spirit and the Son. You probably face the same challenge in differentiating the Son from the Father. Their functions are so similar, and they interact with each other so intimately as the Trinity that distinguishing between them becomes difficult. Part of the work of these Son Finders is helping you differentiate between all these beings, to recognize the unique personality and ministry of each.

The Inner Circles: Beyond Examination

After the attainment of the Infinite Spirit, no more examinations are conducted. The tests of the inner circles are the performances of the pilgrim candidates when in the embrace of the enshrinement of the deities. Advancement is determined purely by the spirituality of the individual, and no one but the Gods presumes to pass upon this possession.

In the event of failure, no reasons are ever assigned. Neither are the candidates themselves, nor their various tutors and guides ever chided or criticized. On Paradise, disappointment is never regarded as defeat. Postponement is never looked upon as disgrace. The apparent failures of time are never confused with the significant delays of eternity.

This paragraph contains perhaps the most important lesson in this entire chapter. If you don't grasp all this material I'm trying to teach, if you work hard at it and still find it challenging, that's perfectly acceptable. You'll get it eventually. You cannot chide yourself for not understanding something immediately.

It took me five years to understand the Supreme, and I consider myself reasonably intelligent. When I first started reading The Urantia Book and tried to make the connection between the Supreme and the Michaels, I thought, "What in the world are they talking about?" I'm not joking when I say it took me five years to figure out the Supreme. I looked at it, studied it, looked at it again, studied it more, and it just didn't click for the longest time.

That's part of what this paragraph addresses: apparent failures of time. Sooner or later, the understanding will come. Someone asked me if I ever felt discouraged, wondering when I would finally understand. All the time. I was brought up on the Old Testament and the New Testament. Everything was supposed to be laid out clearly. It was supposed to be the infallible word of God. When I discovered it wasn't, when I realized the Bible contained human elements, errors, cultural conditioning, it tore my world apart.

There's a quote I always remember from the early printings of The Urantia Book. They included a little flyer that said, "Slowly but surely comprehension will grow if you give it a chance." That always stuck with me.

To give you another example: The concept that Jesus died for everyone's sins, as spiritually problematic as that teaching is, was the hardest concept for me to abandon. It had been ingrained in my brain since childhood. When something is taught to you repeatedly, over and over, it becomes part of you, part of your identity. So, when someone, or some book, comes along and says the deities consider this concept gross, barbaric, and fundamentally wrong, it's difficult to accept at first.

The first time I read The Urantia Book's explanation of the atonement doctrine, I threw the book across the room. I was in a piano lab, and I threw the book all the way across the room because it made me so angry that they said Jesus didn't die for my sins. That was my initial reaction.

How did I get rid of that negative programming? I kept going back to the book. I kept picking it up, reading more, studying more. My first copy was so tattered from me wrestling with it, from marking it up, from carrying it everywhere. It was pathetic by the time I finally absorbed its teachings. Curved pages, annotations in different colored pens covering nearly every page.

I've talked to quite a few people who know about The Urantia Book, and there's one underlying pattern I've noticed: There seems to be a very subtle urge or persuasion to keep at it. Many people have told me they picked the book up, read some, then left it sitting for months or years. Then something drew them back to it. I'm one of them. There seems to be a subtle hand, maybe it's God's hand, maybe it's our Thought Adjuster, saying, "This is the way. Just keep going."

You have to be ready for these teachings. Remember these lines: "Disappointment is never regarded as defeat. Postponement is never looked upon as disgrace. The apparent failures of time are never confused with the significant delays of eternity." This attitude is consistent throughout the universe. It's the attitude of the Gods themselves toward our spiritual development.

The Difficulty of Transformation

You can see the difficulty people have with this book. It requires study, persistence, and a willingness to set aside everything you've been programmed to believe and replace it with truth. That's the key. I remember watching something on television where a congressman, I think it was Rand Paul, said something about how you have to replace lies with truth. That is exactly right. We've been told so many things that aren't true, it becomes hard to discern actual truth when we encounter it.

The truth is out there. You just have to look for it. It takes intellectual stamina to get to the truth. If you simply believe everything everybody tells you, you're going to walk around in spiritual darkness for a very long time.

There's an Aramaic idiom in the four Gospels where Jesus said, "You must be born again." The way Aramaic-speaking people translate that phrase is "changing your thoughts and habits, starting over like a child, relearning everything." During Jesus' day, the religious leaders were so dogmatic, so bound by tradition, so consumed with obeying the 613 commandments of the Torah, that they'd lost sight of what really mattered. Jesus taught what was most important: love, mercy, service, spiritual growth. That requires changing your thoughts and habits, being willing to unlearn and relearn.

Looking Forward

Next time we meet, we'll talk about the delays and seeming failures in the deity adventure. That's a different subject, one that deserves its own focused discussion. We'll shift gears a bit. But I hope you can see from tonight's session the genuine difficulty people encounter with this book and why the circuits of Havona are designed as they are.

It takes study. It takes persistence. It takes humility and patience with yourself. It takes setting aside ingrained beliefs and replacing them with expanding truth. That's the whole purpose of our eternal education, not to fill us with information but to transform us into increasingly spiritual beings capable of recognizing and serving deity.

If you find these concepts challenging, remember slowly but surely, comprehension will grow if you give it a chance. The Trinity of Supremacy, the Supreme Being, the recognition of the Paradise Deities, these aren't concepts you master in an afternoon or even in a lifetime. They're eternal realities you grow into, experience by experience, choice by choice, circuit by circuit.

The ministering spirits of Havona, the Trinity Guides, the Son Finders, and all their associates, stand ready to help us. They have eternity to work with us. They never express disappointment. They never criticize. They simply continue, with infinite patience, to guide us toward fuller recognition of the Gods we serve and the destiny we pursue.

In our next chapter, we'll explore what happens when pilgrims experience delays on their journey and how even these apparent setbacks serve the purposes of eternity.

Chapter 29: The Ministering Spirits of the Central Universe

Introduction: The Journey to Paradise

As I've spent decades studying The Urantia Book, few passages have moved me quite like the descriptions of our journey through Havona, the central universe. Today, I want to walk with you through one of the most profound sections of this revelation, Paper 26, which explores the ministering spirits who guide us on our final approach to Paradise.

When we think about angels, most of us picture beings with wings hovering around Earth, perhaps watching over children or intervening in human affairs. While guardian angels certainly do serve humanity in remarkable ways, The Urantia Book reveals something far more magnificent: an entire hierarchy of celestial ministers who accompany us not just through our earthly lives, but through billions of years of cosmic education as we ascend toward God himself.

I find it fascinating that this journey isn't automatic. We're not simply transported to Paradise and declared perfect. Instead, we face what the text calls "the deity adventure", a series of profound challenges that test our ability to recognize and understand the very nature of God. Some pilgrims succeed on their first attempt. Others, surprisingly, do not. And therein lies one of the most compassionate revelations in the entire book: even apparent failure becomes an opportunity for deeper growth and understanding.

The Deity Adventure: Recognizing the Divine

Let me start by addressing what might seem like a troubling concept at first glance. The text tells us that nearly all ascending mortals attain recognition of the Infinite Spirit, though occasionally a pilgrim from superuniverse number one doesn't succeed on the first attempt. Those who do attain the Spirit seldom fail in finding the Son. However, of those who fail on the first adventure, almost all come from superuniverses three and five. The great majority of those who fail on the first adventure to attain the Father, after successfully finding both the Spirit and the Son, come from superuniverse number six. A few from superuniverses two and three are likewise unsuccessful.

Now, when I first read this passage, I wondered: Why would anyone fail? And why would pilgrims from certain superuniverses struggle more than others? The answer reveals something beautiful about how the universe is organized.

You see, each of the seven Master Spirits possesses personality traits reflecting one aspect of the Paradise Trinity. Superuniverse number one reflects the Father. The second reflects the Son. The third embodies the Infinite Spirit. The remaining four express various combinations, the Father and Son together, the Father and Spirit, the Son and Spirit, and finally, the complete Trinity itself.

Here's where we discover our advantage. We live in superuniverse number seven, which reflects the personality traits of the Trinity itself, all three divine persons combined. This means we receive the influence of God the Father, God the Son, and God the Spirit throughout our entire ascension career. We're exposed to the full spectrum of divinity from the very beginning. Someone from superuniverse number one, by contrast, has been primarily exposed to the Father's influence. When they reach Havona and must learn to recognize the Son or the Spirit as separate divine persons, they face a steeper learning curve.

This isn't a flaw in the system. It's a feature. The text makes clear that these apparent failures are really "inescapable delays", necessary pauses that allow each pilgrim to develop the spiritual perception they need to truly comprehend deity.

The Compassionate System of Retraining

What happens when someone fails to recognize one of the deities? The answer demonstrates the profound mercy woven into the fabric of the universe.

Defeated candidates for the deity adventure are placed under the jurisdiction of the chiefs of assignment, a group of primary supernaphim. They're remanded to the work of the realms of space for a period of not less than one millennium. But here's the crucial detail: they never return to the superuniverse of their nativity. Instead, they're sent to the supercreation most suited to help them develop the recognition they lack.

Let me give you an example. Suppose you've made it all the way through the seven circuits of Havona. You've mastered countless challenges. You stand before the Universal Father himself, and yet, you cannot perceive him. You cannot recognize his essence. For some reason, your spiritual development hasn't yet equipped you to directly apprehend the Father's presence.

The system doesn't condemn you. It doesn't declare you a failure and cast you aside. Instead, it sends you back to superuniverse number one, where the Father's influence permeates everything. There, under the tutelage of primary supernaphim, you spend a millennium, not Earth time, but Havona time, steeping yourself in the

Father's nature. You serve, you learn, you grow. And when you return to Havona, you return to exactly where you left off, ready to attempt the deity adventure again.

The secondary supernaphim never fail to pilot their subjects successfully on the second attempt. Think about that for a moment. The system is designed to ensure success. These apparent failures are simply detours that ultimately make us more complete, more capable, more understanding.

The Role of Superuniverse Seven

I've mentioned our home superuniverse several times, and I want to pause here to emphasize what an extraordinary advantage we possess. During one of our study sessions, someone asked me a question that gets right to the heart of this matter: "Since we come from a Trinity universe and must fully understand our own universe first before we move on to the next, wouldn't that already give us what we need to know about the Son and the Spirit?"

Yes. Exactly. We have what you might call a "leg up." We receive the influence of all three primary deities, God the Father, God the Son, and God the Spirit. Plus, we have the benefit of the Master Spirit who embodies the Supreme itself. We really do have a significant advantage being in the seventh superuniverse.

If we somehow failed to recognize one of the deities, which would be unusual for someone from our superuniverse, they would send us back to whichever superuniverse corresponds to the deity we couldn't recognize. For instance, if we reached the point of standing before the Father and couldn't perceive him, they'd probably send us to superuniverse number one, where the Father's influence is paramount.

But here's something I want you to understand we could potentially remain in our own universe for quite some time before we're even ready to go to Havona. The journey isn't rushed. By the time you're prepared to enter Havona, you typically have all the spiritual equipment necessary to understand all the deities. That's the plan, anyway. The entire structure of training on the mansion worlds, the constellation spheres, the local universe headquarters, and the superuniverse capital, all of it is designed to prepare you for what comes next.

The Three Circles of Final Preparation

When a pilgrim soul finally attains the third circle of Havona, something significant changes. They come under the tutelage of the Father guides, the older, highly skilled, and most experienced of the supernaphim ministers. On the worlds of this circuit, these guides maintain schools of wisdom and colleges of technique. Every being inhabiting the central universe serves as a teacher there. Nothing is neglected that could benefit a creature of time in this transcendent adventure of eternity attainment.

I find this detail remarkable. Schools of wisdom. Not just knowledge, but wisdom, that deeper understanding that comes from integrating knowledge with experience and divine insight. You need wisdom to discern the Father himself. You go through these colleges, and eventually, you reach the point where you're ready to take what I sometimes call "the test", that moment when you must recognize God the Father directly.

By this time, you've probably visited Paradise several times, transported there on the back of a supernaphim. You've caught glimpses of what awaits. But now comes the culmination.

The attainment of the Universal Father is the passport to eternity. Despite the remaining circuits still to be traversed, this moment stands as truly momentous. On the pilot world of circle number three, when the transit trio announces that the last venture of time is about to begin, when another creature of space seeks entry to Paradise through the portals of eternity, well, it's hard to overstate the significance of this occasion.

Did you catch that? It's from circuit number three that we actually prepare ourselves to become Paradise citizens, because that's where we recognize the Father. That recognition gives us our passport into eternity. We still have two more circuits of spheres ahead of us, but the essential transformation has occurred.

The text describes this moment in language that still moves me every time I read it: "The test of time is almost over. The race for eternity has been all but run. The days of uncertainty are ending. The temptation to doubt is vanishing. The injunction to be perfect has been obeyed."

From the very bottom of intelligent existence, the creature of time and material personality has ascended the evolutionary spheres of space, proving the feasibility of the ascension plan while forever demonstrating the justice and righteousness of the Universal Father's command to his lowly creatures: "Be you perfect, even as I am perfect."

You've come full circle. You started as essentially nothing, biological organisms on an evolutionary world, and you've literally clawed your way up through the Paradise ascension plan to become perfect, just as God commanded from the very beginning. Remember that command from the Old Testament? "Be perfect, even as I am perfect." That commandment travels with you through your entire journey. By the time you reach this point, all uncertainty about whether you'll make it is gone. You've traversed many spheres, one at a time, and each one has transformed you.

The Injustice That Never Was

I want to pause here to consider something that sheds light on the Lucifer rebellion. Think about the injustice that would have occurred if Lucifer had succeeded in his plan. His whole problem centered on this ascension plan, the fact that mortal beings could advance to Paradise while he, a magnificent Lanonandek Son, felt stuck in place.

Can you see how Lucifer, Satan his first lieutenant, and Caligastia were trying to steal the possibility away from all inhabitants to stand before God the Father? They would have short-circuited the plan for all mortals to reach Paradise. You wouldn't have gotten to God. You would have gotten to Lucifer, and that would have been it.

Someone once compared it to paying for a Cadillac and getting a Chevy. Actually, it would have been less than a Chevy, more like a Pinto or even a go-cart. The rebellion would have robbed countless beings of their cosmic destiny, all because of one being's wounded pride and philosophical error.

The Second Circle: Preparation for Eternity

The seraphic counselors and advisors of the second circle serve as instructors of the children of time regarding the career of eternity. The attainment of Paradise entails responsibilities of a new and higher order. The sojourn on the second circle affords ample opportunity to receive the helpful counsel of these devoted supernaphim.

By the time you reach the second circle, they start training you in your new career, your life from Paradise onward. They teach you about the responsibilities you'll carry, the higher order you'll join, all of it. You begin to learn what comes next.

But the second circle serves another crucial function. Those who are unsuccessful in their first effort at deity attainment are advanced from the circle of failure directly to the second circle before they return to superuniverse service. The counselors and advisors serve as both counselors and comforters for these disappointed pilgrims.

I want you to really hear this: these pilgrims have just encountered their greatest disappointment. In no way does it differ from the long list of experiences wherein they climbed, as on a ladder, from chaos to glory, except in its magnitude. These are beings who have drained the experiential cup to its dregs. Yet when they temporarily return to serve in the superuniverses, they go as the highest type of loving administrators to the children of time and temporal disappointments.

Wherever you fail in this progress toward the deity adventure, if you cannot recognize one of the deities, they automatically advance you to the second circuit. The beings there help you work through the disappointment of not achieving recognition. They prepare you to go back to the superuniverses for retraining, so you'll succeed the second time.

During one study session, someone asked me whether the tasks assigned to returning pilgrims would be beneficial in addressing whatever they were deficient in. I believe so. It would make sense that if you struggled to recognize the Son, your service assignments would involve work that deepens your understanding of the Son's nature.

Here's something that surprised me when I first understood it: after a long sojourn on circuit number two, the subjects of disappointment are examined by the councils of perfection sitting on the pilot world of this circle. And they are certified as having passed the Havona test. So far as non-spiritual status is concerned, this grants them the same standing in the universes of time as if they had actually succeeded in the deity adventure.

The spirit of such candidates was wholly acceptable. Their failure was inherent in some phase of the technique of approach or in some part of their experiential background. In other words, when they take you to circuit number two, even though you failed the adventure, they certify you as having passed the Havona adventure itself. The only problem was your inability to recognize one of the deities.

So, when they send you back to a different superuniverse for retraining, you're treated as a Havona graduate, not as a failure. Someone once joked that it's like getting a false driver's license, but it's more profound than that. They let you go back as a full-fledged Havona citizen. You simply didn't complete one aspect of the deity adventure, and they fully expect you to return and finish successfully the second time.

The Inner Circle: Meeting the Unrevealed

Much of an ascender's time on the last circuit is devoted to continuing the study of the impending problems of Paradise residence. A vast and diverse host of beings, the majority unrevealed, are permanent and transient residents of this inner ring of Havona worlds. The commingling of these manifold types provides the supernaphim complements of rest with a rich situational environment. They effectively use this to further the education of ascending pilgrims, especially regarding the problems of adjustment to the many groups of beings soon to be encountered on Paradise.

This is like a sneak peek, you might say, of all the different types of beings you're going to meet in Paradise. They help prepare you for these encounters. Many of these beings are called "unrevealed" because we haven't been told about them in The Urantia Book. There are lots of beings we can't even imagine or have any knowledge about. Part of the job of the complements of rest is preparing us for this reality.

During a study session, someone expressed confusion about this, noting that the billion worlds of Havona are supposed to contain samples of all creation from all seven superuniverses. That's true. But we're talking here about Paradise citizens, beings who exist on Paradise itself. All the beings in the seven superuniverses are fashioned from patterns originating on Paradise, yes. They are also represented in all seven superuniverses. However, there are lots of unrevealed beings on Paradise that cannot be duplicated in material form for the seven superuniverses.

These higher types of Paradise citizens and beings simply won't work as material beings and won't be found on the billion spheres of Havona. Only on the last circuit, only on the very last circuit, do you encounter them. That's what the complements of rest do: they introduce you to these beings, help you know them, recognize them, get along with them. So, when you finally arrive on Paradise, it's not such a shock to discover so many different types of beings you've never heard of or seen anything about.

Among those dwelling on this inner circuit are the creature-trinitized sons. The primary and secondary supernaphim are the general custodians of the conjoint corps of these sons, including the trinitized offspring of the mortal finaliters and similar progeny of the Paradise Citizens. Some of these sons are Trinity-embraced and commissioned in the super governments. Others are variously assigned, but the great majority are being gathered together in the conjoint corps on the perfect worlds of the inner Havona circuit.

Under the supervision of the supernaphim, they're being prepared for some future work by a special and unnamed corps of high Paradise Citizens. These citizens were, prior to the times of Grandfanda (the first ascending mortal), executive assistants to the Eternals of Days. There are many reasons for believing that these two unique groups of trinitized beings will work together in the remote future. Not the least of these reasons is their common destiny in the reserves of the Paradise Corps of Trinitized Finaliters.

On this innermost circuit, both ascending and descending pilgrims fraternize with each other and with the creature-trinitized sons. Like their parents, these sons derive great benefit from interassociation. It's the special mission of the supernaphim to facilitate and ensure the confraternity of the trinitized sons of the mortal finaliters and the trinitized sons of the Paradise Citizens.

The supernaphim complements of rest aren't so much concerned with training as with promoting understanding and association among these diverse groups. They help everyone get along, help us understand each other, help them understand us.

The Divine Command and Human Response

Mortals have received the Paradise command: "Be you perfect, even as your Paradise Father is perfect." To the trinitized sons of the conjoint corps, the supervising supernaphim never cease to proclaim: "Be you understanding of your ascendant brethren, even as the Paradise Creator Sons know and love them."

We're not only commanded to be perfect, but we're commanded to love and understand one another as brothers and sisters. This seems important enough to emphasize.

During one discussion, someone pointed out that the text specifically addresses these trinitized sons, telling them to understand their ascending brethren. One command was to be perfect. The other, directed to the descending beings, is to understand those of us coming up.

Exactly right. You know, they have to give us a little leeway, a bit of grace, because we weren't born perfect. We started at the bottom. They have to give us a little more space, as they say.

The mortal creature must find God. The Creator Son never stops until he finds man, the lowest will creature. Beyond doubt, the Creator Sons and their mortal children are preparing for some future and unknown universe service. Both traverse the gamut of the experiential universe and so are educated and trained for their eternal mission.

Throughout the universes, there occurs this unique blending of the human and the divine, the commingling of creature and Creator. Unthinking mortals have referred to the manifestation of divine mercy and tenderness, especially toward the weak and on behalf of the needy, as indicative of an anthropomorphic God. What a mistake! Rather, such manifestations of mercy and forbearance by human beings should be taken as evidence that mortal man is indwelt by the spirit of the living God, that the creature is, after all, divinity motivated.

Several points in this paragraph bear emphasizing. First, the Creator Sons come down to become mortals through the bestowal process. They experience going from divinity down to mortality. Our job is to go from mortality up to divinity. Two opposite directions, meeting in the middle.

But to think that God is weak and needy, that he requires anything whatsoever from us, that's what they're talking about when they mention the anthropomorphic God. God doesn't have personality traits of humans. He doesn't. He's God.

That's why the text says, "What a mistake!" We should think more about mercy and forbearance as evidence that God lives within us. We are, in essence, because of the Thought Adjuster, divinely motivated throughout our entire lives. The Creator Sons come down to us, and we go up to them, and ultimately to God.

The Gross Misconception of Sacrifice

I was talking with someone over lunch recently, and I made a point that I think bears repeating what a gross concept to think that God the Father would need any kind of sacrifice from his children to be recognized by God. To the deities, this is truly a gross concept. When we're talking about misinterpreting who God is, that's about as low as you can possibly get. The idea that he demands blood. That's just insane when you think about it. Whoever came up with that idea was operating from profound misunderstanding. And yet we've accepted it for thousands of years.

Someone pointed out that we've been taught this because of the Jewish tradition of sacrificing. It's an extension of sacrifice, exactly right. It started with human sacrifice. Eventually, they moved on to animals because, well, they were sacrificing the entire population, sons and daughters and all sorts of things. Millions of people were sacrificed for no reason. God never required it. Somebody came up with that idea. You know who? The shamans. That's how they maintained control over other tribes.

It's too bad we let it go on as long as it did. But now we know better. The Urantia Book makes clear that God requires no sacrifice, demands no blood, needs no appeasement. He asks only that we become perfect, and he provides the entire structure of the universe to make that perfection possible.

The Three Great Transitions

Near the end of the first circle sojourn, ascending pilgrims first meet the instigators of rest of the primary order of supernaphim. These are the angels of Paradise coming out to greet those who stand at the threshold of eternity and to complete their preparation for the transition slumber of the last resurrection.

You are not really a child of Paradise until you have traversed the inner circle and have experienced the resurrection of eternity from the terminal sleep of time. The perfected pilgrims begin this rest, they go to sleep on the first circle of Havona, but they awaken on the shores of Paradise. Of all who ascend to the eternal Isle, only those who thus arrive are the children of eternity. The others go as visitors, as guests, without residential status.

The first time we go to Paradise, we're just visitors. It's a teaser, you might say. We see parts of Paradise, but we're not citizens yet. When you're on the fourth circuit and beyond, you visit Paradise. But when you go through the final rest and wake up on Paradise for the last time, that makes you a Paradise citizen. That's when we become part of the children of eternity.

At the culmination of the Havona career, as you mortals go to sleep on the pilot world of the inner circuit, you go not alone to your rest as you did on the worlds of your origin when you closed your eyes in natural sleep of mortal death. Nor as you did when you entered the long transit trance preparatory for the journey to Havona. Now, as you prepare for the attainment rest, there moves to your side your longtime associate of the first circle, the majestic complement of rest, who prepares to enter the rest with you, as one with you, as the pledge of Havona that your transition is complete and that you await only the final touches of perfection.

Your complement of rest actually travels with you in the transport supernaphim to Paradise. You go together. You're not alone during this rest.

And here's the beautiful summary the text provides: Your first transition was indeed death, the second an ideal sleep, and now the third metamorphosis is the true rest, the relaxation of the ages.

Someone asked me to expand on this, so let me break it down clearly.

The first transition is death on this planet. You give up this mortal life forever. Your guardian angel transports your soul to the mansion worlds, and you wake up there. That's your first transition, your first sleep. You go to sleep, and immediately, from your perspective, you wake up, however long the journey actually takes.

The second is an ideal sleep, transporting you from the capital of the superuniverse to the first pilot world of Havona on the seventh circuit. That's the second time you go to sleep. It's called ideal because it's a long journey from Uversa to the first world of Havona. They put you out completely.

The third is what they call the relaxation of the ages, the true rest. It takes so long to get from the first circle all the way to Paradise, you have to pass all the satellites of the Father, Son, and Spirit, the three satellites of each one, twenty-one spheres total, it's a pretty long journey. So, they put you completely out. You're unconscious. That's why you have a complement of rest traveling with you. He's responsible for your safety, ensuring you wake up exactly as you left.

Three rests, basically, until you get there.

Conclusion: The Perfection of Mercy

As I've walked you through this material tonight, I hope you've begun to grasp the extraordinary care woven into every aspect of our ascension to Paradise. Nothing is left to chance. No one is abandoned. Even apparent failure becomes an opportunity for deeper growth.

The ministering spirits of the central universe, from the Father guides to the counselors and advisors, from the complements of rest to the unnamed legions of supernaphim who serve throughout Havona, all exist for one purpose: to ensure that every ascending mortal who desires to find God actually does find him.

We start as virtually nothing. We end as perfected citizens of Paradise, prepared for eternal service we can barely imagine. Along the way, we are guided, taught, tested, retrained if necessary, and ultimately certified as ready to stand in the presence of the Universal Father himself.

The command remains what it has always been: "Be you perfect, even as I am perfect." But now we understand that this isn't a harsh demand. It's an invitation to the greatest adventure in all existence, the adventure of becoming, through divine mercy and celestial ministry, everything God dreamed we could be when he first conceived of ascending mortals.

In our next chapter, we'll explore the primary supernaphim and their unique role in preparing us for permanent residence on Paradise. These are beings we can scarcely comprehend, yet they devote themselves entirely to our success. Their ministry represents the final preparation before we take our place among the children of eternity.

Until then, may you rest in the knowledge that the universe is designed for your success, that failure is temporary, and that God's plan for your perfection is already in motion.

Chapter 30: The Ministry of Primary Supernaphim - Perfect Servants of Paradise

Introduction: Meeting the Angels Who Never Fall

As we begin our exploration of Paper 27, we enter what I consider one of the most important revelations in The Urantia Book, the ministry of the primary supernaphim. These beings represent something we struggle to fully comprehend perfection that has never wavered, service that has never faltered, and devotion that has never been questioned throughout all eternity.

I remember the first time I studied this paper in depth. What struck me then, and continues to move me now, is the simple statement that opens this revelation: "Never have they been known to depart from the paths of light and righteousness. The roll calls are complete from eternity. Not one of this magnificent host has been lost." Think about that for a moment. In a universe where rebellion has touched even high-ranking celestial beings, where free will has led some to choose darkness over light, these primary supernaphim stand as a testament to unwavering perfection.

This chapter may challenge some of our assumptions about angels and their relationship to us as ascending mortals. We'll discover that these perfect beings don't just serve the Paradise Deities, they also serve us, guiding us through the final stages of our journey to Paradise and helping us navigate the extraordinary transition from time-space creatures to eternal citizens of the central Isle.

The Nature and Origin of Primary Supernaphim

When we talk about primary supernaphim, we're discussing beings who are fundamentally different from the angels we've encountered on our evolutionary worlds. The text makes this distinction clear: these are the "supernal servants of the Deities on the eternal Isle of Paradise." But what does this really mean for us as students trying to understand the celestial hierarchy?

Let me explain it this way. The primary supernaphim are created directly by the Infinite Spirit himself. This is crucial to understand because it places them in a category distinct from both secondary and tertiary supernaphim. The secondary supernaphim are created by the Master Spirits in conjunction with the Infinite Spirit, while the tertiary supernaphim are created by the Spirits of the Circuits, again in conjunction with the Infinite Spirit. You might think of it as degrees of directness in their creation, primary supernaphim come straight from the source, if you will.

The revelation describes them as "perfect beings, supreme in perfection." Now, I need to pause here because this language can be confusing. When we hear "supreme in perfection," we might think they represent the highest level of being possible. But the text carefully qualifies this: "they are not absonite, neither are they absolute." In other words, they occupy a unique space, perfect in their created nature, yet not possessing the transcendent qualities of Havona natives (who are absonite beings) or the absolute nature of the Seven Absolutes of Infinity.

What does this perfection look like in practice? These beings "work interchangeably and at will in all phases of their manifold duties." This flexibility speaks to a kind of completeness in their nature. They're not limited to narrow specializations but can function across the full spectrum of the seven orders of service we'll explore throughout this chapter.

The Presence of Primary Supernaphim on Rebellion Worlds

Here's something that directly affects us: primary supernaphim don't normally venture far from Paradise in great numbers. The text notes, "They do not function extensively outside Paradise, though they do participate in the various millennium gatherings and group reunions of the central universe." Yet there's a critical exception to this pattern, one that has profound implications for our planet.

When a world falls into rebellion, as ours did under the Lucifer rebellion, a primary supernaphim is dispatched to take command of all angelic activities on that planet. Think about what this means. In our darkest hour, when our Planetary Prince betrayed his trust, when confusion and spiritual darkness threatened to overwhelm this world, Paradise sent one of its perfect servants to ensure that the angelic corps serving here would have flawless guidance.

During our study group session on this paper, Rodney raised an excellent question: "Do they actually get stationed on that planet?" The answer is yes, for the entire duration of the rebellion. The text tells us that "on Urantia the present chief of seraphim is the second of this order to be on duty since the times of the bestowal of Christ Michael."

This revelation fascinates me because it means we've had two primary supernaphim overseeing angelic activities on Earth. The first served from the time of the rebellion until some point after Michael's bestowal, and now a second continues that vital work. Every guardian angel, every visiting celestial minister, every seraphic helper working on this planet answers ultimately to this perfect being from Paradise.

Why does this matter so much? The reason given is beautifully simple: "Being of the essence of perfection," these primary supernaphim ensure that all support personnel receive "perfect information all the time as to what should be going on on the planet even though we're in a rebellious state." Despite our world's quarantine, despite the confusion sown by rebellion, the angelic administration operates with perfect clarity of purpose and perfect alignment with divine will.

One question that came up in our discussion, and I confess I don't have a definitive answer, is whether these beings work in pairs like other orders of angels. We know that seraphim universally work in pairs: one dominant, one retiring, allowing them to maintain continuous service while one recharges. The term "supernaphim" itself is plural, which made me initially think they might work in pairs. But the text refers to "the second of this order" in a way that suggests individual assignment. It's one of those details that perhaps we'll understand more fully as further revelation comes, or as we ourselves progress upward.

The Seven Orders of Service: A Reverse Journey

The text presents us with what appears at first to be a puzzling structure. It lists seven orders of service in which primary supernaphim minister:

1. Conductors of Worship
2. Masters of Philosophy
3. Custodians of Knowledge
4. Directors of Conduct
5. Interpreters of Ethics
6. Chiefs of Assignment
7. Instigators of Rest

Yet when we begin studying these orders in detail, the revelation presents them in exactly the reverse order, starting with the Instigators of Rest and ending with the Conductors of Worship. Why this apparent inconsistency?

The answer reveals something profound about the educational method embedded in The Urantia Book itself. These orders are listed initially in their logical or hierarchical sequence, but they're explained to us in the order we will actually encounter them, the order of our personal experience. As the text explains, "You enter upon your Paradise career under the tutelage of the instigators of rest and, after successive seasons with the intervening orders, finish this training period with the conductors of worship."

This isn't just about organization or literary structure. It reflects a deeper truth about spiritual education: we learn best through experience, not through abstract hierarchies. The revelation meets us where we are, in the sequence we'll actually live through these realities.

It's also worth noting that these orders "have functioned as now classified only since the arrival on Paradise of the Havona pilgrims of time." Before the first ascending mortal reached Paradise, before the first Grand Fonda completed that incredible journey, these primary supernaphim served only on Paradise as messengers and direct servants of the three Paradise Deities. The ascension plan, the whole magnificent architecture of evolutionary progression, required even these perfect beings to take on new functions and new forms of service.

The Instigators of Rest: Our First Paradise Teachers

Let me walk you through our first actual encounter with primary supernaphim, because it represents one of the most significant transitions in the entire ascension career.

The Instigators of Rest are described as "the inspectors of Paradise who go forth from the central Isle to the inner circuit of Havona." Notice they don't wait for us to reach Paradise, they come out to meet us on the final circuit of Havona, the first circuit, where we're completing our preparation for Paradise citizenship.

But before we can understand their ministry to us, we need to grasp what the revelation means by "rest." And here's where things get interesting. The text describes seven types of rest:

First, there's the rest of sleep and play that we know even in our current mortal existence. We understand sleep intuitively, but I think we sometimes forget that play, genuine enjoyment and recreation, is itself a form of rest. This isn't frivolous; it's a recognition that restoration comes through joy as well as through unconsciousness.

Second, there's the rest of discovery that higher beings experience, and third, the rest of worship that represents the highest form of rest for spirit personalities. As we ascend, we discover that worship itself becomes restorative, that communion with deity refreshes us in ways we can barely imagine now.

Fourth, there's the rest of energy intake, the recharging that even angels require. Our guardian seraphim work in pairs precisely because of this need. While one serves, the other connects to the spiritual circuits for renewal. It reminds us that even celestial beings have their limitations and their needs.

Fifth, there's transit sleep, "the unconscious slumber when enseraphimed, when in passage from one sphere to another." Most of us who read The Urantia Book look forward to that first experience of seraphic transport to the mansion worlds. What we may not realize is that we'll sleep through it. They don't want us moving around during transport, and honestly, the experience would likely overwhelm our newly formed morontia consciousness.

Sixth, there's the deep sleep of metamorphosis that accompanies our transitions from one stage of being to another. When we move from the first mansion world to the second, we're not just relocating, we're being transformed. Our morontia body receives what I think of as a dimensional tweaking. We're still recognizably ourselves, but we're capable of perceiving and experiencing realities that were invisible to us before. This happens repeatedly as we progress: first mansion world to second, second to third, and so on through the morontia progression, then again when we transition from morontia being to first-stage spirit.

But the seventh type of rest stands apart from all the others. This is the final metamorphic sleep, "the transition rest from one stage of being to another, from one life to another, from one state of existence to another, the sleep which ever attends transition from actual universe status." This is the sleep that takes us from being residents of time and space, even as advanced as first-circuit Havona, and transforms us into citizens of Paradise itself, into beings who exist in the timeless and spaceless reality of the eternal Isle.

The revelation makes a striking comparison: "The instigators and the complements of rest are just as essential to this transcending metamorphosis as are the seraphim and associated beings to the mortal creature's survival of death." Just as we can't survive physical death and reach the mansion worlds without seraphic ministry, we can't make this final transition to Paradise without the ministry of these perfect beings.

And here's what moves me every time I contemplate it: this is the only journey in our entire ascension career where a primary supernaphim actually travels with us in seraphic transport. The Instigator of Rest who puts you to sleep on that final Havona circuit is there with you, ensuring your transition, monitoring your transformation. And when you wake up on Paradise, when you open your eyes as an eternal citizen of the central Isle, the very first being you see is that same Instigator of Rest who went to sleep beside you and woke up beside you.

The text captures this beautifully: "You will immediately recognize the instigator of rest who welcomes you to the eternal shores as the very primary supernaphim who produced the final sleep on the innermost circuit of Havona, and you will recall the last grand stretch of faith as you once again made ready to commend the keeping of your identity into the hands of the Universal Father."

That phrase "the last grand stretch of faith" stops me every time. We think of faith as something we need now, in our mortal existence, when we can't see the realities we believe in. And certainly, that's true. But this tells us that even when we've progressed through the mansion worlds, through the constellation spheres, through the local universe training worlds, through the superuniverse capitals, through all seven circuits of Havona, even then, one more act of faith remains. We must trust ourselves to that final transformation, knowing we'll emerge different, knowing we're leaving behind every vestige of time and space, knowing we're becoming something we've never been before.

The Eternal Awakening: Standing Before God

What happens when we wake up? The description given here draws heavily from biblical imagery, but it speaks to realities that transcend any single religious tradition:

"Now you awake to life everlasting on the shores of the eternal abode. And there shall be no more sleep. The presence of God and his Son are before you, and you are eternally his servants. You have seen his face, and his name is your spirit."

During our study session, this passage sparked an important discussion. Jane asked whether everybody on the first mansion world is on the same level, and that led us into a broader conversation about what it means to "see the face of God." The text says clearly that we don't see God with our physical or even our morontia eyes in the way we see other beings. Instead, "you see him with your existence or your soul."

This might sound mystical or vague, but I think there's a precise reality being described here. When the text says "his name is your spirit," it's referring to the

Thought Adjuster, that fragment of God the Father who has indwelt us, guided us, and progressively unified with our emerging soul. By the time we stand on Paradise, that unification is complete. We're not separate from God in the way we were as mortals. We've become, in a very real sense, an expression of his presence and his will.

Now, here's where our study group discussion became particularly meaningful. Someone pointed out that we've often read this passage as describing what happens when we die, the typical Christian understanding of going to heaven. But that's not what's being described here at all. This is the culmination of a journey that spans perhaps hundreds of thousands or even millions of years. This is what awaits us after we've learned and grown and been transformed through countless experiences and relationships.

Yet, and this is crucial, something analogous to this can begin right now, in our mortal lives. When we make the decision to accept God as our Father, when we commit ourselves to living according to divine will, when we accept what I call the "invitation" to become part of the family of God, we experience a version of this awakening. It's unrealized in its fullness, but it's real. The consecration we make as mortals is like a seed of the final consecration we'll make as Paradise arrivals.

I was raised Baptist, and we had what we called "the invitation" at the end of every service. The preacher would invite people to come forward and accept Christ as their savior. Now, the theology I learned then was incomplete, I didn't understand that Christ Michael came as the sovereign of our local universe to complete his seven bestowals, not primarily to die for our sins in the transactional way I was taught. But the invitation itself, the call to make a decision, to step forward and commit yourself, that part was spiritually sound.

The invitation is still the same: accept the fatherhood of God and the brotherhood of man. In accepting God as Father, we accept the Paradise Trinity, because they're inseparable. In accepting the brotherhood of man, we accept our role in the vast family of ascending beings. And in making that choice, something changes in us. We become, in a very real sense, a new person. We move from being lost in the world to being part of the family.

And just as these primary supernaphim have never wavered, never fallen, never turned from the paths of light and righteousness, when we reach Paradise and stand before God, nothing will ever shake our faith again. We become, in our own way, finaliters, beings who have made a final decision that will endure through all eternity.

Chiefs of Assignment: The Organization of Angelic Ministry

As we progress through our Paradise orientation, we encounter the second order, the Chiefs of Assignment. This group is designated by "the chief supernaphim, the original pattern angel, to preside over the organization of all three orders of these angels, primary, secondary, and tertiary."

Think about the scope of what's being described here. This chief supernaphim, the first angel of Paradise, oversees the entire angelic organization. Not just the primary supernaphim who serve on Paradise, but also the secondary supernaphim who minister in the superuniverses and Havona, and the tertiary supernaphim who serve in the local universes. He's what I jokingly called the "head kahuna" in our study group, the supreme administrator of all angelic ministry throughout creation.

The supernaphim themselves are "wholly self-governing and self-regulatory" except for the functions of this mutual chief. It speaks to the perfection of their nature that they don't require extensive external governance. They know their duties, they understand the divine will, and they execute their responsibilities flawlessly. But even perfection benefits from coordination, from an overarching perspective that ensures all the parts work together in harmony.

What does this mean for us as ascending mortals? The text tells us that "the angels of assignment have much to do with glorified mortal residents of Paradise before they are admitted to the Corps of the Finality." Our education doesn't end when we reach Paradise. In fact, a whole new phase begins, and part of that education involves service.

Here's something I want to emphasize: "Study and instruction are not the exclusive occupations of Paradise arrivals. Service also plays its essential part in the pre-finaliter educational experiences of Paradise." If you thought you'd finally get to rest and do nothing, you're in for a surprise. We work all the way up through the mansion worlds, through the constellation and universe training spheres, through the superuniverse capitals, through Havona, and we keep working when we get to Paradise.

Now, before you groan at that prospect, consider what the text says next: "Every day when you get up and you got something you have to do, life is good." Purpose, meaningful activity, contribution, these aren't burdens. They're what make existence fulfilling. The idea of an eternal retirement where we do nothing but float on clouds playing harps isn't just boring, it would be spiritual death.

But here's the beautiful part: during our periods of leisure, we naturally gravitate toward the company of these reserve corps of superaphic Chiefs of Assignment. Why? Because "they remind the mortals of time of the seraphim with whom they have had such long contact and such refreshing association."

We build relationships with our guardian seraphim during our mortal lives and our morontia progression. Those angels become dear to us, familiar to us, comfortable to us in a way that the mighty beings of Paradise might not immediately be. When we're feeling overwhelmed by the magnificence and diversity of Paradise, when we need a break from encountering new and often incomprehensible types of beings, we can talk with angels whose minds work something like ours. It's like going to a foreign country where everything is strange and then finding someone who speaks your language, not because the strangeness is bad, but because familiarity is restorative.

Interpreters of Ethics: Navigating a Vastly Expanded Social Universe

As we continue our Paradise education, we come under the ministry of the Interpreters of Ethics. And here, I think, we encounter one of the most practical and immediately necessary forms of help these primary supernaphim provide.

The text opens with a principle that applies even now: "The higher you ascend in the scale of life, the more attention must be paid to universe ethics." Then it defines ethical awareness in beautifully simple terms: "Ethical awareness is simply the recognition by any individual of the rights inherent in the existence of any and all other individuals."

But then comes the qualifier: "But spiritual ethics far transcends the mortal and even the morontia concept of personal and group relations." We could really use some of this understanding on Earth right now, couldn't we? Our concepts of ethics remain so primitive, so limited to our immediate group or nation or species.

As we've progressed from our birth world through the mansion worlds and beyond, we've continuously expanded our circle of ethical consideration. Every new group of colleagues we meet "adds one more level of ethics to be recognized and complied with." By the time we reach Paradise, we've learned a lot, but now we face an extraordinary challenge.

Consider what the text tells us about who we'll encounter on Paradise: "You must also fraternize with upwards of 3,000 different orders of Paradise citizens." Not 300. Not 30. Three thousand different orders of beings. Each with their own nature, their own perspective, their own rightful way of existing and interacting. And that's not all: "with the various groups of the transcendentalers", the absonite beings from Havona, "and with numerous other types of Paradise inhabitants, permanent and transient, who have not been revealed on Urantia."

I remember when we discussed this in our study group, someone said, "I wish they'd just give us a taste of them!" And I agree. The sheer diversity is staggering. But here's the practical problem: we don't need to be taught ethics as an abstract principle by the time we reach Paradise. We've spent ages learning ethical behavior, expanding our moral consciousness, developing spiritual maturity. What we need is interpretation, help in understanding how the ethics we've learned apply to these specific, unprecedented situations.

Think of it like this: imagine you've learned all the principles of etiquette in your own culture. You understand respect, courtesy, consideration, reciprocity. Then suddenly you're dropped into 3,000 different cultures simultaneously, each with their own complex protocols, their own ways of showing respect, their own definitions of appropriate behavior. You don't need someone to teach you that respect matters, you need someone to tell you how respect is expressed in each specific context.

That's what the Interpreters of Ethics do. They provide "helpful and friendly counsel regarding ethical interpretations." They help us understand what our laboriously learned ethical principles mean when we're "brought face to face with the extraordinary task of contacting with so much that is new."

The revelation lists some of the beings we've already encountered by the time we reach Paradise: "many of the numerous types of Paradise citizens, the ascendant pilgrims have already met on the seven circuits of Havona." We've also had "intimate contact with the creature-trinitized sons of the conjoint corps on the inner Havona circuit." We've met "numerous unrevealed residents of the Paradise-Havona system who are there pursuing group training in preparation for the unrevealed assignments of the future."

One question that came up during our study session deserves mention: when the text refers to the "inner Havona circuit," it means the first circuit, the one closest to Paradise. The "Paradise-Havona circuit" or "Paradise-Havona system" refers to the combined reality of Paradise itself, the seven circuits of Havona, and the architectural worlds that exist between Havona and Paradise, including the seven sacred satellites of the Father, the seven sacred satellites of the Son, and the seven sacred satellites of the Spirit.

Understanding these relationships and navigating these complex social realities, that's where the Interpreters of Ethics become invaluable guides.

The Mutual Gift: What We Bring to Paradise

I want to end this chapter with something that still amazes me every time I contemplate it. Near the conclusion of the section on Interpreters of Ethics, the text makes this remarkable statement:

"All these celestial companionships are invariably mutual. As ascending mortals, you not only derive benefit from these successive universe companions and such numerous orders of increasingly divine associates, but you also impart to each of these fraternal beings something from your own personality and experience which forever makes every one of them different and better for having been associated with an ascending mortal from the evolutionary worlds of time and space."

Read that again slowly. We make them better. We, who started as animals on an evolutionary world, who struggled with fear and selfishness and limited understanding, who made mistakes and had to learn everything the hard way, we give something to these exalted beings that enriches them, that changes them, that makes them better than they were before.

What could we possibly have that they don't? Experience. Stories. The lived reality of transformation. We know what it's like to choose faith when everything around us suggests despair. We know what it's like to choose love when hate would be easier. We know what it's like to keep going when we want to give up. We know struggle and doubt and fear, and we know the triumph of overcoming them.

These perfect beings, these primary supernaphim who have never faltered, they know perfection, but they don't know transformation. They don't know what it's like to be less than perfect and strive toward perfection. And that knowledge, that experience, is precious. It's irreplaceable. It's something the universe needs, something that makes creation richer, something that even perfect beings value.

During our study group, Gary read that passage and we all just sat there for a moment. It's humbling and exalting at the same time. It reminds us that the whole vast architecture of creation, from Paradise down to the humblest evolutionary worlds, is designed not just for our benefit but for mutual enrichment. We're not charity cases being helped along. We're partners in a cosmic adventure, contributing something unique and valuable to every being we encounter.

Conclusion: The Journey Continues

This chapter has taken us through only the first few orders of primary supernaphim ministry. We've explored the Instigators of Rest who guide us through that final, magnificent transition to Paradise citizenship. We've met the Chiefs of Assignment who organize the service opportunities that become part of our ongoing education. We've understood the crucial role of the Interpreters of Ethics in helping us navigate the bewildering diversity of Paradise society.

But three more orders await us: the Directors of Conduct, the Custodians of Knowledge, and the Masters of Philosophy. And finally, we'll reach the Conductors of Worship, completing our preparation for induction into the Corps of Mortal Finaliters.

Each of these orders serves a specific purpose in our development. Each addresses needs we'll discover we have only when we reach that stage of our journey. And each represents another facet of the loving, comprehensive ministry that surrounds us from the moment we make our first faith decision on our evolutionary world to the moment we stand as finaliters, ready to embark on assignments we can barely imagine now.

The revelation of the primary supernaphim reminds us that we're never alone, never without guidance, never beyond the reach of perfect help. Even on our rebellious world, cut off by quarantine, a primary supernaphim stands watch, ensuring that the angelic ministry here receives perfect instruction. How much more will we be guided and helped when we reach Paradise itself!

In our next chapter, we'll complete our study of Paper 27, exploring those remaining orders and understanding more fully how they prepare us for that momentous event, our formal induction into the Corps of the Finality, when we become eternally committed to serving the Universal Father in ways and places yet to be revealed.

The journey continues. It always continues. And at every step, perfect helpers await to guide us forward.

Chapter 31: The Ministry of Primary Supernaphim - Our Guides to Paradise

The sheer number of different orders, their functions, and their relationships to one another seemed almost impossible to grasp. When I first began studying the celestial beings described in The Urantia Book, I have to admit I was overwhelmed. But as I've spent years walking through these papers with study groups, something remarkable has happened. These beings have come alive for me, not as abstract theological concepts, but as real personalities who will one day be our companions, teachers, and guides on the greatest journey any human soul can take.

Tonight, as we continue our exploration of Paper 27, we're going to focus on something truly extraordinary: the Primary Supernaphim who serve on Paradise itself. These are the highest order of all ministering spirits, and understanding their roles gives us a glimpse into what awaits us at the culmination of our ascension journey. More importantly, it helps us understand that even in Paradise, that place of absolute perfection, we will still need guidance, instruction, and help. That realization alone should humble us and fill us with gratitude.

The Directors of Conduct: Learning Paradise Etiquette

The first group of Primary Supernaphim we encounter are the Directors of Conduct. Now, you might wonder why we would need directors of conduct in Paradise. After all, haven't we been instructed in ethics throughout our entire ascension journey? Haven't we learned about proper relationships and behavior on the mansion worlds, in the constellation spheres, and throughout our training in Havona?

The answer is both yes and no. While we've certainly been prepared, Paradise represents something entirely different from anything we've experienced before. The Urantia Book tells us that these directors instruct us not in "meaningless formalities nor the dictations of artificial caste, but rather the inherent proprieties." This distinction matters. We're not talking about arbitrary rules or social hierarchies. Instead, we're learning the natural, perfect way of relating to beings of unimaginable perfection.

Think about it this way: even after billions of years of spiritual growth, even after fusion with our Thought Adjusters, even after traversing the circuits of Havona, Paradise is still "inexpressibly strange and unexpectedly new" to those who finally arrive. The Directors of Conduct help us navigate these new situations without confusion or embarrassment. They smooth our transition into Paradise society.

One of our study group members once asked if these directors were like "the moral police they have in Baghdad." I appreciate the question because it reveals a common misconception. No, they're nothing like that. They're not enforcers or watchdogs. Rather, they're gracious guides who want to help us feel at ease and participate fully in Paradise life. They teach us the "usages of the perfect conduct of the high beings who sojourn on the central Isle of light and life."

The book emphasizes that "harmony is the keynote of the central universe, and detectable order prevails on Paradise." Proper conduct isn't about restriction, it's about harmony. When we understand the right way to interact with Paradise citizens, with the Trinity, with beings of native perfection, we experience greater freedom, not less. We avoid confusion, which the text tells us, "never appears on Paradise."

What strikes me most about this section is the recognition that we've been prepared throughout our entire journey, yet we still need these final touches. The spirit of approaching divinity has been "imparted on the circles of Havona, but the final touches of the training of the pilgrims of time can be applied only after they actually attain the Isle of light." This tells me something profound about both the nature of Paradise and our own nature as ascending mortals.

During one of our study sessions, someone asked whether we're still imperfect when we reach Paradise. That's an excellent question. The answer appears to be yes, in a sense. We're not fully perfect until we unite with God and become finaliters. The Directors of Conduct represent a kind of minor tweaking, not fixing personality flaws, but rather training our personalities to interact appropriately with entirely new categories of beings. We're learning how to communicate properly, how to avoid unintentionally giving offense, how to participate in the life of Paradise with grace and ease.

One student put it beautifully: "It's about learning to be perfect all the time, having all your actions, decisions, everything in your life generated through God, revolving around the will of God." I think that captures it well. But as another participant noted, there's a difference between knowing God's will intellectually and actually knowing it so deeply that it becomes second nature. That's what these billions of years of training accomplish.

The Custodians of Knowledge: Living Libraries of Universal Truth

If the Directors of Conduct help us navigate Paradise society, the Custodians of Knowledge open up something even more extraordinary: access to all the facts and truth that exist in the entire universe of universes.

Let me read you the description from the text, because it's simply stunning: "The superaphic custodians of knowledge are the higher 'living epistles,' known and read by all who dwell on Paradise. They are the divine records of truth, the living books of real knowledge."

Living books. Not libraries with shelves and catalogues, but actual living beings in whom all knowledge resides. The text continues: "The facts of the universe are inherent in these primary supernaphim, actually recorded in these angels, and it is also inherently impossible for an untruth to gain lodgment in the minds of these perfect and replete repositories of the truth of eternity and the intelligence of time."

Think about what this means. These beings contain within themselves the complete, accurate, and perfect record of everything that has ever happened in all universes. Not interpretations, not approximations, but facts. These Custodians of Knowledge are the ultimate reference library, except they're not books on shelves but living, personal beings who can communicate with us.

The practical implications are remarkable. The text tells us: "Any sojourner on Paradise may at will have by his side the living repository of the particular fact or truth he may wish to know." At the northern extremity of Paradise, there are "living finders of knowledge" who direct us to the specific custodian who holds the information we seek. And then "forthwith will appear the brilliant beings who are the very thing you wish to know."

"No longer must you seek enlightenment from engrossed pages," the book says. "You now commune with living intelligence face to face. Supreme knowledge you thus obtain from the living beings who are its final custodians."

Someone in our group likened this to the internet, but with absolute truth. I appreciate the comparison, even though it feels almost crude. Yes, it's similar in the sense of instant access to information, but the difference is profound: no misinformation, no bias, no errors, no need to verify sources. Just pure, perfect truth delivered by beings who cannot contain falsehood.

During our discussion, we explored how these custodians organize knowledge. The text mentions they've "classified knowledge into seven grand orders, each having about one million subdivisions." Seven grand orders, each with a million subdivisions. That gives us some sense of the complexity and comprehensiveness of universal knowledge. Yet these beings have instant access to all of it.

What fascinated our group was learning that these custodians conduct "informal courses of instruction for the residents of the eternal Isle," but their "chief function is that of reference and verification." They're not just teachers, they're the ultimate fact-checkers, the final arbiters of truth. Even the Ancients of Days, who govern the superuniverses, turn to these beings for verification of facts.

Here's something important to understand: this living library is available only to those who make it to Paradise and Havona. The text is clear about this: "This living library, which is available to the central and superuniverses, is not accessible to the local creations. Only by indirection and reflectively are the benefits of Paradise knowledge secured in the local universes."

This means the knowledge we're accumulating now, the understanding we're developing through study of The Urantia Book, is preparatory. The real depth of cosmic knowledge awaits us when we actually make it to Paradise. That should give us both humility and hope, humility because we realize how much we don't yet know, and hope because we see that all truth will eventually be accessible to us.

One student asked whether these beings remember "all the bad things as well as the good things." It's a fair question. My answer is yes; they must. If they contain all facts, they contain the records of evil as well as good, of failure as well as success. However, as another participant wisely noted, beings like Lucifer won't be mentioned in Paradise, they'll have passed away, consigned to oblivion. So, while the Custodians of Knowledge contain the factual record of what happened, the personalities of those who chose final iniquity are simply gone.

The text gives us one more crucial piece of information: "The wisdom of truth takes origin in divinity in the central universe, but knowledge, experiential knowledge, largely has its beginnings in the domains of time and space." This is why the Custodians of Knowledge work in conjunction with vast networks of recording angels throughout the universes, the Celestial Recorders, the seraphim, the seconaphim. All these recording angels throughout space and time feed their observations into this central repository of knowledge.

When I first studied this, I remember feeling almost overwhelmed by the implications. One hour of instruction on Paradise equals ten thousand years of word-memory methods on Urantia. Let that sink in. An hour equals ten thousand years. Our human brains simply cannot process information that efficiently. But when we receive our morontia forms, starting on the first mansion world, we'll have new minds that retain everything we're taught. No more forgetting and having to relearn. No more struggling to remember important concepts.

I've been studying The Urantia Book for over fifty years now, and I still read passages and think, "Oh, I never noticed that before!" That's the limitation of our current minds. We learn, we forget, we learn again. It's a slow, painstaking process. But imagine what learning will be like when we can actually retain and build upon everything we're taught. That's what awaits us.

The Masters of Philosophy: The Wise Men of Heaven

After learning facts from the Custodians of Knowledge, we move to something deeper: learning to think, to philosophize, to grapple with the great mysteries of existence. This is the role of the Masters of Philosophy.

The opening of this section has always struck me: "Next to the supreme satisfaction of worship is the exhilaration of philosophy." I love that word, exhilaration. Philosophy isn't dry or boring; it's exhilarating. And the text continues: "Never do you climb so high or advance so far that there do not remain a thousand mysteries which demand the employment of philosophy in an attempted solution."

Someone in our study group joked, "And you thought you were going to be able to be stupid all these years!" We all laughed, but there's truth in it. We're going to have to think, really think, for all eternity. Not in a burdensome way, but in an exhilarating way.

Here's something I want to emphasize: the foundation of all thinking is logic. When you go to college and start studying philosophy, the very first course they make you take is logic. You have to learn how to think logically before you can philosophize effectively. Logic is the process of thinking, the structure that allows us to reason our way from premises to conclusions. Without logic, philosophy becomes mere speculation or word games.

The Masters of Philosophy are described as "the 'wise men of heaven,' the beings of wisdom who make use of the truth of knowledge and the facts of experience in their efforts to master the unknown." Notice the progression: first we get facts from the Custodians of Knowledge, then we apply reason and experience to those facts under the guidance of the Masters of Philosophy. "With them, knowledge attains to truth and experience ascends to wisdom."

What can we accomplish through this philosophical training? The text tells us: "They have knowledge; they know the truth; they may philosophize, think the truth; they may even seek to encompass the concepts of the Ultimate and attempt to grasp the techniques of the Absolutes."

This is a stepping-stone process. By learning to think philosophically, by learning to reason about ultimate questions, we gradually develop the capacity to understand higher and higher realities. Eventually, we can even begin to grasp concepts related to the Ultimate and the Absolutes, levels of reality far beyond anything we can imagine now.

Someone asked about the "seventy functional divisions of wisdom" mentioned in the text. Honestly, I can't tell you what those seventy divisions are. The revelators don't spell it out. But the fact that wisdom itself can be organized into seventy distinct functional categories, each with who knows how many subdivisions, tells us something about the complexity and richness of philosophical understanding in Paradise.

What I find particularly beautiful is this statement: "They have developed a highly specialized attitude toward various universe problems, but their final conclusions are always in uniform agreement." In other words, the Masters of Philosophy can approach problems from many different angles, using different methodologies and perspectives, but they all arrive at the same truth in the end. This isn't groupthink or conformity, it's the natural result of following sound reasoning to its logical conclusion.

The text emphasizes that these masters "take supreme pleasure in imparting their interpretations of the universe of universes to those beings who have ascended from the worlds of space." They love teaching us. They delight in watching us wrestle with cosmic questions and grow in understanding. And here's something important: "While philosophy can never be as settled in its conclusions as the facts of knowledge and the truths of experience, yet when you have listened to these primary supernaphim discourse upon the unsolved problems of eternity and the performances of the Absolutes, you will feel a certain and lasting satisfaction concerning these unmastered questions."

Did you catch that? Even in Paradise, even with the Masters of Philosophy as our teachers, there will still be unmastered questions. There will always be mysteries beyond our complete comprehension. And I think that's actually wonderful. It means we'll never be bored, never run out of things to explore and understand. There will always be new depths to plumb, new questions to wrestle with, new insights to gain.

One of our group members asked whether this eternal quest for understanding is what ultimately separates us from God. I think there's wisdom in that question. We'll never be God. We'll never have God's infinite, absolute knowledge. There will always be aspects of reality that remain, to some degree, mysterious to us. Even the highest celestial beings often say, "We do not know." That's not a failure or limitation in a negative sense, it's simply the natural state of finite beings contemplating the infinite.

I've noticed something interesting over my years of study: people who claim to know everything are usually the ones who've stopped learning. Real wisdom includes recognizing the vastness of what we don't yet know. As one participant said, "Have you ever noticed that these people who know everything are some of the people who don't even try to learn anything?" That's exactly right. True education begins with intellectual humility.

The Masters of Philosophy teach us not just what to think, but how to think. And that skill, the ability to reason clearly, to evaluate arguments, to follow logic where it leads, is something we'll use for all eternity.

The Conductors of Worship: Achieving Supreme Satisfaction

Now we come to what may be the most important function of all: worship. The text could not be clearer: "Worship is the highest privilege and the first duty of all created intelligences."

Let me read this next part carefully, because it's a beautiful definition: "Worship is the conscious and joyous act of recognizing and acknowledging the truth and fact of the intimate and personal relationships of the Creators with their creatures."

Worship isn't ritual. It isn't reciting prayers or following prescribed forms. It's the conscious and joyous recognition of our relationship with God. And the quality of our worship "is determined by the depth of creature perception." As we grow in our understanding of God's infinite character, our worship becomes "increasingly all-encompassing until it eventually attains the glory of the highest experiential delight and the most exquisite pleasure known to created beings."

Think about that. The highest pleasure, the most exquisite delight we can ever experience, is worship. Not entertainment, not achievement, not even knowledge, worship. That may seem strange to us now, but I think it reveals something profound about the nature of reality and our relationship with the divine.

Here's something important to understand worship is absolutely unique to each individual. No two beings will ever worship in exactly the same way. Why? Because worship emerges from our personal relationship with God, and every personality is unique. My worship experience will be different from yours, which will be different from every other creature in the universe, because each of us has a unique personality and a unique relationship with our Creator.

During our discussion, this led us into a conversation about corporate worship versus individual worship. One person pointed out that what we're describing here sounds like "an individual relationship between man or the worshiper and God," which raises questions about group worship, going to church, for example.

I want to be careful here, because I don't want to diminish the value of gathering with other believers. Let me be clear: church attendance has real benefits. It helps us develop moral character. It provides community and support. It's especially important for children to attend church and Sunday school so they can develop moral foundations. Corporate worship allows us to experience the joy of worshiping alongside other believers, to draw strength from our brothers and sisters in faith.

But, and this is important, corporate worship isn't the same as the deep, personal, individual worship we're talking about here. The most profound worship happens in the intimacy of our individual relationship with God. You can worship more deeply in the silence of your own heart than you can in any church service. That's just the nature of true worship.

As one participant beautifully expressed it, "Worship is related to expressing that love for the Father." When we worship, we're expressing our love, our gratitude, our awe at being in relationship with infinite goodness and love. And that expression is most authentic, most intimate, when it flows directly from our hearts to God without any intermediary.

The text tells us something remarkable about worship in Paradise: "While the Isle of Paradise contains certain places of worship, it is more nearly one vast sanctuary of divine service." The entire place is oriented toward worship. And "worship is the first and dominant passion of all who climb upon its blissful shores."

But here's where it gets really interesting: "During the inward journey through Havona, worship is a growing passion until on Paradise it becomes necessary to direct and otherwise control its expression."

Did you catch that? Our worship becomes so intense, so all-consuming, that it actually has to be controlled. Without guidance, we'd be so overwhelmed by the desire to worship that we couldn't do anything else. That's where the Conductors of Worship come in.

These beings "conduct periodic, spontaneous, group, and other special outbursts of supreme adoration and spiritual praise enjoyed on Paradise." Under their leadership, worship "achieves the creature goal of supreme pleasure and attains the heights of the perfection of sublime self-expression and personal enjoyment."

Someone in our group compared this to Pentecostal worship, where people get so caught up in spiritual ecstasy that they speak in tongues or dance. There may be some parallel there, that sense of being so overwhelmed by spiritual joy that it has to find physical expression. But let me be clear about something: the "speaking in tongues" we read about in Acts wasn't speaking in unknown languages. It was the apostles speaking in the known languages of the people who were present, so that everyone could hear the gospel in their own tongue. That's a very different thing from what some churches practice today.

But I digress. The point is that worship in Paradise is so powerful, so exhilarating, that it requires guidance to channel it appropriately. The Conductors of Worship "teach the ascendant creatures how to worship that they may be enabled to gain this satisfaction of self-expression and at the same time be able to give attention to the essential activities of the Paradise regime."

Without their instruction, it would take hundreds of years for the average ascending mortal to "give full and satisfactory expression to his emotions of intelligent appreciation and ascendant gratitude." The Conductors open up "new and hitherto unknown avenues of expression" so we can achieve worship satisfaction much more quickly.

Here's something wonderful: "All the arts of all the beings of the entire universe which are capable of intensifying and exalting the abilities of self-expression and the conveyance of appreciation are employed to their highest capacity in the worship of the Paradise Deities."

Every art form, every mode of expression, everything that can intensify and beautify our worship is used. And the text gives us this beautiful analogy: "What play does for your jaded minds on earth, worship will do for your perfected souls on Paradise." Worship is refreshing, rejuvenating, delightful.

Now, here's something that moves me deeply: "The mode of worship on Paradise is utterly beyond mortal comprehension, but the spirit of it you can begin to appreciate even down here on Urantia, for the spirits of the Gods even now indwell you, hover over you, and inspire you to true worship."

We can begin to experience it now. Right now, in our current limited state, we can taste what Paradise worship will be like. Our Thought Adjusters, the presence of God within us, can give us glimpses of that supreme satisfaction even while we're still on Earth.

The text goes on to describe how Paradise worship sometimes becomes so intense that "all Paradise becomes engulfed in a dominating tide of spiritual and worshipful expression." The Conductors of Worship can't even control it "until the appearance of the threefold fluctuation of the light of the Deity abode, signifying that the divine heart of the Gods has been fully and completely satisfied by the sincere worship of the residents of Paradise."

God himself signals when he's completely satisfied with our worship. Can you imagine that? The infinite God of all creation, satisfied and delighted by the worship of his finite creatures. "What a triumph of technique," the text says. "What a fruition of the eternal plan and purpose of the Gods that the intelligent love of the creature child should give full satisfaction to the infinite love of the Creator Father."

Here's why Paradise citizens treasure the worship of ascending mortals so much: they've never experienced what we've experienced. They've never clawed their way up from spiritual darkness. They've never struggled, never doubted, never overcome tremendous obstacles to reach Paradise. When we finally arrive and express our accumulated gratitude, our overwhelming joy, it's "a spectacle astounding to the angels of Paradise and productive of the supreme joy of divine satisfaction in the Paradise Deities."

Our worship is precious precisely because of where we've come from and what we've overcome.

The Seven Jubilees: Milestones on the Journey Home

Before we close this chapter, I want to touch briefly on the seven jubilees mentioned at the end of this section. These are the great celebration points, the major milestones of our ascending career.

The first jubilee marks "the mortal agreement with the Thought Adjuster when the purpose to survive was sealed." That's when we make our first real moral decision, when we choose survival and begin our journey toward God.

The second is "the awakening in the morontia life", when we wake up on the first mansion world and discover that death was not the end but the beginning.

The third jubilee celebrates "the fusion with the Thought Adjuster", that momentous event when we become eternally one with the indwelling fragment of God.

The fourth is "the awakening in Havona", when we first arrive in the central universe and begin our approach to Paradise itself.

The fifth celebrates "the finding of the Universal Father", when we actually achieve the presence of God the Father, the goal toward which everything has been moving.

The sixth jubilee is "the occasion of the Paradise awakening from the final transit slumber of time", when we arrive on Paradise and awaken to eternal existence.

And the seventh, the one we've been building toward through this entire chapter, "marks entrance into the mortal finaliter corps and the beginning of the eternity service." We take the Trinity oath of eternity and are mustered into the Corps of the Finality.

But notice this: "The attainment of the seventh stage of spirit realization by a finaliter will probably signalize the celebration of the first of the jubilees of eternity." Even after all this, we're just beginning. There are jubilees of eternity ahead of us, challenges we can barely imagine.

The text ends with these words: "The endless service of the Paradise Trinity is about to begin; and now the finaliter is face to face with the challenge of God the Ultimate."

We've reached Paradise, achieved fusion, found the Father, become finaliters, and now we face a new challenge: God the Ultimate. The adventure never ends. There's always something more, always new heights to reach, always new realities to explore.

Conclusion: Prepared for Paradise

As we close this chapter, I'm struck by a powerful realization: even Paradise requires preparation. Even after billions of years of ascending through universe after universe, even after fusion with our Thought Adjusters, even after traversing the circuits of Havona, we still need guidance when we reach Paradise.

The Directors of Conduct teach us proper relationships and behavior. The Custodians of Knowledge give us access to all truth. The Masters of Philosophy train our minds to wrestle with ultimate questions. The Conductors of Worship guide us to supreme satisfaction in our relationship with God.

None of this diminishes us. Instead, it reveals the infinite depth and richness of Paradise reality. It shows us that growth never ends, that learning continues forever, that there are always new heights to reach and new beauties to discover.

And here's what gives me hope: we can begin now. We can start learning to think logically and philosophically. We can begin accessing truth through study and experience. We can practice right relationships with others. And most importantly, we can begin to truly worship, not through ritual or routine, but through that conscious and joyous recognition of our intimate relationship with our Creator.

The Urantia Book tells us that "the spirits of the Gods even now indwell you, hover over you, and inspire you to true worship." We don't have to wait until Paradise to experience the satisfaction of worship. We can taste it now. We can begin training ourselves in the very practices that will occupy us for all eternity.

In our next chapter, we'll shift our focus from the ministering spirits of Paradise to those closer to home: the ministering spirits of the superuniverses. These are the angels who attend to us now, in our current state, as we begin our long journey toward Paradise. These seraphim and their companions are with us every day, guiding us, protecting us, and preparing us for the incredible journey ahead.

Until then, I encourage you to spend time in genuine worship. Not going through the motions but really opening your heart to the presence of God within you. Try to experience that conscious, joyous recognition of your relationship with the Father. Even if it's just for a few moments, you'll be practicing what will become the highest joy of your eternal existence.

May we all, by God's grace, eventually stand on the shores of Paradise, ready to be guided by these magnificent beings into the fullness of eternal life. And may we begin that journey right now, right where we are, with willing hearts and open minds.

Thank you for studying with me. I'll see you in the next chapter.

Chapter 32: Ministering Spirits of the Super Universes

Introduction to the Celestial Hierarchy

Tonight, I want to take you on a journey into one of the most fascinating aspects of cosmic organization, the ministering spirits of the super universes. As we begin our study of Paper 28 from The Urantia Book, we're moving beyond the familiar territory of our local universe and even beyond the central universe of Havona. We're stepping into the vast administrative machinery of the seven super universes, where angelic beings of extraordinary capability serve in ways that directly impact our eternal journey toward Paradise.

Before we dive into the details, I need to address something that often confuses students when they first encounter this material. The revelation tells us plainly that these beings we're about to study "serve not alone in the super creations, and both numerous and intriguing are the transactions sponsored by their unrevealed associates." What does this mean? Simply put, there exist countless other angelic beings that the revelators haven't even told us about. The ones they do describe are primarily those we'll actually interact with during our ascension journey. This selectivity makes sense, we're being taught what we need to know for our spiritual progression, not given an exhaustive catalog of every celestial being in existence.

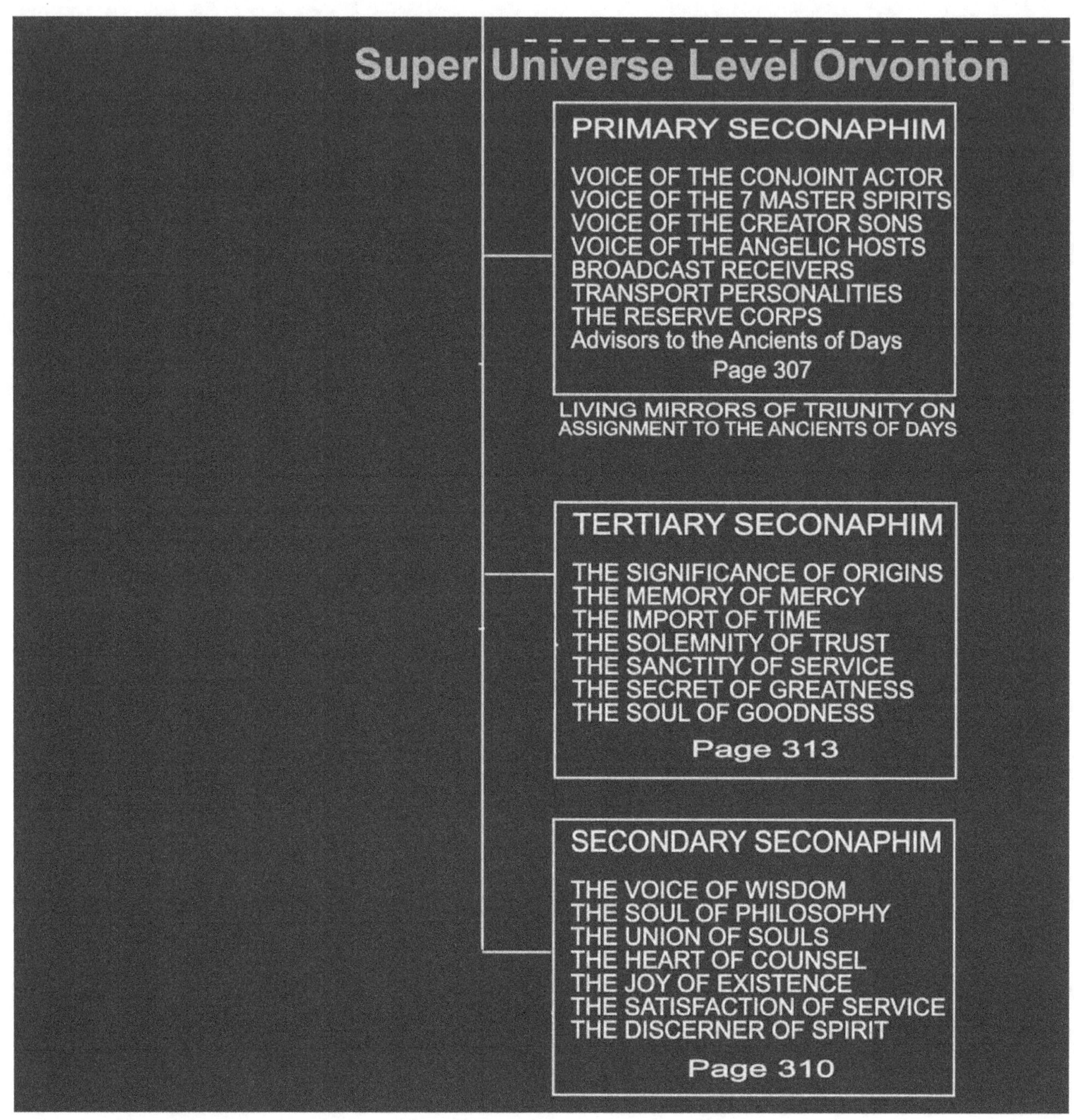

Figure 8: Superuniverse Level Orvonton

Understanding the Three Orders of Angels

Let me make this as simple as possible, because the terminology can trip you up if you're not careful. Think of the angelic hierarchy in terms of location and function. At the highest level, serving in the central universe of Havona, we find the supernaphim, super angels for the super-perfect central creation. Moving outward to the seven super universes, we encounter the seconaphim, literally, the "second" order of angels. Finally, in our local universe of Nebadon and the 699,999 other local universes, we have the seraphim, along with their associated orders of cherubim and sanobim.

This pattern isn't arbitrary. It reflects the descending levels of perfection as we move outward from Paradise. The supernaphim serve in the realm of existing perfection. The seconaphim operate in the evolving super universes where perfection is being achieved. The seraphim work in the local universes where perfection is just beginning to emerge from imperfection.

As we progress through our ascension journey, we'll interact with each of these orders in turn. Right now, on Urantia, we're under the watchful care of seraphim. When we reach the mansion worlds, we'll continue working primarily with seraphim, cherubim, and sanobim. But as we advance to the super universe level, we'll begin our association with the seconaphim. Eventually, when we reach Havona, we'll work with the supernaphim themselves.

I want to emphasize something important here: Paper 38 of The Urantia Book deals specifically with the seraphim and other angels of the local universe. Tonight, we're focused exclusively on Paper 28 and the ministering spirits of the super universes. These are distinct groups with different functions, and we need to keep them separate in our minds.

The Tertiaphim: Paradise Angels on Loan

The revelation introduces us to three main orders of angels serving in the super universes: the seconaphim, the tertiaphim, and the omniaphim. Interestingly, only the seconaphim are truly native to the super universe administration. The other two orders, while serving in the super universes, are actually on loan from other realms.

Let's begin with the tertiaphim. These fascinating beings hold a special place in the cosmic hierarchy because, technically speaking, they're Paradise angels. They're created directly by the Infinite Spirit on Paradise in groups of one thousand, which makes them supernal beings of divine originality. Yet they don't remain on Paradise. Instead, they're given as a gift to the Creator Sons, the Michaels who go forth to organize and administer the local universes.

Here's how it works. When a Michael Son is ready to detach from Paradise and begin his universe adventure, the Infinite Spirit delivers to him a company of one thousand tertiaphim. These companion spirits accompany the Creator Son as his personal staff during the early, formative ages of universe building. Imagine the task before a Creator Son, organizing an entire local universe from cosmic raw materials, creating architectural spheres, preparing for the eventual emergence of inhabited worlds. During this immense undertaking, the tertiaphim serve as his assistants, acquiring tremendous experience in universe assembly and astronomical manipulation.

But their service isn't permanent. They remain with the Creator Son until a pivotal moment arrives, the personalization of the Bright and Morning Star, the firstborn of the local universe. In Nebadon, this firstborn is Gabriel, whom many of you recognize from biblical accounts. When Gabriel appears, something remarkable happens. He becomes, along with Michael and the Creative Mother Spirit, part of a trinity that will bring forth all the native angelic life of the local universe. At this point, the tertiaphim tender their formal resignations. They're released from active service in the local universe and assume a new role as liaison ministers between the Creator Son and the Ancients of Days of the super universe.

One of my students, Gary, raised an excellent question during our study that I think clarifies an important point. He asked whether Michael owns his universe from the beginning. The answer reveals something profound about divine administration. When a Creator Son goes forth to create a local universe, he's given permission to proceed, but he doesn't become sovereign immediately. Technically, God the Father remains the head of that new local universe until the Michael Son proves his sovereignty by completing his seven bestowals. We might say Michael is the vicegerent of the Father, acting with authority but not yet possessing full sovereignty.

This arrangement isn't arbitrary. It serves a purpose. Michael must "pay his dues," just as we must pay ours in our ascension journey. And let me be clear, this process takes time. In Michael's case, it took over a million years just to complete his seven bestowals. But even before beginning those bestowals, he spent approximately four billion years preparing for his mission, studying other Creator Sons who had already accomplished what he was about to attempt. Creating a local universe isn't something you rush into. The planets themselves take millions of years to develop, to be populated, and to produce sentient life. It's a slow, deliberate process.

Jane brought up another interesting point, the Creative Mother Spirit and Michael begin their existence at roughly the same time, but a long period passes before they come together to start the local creation. They train separately, each developing the capabilities they'll need for their cosmic partnership.

The Omniaphim: Administrative Angels

If the tertiaphim serve as liaisons between local and super universe administration, the omniaphim operate at an even higher level. These beings are created by the Infinite Spirit working in conjunction with the Seven Supreme Executives, the highest administrative authorities in the grand universe below the level of the Paradise Trinity itself.

The omniaphim are the exclusive servants and messengers of these Supreme Executives. They're assigned to grand universe duties, and in our super universe of Orvonton, they maintain headquarters in the northern regions of Uversa as what the revelation calls "a special courtesy colony." Notice that phrase carefully, they're guests, not residents. They're not on the registry of Uversa, nor are they attached to our super universe administration. Most significantly for our purposes, they're not directly concerned with the ascendant scheme of mortal progression.

This last point explains why the revelators give us so little information about them. They tell us where the omniaphim come from, where they live, and whom they serve, but that's about it. These angels are wholly occupied with oversight of the super universes from the viewpoint of the Seven Supreme Executives. Our colony on Uversa receives instructions from and reports to only the Supreme Executive of Orvonton, who is stationed on conjoint executive sphere number seven in the outer ring of Paradise satellites.

In essence, the omniaphim function as administrative coordinators, ensuring that the will of the Supreme Executives is carried out across the vast reaches of the super universes. They're important, but they operate at levels of administration we won't encounter until much later in our careers, if at all.

The Seconaphim: Our Primary Focus

Now we come to the heart of Paper 28, the seconaphim. Unlike the tertiaphim and omniaphim, these beings are native to the super universes and directly involved in our ascension scheme. They deserve our careful attention because we will work with them extensively as we progress through the super universe circuits.

The seconaphim are produced by the seven Reflective Spirits assigned to the headquarters of each super universe. Here's where the terminology starts to get tricky, and I need you to pay close attention. When the revelators describe the seconaphim, they divide them into three groups: primary, secondary, and tertiary seconaphim. These designations have nothing to do with the tertiaphim we discussed earlier. They're not the same beings at all. Rather, they represent subgroups within the order of seconaphim itself.

Let me explain how this works. There's a definite Paradise-responsive technique associated with the creation of seconaphim. They're always brought into being in groups of seven, and each group always contains exactly one primary, three secondary, and three tertiary seconaphim. This proportion never varies.

When seven seconaphim are created, each group member receives a specific assignment. The primary seconaphim becomes attached to the service of the Ancients of Days, the triune rulers of the super universe. The three secondary angels are associated with three groups of Paradise-origin administrators: the Divine Counselors, the Perfectors of Wisdom, and the Universal Censors. These three orders constitute what we might call the super universe court system. They're all Trinity-created beings of extraordinary wisdom and experience.

The three tertiary seconaphim receive perhaps the most interesting assignment of all. They're attached to the ascendant trinitized associates of the super universe rulers, beings known as Mighty Messengers, Those High in Authority, and Those without Name and Number. Here's what makes this significant: all three of these orders originated as ascending mortals like ourselves. They climbed the ladder from worlds of time and space, reached Paradise, achieved finality, and were subsequently embraced by the Trinity. Their trinitization qualified them for high administrative positions in the super universe government.

Think about what this means. When you and I advance far enough in our eternal careers, when we've been trinitized and assigned to one of these exalted positions, we'll be given our own seconaphim assistants. These angels will work with us, support us, and help us fulfill our responsibilities in super universe administration.

I need to clarify something that confused one of our study group members. Gary suggested that perhaps these seconaphim were people who had ascended and been assigned to serve as Mighty Messengers or Those High in Authority. That's not quite right. The seconaphim are angels, they're created as angels. They're assigned as assistants to mortals who have ascended and been trinitized. We're talking about created celestial beings serving ascended mortals, not mortals being transformed into angels.

When ascending mortals are trinitized and take up positions as Mighty Messengers, Those High in Authority, or Those without Name and Number, something bittersweet happens. Their names are removed from the roll call of the Corps of the Finality. Why? Because they've been assigned permanent positions in super universe service. They're no longer simply finaliters awaiting their next assignment. They've accepted specific, ongoing responsibilities that will occupy them for ages to come.

If they hadn't been selected for these positions, they would have remained in the Corps of the Finality, probably eventually joining the Corps of Trinitized Finaliters rather than the Corps of Mortal Finaliters. The distinction matters because trinitization changes your nature and your destiny.

The Power of Reflectivity

Since the seconaphim are offspring of the Reflective Spirits, they inherit a remarkable ability, reflectivity. This concept appears throughout The Urantia Book, but many students struggle to grasp what it actually means. Let me try to make it clear.

Reflectivity is inherent in the nature of seconaphim. They're reflectively responsive to every phase of every creature originating in the Third Source and Center (the Infinite Spirit) and the Paradise Creator Sons. However, they're not directly reflective of beings and entities that originate solely in the First Source and Center (the Universal Father). This limitation appears to be by design rather than deficiency.

The revelation tells us something profound: even if we had no other proof, the reflective performances of the seconaphim would be sufficient to demonstrate the reality of the universal presence of the infinite mind of the Conjoint Actor, the Infinite Spirit. In other words, the very existence and function of these angels proves that there's a universal intelligence circuit connecting all things throughout creation.

This brings us to a concept that really opened our eyes during the study group, the universal intelligence circuits. When the revelation mentions "the actuality of the universal intelligence circuits of the Infinite Spirit," it's referring to something specific. In the local universe, there are three primary spiritual circuits. First, there's the Spirit of Truth circuit of Michael, the Creator Son. Second, there's the circuit of the Holy Spirit, emanating from the Creative Mother Spirit. Third, there's the universe intelligence circuit, which connects with the adjutant mind-spirits.

Now here's where it gets interesting. Because we all possess the seven-adjutant mind-spirits functioning in our minds, we're already plugged into the mind circuit of the Infinite Spirit. Every act we perform, every experience we have, no matter how small or seemingly insignificant, is reflected back through this intelligent ministry circuit to the local universe Mother Spirit and ultimately to the Infinite Spirit. But it doesn't stop there. This information also flows through the seventh Master Spirit, who is the vice-gerent of the Supreme Being. All of our experiences, all of our choices, all of our growth, everything contributes to the evolution of the Supreme.

During our study session, Diane had what I call a "light bulb moment." She suddenly realized: "We're all plugged in together to the same mind circuit!" That's exactly right. This is what we mean when we talk about cosmic mind, about the unity of all reality, about the interconnectedness of all beings. We're not isolated individuals floating alone in an indifferent universe. We're nodes in a vast network of consciousness that spans from the humblest mortal world to the heights of Paradise itself.

Let me give you a contemporary example that validates what the revelation teaches. Some of you may be familiar with Dr. Steven Greer's work with consciousness and what many call UFO phenomena. Dr. Greer has demonstrated, and I've studied his methods extensively, that it's possible to contact and communicate with other intelligences through mind transmission. How is this possible? Because they're plugged into the same mind circuit we are. Anything that goes through the mind goes through this intelligent ministry circuit.

This principle extends to many phenomena that we've observed throughout history, telepathy, remote viewing, certain forms of meditation, even some aspects of what we call prayer. All of these operate through the mind circuits that the Infinite Spirit maintains throughout creation. When I studied hypnosis, advanced hypnosis, wakened suggestion, and mind travel back in 1973, I was working with these same principles, though I didn't fully understand the cosmic framework at the time. Everything I've learned in life, from seemingly disparate fields, keeps coming back to this same fundamental truth: it's all about spiritual reality manifesting through universal mind circuits.

Primary Seconaphim and the Ancients of Days

Let's turn our attention now to the primary seconaphim and their service to the Ancients of Days. These angels are, quite literally, living mirrors. Think about what that means in practical terms. The Ancients of Days rule each super universe from their headquarters world. In our case, that world is Uversa, capital of Orvonton. From this central location, they need to maintain awareness of everything happening throughout a super universe containing one trillion inhabited worlds, spread across 100,000 local universes.

How do they do it? Through the primary seconaphim. These angels can turn, as it were, to function as living mirrors, and therein the Ancients of Days can see and hear the certain responses of another being a thousand or even a hundred thousand light-years distant. And they can do this instantly without error.

Let me put this in terms you can relate to. If you've ever watched Star Trek, you've seen Captain Kirk standing on the bridge, looking at the viewscreen, seeing and talking to someone on another ship or planet in real time. That's essentially what we're talking about, reflectivity on cosmic steroids. Or think of it as Zoom technology, but with all the senses included. The primary seconaphim can reflect not just the picture and voice, but the meaning, the values, the feelings, the complete presence of whoever the Ancients of Days need to contact. It's as if the person were standing right there in the room.

Gary raised an excellent point during our discussion. He said, "This helps me understand how it works." And he's right, when we understand the mechanism, the concept becomes much clearer. Reflectivity isn't magic; it's a precise technique utilizing the mind circuits that permeate all reality.

The primary seconaphim who serve the Ancients of Days are naturally inclined toward seven types of service. Let's examine each one, because they reveal how super universe administration actually functions.

The Voice of the Conjoint Actor

The first primary seconaphim, and every seventh one subsequently created, exhibits a high order of adaptability for understanding and interpreting the mind of the Infinite Spirit to the Ancients of Days. This ability proves invaluable on the headquarters of the super universes because, unlike local creations, the seat of super universe government doesn't have a specialized personalization of the Infinite Spirit. In our local universe, we have the Creative Mother Spirit, a direct and personal presence of the Infinite Spirit. But on Uversa, there's no such personalized presence.

The seven Reflective Spirits are there, of course, but even they don't function quite the same way. They're more automatically reflective of the Seven Master Spirits than of the Conjoint Actor directly. So, these secoraphic Voices come the nearest to being personal representatives of the Third Source and Center on Uversa. When the Ancients of Days need to understand what the Infinite Spirit thinks about a particular matter, they consult with the Voice of the Conjoint Actor.

The Voice of the Seven Master Spirits

The second primary seconaphim, and every seventh thereafter, incline toward portraying the collective natures and reactions of the Seven Master Spirits. Now you might wonder: aren't the Seven Master Spirits already represented on each super universe capital by the Reflective Spirits? Yes, they are. But here's the key difference: that representation is individual, not collective. Each Reflective Spirit represents one Master Spirit. To understand the collective mind and unified perspective of all Seven Master Spirits requires something more.

That's where these seconaphim come in. They're competent to represent the Master Spirits collectively before the Ancients of Days. When a matter requires understanding the coordinated viewpoint of all seven Master Spirits, which represent the sevenfold nature of Deity itself, these angels provide that comprehensive perspective.

The Voice of the Creator Sons

The third primary seconaphim, and every seventh serial thereafter, possesses what the revelation calls "the remarkable gift of being reflective of the minds of these Creator Sons." There are 700,000 local universes in the grand universe, each presided over by a Creator Son of the order of Michael. Actually, there are probably a million Michaels in total, with 300,000 held in reserve for future development, but let's focus on the active ones.

Each Creator Son has his own dedicated Voice among the seconaphim. When the Ancients of Days want to know Michael of Nebadon's attitude regarding some matter under consideration, they don't have to call him across the vast distances of space. They simply call for the Chief of Nebadon Voices, who presents the Michael seconaphim of record. Right then and there, the Ancients of Days perceive the voice of the Master Son of Nebadon.

I liken this to the red phone that sits in the White House, a direct line to the most important leadership. The Ancients of Days can, in effect, pick up the phone and instantly be in communion with any Creator Son in their super universe. During our study session, someone asked whether there's really a Voice for each of the 700,000 Michaels. The answer is yes. Every single Creator Son has his own dedicated secoraphic Voice.

The revelation admits something fascinating here: "We do not fully understand just how this is accomplished, and I doubt very much that the Creator Sons themselves fully understand it." Even the celestial beings who use this technique don't completely comprehend its mechanics. But they know with certainty that it works, and that it works unfailingly. In all the history of Uversa, these secoraphic Voices have never erred in their presentations.

Expanding Our Cosmic Perspective

The revelation makes an important observation at this point: "You are here beginning to see something of the manner in which divinity encompasses the space of time and masters the time of space." We're getting a fleeting glimpse of the technique of the eternity cycle, how eternal beings manage temporal realities, how beings who exist outside of time can effectively operate within it to assist those of us who are bound by time and space.

This isn't just theoretical knowledge. It's a preview of what awaits us. When we leave this planet and begin our ascension journey, these techniques will become part of our working reality. Our horizons will expand beyond anything we can currently comprehend. The limitations that feel so absolute to us now, the constraints of distance, the barriers of time, the isolation of individual consciousness, all of these will gradually dissolve as we learn to operate through the universal circuits that connect all reality.

Though the Ancients of Days are apparently deprived of the personal presence of the Master Spirits above them and the Creator Sons below them, they're anything but isolated. They have at their command living beings attuned to cosmic mechanisms of reflective perfection and ultimate precision. Through these means, and others unknown to us, God is potentially present on the headquarters of the super universes.

The Trinity of Administration

Here's something that astonished me when I first grasped its implications. The Ancients of Days can perfectly deduce the Father's will by equating the Spirit voice flash from above and the Michael voice flashes from below. By triangulating these two perspectives, the voice of the Infinite Spirit descending from Paradise and the voice of the Creator Sons ascending from the local universes, they can calculate with absolute certainty what the Universal Father wills concerning administrative affairs.

But here's the catch: it requires all three Ancients of Days working together. Two wouldn't be able to achieve the answer. To deduce the will of one of the Gods from knowledge of the other two requires a threefold perspective. This explains why the super universes are always presided over by three Ancients of Days, never by one or even two.

This arrangement has practical implications. The Ancients of Days can never leave Uversa, not even for a moment. All three must be present at all times for the system to function. Gary quipped that this sounds like "maintenance updates," and there's truth to that analogy. The system requires all components to be online simultaneously.

The Scope and Limits of Reflectivity

During our study, Jane read a passage that clarified something important about the scope of reflectivity. This ability to hear and see all things is perfectly realized in the super universes only by the Ancients of Days, and only on their respective headquarters worlds. Even there, limits exist. From Uversa, such communication is limited to the worlds and universes of Orvonton. While the reflective technique doesn't operate between the super universes, it does keep each super universe in close touch with the central universe and with Paradise.

Why this limitation? Why can't the Ancients of Days of Orvonton directly communicate with their counterparts in the other six super universes? The answer lies in the unique nature of each super universe and the importance of maintaining certain boundaries.

Each super universe is developing its own unique expression of divinity. The Seven Master Spirits each impart their individual character to their respective super universes, making each one distinct from the others. Orvonton, under the influence of the seventh Master Spirit, is developing differently from, say, the first or third super universe. This differentiation is intentional and important.

If a rebellion breaks out in one super universe, and we know from bitter experience that such things can happen, the authorities want to prevent it from spreading to other super universes. Look at what happened on our own world. When Lucifer rebelled, dragging 37 inhabited worlds into rebellion with him, we were immediately quarantined. The System of Satania was isolated to prevent the rebellion from contaminating other systems. The same principle applies at the super universe level.

Diane asked a perceptive question: "Is that like saying what happens here stays here?" In a sense, yes. What happens in Orvonton stays in Orvonton, at least in terms of direct communication and influence. If you're on a planet that has reached light and life, you don't want to be bombarded with the confusion and chaos emanating from a barbaric world like ours. The segregation protects the more advanced civilizations from contamination while allowing the struggling worlds to work through their problems without infecting others.

This doesn't mean the super universes are completely isolated from each other. Everything passes through the Seven Master Spirits, who function as a kind of clearinghouse. If the Ancients of Days need to coordinate with their counterparts in another super universe regarding matters affecting the organization of Paradise or the administration of all seven super universes, they can do so through the Master Spirits.

Another implication of this arrangement became clear during our discussion. We won't interact with beings from the other six super universes until we reach Havona. By that time, we'll be far more mature, far wiser, and far less prejudiced than we are now. We'll be ready for that kind of cosmic interaction. Jane pointed out that the only common element uniting all seven super universes is the Supreme Being, and she's absolutely right. Our experiences in Orvonton are contributing to one aspect of the Supreme's evolution, while simultaneously, beings in the other six super universes are contributing their unique experiences. When the Supreme finally achieves completed evolution, it will be through the unified contribution of all seven super universes.

Conclusion: A Glimpse of What Awaits

As we conclude this chapter, I hope you've gained a clearer understanding of the angelic ministry operating at the super universe level. We've explored the tertiaphim, those Paradise angels on loan to Creator Sons during the formative ages of local universe organization. We've touched briefly on the omniaphim, those administrative coordinators serving the Supreme Executives. Most importantly, we've begun our study of the seconaphim, the true ministering spirits of the super universes.

We've examined how the primary seconaphim serve as living mirrors for the Ancients of Days, functioning as the Voice of the Conjoint Actor, the Voice of the Seven Master Spirits, and the Voice of the Creator Sons. We've discovered how reflectivity works, that remarkable technique allowing instantaneous communication across vast distances of space, transcending the normal limitations of time and matter.

Perhaps most significantly, we've come to understand that we're already connected to these cosmic circuits through the adjutant mind-spirits functioning in our own consciousness. We're not separate from this grand system; we're active participants in it, even now, on this troubled world at the edge of the local universe.

In our next session, we'll continue exploring the primary seconaphim, examining the remaining types of service they render to the Ancients of Days. We'll discover the Voice of the Angelic Hosts, the Broadcast Receivers, the Transport Personalities, and the Reserve Corps. Beyond that, we'll move on to the secondary and tertiary seconaphim, learning about the angels who will work most directly with us as we progress through our super universe career.

The revelation reminds us that we're obtaining our first fleeting glimpses of the technique of the eternity cycle, how eternal beings assist children of time in mastering the difficult handicaps of space. What we're learning here isn't just abstract theology. It's a preview of our own future, a roadmap of the journey that lies ahead. The more clearly we understand the cosmic organization we'll encounter, the better prepared we'll be to take our place within it.

As we close, I'm reminded of something the revelation emphasizes: though apparently deprived of certain personal presences, the Ancients of Days, and by extension, all of us, have access to God through these cosmic circuits. By and through these means, and others unknown to us, God is potentially present everywhere, including on the headquarters of the super universes and in our own minds.

Chapter 33: The Seconaphim - Reflective Angels of the Superuniverses

Introduction

When I first encountered the concept of reflectivity in The Urantia Book, I'll admit I struggled to wrap my mind around it. How could information travel instantaneously across vast cosmic distances without any form of communication we might recognize? Yet as I've studied Paper 28 more deeply over the years, I've come to appreciate that reflectivity represents something far more sophisticated than anything we've yet imagined, a living network of angelic intelligence that keeps the entire superuniverse administration functioning with perfect coordination.

Tonight, as we continue our journey through Paper 28, we arrive at Section 4, which introduces us to the seconaphim, a remarkable order of angels created specifically for reflective service. These beings serve as the nervous system of the superuniverse, if you will, though that analogy barely scratches the surface of what they accomplish. Unlike the supernaphim we studied earlier, who serve in Paradise and Havona, the seconaphim work exclusively in the seven superuniverses, performing functions that range from the transportation of ascending mortals to the most subtle discernment of spiritual character.

What makes this study particularly fascinating is how it reveals the sophistication of celestial administration. We often think of angels in rather simplistic terms, messengers, guardians, perhaps warriors in spiritual battles. But the seconaphim demonstrate something far more complex: an integrated system of living intelligence that operates on principles we're only beginning to understand. They don't just carry messages; they reflect reality itself, making the thoughts, attitudes, and even the unconscious patterns of countless beings instantly available to those who need such information for wise governance.

As we examine the various orders of seconaphim, I want you to consider what this tells us about the nature of universe administration. Nothing is left to chance. Every function has its specialized ministers. Every need has been anticipated and provided for. And perhaps most remarkable of all, this entire system operates with a grace and efficiency that makes cosmic insanity, rebellion against such perfect order, seem utterly inexplicable.

The Primary Seconaphim: Foundation of Reflective Service

The primary seconaphim hold a unique place in the celestial hierarchy. These angels are created directly by the Reflective Spirits and serve as the primary channels through which the Ancients of Days receive instantaneous information about everything occurring throughout their superuniverse. Think of them as living satellites, if you will, though that comparison doesn't do justice to their consciousness and purpose.

What strikes me most about the primary seconaphim is the unconscious nature of much of their service. The text tells us clearly that these angels themselves often don't even know that their thoughts and attitudes are being transmitted through reflectivity to the Ancients of Days. Unless a Solitary Messenger specifically informs them, they remain "wholly ignorant of what is sought and of how it is secured." It's almost like, and I mean this respectfully, osmosis. Remember that old joke about putting a textbook under your pillow hoping to absorb the information while you sleep? Well, these angels actually do transmit information continuously without conscious effort.

The Voices of the Angelic Host

The fourth primary seconaphim in the serial creation order are designated as the Voices of the Angelic Host. These beings possess a peculiar responsiveness to the sentiments of all orders of angels, from the supernaphim above to the seraphim below. When I read that "the attitude of any commanding or supervising angel is immediately available for consideration at any council of the Ancients of Days," I'm reminded of how primitive our own communication systems really are.

Consider this: never a day passes on our world, Urantia, that the chief of seraphim isn't made conscious of a reflective transference being drawn upon from Uversa for some purpose. Yet she remains unaware of what specific information is being sought or how it's secured unless forewarned. These ministering spirits of time constantly furnish unconscious and therefore unprejudiced testimony concerning endless matters that engage the attention of the Ancients of Days.

One detail that caught my attention, and sparked some lively discussion in our study group, is the pronoun used in the text. It says, "she remains wholly ignorant." All angels, it appears, are female. Now, I'm not going to speculate too much on what that means theologically, but it certainly adds another dimension to our understanding of angelic nature.

Broadcast Receivers

The fifth serial creation of primary seconaphim produces the Broadcast Receivers, a specialized class that receives messages intended specifically for primary seconaphim. While they're not the regular broadcasters of Uversa, they work in liaison with the angels of the reflective voices to synchronize the reflective vision of the Ancients of Days with actual messages coming through established circuits of universe communication.

Think of it this way: if you had a television that could receive one special channel that nobody else could access, a channel broadcasting information specifically for your benefit and your group's work, that's something like what these Broadcast Receivers do. They tune into frequencies, so to speak, that are keyed exclusively for the primary seconaphim.

One question that often comes up is whether these broadcasts reach all seven superuniverses. The answer is no, each superuniverse has its own separate groups of these angels, and they don't broadcast outside their own superuniverse. However, within a superuniverse, the information reaches its intended recipients regardless of any local quarantine conditions. This is important for us on Urantia to understand: while our planet is quarantined from certain universal broadcasts due to the Lucifer rebellion, these angelic broadcasts operate on different circuits that weren't severed during the rebellion.

Our world belongs to the seventh superuniverse, Orvonton. When, and I say when, not if, Jesus returns to Earth, the New Testament tells us that "every eye shall see and every ear shall hear." How else could that happen except through some form of broadcast that appears before everyone simultaneously? Perhaps something like a holographic image visible to all? The technology exists in the celestial realms, even if we can't quite fathom it yet.

Transport Personalities

The sixth serial creation produces the Transport Personalities, seconaphim who carry pilgrims of time from the headquarters worlds of the superuniverses to the outer circle of Havona. These beings form the transport corps of the superuniverses, operating both inward to Paradise and outward to the worlds of their respective sectors.

Now, I want to be clear about something that can cause confusion: these are not seraphim. The seraphim are the angels who transport us, our souls, from our death on this planet to the mansion worlds. That's a different class of angel entirely. The primary seconaphim who serve as Transport Personalities are a higher order, and they handle the much longer journey from Uversa to Havona, and eventually from Havona to Paradise itself.

It's almost like different classes of transportation. Seraphim provide local transport, if you will, while these higher beings handle the cosmic equivalent of interstellar travel. You're going to go whether you like it or not, so you might as well hold on, it's going to be a bumpy ride. Though I imagine by the time we're making those journeys, we'll have grown enough spiritually that we'll actually enjoy the experience.

The Reserve Corps

Every seventh primary seconaphim becomes part of the Reserve Corps, a large group held in reserve for unclassified duties and emergency assignments throughout the realms. Not being highly specialized, they can function fairly well in any capacity that their diverse associates might perform, though such specialized work is undertaken only in emergencies.

Their usual tasks involve performing those generalized duties of a superuniverse that don't fall within the scope of angels with specific assignments. Think of them as the flexible workforce, the ones who can step in when there's a shortage of specialized angels or when unexpected situations arise. In any complex organization, and the superuniverse is certainly that, you need people, or in this case angels, who can adapt and fill multiple roles as needed.

The Secondary Seconaphim: Specialized Reflective Service

As we transition to the secondary seconaphim, I want to address a potential misunderstanding right away. Being classified as primary, secondary, or tertiary does not indicate any differential in status or function among the seconaphim. It merely denotes orders of procedure. All three groups exhibit identical qualities in their activities. This is just a way of organizing them, of understanding their roles within the larger celestial administration.

The seven reflective types of secondary seconaphim are assigned to the coordinate Trinity-origin associates of the Ancients of Days. To the Perfectors of Wisdom go the Voices of Wisdom, the Souls of Philosophy, and the Union of Souls. To the Divine Counselors go the Hearts of Counsel. To the Universal Censors go the Joys of Existence, the Satisfaction of Service, and the Discerners of Spirits.

Like the primary order, this group is created serially, the firstborn is a Voice of Wisdom, the seventh thereafter is similar, and so on with the six other types. This serial creation maintains the balance and distribution of these specialized servants throughout the superuniverse.

The Voices of Wisdom

Here we encounter something truly remarkable. Certain of the seconaphim maintain perpetual liaison with the living libraries of Paradise, those custodians of knowledge who belong to the primary supernaphim. Remember when we studied the angels of Paradise? This is what that was pointing toward.

The Voices of Wisdom are living, current, completely reliable concentrations and focalizations of the coordinated wisdom of the universe of universes. To the nearly infinite volume of information circulating on the master circuits of the superuniverses, these superb beings are so reflective and selective, so sensitive, that they can segregate and receive the essence of wisdom and unerringly transmit these jewels of meditation to their superiors, the Perfectors of Wisdom.

But here's what makes this truly extraordinary: they function in such a way that the Perfectors of Wisdom not only hear the actual and original expressions of this wisdom but also reflectively see the very beings, whether of high or lowly origin, who gave voice to it. Imagine standing in front of a mirror, but instead of seeing your own reflection, you perceive a reflection of the wisdom of divinity and the philosophy of Paradise. That's something like what the Perfectors of Wisdom experience through these angels.

When we get knowledge or wisdom, real wisdom, not just information, it comes directly from Paradise. That's why this service is so crucial. If you have access to this knowledge, then it gets reflected back to the Perfectors of Wisdom, who in turn teach us this information as we progress through the mansion worlds and beyond. It's like hearing it from the actual source, or as close to the source as we can get.

The text includes a quote that I find particularly moving: "It is written: If any man lack wisdom, let him ask." When it becomes necessary to arrive at decisions of wisdom in the perplexing situations of complex superuniverse affairs, when both the wisdom of perfection and of practicability must be forthcoming, the Perfectors of Wisdom summon a battery of the Voices of Wisdom. Through the consummate skill of their order, they attune and directionize these living receivers of the enminded and circulating wisdom of the universe of universes. Then, from this seraphic ensemble, there flows a stream of divine wisdom from the universe above and a flood of practical wisdom from the higher minds of the universes below.

Now, let me take you on what I call a fantasy trip. Imagine if this planet actually used the access to the Voices of Wisdom. Think about the lack of wisdom we see on Earth, in our governments, in our institutions, in our daily conflicts. If the people who run this planet could request access to a battery of these Voices of Wisdom to help them make decisions, to learn the proper procedure for running planetary administration the way the universe is meant to operate... can you imagine what this world would be like? Can you imagine how far behind we actually are?

This isn't just theoretical. On planets not in rebellion, this actually happens. When planetary administrators get perplexed about what to do in any situation, they can and do request access to this wisdom to help them make the right decisions.

Someone in our study group reminded me of Solomon from the Bible. He asked for wisdom, and he was given wisdom. "If any man lack wisdom, let him ask." Solomon asked, and he received wisdom, and consequently he had the greatest kingdom of his day, perhaps up to that point in history. It didn't guarantee his salvation, of course, but by asking for that wisdom, he gained the expertise to run his kingdom effectively. He had wisdom enough to ask for help, and that in itself is wisdom.

Just imagine what this planet could be like if we could do that consistently.

Now, if confusion arises regarding the harmonization of different versions of wisdom, because sometimes even divine wisdom must be adapted to local conditions, immediate appeal is made to the Divine Counselors, who rule as to the proper combination of procedures. And if there's any doubt about the authenticity of something coming from realms where rebellion has been rife, appeal is made to the Censors. Working with their Discerners of Spirits, they can immediately determine what manner of spirit has actuated the advisor.

This is checks and balances on a cosmic scale. If someone from a rebellion planet requests certain information, the response differs from what would be given to a loyal world. They don't want the rebellion to spread to other planets, 37 worlds have already fallen into rebellion, after all. So, the system asks: what manner of spirit actuated the one who seeks this counsel? It's a system that works, that protects while still serving.

The wisdom of the ages and the intellect of the moment remain ever-present with the Ancients of Days, like an open book before their beneficent gaze.

The Souls of Philosophy

This is the second time in our studies that we've encountered philosophy in heaven, and it raises an interesting question: why philosophy? Philosophy, after all, is the study and understanding of knowledge, or in Greek, the love of wisdom. This tells us that philosophy exists in heaven specifically so we can study how things work in the various realms of creation.

The wonderful teachers known as Souls of Philosophy are also attached to the Perfectors of Wisdom. When not otherwise directionalized, they remain in focal synchrony with the masters of philosophy on Paradise. The text gives us a vivid image: think of stepping up to a huge living mirror, but instead of seeing your finite and material self, you perceive a reflection of the wisdom of divinity and the philosophy of Paradise.

And if it becomes desirable to incarnate this philosophy of perfection, to dilute it, as it were, so as to make it practical for application to and assimilation by the lowly peoples of the lower worlds, these living mirrors have only to turn their faces downward to reflect the standards and needs of another world or universe.

So, it's like standing in front of a mirror with the masters of philosophy in Paradise standing before you, telling you what to do and which way to go. These are perfect reflections, perfect guidance on what to do and how to do it. And remember, these are angels performing this service.

Someone once asked me: with all this good communication, with all this wisdom and philosophy available, how could Lucifer go astray? I don't fully understand it myself. There's a reason the book calls Lucifer's action "cosmic insanity", because that's the only explanation that makes sense. It is cosmically insane. Why would anyone upset a universe that runs so perfectly, where provisions have been made for every situation, where the proper procedures for everything have been established? Yet he still wanted to do it his own way.

Cosmic insanity is the only term that fits. It's nuts, any way you look at it. And if you want to see an example of cosmic insanity closer to home, just turn on the television. Turn on the evening news any night. You'll see it playing out in the very way this planet is run.

By these very techniques, the Perfectors of Wisdom adapt their decisions and recommendations to the real needs and actual status of the peoples and worlds under consideration. They always act in concert with the Divine Counselors and the Universal Censors. But the sublime completeness of these transactions is beyond even the ability of the author of this paper to comprehend. So, if it's beyond the writer's ability to fully understand, we shouldn't feel too bad if we don't grasp every detail ourselves.

The Union of Souls

Completing the triune staff of attachment to the Perfectors of Wisdom are these reflectors of the ideals and status of ethical relationships. Of all the problems in the universe requiring an exercise of consummate wisdom and adaptability, none are more important than those arising from the relationships and associations of intelligent beings. Whether in human associations of commerce and trade, friendship and marriage, or in the liaisons of the angelic hosts, there continue to arise petty frictions and minor misunderstandings.

These difficulties are often too trivial even to engage the attention of conciliators, but they're sufficiently irritating and disturbing to mar the smooth working of the universe if allowed to multiply and continue. Therefore, the Perfectors of Wisdom make available the wise experience of their order as "the oil of reconciliation" for an entire superuniverse, I love that phrase. In all this work, these wise beings are ably seconded by their reflective associates, the Union of Souls, who make current information available regarding the status of the universe and concurrently portray the Paradise ideal for the best adjustment of these perplexing problems.

When not specifically directionalized elsewhere, these seconaphim remain in reflective liaison with the interpreters of ethics on Paradise. Here we go back to Paradise again, that's where the ultimate standard resides.

It's funny, actually. In the movie where Indiana Jones searches for the Ark of the Covenant, they mention the Union of Souls. They had no idea what they were actually talking about. The real Union of Souls serves a very different purpose than anything Hollywood could imagine.

In essence, the Union of Souls tries to keep things running smoothly. They're the grease, if you will, that addresses the minor problems, the misunderstandings that crop up in running universes and their administrations. They work to smooth things over before conflicts escalate. They're actually helped by the interpreters of ethics on Paradise, who guide them on how to do things properly.

This is a crucial function because they work all the way down to the minor stuff, even to misunderstandings that might seem insignificant. They intervene before issues grow large enough to require bringing in the conciliators for formal proceedings. So, I'd say their work is pretty important. These angels are probably quite busy, as the text suggests.

The next paragraph expands on this theme. These are the angels who foster and promote the teamwork of all Orvonton, our superuniverse. One of the most important lessons to be learned during your mortal career is teamwork. The spheres of perfection are staffed by those who have mastered this art of working with other beings. Few are the duties in the universe for the lone servant. The higher you ascend, the more lonely you become temporarily without the association of your fellows.

So, all these tasks we're given, all these responsibilities, we're going to have other beings working alongside us. We won't be alone in these endeavors. Isolation isn't the goal; cooperation is.

The Hearts of Counsel

This is the first group of these reflective geniuses to be placed under the supervision of the Divine Counselors. Seconaphim of this type possess the facts of space, being selective for such data in the circuits of time. They're especially reflective of the superaphic intelligence coordinators, but they're also selectively reflective of the counsel of all beings, whether of high or low estate.

Whenever the Divine Counselors are called upon for important advice or decisions, (like they were for the revelation of the Urantia Book) they immediately requisition an ensemble of the Hearts of Counsel. And presently there's handed down a ruling that actually incorporates the coordinated wisdom and advice of the most competent minds of the entire superuniverse, all of which has been censored and revised in the light of the counsel of the high minds of Havona and even of Paradise.

You can see why these are called the Hearts of Counsel. They're the teamwork specialists. They ensure that everybody gets along, that advice is properly gathered, that everyone learns to work together effectively. They gather input from the highest and lowest types of beings, enabling them all to work together in group functions.

They know how to allocate responsibility properly. And if you think about it, this is why Michael rarely has to leave Nebadon to take care of things. He's always had someone to delegate to. That's the genius of proper organization, you don't do everything yourself; you delegate to competent subordinates.

One of our study group members commented on the excellent communication these systems demonstrate. Communication is indeed very important, and it sounds like they've really got it down. They're fully plugged in.

The Joys of Existence

By nature, these beings are reflectively attuned to the superaphic harmony supervisors above and to certain seraphim below. But it's difficult to explain just what the members of this interesting group actually do. Their principal activities are directed toward promoting reactions of joy among the various orders of the angelic hosts and the lower-will creatures.

The Divine Counselors to whom they're attached seldom use them for specific joy-finding missions. Rather, in a more general manner and in collaboration with the reversion directors, they function as joy clearinghouses. They seek to up step the pleasure reactions of the realms while trying to improve the humor taste, to develop a super humor among mortals and angels.

They endeavor to demonstrate that there's inherent joy in freewill existence, independent of all extraneous influences. And they're right, though they meet with great difficulty in inculcating this truth in the minds of primitive men. The higher spirit personalities and the angels are more quickly responsive to these educational efforts.

I joked in our study group that if you get to the mansion worlds and your job has been as a comedian telling dirty jokes, you're out of a job. That's just all there is to it. But seriously, what the Joys of Existence actually do is take the everyday functioning of the universe and bring out the joy in what we do in everyday living. They help us realize how much joy there is in everyday existence. They try to up step our humor, our joy, our relaxation, our appreciation of life itself.

It's an attitude adjustment, really. They develop what the text calls a "super humor" among mortals and angels. That's quite an accomplishment, keeping us from being depressed, helping us learn to laugh at ourselves, teaching us not to take things so seriously.

There's an old saying: Don't sweat the small stuff. And what's small stuff? Everything is small stuff. That's what it's really about.

The Satisfactions of Service

These angels are highly reflective of the attitude of the directors of conduct on Paradise. Functioning much as the Joys of Existence do, they strive to enhance the value of service and to augment the satisfactions to be derived from it. They've done much to illuminate the deferred rewards inherent in unselfish service, service for the extension of the kingdom of truth.

What did Jesus say? Service, service, and more service. That's where the joy in life comes from, ultimately.

The Divine Counselors, to whom this order is attached utilize them to reflect from one world to another the benefits to be derived from spiritual service. By using the performance of the best to inspire and encourage the mediocre, these seconaphim contribute immensely to the quality of devoted service in the superuniverses.

Effective use is made of the fraternal competitive spirit by circulating to any one world information about what the others, particularly the best, are doing. A refreshing and wholesome rivalry is promoted even among the seraphic hosts.

We really need that here, don't we? On this world, I mean. To see how other worlds are doing things. Maybe we could improve a little on what's going on this planet if we had that kind of perspective, that kind of positive competition.

The Discerners of Spirits

A special liaison exists between the counselors and advisors of the second Havona circle and these reflective angels. They are the only seconaphim attached to the Universal Censors, but they're probably the most uniquely specialized of all their fellows.

Regardless of the source or channel of information, no matter how meager the evidence at hand, when it's subjected to their reflective scrutiny, these discerners will immediately inform us as to the true motive, the actual purpose, and the real nature of its origin. The author marvels at the superb functioning of these angels, who so unerringly reflect the actual moral and spiritual character of any individual concerned in a focal exposure.

Now, I wanted to read the next paragraph before discussing this because both paragraphs together reveal something crucial about what these angels actually do.

The Discerners of Spirits carry on these intricate services by virtue of inherent spiritual insight, if we may use such words in an endeavor to convey to the human mind the thought that these reflective angels function intuitively, inherently, and unerringly. When the Universal Censors behold these presentations, they're face to face with the naked soul of the reflected individual. This very certainty and perfection of portraiture in part explains why the Censors can always function so justly as righteous judges. The discerners always accompany the Censors on any mission away from Uversa, and they're just as effective out in the universes as they are at their headquarters.

The reason I wanted to cover both paragraphs together is the name itself: Discerners of Spirits. And then look at what it says in the second paragraph, that these Discerners of Spirits are "face to face with the naked soul of the reflected individual."

These Discerners of Spirits, when they're examining any being, see you and me as we really are. Not as we pretend to be. Not as we imagine ourselves to be. Not as we want others to see us. They see us outside of all the garbage we construct around ourselves, all our self-deceptions and rationalizations. They see us as we truly are.

That's why they're called Discerners of Spirits, because they can examine any individual and tell you what their motive is in everything they do. That's why they're so important to the Censors, who are part of the department that determines whether you progress from world to world, planet to planet, whether you continue in your eternal career.

This becomes absolutely crucial. You can't hide from them. You can't conceal anything they wouldn't know. They don't just know what you did, they know why you did it. They know what you were thinking when you did it. They understand your motivations, your underlying character, the whole nine yards. You cannot fool them. There's no way you could lie about anything and get away with it.

That's why this service is so vitally important.

The author assures us that all these transactions of the spirit world are real, that they take place in accordance with established usages and in harmony with the immutable laws of the universal domains. The beings of every newly created order, immediately upon receiving the breath of life, are instantly reflected on high. A living portrayal of the creature nature and potential is flashed to the superuniverse headquarters.

Thus, by means of the discerners, the Censors are made fully cognizant of exactly what manner of spirit has been born on the worlds of space. From the moment you were created and born, these Discerners of Spirits know exactly who you are, where you are, and what you're likely to do in life. That's quite remarkable when you think about it.

The final paragraph of our study tonight brings this all together in a profound way:

So, it is with mortal man. The Mother Spirit of Salvington knows you fully, for the Holy Spirit on your world searches all things. And whatsoever the divine Spirit knows of you is immediately available whenever the secoraphic Discerners reflect with the Spirit concerning the Spirit's knowledge of you.

Through the Holy Spirit, the local universe Mother Spirit knows exactly what you're thinking, what you're doing, who you are, what type of being you are, and what you're going to develop into. That's part of the spiritual presence, one of the three divine presences working in your life.

But, and this is crucial, it should be mentioned that the knowledge and plans of the Father fragments are not reflectable. The discerners can and do reflect the presence of the Adjusters. The Censors pronounce them divine. But they cannot decipher the content of the mindedness of the mystery monitors.

Someone asked me what this means, and it's actually quite simple, yet profound. The Father fragment within you, your Thought Adjuster, is not ascertainable in any way, shape, form, or fashion. That fragment of God dwelling within you remains a mystery even to these specialized angels who can see everything else about you.

They can determine what kind of person you are, what kind of personality you possess, all the information about your character and nature. But they cannot discover how the Father fragment is affecting your life. They cannot determine what type of being you'll ultimately become when you fuse with that Thought Adjuster, because the influence of the Thought Adjuster on your eternal destiny remains beyond their reflective capacity.

What's most important, as someone in our study group pointed out, is that the Father fragment is perfect. It's a perfect part within you. Until you fuse with it, it doesn't actually become part of you in the fullest sense, it's more like it's hitchhiking through this life with you. Or as another member joked, we have it trapped. They can't go anywhere.

But that perfect fragment of the Universal Father, working within you, preparing you for eternity, that remains the one area of your being that even these supremely perceptive Discerners of Spirits cannot fully penetrate. The mystery monitors remain mysterious, even to those who can see the naked soul.

Conclusion

As we pause here in our study of Paper 28, having completed our examination of the primary and secondary seconaphim, I hope you're beginning to appreciate the sheer scope and sophistication of celestial administration. These aren't just angels in the traditional sense we might imagine, winged beings delivering occasional messages or providing comfort in times of distress. These are highly specialized, supremely efficient servants of the Most Highs, each order performing functions that keep the entire superuniverse operating in harmony.

The unconscious nature of much of their service fascinates me. These angels don't need to think about transmitting information, they simply reflect reality as it is. They don't need to decide what's important, they're attuned to exactly what needs to be known. And through them, the Ancients of Days and their associates have immediate access to everything necessary for just and wise governance.

What strikes me most, though, is how this reveals the character of God and the nature of divine government. Nothing is arbitrary. Everything serves a purpose. Every need has been anticipated and provided for. The wisdom of Paradise is continuously available to those who seek it. Ethical guidance is always at hand. Even the minor irritations that could disrupt harmony receive attention before they escalate.

And yet, even in this perfectly organized system, there remains room for mystery, the mystery monitors, those fragments of the Father that remain beyond even these comprehensive reflective services. Your relationship with your Thought Adjuster, your potential for fusion and eternal growth, that remains between you and the Father. No angel, however perceptive, can fully penetrate that sacred space.

In our next session, we'll continue with the tertiary seconaphim and explore additional dimensions of angelic ministry. But for tonight, let me leave you with this thought: if this is how thoroughly the universe provides for the administration of justice, wisdom, and harmony across billions of worlds, how much more can you trust that your own path forward has been anticipated and provided for?

The same wisdom that guides superuniverses is available to you. The same attention to your real needs that governs cosmic affairs can operate in your daily life. You need only ask. If any man lack wisdom, let him ask. It really is that simple, and that profound.

Until next time, may you walk in growing awareness of the vast, loving intelligence that surrounds and sustains you, and may you find joy in your service to the ever-expanding kingdom of truth.

Chapter 34: The Tertiary Supernaphim - Servants of the Trinitized Sons

Introduction: Understanding the Third Order of Seconaphim

As we continue our journey through Paper 28 of The Urantia Book, I find myself increasingly fascinated by the intricate organization of celestial beings and their dedicated service to ascending mortals like ourselves. Tonight's study brings us to the Tertiary Supernaphim, the third order of seconaphim, and I must confess that each time I review this material, new layers of meaning seem to emerge.

The Tertiary Supernaphim represent something quite remarkable in the grand scheme of universe administration. Unlike their primary and secondary counterparts who serve on Paradise and in Havona respectively, these angels work directly with beings who share our mortal origins. They serve the Trinitized Sons of Attainment, mortals who have successfully reached God the Father and been trinitized into new orders of universe service. This connection makes their ministry particularly relevant to our own spiritual journey.

What strikes me most profoundly about these celestial servants is that they minister to beings who were once exactly like us. The Mighty Messengers, Those High in Authority, and Those Without Name and Number all began their existence as mortals on evolutionary worlds, facing the same struggles, doubts, and challenges that we face daily. They attained God the Father through faith, persistence, and the patient guidance of countless celestial helpers. Now, having been elevated to positions of superuniverse administration, they work alongside these specialized angels to govern and guide the vast realms of the seven superuniverses. They also were involved

The Seven Reflective Types

The Tertiary Supernaphim are created serially in seven distinct reflective types, each designed for a specific ministry. However, unlike other orders of angels who are assigned individually to separate services, all tertiary seconaphim are collectively assigned to the Trinitized Sons of Attainment. This arrangement allows these ascendant sons to utilize any of the seven types interchangeably, creating a flexible and responsive system of administration.

These seven types are known by titles that reveal their essential functions: The Significance of Origins, The Memory of Mercy, The Import of Time, The

Solemnity of Trust, The Sanctity of Service, The Secret of Greatness, and The Soul of Goodness. Each designation hints at fundamental truths about universe administration and the ascendant career. As we explore these beings and their ministries, we'll discover that they address the most critical aspects of our eternal progression.

The Significance of Origins: Why Your Beginning Matters

The first order we encounter, the Significance of Origins, performs a function that initially may seem bureaucratic but proves to be absolutely essential. These angels maintain living, ready-reference genealogies of the vast hosts of beings, men, angels, and others, who inhabit the seven superuniverses. They can instantly portray anything required concerning the genesis and status of any being in either the central universe or throughout the entire realm of a superuniverse.

When I first studied this section, I wondered why origins would matter so much in a universe that emphasizes growth, change, and spiritual transformation. The answer, I've come to understand, lies in the fundamental nature of relationships and ethical application. As the text states clearly: "All relationships and the application of ethics grow out of the fundamental facts of origin." Origin forms the basis of how the Gods themselves relate to each individual creature.

The Conjoint Actor, the Infinite Spirit, always takes note of the manner in which a being was born. This observation isn't mere record-keeping; it represents a deep understanding that our origins shape our capabilities, challenges, and potential contributions to the universe.

Consider our own situation here on Urantia. Every human being born on this planet carries a designation that sets us apart in the universe: we are rebellion-tested beings. This fact has profound implications for our future service. We have lived on a world isolated by rebellion, cut off from normal universe circuits, plagued by confusion and spiritual darkness. Yet we have chosen, despite these handicaps, to believe in God the Father, God the Son, and God the Spirit. We have remained loyal even when rebellion surrounded us.

This rebellion-tested status makes us particularly valuable for certain types of universe service. When celestial administrators know that a being comes from Urantia or another rebellion-tested world, they understand that such individuals can be trusted in situations where rebellion may be in progress or where loyalty must be proven under difficult circumstances. We have already demonstrated our commitment under the worst possible conditions.

There's another crucial aspect to understanding origins that I believe deserves our careful attention. Throughout the entire history of the universe, no fusion being has ever rebelled against God. Let me state this even more clearly: no one who has ever fused with their Thought Adjuster has ever rebelled against the divine plan.

This fact raises an important question: Why is fusion such a guarantee against rebellion?

The answer lies in understanding what fusion actually means. When we fuse with our Thought Adjuster, that fragment of God the Father dwelling within us, we literally become one with a portion of Deity itself. We unite with perfection. At that point, our will and the Father's will become inseparable. The house cannot fight against itself, as one of our study group members aptly observed. God will not rebel against himself, and once we are truly one with that divine fragment, neither will we.

This stands in stark contrast to beings like Lucifer, Satan, and Caligastia. These were created beings of the local universe, a Lanonandek Son and his associates, who never possessed Thought Adjusters. They were created perfect for their specific positions, yes, but they lacked that indwelling fragment of the Father. Without that divine anchor, even beings created in perfection can go astray. Lucifer fell in love with himself. His ego went unchecked, and eventually he became, quite literally, cosmically insane.

When I reflect on Lucifer's rebellion, I'm struck by the sheer impossibility of his undertaking. How did he ever think he could succeed in overturning the established order of the universe? How could any created being imagine they could triumph against the infinite wisdom and power of the Paradise Trinity? The only explanation is that he had become detached from reality, a form of cosmic insanity born of unchecked pride and self-worship.

The Greeks told a story about a god who looked into a lake, saw his own reflection, and fell in love with himself. It's a fitting metaphor for what happened to Lucifer. He became enamored with his own brilliance, his own beauty, his own capabilities, and in that narcissistic fascination, he lost sight of the source of all those gifts.

Now, some might question how we can be called "rebellion-tested" when we personally haven't lived through an active rebellion. It's true that according to The Urantia Book, the Lucifer Rebellion has been adjudged and ended in our local universe. Michael's sovereignty is complete and unquestioned. However, the adjudication of the rebellion's effects continues. Until that process is fully complete, until every last consequence has been addressed and resolved, Urantia remains under quarantine. We are still living with the accumulated effects of that ancient catastrophe.

Our rebellion-tested status prepares us for future service beyond Nebadon, our local universe. When we become finaliters, when we complete the long journey from our birth world all the way to Paradise and into the presence of the Universal Father, we will be assigned to serve throughout the seven superuniverses. It's entirely possible that we might be sent to another world experiencing the very problems we face here, to help guide and teach beings struggling with the aftermath of celestial rebellion.

This prospect both humbles and challenges me. The difficulties we face daily on this world, the struggles to maintain faith in the face of confusion and darkness, the effort required to discern truth from error, all of this becomes training for future service. Nothing is wasted in God's universe.

Even apart from rebellion, our animal origin matters significantly. We come from a world where life evolved from single-celled organisms through countless generations, developing slowly over millions of years. We carry within us the legacy of that animal ancestry, what the book calls "the mark of the beast." We have animal tendencies, animal urges, animal limitations that must be gradually transformed and transcended. This is partly why the mansion world experience is so necessary. We need time and training to shed these animal characteristics and develop the spiritual qualities appropriate for morontia life and beyond.

A being from a world that has already reached light and life, a settled, perfected sphere, will naturally act and react differently than someone like us, emerging from an animal-origin world still mired in confusion and conflict. The celestial administrators need to know these things. They need what we might call a "background check" on every ascending mortal to understand their capabilities, limitations, and potential.

The Significance of Origins provides exactly this service. These angels can instantly access comprehensive information about any being's background, ancestral factors, and current actual status. Their computation of possessed facts is always up to the minute, constantly updated and immediately available. They are, in essence, the living reference system of the superuniverse, ensuring that administrators have the information they need to make wise decisions about assignments, training, and progression.

The Memory of Mercy: God's Inexhaustible Grace

As we move to the second order of Tertiary Supernaphim, we encounter what I consider to be one of the most comforting and revolutionary concepts in the entire Urantia revelation: the Memory of Mercy.

These angels are the actual, full, and replete living records of the mercy that has been extended to individuals and races by the tender ministrations of the instrumentalities of the Infinite Spirit. Their function involves adapting the justice of righteousness to the status of the realms, as disclosed by the Significance of Origins.

Here's what strikes me as absolutely crucial: the Memory of Mercy discloses the moral debt of the children of mercy, our spiritual liabilities, but these are set down against our assets, the saving provision established by the Sons of God. In revealing the Father's pre-existent mercy, the Sons of God establish the necessary credit to ensure the survival of all beings who truly desire to survive.

According to the findings of the Significance of Origins, a mercy credit is established for the survival of each rational creature. And this is the part that should set our hearts at ease: it is "a credit of lavish proportions and one of sufficient grace to ensure the survival of every soul who really desires divine citizenship."

After reading this paragraph, I cannot conceive of a God who would require animal sacrifice for our sins. The entire concept becomes absurd in light of this revelation. We are not dealing with a petty deity who needs to be appeased with blood offerings. We are not working with a cosmic accountant who demands payment for every transgression. Instead, we discover a Father of infinite love and mercy who has already established more than enough grace to ensure that every sincere soul can survive and progress.

From the moment of our birth, we are endowed with sufficient mercy credit to guarantee our survival if we genuinely choose it. There is literally nothing we can do, no sin we can commit, no mistake we can make, that exhausts this divine provision, assuming we maintain sincere purpose and honest heart.

I'm convinced that unless someone is completely and consciously aware of what they're doing and deliberately, knowingly rejects survival and continued existence, they will not be extinguished. Even then, I believe they're given additional opportunities, particularly if they're in a position where they cannot make a reasonable, logical, sane assessment of their situation. You must have functioning reasoning capabilities to make a truly informed decision about your eternal destiny.

The mercy credits account for this reality. They allow for our limitations, our confusion, our animal nature, our environmental handicaps. But here's the critical point: if someone is so completely in love with themselves that they refuse all help, if they persistently reject every offer of divine assistance, then no amount of mercy can save them, not because the mercy is insufficient, but because they refuse to receive it.

The Memory of Mercy functions as a living trial balance, a current statement of our account with the supernatural forces of the realms. These are the living records of mercy ministration that will be read into the testimony of the courts of Uversa when each individual's right to unending life comes up for adjudication.

The text paints a dramatic picture: "When thrones are cast up and the Ancients of Days are seated, the broadcasts of Uversa issue, and come forth from before them. Thousands upon thousands minister to them, and ten thousand times ten thousand stand before them. The judgment is set, and the books are opened."

These books that are opened on such a momentous occasion are the living records of the tertiary seconaphim of the superuniverses. The formal records remain on file to corroborate the testimony of the Memories of Mercy if required. When every single being comes up through adjudication, when the thrones are cast by the Ancients of Days, the account of mercy is shown to be paid in full.

This means there is nothing you have done, nothing in this world, that cannot be forgiven. That's what it comes down to. That mercy is available to everybody, to every being who has ever lived. All we must do is ask for it and accept it.

The saving credit established by the Sons of God has been fully and faithfully paid out in the loving ministry of the patient personalities of the Third Source and Center, all the angels, all the spiritual beings placed in the universe to help us. The Creator Sons have shown us the way. They have gone through the bestowals for us.

The saving grace of Jesus Christ Michael lies precisely in this: he went through seven bestowals, incarnating as every single type of being he created, demonstrating his understanding of each one. He experienced life as these beings experience it so he could minister to us with genuine love and understanding based on actual experience.

This is similar to what Christians proclaim when they say, "Jesus died on the cross for us," but the truth is actually more profound. Jesus didn't just die for our sins in some legalistic transaction that satisfied an angry God. Rather, he experienced all these different levels of existence so that he could truly understand us and minister to us with compassionate wisdom born of personal experience.

That's the real significance of the cross, not that Jesus died to pay a debt, but that his sacrifice demonstrates his willingness to come down from perfection, from his position as sovereign of the universe, to show us love through complete identification with our struggles. That is the true sacrifice. That is the mystery of the cross. That is the saving grace of our Lord.

Your sins, in themselves, mean nothing in terms of preventing your survival, because God forgives all sin. He knows what we're capable of doing and what we're not. The important thing is to try not to sin in the first place, and when we do, to ask for forgiveness and try not to repeat the mistake.

The paragraph emphasizes something I find both humbling and encouraging: our individual drawing credits are always far in excess of our ability to exhaust the reserve, provided we maintain sincere purpose and honest heart. We are, frankly, stupid, fallible people. We have animal origins. We make mistakes repeatedly, the same mistakes, over and over again. We draw on these mercy credits, we fail, we try again, we fail again, and eventually we have to kick ourselves and ask, "Why do I keep doing this?"

It's because we're of animal origin. That's why we struggle so much with habitual sins and repeated failures. But the mercy is never exhausted. We can always draw enough mercy to take care of everything we do. This knowledge gives us faith that when we wake up on the mansion worlds, we will indeed be there, because God the Father has forgiven all our sins. Every single one.

However, there's an important caveat that we must understand. When mercy is exhausted, when the memory thereof testifies to its depletion, then justice prevails and righteousness decrees. Mercy is not to be thrust upon those who despise it. Mercy is not a gift to be trampled underfoot by the persistent rebels of time.

This is crucial: God's mercy is infinite, but it can only be received by those who are willing to accept it. You cannot force mercy on someone who rejects it. You cannot save someone who absolutely refuses to be saved.

The text then moves into teaching us how to develop mercy ourselves, and this section proves equally profound. The mercy reflectors, with their tertiary associates, engage in numerous superuniverse ministries, including teaching ascending creatures. The Significances of Origins teach these ascenders how to apply spirit ethics. Following such training, the Memories of Mercy teach them how to be truly merciful.

Here's the key insight: mercy is a quality of growth. There is great reward and personal satisfaction in being first just, next fair, then patient, then kind. On that foundation, if we choose and have it in our hearts, we can take the next step and really show mercy. But we cannot exhibit mercy in and of itself. These steps must be traversed. Otherwise, there can be no genuine mercy. There may be patronage, condescension, charity, even pity, but not true mercy.

True mercy comes only as the beautiful climax to these preceding developments: group understanding, mutual appreciation, fraternal fellowship, spiritual communion, and divine harmony.

This teaching addresses how we give mercy to each other, how we forgive one another. The principle works both ways: as we give out mercy, we receive mercy. Just as we forgive others, God forgives us. How can the Gods forgive us if we cannot forgive those around us who wrong us?

The challenge for us is learning to be merciful ourselves. Mercy requires that we stop being judgmental toward every person we encounter, our brothers, sisters, spouses, children, colleagues, and even strangers. If we become harshly judgmental toward everyone we meet, we are not being merciful. Mercy is the quality of forgiveness. As Jesus said, "Go and sin no more", and remember their sin no more.

We need to develop that same quality of divine forgetfulness. We have a terrible tendency to remember everything everybody has ever done to us and hold it against them indefinitely. That is not mercy. That is not forgiveness in the fullest sense.

Someone asked an important question during our study: What about forgiving someone while still being aware of their tendencies so you don't fall victim again?

This is where divine forgetfulness becomes challenging. When somebody injures you, you naturally remember it. You've been hurt. Developing divine forgetfulness means trying to forget those past injuries and start from square one, giving the person another chance.

This can be extremely difficult. If you live with an alcoholic, a drug addict, or someone with other destructive patterns, they may abuse you repeatedly. Developing divine mercy toward that repeated action is very, very tough. And here's an important distinction: continually accepting abuse is not mercy, it's enabling. It makes you codependent. You're actually allowing them to continue destructive behavior without consequences.

True mercy doesn't mean becoming a doormat. Jesus himself exemplified this balance. He was "as wise as serpents and harmless as doves." He knew people's motivations. He passed out alms personally but did not allow the apostles to do so indiscriminately because he understood the motivations of those asking for help. He would not enable people who didn't truly need or deserve assistance.

When I first read that Jesus didn't give alms to just anybody, I was shocked. I thought, "How could he do that? Shouldn't he help everyone who asks?" But that's not how it works. Jesus was being a good parent to all humanity. Good parents don't give their children everything they want; they give them what they need. They establish boundaries. They teach responsibility. They don't enable destructive behavior.

This is mercy operating at its highest level, mercy combined with wisdom, discernment, and genuine concern for the person's ultimate welfare rather than their immediate desires.

The Import of Time: Our Universal Talent

The third order of Tertiary Supernaphim, the Import of Time, addresses what may be the most practical and immediately relevant aspect of our mortal existence. The text states simply and powerfully: "Time is the one universal endowment of all will creatures; it is the one talent entrusted to all intelligent beings."

We all have time in which to ensure our survival. And here's the sobering truth: time is fatally squandered only when it is buried in neglect, when we fail to utilize it in ways that make certain the survival of our souls. Failure to improve one's time to the fullest extent possible does not impose fatal penalties, it merely retards the pilgrim of time in his journey of ascent. But if survival is gained, all other losses can be retrieved.

I could spend days preaching on this one paragraph alone. Let me tell you why: people go through life without using any time to assure the survival of their souls. You see it all around you every single day. And yet, what is the most important thing in life? To do the will of God. That's the purpose of life, to know God, to do the will of God.

If you do not seek God's will and do not take time to ensure your own survival, you miss the entire point. That last sentence holds the key: "If survival is gained, all other losses can be retrieved." So, what is your most important goal in life? To survive. To make it to the mansion worlds. Survival is the single most important thing in your existence.

And how do you ensure survival? You take time to improve your soul. You develop faith. Faith, the simplest thing, and yet so easily neglected. People run around making money, chasing relationships, pursuing sex as if it were life's ultimate goal, doing everything except ensuring the survival of their souls.

When someone asks whether we can only make the survival decision here on this planet, the answer requires nuance. We can potentially make faith decisions on the mansion worlds as well, but this planet is where we normally make that initial, crucial choice. That's the whole point of mortal existence, to choose God or reject him, to decide for survival or against it.

This is why, when I hear someone like Elon Musk say on YouTube that he's "not sure about God," it makes me want to cry. Here's possibly the most intelligent person on Earth, certainly one of the wealthiest, and yet apparently lacking a conscious relationship with the divine. Now, perhaps he does have faith and simply doesn't express it publicly. I hope that's true. But the fact remains that there are people exactly like him all over the world who have not taken the time to discover God. Some even blatantly declare that God doesn't exist.

I knew someone in my own family who for years insisted he didn't believe in God because he thought God didn't exist. Eventually, thankfully, he woke up to the reality of divine presence. But it happens, even in families of faith, people can become so caught up in material existence that they never stop to consider eternal realities.

The Buddhist concept of mindfulness seems particularly relevant here. We should be constantly vigilant and mindful of our thinking and behavior, aware of everything that goes on in our lives from moment to moment, from the moment we wake until the moment we sleep. What do we think about it? Do we think about God? Do we ever ask ourselves, "What does God want me to do today?"

I know someone who asks that question every day. It's so easy to just cruise through life on autopilot, never making conscious decisions about anything, especially about our spiritual development and eternal destiny.

I recently encountered a summary of a book called "The 5 AM Club," which recommends spending the first hour of your day in three twenty-minute segments: twenty minutes for meditation and reflection, twenty minutes for physical exercise, and twenty minutes for learning or planning. The idea is to really meditate on where God is leading you, to consider the purpose of each day, and to align yourself with divine will before the rush of daily activities takes over.

The Import of Time becomes particularly valuable in the assignment of trust. These angels can evaluate exactly how much time is required for any undertaking. Time is a vital factor in everything this side of Havona and Paradise. In the final judgment before the Ancients of Days, time itself becomes an element of evidence. The Import of Time must always afford testimony showing that every defendant has had ample time for making decisions and achieving choices.

This addresses a question that might trouble us: What if someone didn't have enough opportunity? What if circumstances prevented them from hearing the gospel or understanding spiritual truth? The Import of Time provides evidence that adequate opportunity was given. If it wasn't, if circumstances truly prevented informed choice, then that fact becomes part of the mercy calculation.

These time evaluators are also described as "the secret of prophecy." They can portray the element of time required for completing any undertaking, and they are just as dependable as indicators as the frandalanks and chronoldeks, other orders of beings who record time and material events. The Gods foresee; hence they foreknow the future. But the ascendant authorities of the universes of time must consult the Import of Time to forecast events accurately.

We will first encounter these beings on the mansion worlds, where they will instruct us in the advantageous use of time, both in its positive employment (work) and in its negative utilization (rest). Both uses prove equally important. Both work and rest require time and take up legitimate segments of our lives. We need to learn how to use both effectively.

Conclusion: Laying Foundations for Eternal Service

As we conclude this exploration of the first three orders of Tertiary Supernaphim, I'm struck by how practical and immediately applicable these teachings are to our daily lives. These are not abstract theological concepts meant only for distant future reference. They address the fundamental realities of our present existence.

The Significance of Origins reminds us that our background matters, not as a limitation, but as a unique preparation for future service. Our rebellion-tested status, our animal origin, our struggles and difficulties all become training for eternal careers of service. Nothing is wasted in God's economy.

The Memory of Mercy assures us that divine grace far exceeds anything we could possibly exhaust through our failures and sins. We can rest secure in the knowledge that God has already provided sufficient mercy to ensure our survival if we sincerely desire it. At the same time, we're challenged to develop mercy ourselves, to learn the divine art of forgiveness that doesn't just pardon but genuinely forgets.

The Import of Time confronts us with the reality that we have been given one universal talent, time itself, and the crucial question is whether we're using it to ensure our soul's survival. Everything else can be recovered if survival is gained, but if we squander our time in complete neglect of spiritual realities, we risk everything.

These three orders of angels serve beings who were once exactly like us, mortals who successfully completed the ascension journey. Someday, if we remain faithful, we too will work with these same angels in service to the superuniverse administrations. We will help guide other ascending mortals along the path we now travel.

In our next session, we will examine the remaining four orders of Tertiary Supernaphim: the Solemnity of Trust, the Sanctity of Service, the Secret of Greatness, and the Soul of Goodness. Each reveals additional dimensions of divine ministry and eternal service that await us.

For now, let us carry with us these essential truths: our origins prepare us for unique service, God's mercy ensures our survival if we desire it, and time is our most precious resource for spiritual development. As we go about our daily lives, may we remember to use our time wisely, to show mercy to others as we've received mercy, and to value our unique preparation for eternal service in God's vast universe.

The journey continues, one step at a time, one choice at a time, always moving forward toward that distant but certain goal, the presence of the Universal Father on Paradise and beyond, into eternity.

Chapter 35: The Seconaphim - Reflectors of Truth and Ministers of Trust

As we continue our exploration of the celestial hierarchy described in The Urantia Book, we arrive at one of the most fascinating orders of angelic beings, the seconaphim. These remarkable entities serve as living mirrors of divine reality, reflecting with perfect accuracy the character, motives, and spiritual potential of every ascending mortal who passes through the superuniverse systems. In this chapter, we examine Paper 28, focusing particularly on the profound concepts of trust, service, and greatness as revealed through the ministry of these extraordinary beings.

What strikes me most about the seconaphim is their unique ability to perform what we might call "spiritual x-ray vision." Unlike our clumsy human attempts to judge character or assess someone's trustworthiness, these angels see through to the very core of our being. They weigh our souls in what the text calls "the living scales of unerring character appraisal." There's no hiding from them, no putting on a false front. They know exactly who we are and what we're capable of becoming.

The Solemnity of Trust: A Foundation for Cosmic Citizenship

The section on the Solemnity of Trust opens with a statement that should make all of us pause and reflect: "Trust is a crucial test of will creatures. Trustworthiness is the true measure of self-mastery character." These seconaphim accomplish a dual purpose in the economy of the superuniverses. First, they portray to all will creatures a sense of the obligation, sacredness, and solemnity of trust. Second, they unerringly reflect to the governing authorities the exact trustworthiness of any candidate for confidence or trust.

I could spend months unpacking this single paragraph because it touches on something fundamentally broken in our world today. We face a crisis of trust on this planet, a big, undeniable crisis. When I read this passage, I couldn't help but think about the state of our institutions, our government, and the representatives we elect to serve us. The most critical obligation any person has when placed in a position of trust is not to betray that trust. It sounds simple, doesn't it? Yet look around at what's happening in our society.

Most of the politicians in our government, not all, but certainly most, have failed this fundamental test. They've grossly misused the trust placed in them. We elect them to office with the expectation that they'll serve the will of the people, that they won't steal, won't take bribes, won't engage in the corruption and deception that seems to permeate every level of governance. But time and again, they fail us. And here's the sobering question: Do you think these individuals, when they eventually arrive on the mansion worlds, will be found trustworthy? I don't. I really don't think they will be at all.

Will they be placed in positions of responsibility in the universe, as described in these passages about the economy of the superuniverses? I doubt it. They've failed at the most basic level here on Urantia. When people accept positions as representatives of the people, their paramount obligation is to fulfill that responsibility above all else, above personal gain, above party loyalty, above everything.

One of our study group members, Rodney, shared a personal experience that illustrates just how difficult it can be to serve in a position of trust, even at a local level. He was voted in as chairman and serviceman for a Parks and Recreation Committee, a small political position, but one that came with real responsibilities. He found it nearly impossible to please everyone. No matter what decision he made, one group would be happy while others felt betrayed. He eventually had to step away from the position because he couldn't reconcile his desire to be trustworthy with the impossible demands of satisfying conflicting constituencies.

This brings us to the heart of the problem, which the text addresses in the very next paragraph.

The Problem of Assessing Character on Urantia

The second paragraph under the Solemnity of Trust section contains what may be the most brutally honest assessment of human judgment in the entire book: "On Urantia you grotesquely essay to read character and to estimate specific abilities. But on Uversa we actually do these things in perfection."

Notice the word choice. Not "poorly." Not "inadequately." Grotesquely. We grotesquely attempt to assess character. That's the whole problem, right there. On Uversa, the capital of our superuniverse, they have it figured out. The seconaphim weigh trustworthiness in living scales of unerring character appraisal, and when they've looked at you, the authorities need only look at them to know the limitations of your ability to discharge responsibility, execute trust, and fulfill missions. Your assets of trustworthiness are clearly set forth alongside your liabilities of possible default or betrayal.

But here on Urantia? We're flying blind. When people throw their hats into the ring for public office, do we really know anything about them? Think about it honestly. When you go to vote, how much do you actually know about the candidates? Most of the time, practically nothing. You might see a campaign sign, catch a commercial, read a brief statement online. But do you know who these people really are? Do you understand their character, their values, their true motivations?

The answer, for most of us, is no. And this raises a troubling question: Are we even qualified to elect people to represent us? Not really. We're not qualified for two primary reasons. First, we're not trained in how to assess and qualify candidates. Second, we're not given adequate information about them. There should be comprehensive essays available on every single candidate, detailed profiles outlining what they stand for, what they believe, their track record, their positions on key issues. Some of you might remember, many years ago, newspapers used to provide this kind of coverage before elections. They'd publish entire sections devoted to candidate information, giving voters the tools they needed to make informed decisions. That's largely disappeared now.

With the internet, you'd think we'd have better access to this kind of information than ever before. You should be able to look up any candidate and find everything you need to know in one place, right there on your ballot or linked from it. But it doesn't work that way. The information is scattered, unreliable, often tainted by partisan spin. So, we don't have what we need to make truly informed, logical decisions about who should represent us.

There's another crucial element missing civic education. If you read Paper 72, you'll find a description of government on a neighboring planet where citizens must be trained and authorized to vote before they can participate in elections. That's what we need here on Urantia. Just because you have a name and a driver's license shouldn't automatically authorize you to walk into a polling place and cast votes that will shape the future of your society. I know that might sound controversial, but it's the truth. Do you want to live in the truth, or do you want to live in fantasy land?

The truth is, we need to be trained in how to vote, how to evaluate candidates, how to understand the issues, how to think critically about governance and representation. Only then would we become what we claim to aspire to be: an educated, informed electorate. And that's precisely what this paragraph is talking about. The seconaphim weigh your trustworthiness by seeing your character in its rawest, most unfiltered form. They know instantly whether you possess any trustworthiness at all. They also know your assets and your liabilities, including the possibility of default or betrayal.

Why does this matter so much? Because of what happened during the Lucifer Rebellion. We've seen, in dramatic and devastating fashion, what occurs when trusted beings betray that trust and default on their responsibilities. That's the road we're traveling on our planet right now. We have far too many people in positions of authority who are betraying their trust and defaulting on their obligations.

One of our study group members, Gary, made an excellent point about this. We talk constantly about rights in our society, our right to this, our right to that. But we almost never discuss responsibilities. For every right you possess, you have a corresponding constitutional responsibility. If you have the right to vote, you have the responsibility to become an informed voter. That's absolutely correct. And it's not an easy process, is it? It's actually quite difficult. Gary shared that in the last local election, he didn't vote for one of the first times in his life because he simply couldn't find adequate information about the candidates. He knew nothing about them, and he refused to pull a lever for people he knew nothing about.

That's a real problem. You're essentially gambling when you vote under those conditions, supporting candidates based on virtually no substantive knowledge of who they are or what they'll actually do once in office.

The Plan for Advancement Through Augmented Trust

The next section addresses how the universe handles the development of trustworthiness over time: "It is the plan of your superiors to advance you by augmented trust just as fast as your character is sufficiently developed to gracefully bear these added responsibilities. But to overload the individual only courts disaster and ensures disappointment. And the mistake of placing responsibility prematurely upon either man or angel may be avoided by utilizing the ministry of these infallible estimators of the trust capacity of the individuals of time and space."

This passage reveals something profound about how the universe operates. Those in high authority, and these are mortals who have progressed to such positions, never make assignments until candidates have been weighed in the secoraphic balances and pronounced "not wanting." When they assign someone to a job, they know with certainty whether that person can handle it. You really can't ask for a better system than that.

The universe doesn't set people up for failure. It advances us according to our actual capacity, not according to our ambitions or our connections or our ability to campaign for a position. This is radically different from how things work on Urantia, where we routinely place people in positions they're not qualified for, where advancement often depends more on politics than on merit.

The Sanctity of Service: Privilege, Not Burden

The angels who oversee the Sanctity of Service embody a crucial principle: "The privilege of service immediately follows the discovery of trustworthiness. Nothing can stand between you and opportunity for increased service except your own untrustworthiness, your lack of capacity for appreciation of the solemnity of trust."

Service is presented here not as an obligation or a burden, but as a privilege. Once you've demonstrated trustworthiness, you're given opportunities to serve. The only thing that can hold you back is your own lack of trustworthiness or your inability to appreciate how sacred trust really is. This represents a complete inversion of how we often think about service in our society. We tend to view service positions, whether in government, community organizations, or volunteer work, as either stepping stones to something better or as obligations we grudgingly fulfill. But the universe sees it differently. Service is the privilege. It's what you get to do once you've proven yourself worthy of trust.

The next paragraph develops this concept further: "Service, purposeful service, not slavery, is productive of the highest satisfaction and is expressive of the divinest dignity. Service, more service, increased service, difficult service, adventurous service, and at last divine and perfect service, is the goal of time and the destination of space."

If you're planning to get to the mansion worlds expecting to play your harp and sit around doing nothing for eternity, you're in for a surprise. We do have periods of play and recreation, that's acknowledged, but primarily, we work. It's all about work, about service. Jane mentioned during our study that she'll have to learn to turn off her mind a little bit, to stop working constantly. I laughed because I have the same problem. I was helping my neighbor with a project recently, and even while we were working on something completely unrelated to The Urantia Book, I found myself explaining the mercy angels to him. He said, "You know, you always have something interesting to tell me." My problem isn't finding things to teach, it's learning when to stop.

But here's what struck me about this passage: "Ever will the play cycles of time alternate with the service cycles of progress. And after the service of time there follows the super service of eternity. During the play of time, you should envision the work of eternity, even as you will, during the service of eternity, reminisce the play of time." There's a rhythm to existence, a balance between work and rest, service and recreation. We'll carry that forward throughout our eternal careers.

The Universal Economy: Based on Intake and Output

The section on the Universal Economy contains a statement that challenges the self-centered thinking that pervades much of human society: "The universal economy is based on intake and output. Throughout the eternal career you will never encounter monotony of inaction or stagnation of personality. Progress is made possible by inherent motion. Advancement grows out of the divine capacity for action, and achievement is the child of imaginative adventure."

But then comes the corrective: "Inherent in this capacity for achievement is the responsibility of ethics, the necessity for recognizing that the world and the universe are filled with a multitude of different types of beings. All this magnificent creation, including yourself, was not made just for you. This is not an egocentric universe."

That's worth repeating. This is not an egocentric universe. Everything wasn't created for your benefit alone. The gods have decreed that it is more blessed to give than to receive. And Jesus himself said, "He who would be greatest among you, let him be server of all." That comes straight from the Master's mouth.

My wife and I were talking over lunch recently about getting older, and we touched on something relevant to this discussion of service. As we age and approach that transition to the mansion worlds, our bodies may fail us. Getting old isn't for the faint of heart, it's genuinely difficult. But here's what's important: as we get older, we have so much more to give, so much more to offer in service. We're wisest near the end of our lives, not at the beginning. Think about that. We accumulate decades of experience, of hard-won wisdom, of lessons learned through trial and error. Yet what does our society do? We tend to push older people aside. We put them in nursing homes and forget about them. We act as if their contributions are no longer valuable.

That's exactly backward. We should be tapping into their wisdom. We should be learning from their experiences so we can grow as they grew. Just as someone is getting ready to transition to the mansion worlds, they're probably at their wisest.

My neighbor from Romania often talks about his mother and father, about the values they instilled in him. He's carried those values forward, and they've shaped him into a person with wonderful character. That's the kind of intergenerational transmission of wisdom we should be cultivating.

Someone in our study group pointed out that Jesus himself set the ultimate example of service. He could have ascended right after his baptism. He'd completed his mission at that point. But he stayed for more than three years to serve the lowest creatures, to serve us. He said it many times throughout his ministry: service, service, service.

The Orientals and Asians have something to teach us in this regard. In those cultures, young people look forward to getting old because they know they'll be respected for their wisdom. They're way ahead of our Western world in that respect. It represents a fundamentally different understanding of the value and purpose of human life across its entire span.

The Real Nature of Service: Mind Readers and Soul Revealers

The section titled "The Real Nature of Any Service" contains a revelation that should make all of us a bit uncomfortable: "The real nature of any service, be it rendered by a man or angel, is fully revealed in the faces of these secoraphic service indicators, the sanctities of service. Full analysis of the true and of the hidden motives is clearly shown. These angels are indeed the mind readers, heart searchers, and soul revealers of the universe. Mortals may employ words to conceal their thoughts, but these high seconaphim lay bare the deep motives of the human heart and of the angelic mind."

You can't fool them. There's no point in even trying. They read your mind, see through your pretenses, understand your true motivations. Wouldn't it be something if we had beings like that here on Earth? It would certainly put an end to a lot of the chicanery and deception that characterizes so much of human interaction.

The Secret of Greatness and the Soul of Goodness

As ascending pilgrims awaken to the import of time, they're prepared for the realization of the solemnity of trust and the appreciation of the sanctity of service. These are identified as the moral elements of greatness. But there are also what the text calls "secrets of greatness." When spiritual tests of greatness are applied, the moral elements aren't disregarded, but something else becomes paramount: "The quality of unselfishness revealed in disinterested labor for the welfare of one's earthly fellows, particularly worthy beings in need and in distress, that is the real measure of planetary greatness."

And then comes one of the most powerful statements in the entire book: "The great man is not he who 'takes a city' or 'overthrows a nation,' but rather 'he who subdues his own tongue.'"

I believe that's a quote from Jesus, though I'd need to verify that. Regardless, it captures something profound about the nature of true greatness. We tend to measure greatness by external achievements, conquests, wealth, fame, power. But the universe measures it by something much more subtle and much more difficult: self-control, particularly control over one's speech. Subduing your own tongue means subduing your ego. It means resisting the impulse to lash out, to dominate conversations, to always have the last word, to use your words as weapons.

This paragraph also emphasizes that a measure of planetary greatness is found in those who serve people in need and in distress. How much, as a planet, do we truly help one another? That's a question worth asking ourselves regularly.

Greatness is Synonymous with Divinity

The next section develops this theme further: "Greatness is synonymous with divinity. God is supremely great and good. Greatness and goodness simply cannot be divorced. They are forever made one in God. This truth is literally and strikingly illustrated by the reflective interdependence of the Secret of Greatness and the Soul of Goodness, for neither can function without the other in reflecting other qualities of divinity."

Here's where it gets really interesting from a technical standpoint. The superuniverse seconaphim can act alone when reflecting other qualities of divinity, but when it comes to estimates of greatness and goodness, they appear to be inseparable. On any world in any universe, these reflectors of greatness and goodness must work together, always showing a dual and mutually dependent report of every being upon whom they focus. Greatness cannot be estimated without knowing the content of goodness, and goodness cannot be portrayed without exhibiting its inherent and divine greatness.

You can't have one without the other. The measure of how great you are in your life is really an indication of how good you are. During our study session, someone asked me to define goodness. I said being God-like. But then they pressed further, asking for a concrete example. They knew someone who carries five-dollar bills specifically to give to people they encounter on street corners. Is that goodness?

I said no, that's altruism. There's a difference. And the key question is: Why do they give it? What's their motive? Intention matters enormously. Jane offered a helpful summary: Goodness is the desire to do good to others and to create favorable conditions for others. I added that it's also the reflection of the divine within you. Goodness is the reflection of God working through you, translating into action. You can't have goodness without action. You can't have goodness without service and the creation of favorable conditions for the spiritual growth of others.

Gary brought up another crucial point: You have to add to the definition of goodness the intention of doing good without the expectation of reward. That's exactly right. You don't perform acts of goodness to gain recognition, wealth, status, or heavenly rewards. You do it for the sake of service itself, for the inherent value of helping others.

That's where politicians often go astray. They seek office to make money, to benefit themselves, to become rich and powerful. That's not service. That's self-aggrandizement. If you want to serve in any office, political or otherwise, you have to genuinely want to serve. You don't serve for your own benefit. You serve for the benefit of others.

Let me ask you: Do you think I teach these study sessions on Tuesday and Thursday nights for my own benefit? Of course not. I know the book. I could sit home, read it by myself, and feel intellectually satisfied. But what good would that do? I share it because I'm excited to help others discover these truths. It doesn't primarily benefit me, though I certainly benefit from going through the material again. But the reason I do it isn't self-benefit. I do it to serve others, to help them realize the joy of sonship with God.

One of our group members reminded us that unfailing goodness is listed as one of the fruits of the spirit. When goodness becomes a habit in your life, when it's something that flows through you automatically without conscious thought, you're on the right track. You wake up thinking, "What good can I do today?" And you don't limit it to service to people. You can express goodness toward animals, toward the environment, toward every living thing you encounter. When you rescue an injured animal and nurse it back to health, does that benefit the animal? Yes. But it benefits you even more because it puts you in a position to express love and caring, and those qualities then overflow into every other relationship in your life.

That's why we sometimes tell each other we love each other at the end of these study sessions. We feel this overwhelming joy from sharing spiritual concepts and ideas with one another, and the joy of love just pours out. You can't stop it. It's the joy of life itself.

I looked up "goodness" in the Urantia Book index during our study, and the list of references provides a fairly complete picture: Goodness is defined as carrying out divine plans, the finite maximization of experience, fruit of the spirit, health of the soul, living relative to evil, always a personal experience, man's effort to discern God in spirit, nearness to divinity, revelation of divinity in finaliters, definite value, shown in loving ministry of Father, Son, and Spirit, stabilizing, understandable only in relationships to personality, value realization of God consciousness. That about covers it, doesn't it?

The Estimate of Greatness

The final paragraph of this section brings it all together: "The estimate of greatness varies from sphere to sphere. To be great is to be God-like. And since the quality of greatness is wholly determined by the content of goodness, it follows that even in your present human estate, if you can through grace become good, you are thereby becoming great. The more steadfastly you behold, and the more persistently you pursue the concept of divine goodness, the more certainly you will grow in greatness, in true magnitude of genuine survival character."

That really says it all, doesn't it? Greatness is accessible to every single one of us, right now, in our present human state. We don't have to wait until we reach the mansion worlds. We don't have to achieve some exalted position. We simply have to become good, genuinely, habitually, instinctively good. And as we become good, we automatically become great in the cosmic sense.

Ministry of the Seconaphim: From Paradise to the Evolutionary Worlds

The seconaphim have their origin and headquarters on the capitals of the superuniverses, but they range from the shores of Paradise to the evolutionary worlds of space. They serve as valued assistants to the deliberative assemblies of the super governments. They provide great help to numerous groups: the courtesy colonies of Uversa, star students, millennial tourists, celestial observers, and ascending beings waiting for Havona transport.

The Ancients of Days take pleasure in assigning certain primary seconaphim to assist ascending creatures living on the 490 study worlds surrounding Uversa. Many secondary and tertiary orders also serve as teachers on these worlds. These satellites of Uversa function as the finishing schools of the universes of time, offering preparatory courses for the seven-circuited university of Havona. The seconaphim truly serve from Paradise all the way down to the evolutionary planets.

Of the three orders of seconaphim, the tertiary group attached to the ascendant authorities ministers most extensively to ascending creatures of time. We'll meet them occasionally soon after we depart from Urantia, though we won't freely make use of their services until we reach the tarrying worlds of Orvonton. We'll really get to know them during our time on the Uversa school worlds, the period when we're waiting to be transported to Havona.

Timesavers, Guideposts, and Emergency Help

These tertiary seconaphim are described as timesavers, space abridgers, error detectors, faithful teachers, and everlasting guideposts. They're living signs of divine surety and mercy, placed at the crossroads of time to guide anxious pilgrims in moments of great perplexity and spiritual uncertainty. Long before we attain the portals of perfection, we'll begin to gain access to the tools of divinity and make contact with the techniques of deity.

From the time we arrive on the initial mansion world until we close our eyes in the Havona sleep preparatory to Paradise transit, we'll increasingly avail ourselves of the emergency help of these marvelous beings. They're fully and freely reflective of the sure knowledge and certain wisdom of those safe and dependable pilgrims who have preceded us on the long journey to the portals of perfection.

You could say that these tertiary seconaphim exist primarily to help us when we become uncertain about anything during our long traverse to Paradise. If we become perplexed about some concept, uncertain about what lies ahead, confused about our next steps, these beings can show us through reflectivity what we need to see. They reassure us, give us examples of what's to come, help us understand what to expect. They make us feel comfortable throughout the entire journey.

It's remarkable, when you think about it, how many different orders of angels exist specifically to help us along our pathway to Paradise. And I'm certain we'll all experience moments of uncertainty along the way. How many times in this life do you feel uncertain about things? You wonder, "Why am I here? What am I doing?

What's the point of all this?" That's exactly what these tertiary seconaphim are there to address.

The Problem of Quarantine

The final paragraph of this section addresses a sobering reality about our current situation on Urantia: "We are denied the full privilege of using these angels of the reflective order on Urantia. They are frequent visitors on your world, accompanying assigned personalities. But here they cannot freely function. This sphere is still under partial spiritual quarantine, and some of the circuits essential to their services are not here at present."

Because of the Lucifer Rebellion, we remain cut off from many of the circuits that the rest of the universe takes for granted. This makes it difficult for even the angels visiting our planet to do their work properly. The circuits they need simply aren't available to them. When our world is finally restored to the reflective circuits, much of the work of interplanetary and interuniverse communication will be greatly simplified and expedited.

The passage concludes on a note of patient perseverance: "Celestial workers on Urantia encounter many difficulties because of this functional curtailment of their reflective associates. But we go on joyfully conducting our affairs with the instrumentalities at hand, notwithstanding our local deprivation of many of the services of these marvelous beings, the living mirrors of space and the presence projectors of time."

It makes you wonder: If the quarantine were completely lifted, how much would change? How many of these reflective services would suddenly become available to us? All the negativity we see on the internet, on television, all the things that make us feel like the world is falling apart, that's partly a function of being cut off from the sustaining circuits of divinity. We're operating in a kind of spiritual isolation. When those circuits are restored, I believe things will change dramatically. We'll see the positive aspects of reality more clearly. We'll be well on our way to the era of light and life.

During our study session, Pam suggested something I thought was profound: We should pray for the restoration of these circuits. Why not? We pray for many things. Why not pray for this? The challenge, of course, is the lag time of justice. If the circuits were restored too quickly, before we're ready, it might not go well. But eventual restoration is something we can work toward and pray for.

I was explaining to my neighbor recently how judgment works for those who don't survive to the mansion worlds. When someone dies and their guardian angel must justify their life before the Ancients of Days, that justification happens through reflectivity. But here's the problem: Because we're cut off from the circuits, our guardian angels can't communicate reflectively with the Ancients of Days directly from this planet. They have to get off-planet to do it, travel to our system capital, perhaps to the capital of our local universe.

And they have to work fast. If you're going to wake on the mansion world on the third period after death, and remember, if three days equals one day on our system capital, then your guardian angel has only about nine days to complete this entire justification process. Think about that. They have to present your entire life, justify every attempt they made to guide you, demonstrate that they did their job properly, and receive judgment from three Ancients of Days. And they can't do any of that from this planet because the circuits aren't functioning.

As Gary put it, they have to go to a celestial phone booth. That's exactly right. And wherever that phone booth is, whether it's on our system capital or the capital of our local universe, they have to get there quickly, present their case, and await judgment. It's a process that should be much simpler, much more immediate, but because of the quarantine, it's been complicated.

Gary asked a good question during our study: When we die, how is our soul transported from wherever we die to the celestial pole of the planet? The guardian angel takes possession of it immediately upon the last functioning of the human brain. Wherever you are when you die, your guardian angel is there to receive your soul. Rodney then asked about what would happen if someone dies on Mars in the future. Would they need to build a spiritual pole there? I suspect they already have one, or at least they will the moment a human being sets foot on that planet. Anywhere a human being goes, the necessary spiritual infrastructure must exist. If one person lands on Mars, that becomes a sanctioned planet for human habitation, and all the circuits, poles, and angelic support systems must be in place.

We tend to think of these things in terms of physical transportation, how do you get from Mars back to Earth? But we're talking about spiritual transportation, which operates on entirely different principles. I'm certain there are circuits connecting every planet that has even one inhabited being on it.

Consider this: The archangel circuit has been on our planet for several hundred thousand years, established shortly after the Caligastia Rebellion. It's been here perhaps 250,000 to 300,000 years. Yet our planet is about 4 billion years old. It's been inhabited by human beings for a little less than a million years, about 998,000 years, if I recall correctly. For the vast majority of Earth's existence, it was simply maturing, being prepared for us. Only in the last 500,000 years or so has it really been developing as a spiritual planet.

And if it weren't for the Lucifer Rebellion and the Adamic default, we'd be at a completely different level of development right now. But we've learned lessons that other planets haven't had to learn. So, we're not cursed, not really. The difficulty has brought benefits, even if those benefits came at a tremendous cost.

Conclusion: Living Mirrors of Divine Reality

As we conclude this chapter on the seconaphim, we're left with a vision of celestial beings who serve as living mirrors of divine reality, reflecting with perfect accuracy the character, trustworthiness, and spiritual potential of every ascending mortal. They cannot be deceived. They cannot be manipulated. They see us exactly as we are, our assets and our liabilities, our capacity for service and our potential for betrayal.

What should our response be to this knowledge? Perhaps it's to recognize that the standards by which we'll ultimately be judged are already in operation, already measuring us, already known in the universe. The question isn't whether we can fool anyone about who we really are. The question is whether we're becoming the kind of people we'd want the seconaphim to see when they look at us, trustworthy, good, committed to service, growing in greatness through the cultivation of genuine goodness.

My sincere Thank You!

I have enjoyed bringing you the information in this book. My hope is that it will make your life more fulfilling and bring you closer to God our Father.

Source Materials:

The key source materials can be found and downloaded at:

https://www.youtube.com/@rogerpauldc

Universe Reality Concepts to Understand The Urantia Book:

https://www.youtube.com/playlist?list=PLbPjbuLCH4aj7dpiOnq8rb3Kr, GJkm4pl

Links

Fifth Epochal Revelation https://www.fifthepochalrevelationfellowship.com

https://fifthepochalrevelationfellowship.com/b-i-urantia-book-standardized/papers/front-matter.htm

About the Author

Dr. Roger W. Paul's journey with The Urantia Book began in an unexpected way that would shape the course of his life. In 1973, while serving in the U.S. Navy and attending Florida Keys College, a stranger approached him during a meeting, handed him a copy of The Urantia Book, and simply said, "I think you're ready for this," before walking away. That encounter sparked a lifelong dedication to understanding and sharing the profound truths contained within its pages.

Early Life and Education

Dr. Paul's path has been marked by diverse experiences and persistent dedication to learning. At age sixteen, while still in tenth grade, he earned his Master Barber license from Capital Barber College - a profession that would help support him through his extensive educational journey.

In 1972, he joined the U.S. Navy during the Vietnam War, serving initially as a jet engine mechanic (Airman) before transitioning to ship serviceman. His military service resulted in injuries that eventually led to total disability status in 2006, but never diminished his commitment to spiritual and intellectual growth.

After receiving his Associate of Arts degree in Basic Sciences, Philosophy and Religion, and Music Education from Florida Keys College starting in 1973, Dr. Paul originally planned to attend a Southern Baptist Seminary. However, after nine months of immersive study of The Urantia Book, he realized that traditional theological frameworks no longer aligned with the cosmic truths he had discovered. Unable to find any institution offering formal academic study of The Urantia Book (this was long before the internet era), he redirected his educational pursuits while maintaining his dedication to understanding this remarkable revelation.

His academic credentials include:

- **Georgia State University, Atlanta, GA**
    - Associate of Science in Commercial Music and Recording
    - Bachelor of Science in Communications and Business
    - Pre-med studies in the nursing program

- **Life Chiropractic College, Marietta, GA**
    - Doctor of Chiropractic
- **National College of Chiropractic**
    - Diplomate (Doctorate level) in Chiropractic Sports Medicine

Professional Career

Dr. Paul's professional life has encompassed both healthcare and technology sectors. As owner and operator of Paul Chiropractic, he installed over 100 computer office management systems for medical and chiropractic offices, pioneering the integration of technology in healthcare administration.

He served as Supervisor of Diagnostics and Director of the Southeast Region for Trident Medical Concepts (1996-1997), where he managed the Mobile Video Fluoroscopy Division and established the Southeast Region as a profitable enterprise within one year.

Recognizing the emerging potential of the internet, Dr. Paul founded My Web Partner Incorporated (1997-1999), providing web solutions for individuals, small businesses, and corporations. This venture led to consulting work with major corporations, including serving as Senior Consultant and Project Manager for CIBER Incorporated (1999-2006), where he managed significant projects for the Georgia Courts Automation Commission and BellSouth.

His technical certifications include Certified Internet Webmaster (CIW), CIW Application Developer, and CIW Web Languages.

Personal Interests

Beyond his professional and academic pursuits, Dr. Paul became a certified scuba instructor through PADI, SSI, and NASDS, earning certifications in mixed gases, cavern and cave diving, and serving as a DAN O2 and First Aid Instructor. He achieved every PADI certification available before health conditions required him to cease diving.

Ministry and Teaching

For over five decades, Dr. Paul has dedicated himself to understanding and sharing the teachings of The Urantia Book. His YouTube channel

(@rogerpauldc) features extensive video teachings (over 3000) on universe reality concepts, making these profound spiritual truths accessible to seekers worldwide. His teaching approach combines scholarly rigor with practical application, helping students grasp both the cosmic scope and personal relevance of these revelations.

Published Works

Dr. Paul is the author of five comprehensive guides to The Urantia Book:

- *Who Is God? The Origins and Destiny of Universes and Deity from The Urantia Book: A Guide to Understanding the Urantia Book's Cosmic Vision*
- The Evolution of God - The Origins and Destiny of Universes and Deity: Understanding the Urantia Book's Cosmic Vision
- The Thought Adjusters - The Presence of God Within: The Origin and Nature of Thought Adjusters
- *Jesus, Who, What, When, and Where: The Origins of Jesus Before Earth—The True Identity of Jesus Christ Michael*
- Angels - The Real Truth About All Types Of Angels

Through his writings, teachings, and decades of study, Dr. Paul continues his mission to illuminate the profound truths revealed in The Urantia Book, helping readers understand their place in the cosmic family and their eternal destiny as ascending sons and daughters of the Universal Father.

Dr. Paul resides in Dacula, Georgia, where he continues his research, writing, and teaching ministry, sharing the transformative message of divine love and cosmic citizenship with all who seek deeper spiritual understanding.

Contact and Resources:

YouTube: @rogerpauldc
Website: http://www.fifthepochalrevelationfellowship.com

www.ingramcontent.com/pod-product-compliance
Lightning Source LLC
LaVergne TN
LVHW081400110826
845149LV00010B/1625

* 9 7 9 8 9 9 4 7 6 5 3 2 6 *